THE
THEORY
OF
MACROECONOMIC
POLICY

SECOND EDITION

Nancy Smith Barrett

Professor of Economics, The American University

Prentice-Hall, Inc., Englewood Cliffs, New Jersey

Library of Congress Cataloging in Publication Data

Barrett, Nancy Smith.
  The theory of macroeconomic policy.

  Includes bibliographies.
  1. Macroeconomics.   2.   Economic policy.   I. Title.
HB171.5.B3   1975   330   74–19019
ISBN 0–13–913830–7

Printed in the United States of America

10   9   8   7   6   5   4   3   2   1

Prentice-Hall International, Inc., *London*
Prentice-Hall of Australia, Pty. Ltd., *Sydney*
Prentice-Hall of Canada, Ltd., *Toronto*
Prentice-Hall of India Private Limited, *New Delhi*
Prentice-Hall of Japan, Inc., *Tokyo*

. . . the ideas of economists and political philosophers, both when they are right and when they are wrong, are more powerful than is commonly understood. Indeed, the world is ruled by little else. Practical men, who believe themselves to be quite exempt from any intellectual influences, are usually the slaves of some defunct economist. Madmen in authority, who hear voices in the air, are distilling their frenzy from some academic scribbler of a few years back. I am sure that the power of vested interests is vastly exaggerated compared with gradual encroachment of ideas.

John Maynard Keynes

The General Theory of Employment, Interest, and Money

Contents

Preface

In no other area of economics has there been so much change in the past few years as in macroeconomic theory and policy. Three major developments stand out. First, inflation has become the predominant problem for stabilization policy. Economists have recognized some fundamental changes in the structure of the inflationary process in the U.S. economy, and their policy models have suggested new remedies, different from previous experience. A second problem has been the recognition that aggregate demand measures alone are no longer able to bring unemployment to an acceptably low level. Furthermore, because the burden of unemployment is not uniformly distributed among different demographic groups in the labor force, the welfare implications associated with high unemployment rates may be different from those suggested by the standard macroeconomic models that assume a homogeneous labor force. Finally, the growing influence of monetarism both as a theoretical model of the macroeconomy and as a guide to macroeconomic policy has made it necessary to rethink certain conclusions that one has taken for granted in a country where Keynesianism has assumed a certain orthodox respectability and political legitimacy.

The second edition of *The Theory of Macroeconomic Policy* has attempted to keep pace with these changes. Chapter 10 on the theory of inflation has been completely rewritten to incorporate the latest developments in Phillips curve analysis and the role of expectations. Chapter 12 contains a thorough discussion of the theory of wage-price controls with a detailed evaluation of the Nixon price program and a comparison with the Kennedy-Johnson guideposts. A new chapter on the labor market incorporates a discussion of the turnover-flow approach to unemployment, search theory, and the natural rate of unemployment hypothesis.

In the development of the theory of income determination, the monetarist model is explored in more detail than in the earlier edition. Although the approach of the book remains Keynesian, the underlying microeconomic assumptions of both the Keynesian and monetarist approaches are emphasized and critically evaluated.

Mixed reactions to placing the treatment of the national accounts in an appendix resulted in some reorganization of the discussion of data sources in this edition. A brief discussion of the national accounts appears in Chapter 2, and there is a detailed treatment of statistical price indices and unemployment data in Chapters 10 and 11. However, for the reader interested in a thorough treatment of national accounting, the material remains as Appendix B. Following the incorporation of the monetarist approach in the theoretical chapters, a discussion of flow-of-funds accounting has been added.

Despite these important changes and the usual updating of empirical material, the emphasis of this edition remains the same as in the original. The recognition of the need for government intervention in the economy that was the Keynesian legacy implies a theory of regulation. Because it demonstrates a need for active government intervention, modern macroeconomic theory requires a complementary theory of economic policy. Public policy cannot proceed on an *ad hoc* basis but must be based on some underlying theory of the structure of macroeconomic behavior and processes. It is the basic premise of this book that the success of any policy model depends upon the validity of the macroeconomic theory from which it is derived.

As a complement to the theoretical specification, we emphasize the importance of reliable empirical estimation of the policy model. Chapters 5 and 6 treating empirical specification of consumption and investment functions as well as Appendix A on economy-wide econometric models have been updated and expanded.

Many people have sent me advice and suggestions that have been extremely useful in developing this revision. Unfortunately, space does not permit my naming them individually. Rayford Boddy, George Iden, and Jon Wisman all used the first edition in their classes and made detailed comments on the revised manuscript. Many of their suggestions were incorporated into the final product. But my best critics have been the students who have learned or have tried to learn macroeconomics from this book. They have pointed out the rough spots, inconsistencies, and difficulties in the exposition. It is hoped that those who read this second edition will benefit from the critical commentary of those who went before them.

November, 1974
Washington, D.C.

1

The Method
and Scope
of Macroeconomic
Theory

John Kenneth Galbraith once remarked that the bumblebee does indeed fly, defying those laws of aerodynamics which would conclude that he cannot.[1] The success of mature or industrially developed economies in maintaining high levels of production and employment in the face of affluence is similarly in contradiction to the conclusions of the "dismal" economists of the nineteenth century who foresaw overproduction, falling profit rates, and stagnation as the inevitable result of the process of economic development. To some extent, Keynes echoed the teachings of economists such as Ricardo, Malthus, and even Marx in his speculation that private demand in a mature economy would generally be inadequate to warrant full employment of the labor force. He showed, however, that the public sector has a macroeconomic role in a *laissez-faire* economy that, from a theoretical perspective, at least, will enable it to achieve full employment and rising incomes indefinitely without destroying its capitalistic or free-enterprise institutions. In the Keynesian view, public policy is the key to the maintenance of affluence.

Although the Keynesian model was orginally designed to demonstrate the invalidity of Say's Law (the hypothesis that free-market forces automatically produce full employment) and to show the need for government intervention, it is readily adaptable into a model for practical policy design. The focus of this text is to relate macroeconomic theory to

---

[1] John Kenneth Galbraith, *American Capitalism: The Concept of Countervailing Power* (Boston: Houghton Mifflin Company, 1962), p. 1.

policy planning. Implicit in the theory is economic policy; and we shall show that the success of any policy model depends ultimately on whether the underlying theory is an accurate representation of macroeconomic processes. Consequently, to evaluate any policy measures, one must first understand the theory on which they are based.

1-1   THE METHODOLOGY OF ECONOMIC THEORY

This text is concerned with how economic policy can be used to reach certain goals. But to understand how policy decisions affect these designated objectives, one must first develop a model to represent the structural processes of the economic system.

In order to model an economic structure one must first formulate hypotheses about the behavior of decision-making units in the economy. Next, relationships between these decision-making units must be specified. Finally, implications from these various hypotheses and interrelationships must be derived.

A descriptive hypothesis may have more than historical interest. Suppose the policy planner wants to know whether a transfer of income from high-income to low-income families will stimulate total spending. He wishes to test the hypothesis that the proportion of an additional dollar of income which will be spent by low-income families will exceed the percentage decrease in spending by high-income families per dollar of tax collected. While the hypothesis is purely descriptive, it must be tested to gauge the impact of a potential economic program.

Some hypotheses are part of a larger analytical framework. The hypothesis that consumption increases with disposable income, together with the recognition that aggregate demand is composed of consumption and investment, leads ultimately to the conclusion that an increase in investment, by increasing income, will stimulate additional consumption and result in an increase in national income that is greater than the original change in investment. This result, known as the *multiplier effect,* is derived from the formulation of a behavioral hypothesis about consumption, the recognition of the interrelationship between aggregate demand, income, consumption, and investment, and the deduction of its implications. This approach to economic theory also yields fruitful insights for forecasting and policy planning.

Both deductive and inductive reasoning are important in the construction of useful hypotheses. A hypothesis is useful if it provides a reasonably accurate description of reality, particularly when predicting future events on the basis of past information. The observation that, in the past, consumption has been closely related to disposable income is useful to the forecaster only if the relationship is expected to continue into the future. A hypothesis based on past experience alone reflects an inductive, *a posteriori,* relationship. Unless a hypothesis also has some deductive, *a priori,* basis, its reliability as a predictor of future events is questionable. The hypothesis that consumption is related to disposable income is reasonable, *a priori,* that is, on a logical basis in the absence of empirical confirmation. Since this particular relationship has considerable *a priori* appeal, and since it has stood up well to *a posteriori* testing, that is, data on past consumption and income reflect the relationship, it has become a useful forecasting tool.

Suppose a study in a small town showed that, over a period of five years, consumption was closely related to the number of high school dropouts. Since the hypothesis that an increase in the dropout rate stimulates consumption has little to recommend it *a priori,* it would be inadvisable for a policy planner to use the dropout rate as an indicator of future consumption, especially when generalizing from the sample to the economy as a whole. Instead, he might suspect that the observed relationship for the particular sample studied was a coincidence rather than a reliable behavioral relationship.

Empirical testing of theoretical relationships is important for policy planning, however. The theorist may deduce that consumption is a function of disposable income, but the policy planner wants to know exactly how much consumption spending will increase in response to a tax cut or an income transfer. The exact magnitude of the response to be expected cannot always be determined on the basis of *a priori* or deductive reasoning alone. Instead, past experience must be examined.

MICROECONOMICS AND MACROECONOMICS

It is important to keep in mind that economic decisions—what and how much to produce and consume—are made by individuals. Any theoretical model of an economy must take individual behavior into account. Macroeconomic theory is concerned with the aggregate effects of individual actions. The aggregate level of employment, for instance, depends on the total number of workers that all the firms in the economy decide to hire. The level of aggregate output is the sum of all goods and services produced in the economy. Aggregate demand is total purchases of goods and services by all the households in the economy.

Suppose we want to consider a theoretical explanation of aggregate consumption. Clearly the theory must be related to a theory of household behavior. Microeconomic theory that describes individual household behavior would suggest that if a household gets more income, it would increase purchases of goods and services and also save some of the increase for future consumption. Thus, the hypothesis that an increase in aggregate income will increase aggregate consumption by an amount that is slightly less than the income change is consistent with microeconomic theory.

Sometimes, however, aggregate behavior is different from that implied by a microeconomic model. For example, microeconomic theory would predict that a firm will hire more workers if wages fall. This may be true for a single firm in an isolated labor market. For instance, if the neighborhood children offer to clean my attic one Saturday afternoon, the lower the wage for which each is willing to work, the more of them I am likely to hire. Suppose, on the other hand, wages fall economy-wide. The effect will be to reduce incomes of all households, resulting in a decline in demand for goods and services. If firms experience a decline in demand for their output that is proportional to the fall in wages, they will not necessarily hire more workers, since fewer are needed to produce the reduced output. Keynes pointed to this "fallacy of composition" when criticizing the policy of wage deflation proposed by his contemporaries to eliminate unemployment in the Depression of the early 1930's. For a single firm, wage deflation will increase employment, but in the aggregate, from a *macroeconomic* perspective, wage deflation will cause a decline in demand for goods and services and hence will not cause an increase in the aggregate demand for labor. Applying macroeconomic theory to the problem, Keynes concluded that a policy to stimulate aggregate demand by *raising* the incomes of households is preferable to wage deflation (that reduces household incomes) as a measure to reduce aggregate unemployment.

Macroeconomic theory must be consistent with individual or microeconomic behavior but must also recognize the fallacy of composition. In addition, a macroeconomic theory, unlike microeconomics, must select a method of aggregation. While a microeconomic model examines individual decision-making units, a macroeconomic model analyzes the behavior of groups. One macroeconomic model is distinguished from another by the way in which decision units are aggregated or grouped.

A Keynesian model, for instance, groups spending units in terms of the types of goods purchased—consumption, investment, public goods, and exports. A Ricardian model aggregates spending units in terms of the sources of the income received—wages, rent, and profits. A monetarist model aggregates not over spending units, but over decisions to purchase goods and services on the one hand and to hold money balances on the other.

In some ways, macroeconomic theory is more difficult to understand than microeconomic theory because there are often many different models with conflicting policy implications. This is in part because they are based on different microeconomic assumptions about individual behavior. But more often it is because they identify different aggregates. Sometimes the models do not conflict at all when they are appropriately disaggregated. But there is no doubt that the way macroeconomic models are aggregated often conceals important influences.

For instance, a Keynesian model postulates that consumption depends on income. In a Ricardian model, the propensity to consume out of wages is much greater than the propensity to consume out of rental income.[2] A Ricardian would say to a Keynesian that the aggregate propensity to consume (a Keynesian concept) depends on income distribution. The Keynesian may well agree and reply that such a conclusion depends on the level of disaggregation one desires. To analyze, for instance, the impact of an across-the-board spending increase in consumption, one can aggregate across income groups since relative income shares are presumably not affected by the policy measure. If, on the other hand, a policy measure is known to affect relative income shares, then a Ricardian type of disaggregation might be appropriate.

ECONOMIC MODELS

The hypotheses and interrelationships of economic theory can be used to construct models of economic behavior. The scope of the model depends on the particular aspect of economic behavior being examined, and the dimensions of disaggregation depend on the problem addressed. The model will consist of hypotheses about behavior, or *behavioral relationships,* definitions or *identities,* and *equilibrium conditions.*

Suppose we want to model an economy with no government and no foreign trade. We want to answer the question: How will a change in the level of investment affect the aggregate demand for goods and services?

First, we must decide on the appropriate dimensions of aggregation. Suppose we divide total aggregate demand, D, into consumption, C, and investment, I, that is

$$D = C + I$$

If investment is defined as the use of goods and services for purposes other than consumption, this equation is a definition, or identity.

Second, we shall introduce a hypothesis about aggregate consumption behavior based on microeconomic theory. We will postulate that consumption is a linear function of income, Y, or

$$C = a + bY$$

[2] In less technical terms, wage-earners spend a higher proportion of their income on consumption than landlords.

where

$$a > 0$$

and

$$0 < b < 1$$

Finally, we will specify an equilibrium condition, that national income will eventually settle at the level of aggregate demand,[3] that is

$$Y = D$$

For any level of investment, I_0,

$$I = I_0$$

the complete model

$$D = C + I$$
$$C = a + bY$$
$$Y = D$$
$$I = I_0$$

is consistent. Since there are four equations and four unknowns, the level of aggregate income can be found when I is known (except in special cases).

In this case, national income is seen to be a function of I, since

$$Y = D = C + I_0$$
$$= a + bY + I_0$$

or

$$Y = \frac{I_0 + a}{1 - b}$$

For any change in I, ΔI, the resultant change in Y, ΔY, is

$$\Delta Y = \frac{\Delta I}{1 - b}$$

since Δa is zero.

Notice that the effect of a change in investment on income depends on b, which is a behavioral coefficient or parameter in the consumption equation. That is, the link between the variable being changed and that

---

[3] A detailed explanation of this equilibrium condition is given in Chapter 3.

which it affects depends on a behavioral relationship in another sector altogether. We shall see that the equations that link policy variables to policy objectives (sometimes called *reduced form equations*) often contain behavioral coefficients from a structural model of the economy. These coefficients can be estimated statistically from examining past behavior. Clearly, behavioral parameters can be crucial to a policy model.

1-2   ECONOMIC THEORY AND THE KEYNESIAN REVOLUTION

Macroeconomics studies the aggregate results of individual behavior.[4] Although economists have always been interested in macroeconomic phenomena, John Maynard Keynes, with his 1935 classic, *The General Theory of Employment, Interest, and Money,* might be called the father of modern macroeconomic theory. By drawing attention to the fallacy of composition, Keynes argued that macroeconomic phenomena cannot be treated solely as an extention of microeconomic principles.

Keynes' role in macroeconomics is threefold. First, he was the first to question the validity of Say's Law—the principle that full employment could be achieved without government intervention through the price mechanism. Economists before Keynes had traditionally ignored national income and other aggregate concepts, such as employment, output, and prices, and had concentrated their attention instead on the markets for individual goods and services.[5] Price fluctuations within these markets served to clear them, that is, to equate supply and demand. Only monopoly influences or market imperfections which promoted price rigidity could produce excess supply in any particular market.

Thus, traditional (or classical) economic theory concluded that, if prices were permitted to fluctuate freely, particularly in the downward direction, and if monopoly influences were eliminated, there would be no excess supply in any commodity or factor market. If wages were to fall sufficiently, then there would be no unemployment. Since the notion did not arise that what was true for individual markets might not be valid for the economy as a whole (in the aggregate), the economists of the 1930's urged a policy of wage and price deflation as the best remedy for the Great Depression.

---

[4] Individuals may act independently or in collusion. Macroeconomics looks at the sum total of their actions.

[5] This is not true of economists of the late eighteenth and early nineteenth centuries, such as Hume, Ricardo, and Malthus. While there are some marked similarities in the Keynesian and Malthusian analyses, the passage of over a century between them represented enough of a discontinuity in the tradition that it is legitimate to refer to the Keynesian contribution as a revolution in the development of economic theory.

A theory which left the job of clearing all markets to a freely fluctuating price system was ill-equipped to handle a depression such as the world faced in the 1930's. There was a substantial excess supply of labor—over 25 percent of the labor force was unemployed in most industrial countries. Classical theory, based on extrapolation from the model of a single market, implied that a decline in the general wage level would solve the problem. All one had to do to get a job was to offer to work for a lower wage. Practical policy makers intuitively felt that the heart of the difficulty was an inadequate demand for goods. Wage cuts, in the face of insufficient demand, would reduce purchasing power and, therefore, would only aggravate the situation.

Even before the publication of *The General Theory,* Keynes appeared before national radio audiences in Britain advocating public works programs and deficit spending by the government. Economic policy makers agreed with these recommendations, and all but the most orthodox economists had to admit that intuitively his suggestions made sense. *The General Theory* presented a theoretical model which corroborated the Keynesian policy prescriptions. The theoretical model served two purposes. First, it gave respectability to the measures designed by the policy planners to reduce the unemployment rate. These measures attempted to stimulate demand without reducing prices and wages. Although few people actually read *The General Theory,* the very fact of its publication made everyone feel more comfortable about what they were doing. In addition, the theoretical analysis, including hypotheses about aggregate behavior as well as the specification of key macroeconomic identities and equilibrium conditions, provided the basis for the development of a macroeconomic model for policy planning and forecasting. If the relationships specified *a priori* in *The General Theory* could actually be determined from historical data, then policy decisions would not have to be made on an *ad hoc* basis.

Thus, in addition to providing a justification for government intervention (by showing that the classical justification for *laissez-faire* was based on the fallacy of composition), Keynes developed a macroeconomic model of the economy that was adaptable into a policy-planning model. That is, he defined certain dimensions of aggregation, formulated hypotheses about aggregate behavior, and pinpointed relationships between various macroeconomic variables.

For a long time, the Keynesian model was the only one equipped to deal with the problems of unemployment and macroeconomic instability. Consequently that model, and the policy remedies implicit in it, gained a certain intellectual respectability and political legitimacy others lacked. This influence explains why it is extremely difficult to sell non-Keynesian policy schemes, even when the Keynesian model is clearly not an accurate structural representation of the problems at hand.

Keynesian economics implied an active role for public policy. The economist of today is far different from the armchair sage of the nineteenth century, who was concerned with proving theorems about optimal resource allocation in a market system. Instead, the large majority of economists are found outside the university, and many of these are concerned with the day-to-day business of planning practical ways to achieve the economic goals society has put before them.

To summarize the three-fold influence of Keynes' *General Theory*, it:

1. provided a rationale for government intervention in a free-enterprise economy.
2. presented a macroeconomic model for policy planning.
3. legitimatized certain types of monetary and fiscal policy and (by implication) excluded other forms of government intervention.

KEYNESIAN ECONOMICS
AND CONTEMPORARY MACROECONOMICS

It has become fashionable in contemporary macroeconomics to reject the Keynesian model as outdated orthodoxy.[6] And there is no doubt that the application of uncritical naïve Keynesianism to many problems produces incorrect policy recommendations. Nowhere is this more obvious than in an analysis of inflation in a recession, a possibility not consistent with Keynesian reasoning.

Yet, despite its limitations, the Keynesian model and its associated policy measures have, at least in the capitalist countries, a certain political and intellectual respectability. Consequently, an understanding of the basic Keynesian approach is important for evaluating real-world macroeconomic policy. If its assumptions are weak, those weaknesses must be understood if the model is to be changed to take them into account and if appropriate policy recommendations are to be forthcoming.

Developing macroeconomic theory within a Keynesian framework is also useful from a pedagogical perspective. Since Keynes was the first to establish the invalidity of Say's Law, Keynesian theory is useful for analyzing that issue. In the first place, the refutation of Say's Law must be established before one can rationalize certain types of public policy. In addition, as we have seen, there are many possible ways to disaggregate macroeco-

---

[6] It is also fashionable to reinterpret *The General Theory* and attribute to it implications that were not perceived at the time. See, for instance, Axel Leijon-hufvud, *On Keynesian Economics and the Economics of Keynes* (New York: Oxford University Press, 1968).

nomic relationships. The Keynesian method is one such approach, and it is useful to rely on one framework throughout for consistency. One might view it simply as a prototypical macroeconomic model.

Whether one wishes to accept the Keynesian structure as the best description of a capitalist system or whether one simply views it as one among many alternative views of the world, one cannot fail to recognize its extraordinary influence on economic policy. From a practical perspective, it is much more difficult to convince non-economists of the weaknesses of the model than of its strengths, which is perhaps the most important reason why contemporary economists cannot ignore it. Even Milton Friedman, one of the strongest critics of the Keynesian view, has said, "We are all Keynesians now." [7]

1-3 THE GOALS OF MACROECONOMIC POLICY

The Employment Act of 1946 reflected the official acceptance of Keynesian economics in the United States. Based on the recognition that full employment must be a concern of public policy, it admitted that a free-market system might not automatically generate enough jobs to employ the entire labor force and implicitly rejected wage deflation as a policy to promote full employment. The Act reads in part:

> The Congress declares that it is the continuing responsibility of the Federal Government to use all practicable means . . . to promote maximum employment, production and purchasing power.

Besides the goal of full employment, macroeconomic policy is concerned with controlling inflation, avoiding unmanageable balance-of-payments deficits, and promoting growth. Each of these goals will be considered briefly. [8]

FULL EMPLOYMENT

Economists have always been concerned with full employment, although their view of the problem associated with unemployment keeps

---

[7] Milton Friedman, *Dollars and Deficits* (Englewood Cliffs, New Jersey: Prentice-Hall, Inc., 1968), p. 15.

[8] We have not addressed the question of what constitutes a national goal or who decides what are the goals and how national priorities are established. The objectives considered in this section are those to which national economic policy is most often addressed in the United States. Also, there are other goals, such as income redistribution that are more controversial and less explicitly the concern of Keynesian macroeconomics. This is not to suggest other goals are not important.

changing. Unemployment is defined as a situation in which people are seeking jobs, are willing to work for the prevailing wage (or less than the prevailing wage), but cannot find work. Unemployment, so defined, recognizes the value of leisure and the right of an individual not to work if this is his preference. Unemployment is a problem for remedial action only when it is involuntary.

Pre-Keynesian economists viewed unemployment as symptomatic of a malfunctioning of the labor market that was supposed to achieve equilibrium automatically. It was attributed to monopoly influences that were undesirable because they interfered with efficient resource allocation.

Keynes contended that unemployment represents a welfare loss to society because of the output foregone when labor resources are left idle. Goods are scarce because resources are scarce. If economic welfare can be increased by reducing the scarcity of goods, then policies designed to provide jobs to individuals who wish to work will increase the amount of goods available and, hence, the general welfare.

More recently, economists have been concerned with the welfare burden borne by those individuals experiencing unemployment (rather than the society at large that obtains less goods). The problem has been compounded in recent years with the recognition that unemployment is not uniformly distributed among various demographic groups in the labor force, with blacks, women, and young people bearing a disproportionate burden.

PRICE STABILITY

Price stability is important in an economy which uses money as a store of value. Since prices drift upward more easily than downward, inflation is a primary target of remedial government policy.

Inflation has serious distributive consequences. It penalizes those whose incomes are fixed in money terms. Workers whose wage contracts contain cost-of-living escalator clauses will receive money wage increases when prices rise, but this is not true of individuals relying on pensions and annuities. Inflation hurts creditors and reduces the real obligations of debtors.

Aside from its impact on income distribution (which could theoretically be remedied by appropriate redistributive policies), the primary concern is that inflation not become so rampant that the currency becomes unacceptable. If prices are rising and consumers and investors expect the trend to continue, they may be encouraged to spend immediately, exchanging money for goods, driving prices up still further. Such an occurrence would lead to breakdown or panic in financial markets which would have a deleterious effect on investment, the basis for growth. It would also have a disastrous impact on the balance of international payments and the international acceptability of the currency. In a rare instance, such as the runaway inflation in Germany in the 1920's, the economic fabric of the society may be destroyed, with dire political and social consequences.

Although it is unlikely that the events in post-World War I Germany will occur in the United States today, inflation does tend to reinforce itself. Unless it is controlled, the uncertainty it generates may itself have undesirable social and political, as well as economic, consequences. Measures to control inflation may produce recession and unemployment and other social problems. Experience with price controls has not been without difficulties. Recent attempts to control prices directly have resulted in panic buying and withholding of supply, producing shortages, inefficiency, uncertainty, and widespread frustration.

AVOIDING EXCESSIVE BALANCE-OF-PAYMENTS DEFICITS

In the United States, the foreign sector comprises less than 5 percent of national income. However, as long as the international gold standard is in effect and if the dollar is to maintain its position as a reserve currency, the United States must maintain confidence in the value of the dollar abroad by preventing large outflows of dollars and gold.[9] A loss of confidence in the dollar, given current international monetary arrangements, would have considerable destabilizing effects on world markets.

For countries which transact a larger part of their business in world markets, balance-of-payments equilibrium is a more important national goal. This is particularly true for countries that are dependent upon imports for food, capital equipment, and other essential items. If their currency becomes unacceptable or if creditors doubt their ability to pay because of excessive payments deficits, these countries may have difficulty finding import sources.

ECONOMIC GROWTH

Growth of productivity, or output per worker, is generally considered to be an improvement in economic well-being. If productivity increases are matched by increases in wages, workers can realize either an increase in real income or in lesiure. It is not always true, however, that economic

---

[9] Many economists argue that maintenance of a gold standard and the dollar's position as a reserve currency is not a desirable policy objective. Currently, however, it is a stated policy goal, and macroeconomic policy must be designed accordingly.

growth reflects an increase in welfare, particularly if that growth is accompanied by undesirable changes in the distribution of income. Nevertheless, if economic growth can be achieved, a redistributive incomes policy could ensure that it represents an increase in national economic welfare.

CONFLICTS IN ECONOMIC GOALS

The goals of economic policy may be conflicting. It is not always possible to achieve all our goals simultaneously. This being the case, it is necessary to accept a trade-off between them. For instance, Figure 1-1 shows the relationship between increases in the price level and the unemployment rate for the United States over the period 1935–1960. This downward-sloping curve, often called a "modified Phillips curve," [10] indicates that periods of low unemployment are associated with rising prices. In a period of rising demand and employment, labor markets tighten, wage increases are demanded and achieved, and prices drift upward. In tight labor markets, unemployment is due primarily to structural influences such as rapid technological change and shifts in demand, which provide new jobs requiring special skills in some areas while rendering other skills obsolete. It is generally recognized that macroeconomic measures to stimulate aggregate demand will not eliminate structural unemployment. New jobs may be created, increasing the demand for labor in some occupations. As money wages increase in these markets, unions in the declining sectors demand and achieve wage increases, thus reducing the quantity of labor demanded and accentuating the problem of structural unemployment. Furthermore, firms may respond to the wage increases by raising product prices. In this instance a policy which stimulates aggregate demand could have the disastrous effect of increasing the rate of inflation *and* the unemployment rate at the same time. Although many economists have questioned the validity of the Phillips curve concept in the light of recent experience (see Chapter 10), the recognition that the cost of price stability may be unemployment and a reduced rate of growth is certainly implicit in our policy decisions.

A policy which stimulates demand may reduce the unemployment rate at the expense of the goal of price stability. It may also increase the rate of economic growth. Whether or not this represents an improvement in the economic welfare of the community depends upon the output mix and how it is distributed. A reduction in taxes at all income levels by a fixed percentage of income, for instance, will increase disposable income for all

---

[10] A "modified Phillips curve" relates price changes to the unemployment rate, while a "Phillips curve" relates wage changes to the unemployment rate. For the original derivation, see A. W. Phillips, "The Relation Between Unemployment and the Rate of Change of Money Wage Rates in the United Kingdom, 1861–1957," *Economica* (n.s.), XXV (November, 1958), 283–299.

tax payers without affecting income distribution. This might be compared with an increase in military spending for materials of war. In both cases, spending increases will stimulate employment and growth of output; however, it will be distributed differently among the various sectors. In one case, the demand and output will increase in the consumer goods industries, while in the other, more war materials will be produced. Some people feel that the production of more war materials does not constitute an improvement in social welfare.

Macroeconomic policy to stimulate growth may also conflict with the goal of balance-of-payments equilibrium. As demand increases, imports

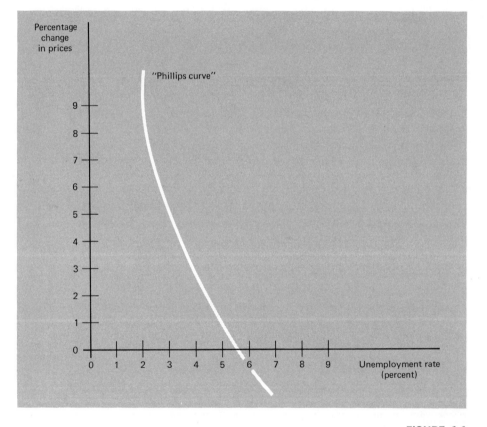

FIGURE 1-1

Relationship Between Changes in the Price Level
and the Unemployment Rate

Source: Paul A. Samuelson and Robert M. Solow, "Analytical Aspects of Anti-Inflation Policy," *The American Economic Review*, L (May, 1960), 177–194.

rise, while rising prices at home discourage exports and further encourage imports.

Thus, macroeconomic policy is framed in large measure in terms of trade-offs between the various goals. In some cases the planner may be able to reduce the amount of the trade-off. For instance, training programs which increase labor mobility may reduce the rate of structural unemployment and consequently lower the rate of inflation associated with expansionary public policy. This would, in effect, shift the Phillips curve leftward, or make it more L-shaped. Policies to stimulate investment during boom periods enable supply to increase with demand, again serving to promote price stability.

INSTRUMENTS OF ECONOMIC POLICY

An economic model essentially pinpoints the relationship between policy targets, or goals, and the policy instruments at the disposal of the planner. Suppose each target is represented as a variable in a linear model.[11] Furthermore, for each target there is an equation which specifies its relationship to the policy instruments. For instance, employment, N, and prices, p, might be related to government spending, G, and interest rates, i. The relationship can be represented algebraically:

$$a_1 G + a_2 i = N$$
$$b_1 G + b_2 i = p$$

Suppose target values for N and p are specified so that

$$N^* = 75 \text{ million}$$
$$p^* = 100$$

where p is a price index. Then the system becomes

$$a_1 G + a_2 i = 75$$
$$b_1 G + b_2 i = 100$$

and, generally, a solution can be found. Note that two instrumental variables are required if two targets are to be fulfilled. Since there must be as many equations as there are unknowns to determine a solution to a linear system, there must be as many instruments as targets in the planning of practical policy.

---

[11] Policy planners prefer to work with linear models because they are easier to estimate and solve than nonlinear models.

While the equality between instruments and targets is a necessary precondition for successful planning, it is not sufficient. As we have seen, some targets are inconsistent. Furthermore, there are often political or economic constraints on our instruments. Suppose, for example, the solution of the model requires a negative rate of interest. This would mean subsidizing borrowers and extracting an interest payment from lenders, a practice which is quite alien to established financial practice. Furthermore, it would not be behaviorally feasible, since it is unlikely that lenders would be willing to pay borrowers to take their money. There may also be political constraints on economic policy. For instance, it may not be politically feasible to cut government spending in certain areas, such as national defense or social development programs. Policy instruments are generally assumed to be economic activities or parameters which planners can manipulate at will, at least within certain boundaries. However, even presidential advisors have found it nearly impossible to predict the level of federal spending, taxes, or interest rates within a planning period. In the last year of the Johnson administration, with the Vietnam War a hot political issue, the President's Council of Economic Advisors was criticized for its apparent underestimate of aggregate demand and its failure to recommend measures which would have prevented the economy from "overheating." Much of the difficulty, however, was due to the fact that the administration consistently underestimated defense spending. In this instance the planners found it easier to forecast spending by the private sector than to forecast public spending, which was theoretically a "known" parameter in their model.

Thus, to achieve policy targets, planners must have sufficient policy instruments at their disposal. More policy instruments than targets may be required if the instruments are not flexible or if they are constrained by political and economic influences. Generally, the planner is faced with too many objectives and too few flexible policy instruments.

1-4   TOWARD A THEORY OF MACROECONOMIC POLICY

One reason for the remarkable influence of the Keynesian model is that it analyzes the very macroeconomic variables—employment, national income, output, and prices—that reflect national policy objectives. In addition, of course, it provides the rationale for fiscal and monetary policy and hence legitimizes the work of the policy planner. Consequently, the most influential real-world macroeconomic policy-planning and forecasting models consist of the relationships specified by Keynes in *The General Theory*. The actual parameters of these models are, of course, derived from historically generated information using the techniques of statistical inference.

For example, Keynes suggested that consumption is primarily a function of disposable income. Algebraically,

$$C = a + bY$$

where C is aggregate consumption and Y is aggregate disposable income. A policy planner, using the basic Keynesian hypothesis about consumption, will examine actual data measuring income and consumption.

Figure 1-2 is a scatter diagram of consumption and income data such as a planner might use in attempting to specify a consumption function for his model. Each point in the scatter represents a pair of observations on consumption and income at a particular point in time. Approximating the scatter with a straight line, the actual values for the constant a (the intercept) and b (the slope) of the relationship can be identified.

If public policy is to be used to achieve economic goals, it must be planned. Economists are not omniscient, however, and their models are not perfect. Consequently, their forecasts are not always accurate, and public policy may be of the too-much-too-soon or too-little-too-late variety.

Inaccurate forecasts and inappropriate policy recommendations may be due to such factors as:

1. poor theoretical construction, inconsistency, or error in the logical basis of the forecasting and planning model.
2. incorrect *a posteriori* specification of the model due to poor data or inappropriate statistical procedure.
3. random, unexpected, or unknown events or behavior.
4. political or institutional constraints on the policy instruments.

When all the potential sources of error are considered, however, the record of policy planning since the Keynesian revolution has been remarkable. Since World War II, there has been no serious depression or financial panic. Unfortunately, recent attempts at achieving price stability have not been as successful as measures to promote full employment, and even in the area of unemployment many economists are urging non-Keynesian remedies for the rising so-called "full-employment unemployment rate." (See Chapter 11.)

One reason that macroeconomic policy has been more successfully applied to the full-employment goal than the price stability goal is that Keynesian theory is concerned primarily with the causes of unemployment rather than inflation. But although recent experience with an inflation that has not been slowed by Keynesian remedies has stimulated economists to develop new theoretical models of the inflationary process (see Chapter 10), such models lack the legitimacy of the Keynesian model, and the policy remedies are still viewed with suspicion.

In this text we will develop a theory of inflation along with the Keynesian model, even though the analysis presented in *The General Theory* focused on unemployment. Hopefully, this will make the Keynesian approach more relevant to the contemporary reader. After developing the complete model, we shall return to a consideration of policy planning in the final chapter. Appendix A, on the construction and use of macro-

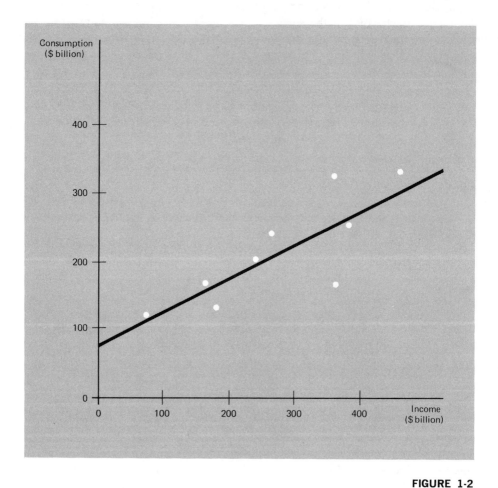

FIGURE 1-2

Scatter Diagram of Consumption and Income Data

economic models, ties the policy-planning approach to the development of the model in each of its phases.

QUESTIONS FOR STUDY AND REVIEW

1. "Economic planning is not inconsistent with a free-enterprise economy; indeed, it is the key to its long-run survival. The main problem with 'automatic mechanisms' is that they are insufficient in perspective." Discuss.

2. What is an *economic model?* Discuss some of the advantages and limitations of using economic models in the planning of national economic policy.

3. The hypothesis that consumption is a function of income is central to the Keynesian theory. If you were developing a model of the economy to be used for forecasting and policy planning, how would you test the validity of the hypothesis? What problems would you expect to encounter in your effort to achieve realistic specification of the consumption equation?

4. "An effective economic policy program must contain at least as many policy instruments as there are goals to be attained. With enough instruments, any targets can be reached." Discuss the validity of each of these statements.

5. "Macroeconomic policy must be based on some theoretical view of macroeconomic processes. The success of any policy package depends ultimately on the validity of its theoretical underpinnings." Illustrate this proposition with specific examples.

6. "Macroeconomic theory encompasses all of microeconomic theory and more." Explain.

ADDITIONAL READING

BEACH, E. F., *Economic Models.* New York: John Wiley & Sons, Inc., 1957, Part I.

"The Employment Act: Twenty Years of Policy Experience," *Economic Report of the President.* Washington, D.C.: Government Printing Office, January, 1966, Chapter 7.

KUHN, THOMAS S. *The Structure of Scientific Revolutions. International Encyclopedia of Unified Science.* Vol. 2. Number 2. Chicago: University of Chicago Press, 1970.

SMITHIES, ARTHUR, "Reflections on the Work and Influence of John Maynard Keynes," *The Quarterly Journal of Economics,* LXV (November, 1951), 578–601.

2

The Analytics
of Income Determination:
Aggregate Supply
and Aggregate Demand

To achieve the goals of full employment and stable prices, the policy maker must have a clear understanding of macroeconomic relationships. Employment and the level of prices are two variables of concern to policy makers. Both are linked directly to output. Employment is tied to output through the production function, while prices and output are simultaneously determined in product markets. Because of their connection with employment and the price level, real output and the value of output or, equivalently, of income become the focal point of macroeconomic analysis. In equilibrium, when the plans of firms and households are realized, the level of money income is determined by aggregate demand. Employment, in turn, depends upon the equilibrium relationship between aggregate demand and aggregate supply.

In Chapters 2 and 3 the basic model of income and employment will be developed. After a preliminary discussion of the aggregate supply and aggregate demand functions in this chapter, the equilibrium model will be presented in Chapter 3. Although these chapters are concerned primarily with the relationship between income and employment, the foundation is laid for an analysis of the price level in Chapter 10.

2-1 THE ACCOUNTING FRAMEWORK AND NATIONAL ACCOUNTS

As goods are produced, factor services are performed, and income, in the form of wages, rent, interest, and profit, is earned. Part of income is the

TABLE 2-1

Accounts of the Farmer

Sales		Expenses and Profit	
100 bushels of wheat	$100	Expenses:	
		Rent	$ 50
		Profit:	$ 50
Total sales	$100	Total expenses and profit	$100

return to factors—labor, land, and capital—in the form of wages, rent, and interest for services rendered in the process of production. The remaining part of income, profits, is the residual between the value of output and payments to factors. Thus, when profit is included in income, income will always be exactly, or *identically,* equal to the value of output.

Consider the following example: A farmer produces 100 bushels of wheat with his own labor on an acre of land belonging to a landlord. He sells the wheat to a miller for $100, paying the landlord a rent of $50 and earning a profit of $50. The farmer's accounts are shown in Table 2-1. Sales, or the value of output, is exactly equal to total income in the form of profits and rent.

The miller who buys the wheat produces 500 pounds of flour which he sells to a baker for $300. The miller's accounts are shown in Table 2-2. The value of output of the miller is $300 and total income earned (wages, $100; overhead, $50; profits, $50) is $200. Does this violate the output–income identity? Not if we remember that part of the value of the flour

TABLE 2-2

Accounts of the Miller

Sales		Expenses and Profits	
500 pounds of flour	$300	Expenses:	
		100 bushels of wheat	$100
		Wages	$100
		Overhead (interest and rent)	$ 50
		Total expenses	$250
		Profit:	$ 50
Total sales	$300	Total expenses and profit	$300

TABLE 2-3

Income Earned in the Production of Flour

Wheat production:	
Rent	$ 50
Profit	$ 50
Total income	$100
Milling process:	
Wages	$100
Overhead (interest and rent)	$ 50
Profit	$ 50
Total income	$200
Total income earned in flour production	$300
Total value of flour	$300

is derived from the value of the wheat. As shown in Table 2-3, income earned in the total process, including wheat production, is $300, which is exactly equal to the value of the flour.

In actual practice, it would be difficult to account for all income earned in the intermediate stages of the production process. Instead, keeping in mind that the value of output is always equal to income, the accounts can be balanced by subtracting the value of intermediate products from the value of the final product to obtain *value added* at each stage.

TABLE 2-4

Value Added and Income in the Production of Flour and Wheat

	Flour		
Value of Output		*Income*	
Flour	$300	Wages	$100
		Overhead	$ 50
Wheat	−$100	Profit	$ 50
Value added	$200	Total income	$200

	Wheat		
Value of Output		*Income*	
Wheat	$100	Rent	$ 50
		Profit	$ 50
Value added	$100	Total income	$100

TABLE 2-5

Accounts of the Baker

Sales		Expenses and Profit	
1000 loaves of bread	$500	Expenses:	
		500 pounds of flour	$300
		Wages	$ 75
		Overhead (interest and rent)	$ 40
		Total expenses	$415
		Profit	$ 85
Total sales	$500	Total expenses and profit	$500

Value added will exactly equal income for each stage of production, as seen in Table 2-4.

The sum of the value added at each stage is equal to the value of total output which is equal to the total income earned. The value-added approach is used to avoid "double counting" of intermediate outputs while still accounting for all income earned at all stages of production.

The baker who buys the flour sells 1000 loaves of bread for $500. His accounts are shown in Table 2-5. Value added in this stage of production is $200 and income earned is $200. As shown in Table 2-6, the value of the bread, $500, is equal to the sum of the value added at each stage, which is equal to total income earned.

THE NATIONAL ACCOUNTS

In macroeconomic theory we are interested in aggregate or economy-wide measures of output and income. For a real-world economy these

TABLE 2-6

Value Added and Income in All Stages of Bread Production

Value of Final Product		Value Added		Income	
Bread	$500	Wheat	$100	Wheat	$100
		Flour	$200	Flour	$200
		Bread	$200	Bread	$200
Value of output	$500	Total value added	$500	Total income	$500

measures are called the *national accounts.* Since economy-wide there are many different stages of production with the same firm often producing goods at various stages, the concept of value added is extremely important in national accounting. It would be impossible to distinguish between intermediate and final products, for instance, in actual practice. General Motors produces automobiles both for households and for taxicab companies. But if we were to count the value of output of both General Motors *and* taxicab companies, we would be double counting those automobiles that were produced by General Motors and then used by the taxicab companies and entered into a calculation of their production costs. Consequently, the value-added approach becomes the technique used by national accountants to estimate *Gross National Product,* which is a measure of national output in value-added terms.

Equivalently, *National Income* measures the aggregate payments to the factors of production in wages, profit, interest, and rent. As we have seen in our example, National Income should equal Gross National Product, since in an accounting framework value added is equal to income or factor costs. Because of some definitional differences, however, the two measures are not exactly the same in practice, primarily because Gross National Product includes and National Income excludes a capital depreciation allowance. In Appendix B, we discuss the national accounts definitions in more detail, and the interested reader should refer to it at this point.

In addition to measuring aggregate output and income, the national accounts provide estimates of other aggregate activities such as consumption and investment that are useful for policy analysis in a Keynesian model. These are discussed in Appendix B. In addition, some issues relating to the interpretation of national accounts aggregates as measures of economic welfare and performance are also explored.

ANALYTICAL USE OF THE OUTPUT-INCOME IDENTITY

In the study of macroeconomic relationships it is sometimes convenient to use income rather than output value as a variable. Since income and output values are identical within a given time period, it will not matter which variable is considered.

Analytically, the output–income identity is represented by means of a 45° line which bisects the positive quadrant of a graph with output on one axis and income on the other. Since income and output never take on negative values, only the positive quadrant is of interest. In Figure 2-1, any point on the 45° line is equidistant from the two axes. If income is known to be Y_0, the corresponding level of output, Q_0, can immediately be determined from the graph.

In the discussion which follows, it is convenient to treat the aggregate demand for goods and services as a function of income and to treat the supply in terms of output value. This will pose no analytical difficulties if the output–income identity is kept in mind.

2-2 AGGREGATE SUPPLY AND EMPLOYMENT

Output or income is an aggregate measure of the level of product market activity, either in real terms (output) or money terms (the value of output, income). Employment, on the other hand, is an aggregate measure of

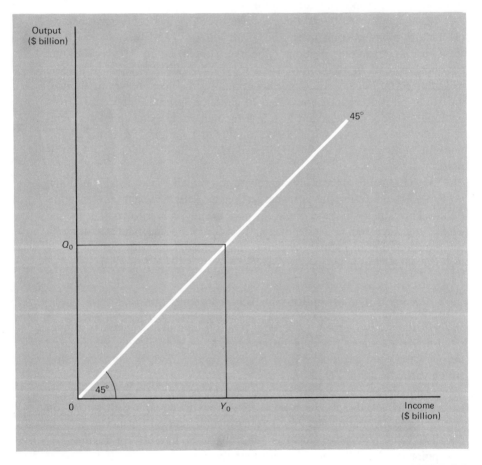

FIGURE 2-1

The Output–Income Identity

labor market activity. In the Keynesian model of income determination it is implicitly assumed that changes in the aggregate level of product market activity directly affect aggregate employment. This provides the rationale for using measures that affect aggregate demand to influence employment. Before we turn to consider the determinants of product market demand, it is first necessary to see how it is related to the aggregate demand for labor.[1]

To produce a given output, a firm will require a certain amount of factor services. The demand for any factor of production will depend upon the cost of that factor per unit of output as well as upon the price at which the product is sold. Consequently, it is the expected value of sales that determines the amount of a factor a firm will hire when the factor cost is known.

Suppose the capital stock is fixed so that the firm can vary the amount of goods it produces and sells only by varying the number of workers it employs. The *aggregate supply function* relates the number of workers that firms wish to hire and the amount of total revenue firms expect to receive from sales. For any level of expected sales, or total spending, the aggregate supply function provides an estimate of the number of workers that will be employed.

The shape of the aggregate supply function will be of interest. If entrepreneurs become pessimistic about the prospects for total sales in the next quarter, how will their pessimism affect employment?

Assuming that the firm will attempt to maximize profits, it will hire additional workers only if the expected contribution of those workers to total revenue exceeds their addition to the total wage bill. This suggests that firms will hire additional workers only if they expect sales revenue to increase. Consequently, we expect the aggregate supply curve to be upward sloping as in Figure 2-2.

In constructing our complete model of income and employment in Chapter 8 and in our analysis of price level changes in Chapter 10, we will need to know more about the shape of the aggregate supply function. Will changes in employment be proportional to expected changes in total revenue or will the demand for labor in response to a given change in expected sales depend upon how much labor is already employed? The possibilities are indicated in Figure 2-3.

Changes in employment will be proportional to changes in total revenue only if the aggregate supply function is a straight line, such as Z_2 in Figure 2-3. In this case the change in employment associated with any given change in product demand is independent of the number of workers

---

[1] In this section we will assume some involuntary unemployment, that is, an excess supply of labor at the prevailing wage. Firms can hire all the labor they want at a fixed wage, so that changes in the demand for labor are reflected in changes in employment. We will drop this assumption in Chapter 10.

already employed. If the aggregate supply function is convex to the employment axis, such as Z_3, for a given change in expected total revenue (product demand), the demand for additional workers will be smaller the more labor is already employed. If the function is concave, such as Z_1, the opposite will be the case.

DERIVATION OF THE AGGREGATE SUPPLY FUNCTION

A firm will continue to hire additional workers until the contribution of the last worker to total revenue is just equal to his cost, or wage. Let us

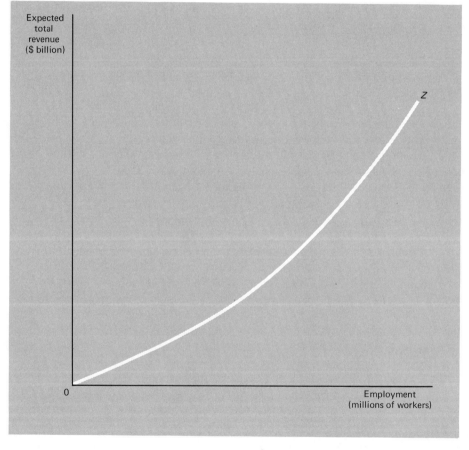

FIGURE 2-2

The Aggregate Supply Function

assume that the firm is a perfect competitor in both the product market and the labor market. This means that he can sell all his output at some constant price, p, and hire all his labor at a constant wage, w. Given these assumptions, the contribution to total revenue of the last worker hired is equal to the added output resulting from his employment, or the marginal product, MP, multiplied by price of the output. The profit-maximizing firm will hire workers up to the point at which the value of the marginal product is just equal to the wage, or algebraically,

$$p \times MP = w$$

for the last worker hired.

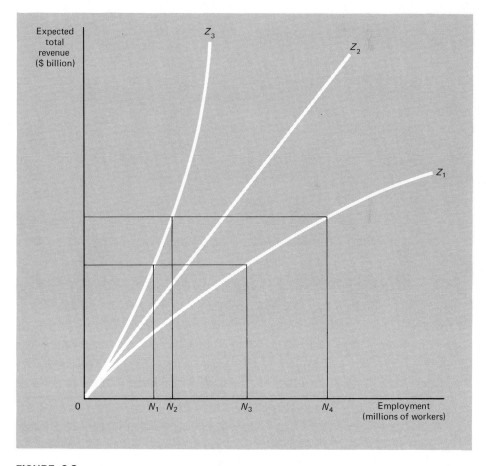

FIGURE 2-3

Alternative Specifications of the Aggregate Supply Function

To derive the shape of the aggregate supply function, something must be known about the relationship between employment and marginal productivity. Since the capital stock is assumed to be fixed, the *law of diminishing returns* should take effect as more workers are employed. In

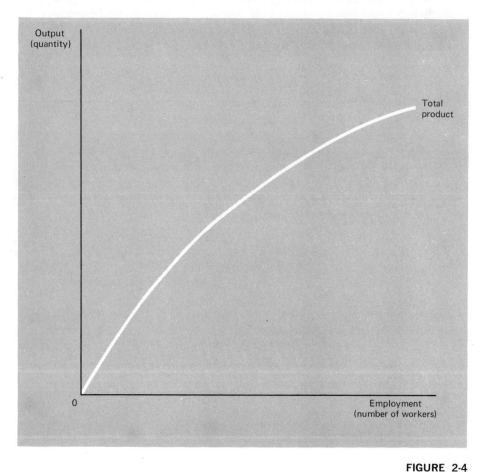

FIGURE 2-4

Typical Production Function for a Firm with a Fixed Stock of Capital

other words, we would expect output to increase with employment, but at a decreasing rate. The marginal contribution of each additional worker, although positive, will decrease as employment increases. Figure 2-4 represents a typical production function (the relationship between input and output) displaying diminishing returns to employment. The decreasing

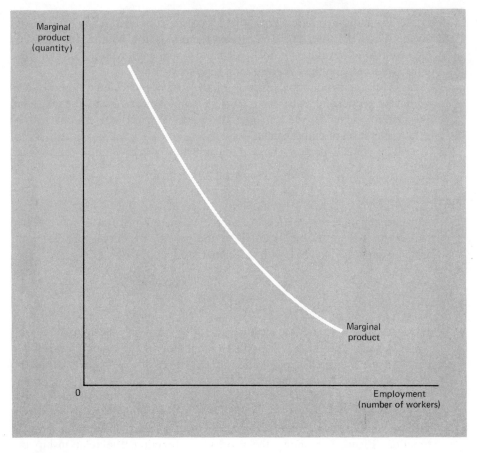

FIGURE 2-5

Marginal Productivity of an Additional Worker

marginal product per worker associated with this production function is
shown in Figure 2-5.[2]

___

[2] The marginal product is the change in total product associated with a change
in employment. Algebraically,

$$MP = \frac{\Delta TP}{\Delta N}$$

where ΔTP is the change in total product and ΔN is the change in employment.
Thus, the marginal product for any level of employment, N, is the slope of the
total product function there, and the marginal product function can be derived
from the production function. Notice that if the production function displays
diminishing returns, its slope is constantly falling, and the marginal product function
will be downward sloping.

Given these relationships, the aggregate supply function can be derived. We shall begin the analysis by examining the relationship between expected total revenue (product demand) and employment for the firm. This relationship is the *expected total revenue function.*

From the production function of the firm we can determine the level of output associated with each level of employment. From the marginal productivity schedule we can find the price at which the output will be sold at any level of employment.

The firm in perfect competition will hire workers until, for the last worker,

$$p \times MP = w$$

This implies that, for any level of employment, the price at which the firm expects to sell its output is equal to the cost of producing the last unit, which is the wage divided by the marginal product of labor, or

$$p = \frac{w}{MP}$$

If we assume that the wage which the firm must pay is uniform for all workers (since the firm is a perfect competitor in the labor market), we can find the expected supply price at any level of employment from the marginal productivity schedule.

With our knowledge of the firm's production function and the assumption that the firm is a perfect competitior,[3] attempting to maximize profits, we can now proceed to derive the firm's expected total revenue function. Figure 2-6 shows the production function, the relationship between output and employment, as well as the relationship between expected supply price and employment. Since output multiplied by expected supply price is equal to expected total revenue, we have all the information required to derive the expected total revenue function.

The production function relating labor input to output is shown in Figure 2-6(A). When N_0 workers are employed, output will be q_0, read from the production function. Figure 2-6(B) shows the marginal product, also as a function of employment. The marginal product function is derived from the production function. At N_0, the marginal product is MP_0. Remember that the firm will employ workers until the value of the marginal product just equals the wage. If the wage is known, and since for any level

---

[3] Other assumptions about the market behavior of firms can be introduced. This will change the specification of the aggregate supply function. However, as long as firms raise product prices when labor costs increase, the aggregate supply function will be positively sloped. But it is important to keep in mind that the relationship between the product market and the labor market depends on the microeconomic model of market behavior one assumes to be most prevalent.

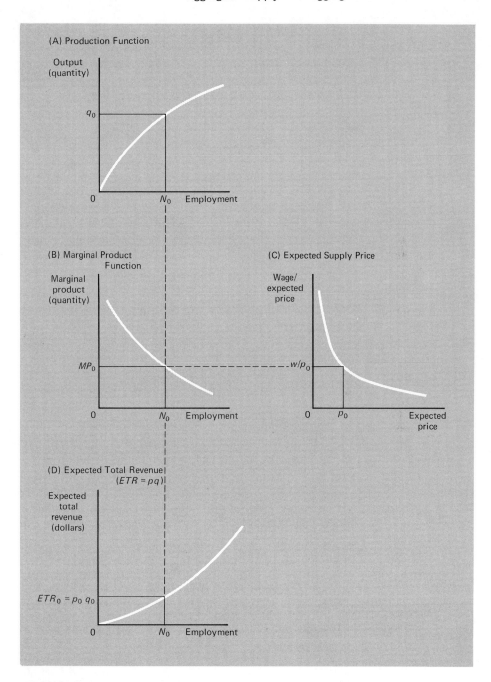

FIGURE 2-6

The Derivation of the Expected Total Revenue Function
from the Production Function for a Firm

of employment the marginal product is also known, then for any level of employment the price at which the firm expected to sell its output is determined. Algebraically,

$$p_0 = \frac{w}{MP_0}$$

which implies

$$MP_0 = \frac{w}{p_0}$$

Graphically the relationship is found in the following way. Figure 2-6(C) shows the ratio w/p_0 plotted as a function of p_0. This is simply the graph of a hyperbola when w is a constant. Since the marginal product, MP_0, is determined by the level of employment, N_0, in (B), and

$$MP_0 = \frac{w}{p_0}$$

the price p_0 at which the firm expects to sell its output when employment is N_0 can be found from (C). Expected total revenue associated with employment of N_0 workers is $p_0 q_0$ as seen in Figure 2-6(D). The expected total revenue function is the product of expected supply price and output, similarly derived for each hypothetical level of employment.

The derivation of the relationship between expected total revenue and employment for the firm can also be illustrated by means of a hypothetical example. Suppose that the firm can hire workers at the rate of $2 per hour. Columns 1 and 2 of Table 2-7 show the production function, the relationship between employment and output per man-hour. From this informa-

TABLE 2-7

The Derivation of Expected Total Revenue as a Function of Employment for a Firm

(1)	(2)	(3)	(4)	(5)	(6)
			Addition to		
		Marginal	Wage Cost	Expected	Expected
		Product (for	(for each 10	Market	Total
	Output	each 10 addi-	additional	Price =	Revenue =
Employment	(per hour)	tional workers)	workers)	(4)/(3)	(2) × (5)
0	0	0	$ 0.00	$0.00	$ 0.00
10	100	100	$20.00	$0.20	$ 20.00
20	190	90	$20.00	$0.22	$ 41.80
30	270	80	$20.00	$0.25	$ 67.50
40	340	70	$20.00	$0.29	$ 98.60
50	400	60	$20.00	$0.33	$132.00

tion the marginal product for each group of 10 additional workers can be derived. The result is shown in column 3. For example, if employment is 20, output is 190. By hiring 10 more workers, the firm can increase output to 270, resulting in a marginal product for the 10 workers of 80. For each level of employment, the price at which firms expect their output to be sold, column 5, is determined by dividing the addition to the total wage cost, column 4, by the marginal product, column 3. Then, expected total revenue in column 6 can be calculated as expected market price multiplied by output for each level of employment.

Figure 2-7 shows the relationship between expected total revenue and employment for our hypothetical firm. An increase in expected total revenue from $67.50 to $98.60 per hour, for example, would induce the firm to hire 10 additional workers. As employment increases, the firm requires successively greater increments to expected total revenue to induce it to hire 10 additional workers. Therefore, the expected total revenue function of the firm is convex to the employment axis, as seen in Figure 2-7.

The aggregate supply function can be derived from the expected total revenue functions of the individual firms in the economy. An aggregate supply function, such as that shown in Figure 2-8, is obtained by aggregating the expected total revenue functions of the individual firms.

THE SHAPE OF THE AGGREGATE SUPPLY FUNCTION

Although we know *a priori* that the aggregate supply function is upward sloping, its actual shape will be determined by the aggregate production function of all the firms in the economy and the money wages.[4] Assuming again that our firms are perfect competitors maximizing profits, price will be equal to the cost of the last unit produced [5] or

$$p = \frac{w}{MP}$$

Multiplying both sides of the profit-maximizing equation by output, q, the value of output, pq, will be equal to the cost of the last unit multiplied by the number of units, or

$$pq = \frac{wq}{MP}$$

---

[4] The derivation which follows is taken from Paul Davidson and Eugene Smolensky, *Aggregate Supply and Demand Analysis* (New York: Harper & Row, Publishers, 1964), pp. 125–128.

[5] If the capital stock is fixed, the wage divided by the marginal product of labor represents the cost of the last unit, or the marginal cost, MC. Thus, in perfect competition, firms will produce until price is equal to marginal cost or

$$p = \frac{w}{MP} = MC$$

Since output per worker, q/N, is called the average product of labor, AP, or

$$AP = \frac{q}{N}$$

the relationship can be expressed as

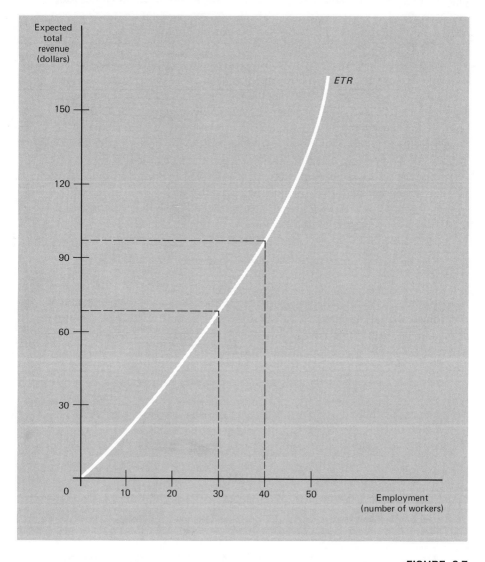

FIGURE 2-7

Relationship Between Expected Total Revenue and Employment for a Hypothetical Firm

$$pq = \frac{wq}{MP}\frac{N}{N} = \frac{w}{MP}\left(\frac{q}{N}\right)N = w\left(\frac{AP}{MP}\right)N$$

The expression $w(AP/MP)$ represents the slope of the aggregate supply function. It indicates the change in employment which will occur in response to expected changes in total revenue or sales. The slope depends upon the money wage, w, as well as the ratio AP/MP. The behavior of the ratio AP/MP as employment changes depends upon the production function and reflects the importance of diminishing returns to labor as employment increases with a fixed capital stock.

If the money wage is assumed to be fixed, the aggregate supply function will be a straight line (having a constant slope) only if the $AP/$

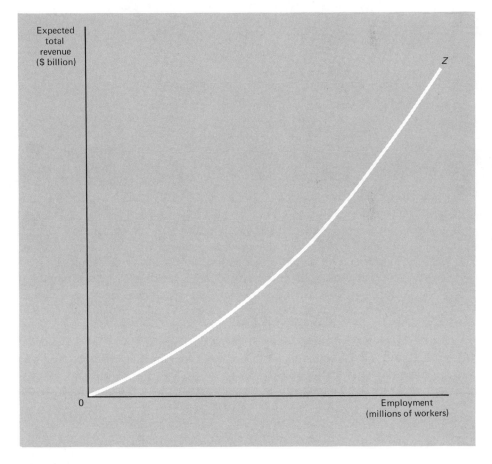

FIGURE 2-8

An Aggregate Supply Function

MP ratio is constant for all levels of employment. This property characterizes certain special types of production functions, including thet Cobb–Douglas production function which is extensively used in empirical research.[6]

If the slope increases with employment, the aggregate supply function will be convex to the employment axis. If the money wage is fixed, this will be the case if the ratio AP/MP rises as employment increases. The ratio will rise if diminishing returns become more important as successive increments of labor are added to a fixed capital stock. In our hypothetical example, marginal productivity decreases faster than average productivity as employment increases, and the expected total revenue function is convex to the employment axis. The slope will also increase with employment if money wages tend to rise as labor markets tighten.

It is unlikely that the slope of the aggregate supply function will decrease with employment, making it concave to the employment axis. This implies that diminishing returns become less important as more and more labor is added to a fixed capital stock, making AP/MP a decreasing function of employment. Alternatively, it suggests that money wages tend to fall as labor markets tighten, an unlikely occurrence.

Assuming a fixed money wage, the relationship between the aggregate production function and the aggregate supply function is shown in Figure 2-9. Z_3, derived from a production function in which diminishing returns become progressively more important as employment increases, implies that successively greater increments in expected total revenue will be necessary to induce firms to hire additional workers. Z_2 implies that diminishing returns are of equal importance at all levels of employment. Firms will always employ the same number of additional workers for equal increments in expected total revenue at all levels of employment. Both Z_3 and Z_2 are likely shapes that an actual aggregate supply function might take.

The function Z_1, based on a production function displaying diminishing returns that become less important as employment increases, implies that firms require successively smaller increments in expected total revevnue to induce them to hire additional workers. This is not likely on an *a priori* basis, and consequently, we shall generally reject the notion of a concave aggregate supply function, unless, of course, an empirical investigation should demonstrate otherwise.

While the exact shape of the aggregate supply function must be de-

---

[6] A Cobb–Douglas production function is of the form

$$q = Ax_1^\alpha x_2^{1-\alpha}$$

where x_1 and x_2 are factor inputs, A is a constant which reflects the general efficiency of the technology and α is a constant which reflects relative factor shares in the total product.

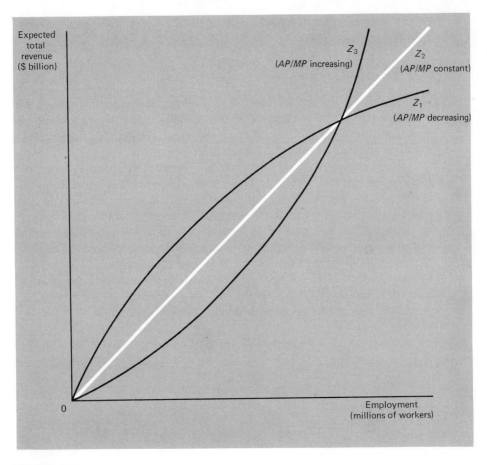

FIGURE 2-9

Relationship Between the Aggregate Production Function
and the Aggregate Supply Function

termined empirically, *a priori* reasoning suggests that it will be positively
sloped, originating from the origin and either linear or convex to the
employment axis.

2-3   THE COMPONENTS OF AGGREGATE DEMAND

From the aggregate supply function, the level of employment can be determined if expected total revenue is known. To estimate how much
revenue firms can expect, the buyers' side of the market must be examined.

Of course, total revenue of firms will be identically (always) equal to total spending of buyers.

In this section the spending decisions of major economic groups will be investigated. Total spending by all economic groups is *aggregate demand,* and the *aggregate demand function* is the relationship between total spending and income for the economy as a whole.

It is important to note that total income and spending are *functionally* related, not identical. This means that spending and income are not necessarily always equal, but are equal only at some particular level of spending and income. In the Keynesian model, the relationship between spending and income is based on a hypothesis about the behavior of spending units. Total income, however, is identically, or definitionally, equal to the value of output, and this implies that total spending is not always equal to the value of output. Therefore, all goods will not be purchased at all levels of output.

Denoting an identity relationship by the symbol $\equiv$, then

$$\text{Income} \equiv \text{Value of output}$$

and

$$\text{Total spending} \equiv \text{Total revenue}$$

Therefore, if

$$\text{Income} \neq \text{Total spending}$$

then

$$\text{Total revenue} \neq \text{Value of total output}$$

It is the aggregate demand *function* of the Keynesian analysis that represents the basic departure from the classical point of view. By stating that total income is equal to total spending only at a single level of income, Keynes was in effect denying the validity of Say's Law on which classical macroeconomics was based. Say's Law, held by classical economists to be a basic macroeconomic principle, asserted that "supply creates its own demand." This can be interpreted to mean that spending is *identically,* not functionally, related to income, or that all goods produced will be purchased regardless of the level of output and income.

It is convenient to divide buyers into four categories, since the spending decisions of economic units within each of the four groups are based upon similar factors, while the determinants of demand for each group are sufficiently different to warrant analyzing them separately. The consumer sector, or household units, purchases consumption goods; the business sector purchases capital, or investment goods; the foreign sector, economic units abroad, purchases our exports; and the public sector, or government, purchases "public goods." Total spending, or aggregate demand, D, can be treated as the sum of consumption, C, investment, I, net exports, X_n,[7] and government spending, G:

$$D = C + I + X_n + G$$

Since each spending group is motivated by different factors, the analysis of aggregate demand will involve the consideration of each of its components separately. Chapters 5 and 6 will look at factors affecting consumption and investment in some detail. However, to develop the preliminary model of income determination in the next chapter, something about the shape of the aggregate demand function must be known. Government spending will be treated as a policy variable that can be controlled by a central authority. It will be apparent that one goal of government expenditure policy will be to control the level of aggregate demand. The remainder of this chapter will take a preliminary look at factors affecting spending in the consumer and business sectors.

THE CONSUMPTION FUNCTION

Expenditures by the consumer sector represent the largest component of aggregate demand in most economies. Empirically the *consumption function,* or the relationship between aggregate consumption and aggregate income, is one of the most stable or reliable of all macroeconomic relationships. Consequently, if the amount of income earned in a particular period is known, a forecaster can predict consumption, the major component of total spending, with a fair amount of accuracy.[8]

Keynes postulated that consumption is a function of income. He

---

[7] Only *net* exports, that is, total exports minus imports should be included in aggregate demand. Since some of the demand in the domestic sectors, C, I, and G, is met by imports, spending on imports must be subtracted from total aggregate demand to obtain domestic aggregate demand. Treating exports as net exports, that is,

$$X_n = \text{total exports} - \text{total imports}$$

does, in effect, reduce the aggregate demand equation by the amount spent on imports.

[8] One reason that such good estimates of consumption can be obtained when income is known is that consumption itself represents a high percentage of income. In most years, consumption represents over 90 percent of the after-tax income of households in the United States. It is more difficult to predict *changes* in consumption where a change in income is expected.

believed that, barring sudden changes in tastes and institutions, consump-
tion°could be expected to increase as income increased.

A consumption function such as Keynes suggested is shown in
Figure 2-10. The consumption function intersects the consumption axis
above the origin and has a slope that is less than 1. (The 45° line has a
slope equal to 1.)

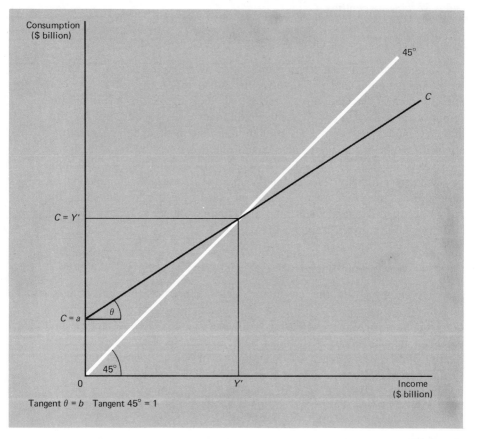

FIGURE 2-10

The Keynesian Consumption Function

Keynes reasoned that while people with high incomes consume
more than people with low incomes, high-income families consume a
smaller *proportion* of their income than low-income families. He believed
that the same type of behavior would characterize whole economies. The
higher the level of aggregate income, the greater would be the proportion

saved, in the aggregate. A poor society might actually consume more than its current income by borrowing from abroad. A rich economy, on the other hand, would not spend all of its income on consumption goods.

In Figure 2-10, if aggregate income is less than Y', consumption will be greater than income and must be financed by borrowing or utilizing accumulated assets. If income is above Y', it is not all spent. A moment of reflection will reveal that the vertical distance between the consumption function and the 45° line measures saving when income is above Y' and dissaving or borrowing when income is below Y'. Only when income is Y' will income and consumption be equal.

Keynes labeled the proportion of income consumed at any income level the *average propensity to consume, APC*. Since saving is defined as income not consumed, the reader should verify that

$$APC + APS = 1$$

where *APS* is the *average propensity to save*, defined as the proportion of income saved. In Figure 2-10 the *APC* is a decreasing function of income. This implies that the *APS* increases with income.

The *marginal propensity to consume, MPC,* is the proportion of an increment of income spent on consumption. If a family receives an extra dollar of income (e.g., in the form of a tax rebate), the proportion of the *additional* dollar spent on consumption is the *MPC*. The *MPC* is of particular interest to forecasters and policy planners who are concerned with the effect of tax cuts and changes in government spending on consumption. Since the *APC* decreases with income, the *MPC* will be less than the *APC*. Defining the *marginal propensity to save, MPS,* as the proportion of an increment of income saved, it is clear that

$$MPC + MPS = 1$$

For a linear or straight-line consumption function the *MPC* will be constant and equal to its slope.

Consider the algebraic representation of Figure 2-10:

$$C = a + bY$$

The constant, *a*, represents the point of intersection with the consumption axis and indicates the amount of consumption that would take place even if no income were earned. The slope of the function, *b*, represents the ratio of vertical to horizontal change along the function.[9] Notice that *b* is the *MPC*, since

---

[9] The slope of the function is the tangent of the angle of inclination.

$$MPC = \frac{\Delta C}{\Delta Y} = b$$

where ΔC and ΔY signify change in C and Y, respectively. The expression $(1 - b)$ is the *MPS*, since

$$MPS = 1 - MPC = 1 - b$$

Along this function the *APC*, C/Y, declines with income since

$$APC = \frac{C}{Y} = \frac{a + bY}{Y} = \frac{a}{Y} + b$$

and the expression $(a/Y) + b$ declines with income if a and b are positive.

A linear consumption function with a positive intercept and positive slope less than 1 reflects Keynes' postulates about consumption behavior. It is realistic to assume that there will be some positive consumption forthcoming even if there is no current income, at least in the short run, so that

$$0 < a$$

It is also reasonable to assume that

$$0 < MPC = b < 1$$

That is, some of an increment to income is always saved even if the *APC* is greater than 1. Given such a consumption function, the *APC* will decline with income and the *MPC* will be constant. As discussed in Chapter 5, there is empirical evidence in support of such a linear consumption function for many economies, particularly for short-run situations in which practical policy planning and forecasting take place.

THE INVESTMENT DECISION

Investment, or expenditure on capital equipment and inventories, is undertaken for the purpose of producing other goods and services rather than for directly satisfying human wants. Although smaller in magnitude than consumption spending, investment presents more difficult problems to the forecaster because its relationship to income is more complicated and less reliable. It is financed by depreciation allowances, profits, and borrowing. *A priori* reasoning suggests that investment will increase with rising sales and profits, making more funds available. Consequently, investment will be an increasing function of income. Since some expenditure on capital equipment is financed by borrowing, investment should also be sensitive to credit conditions, reflected in the market rate of interest. Investment should be a decreasing function of the rate of interest, since as the interest rate rises, firms will be discouraged from borrowing and consequently will invest less. Furthermore, some additional investment may be forthcoming that is independent of the level of sales or credit conditions. This may occur as old machines wear out or become obsolete, or when firms undertake innovative investment to capture a larger market share.

These considerations are reflected in a hypothetical *investment function* which relates aggregate investment with aggregate income and the interest rate. Algebraically,

$$I = g + dY - ei$$

where g, the constant term, represents investment taking place independently of income and the interest rate, and i is the market rate of interest. We expect the constant d to be positive and less than 1; that is,

$$0 < d < 1$$

since firms will most likely invest some, but not all, of an increment in national income. While firms may invest all or more of their own income, the share of national income at their disposal is relatively small, generally not exceeding 15 percent.[10] The effect of the interest rate should be negative, reflecting the hypothesized inverse relationship between investment and the interest rate.

To portray the investment function graphically, the equation must be reduced to two variables. For any given interest rate, the investment represented by the expression ei can be combined with g, and the investment function can be written as

$$I = (g - ei) + dY$$
$$= h + dY$$

where

$$h = g - ei$$

In this way investment is broken down into a function of income as well as a component which is independent of income.

This investment function is shown in Figure 2-11. The slope of the investment function, d, is the *marginal propensity to invest* or the propor-

---

[10] See Appendix A (Section A-4) for a discussion of the relationship between income shares and the marginal propensity to spend out of national income.

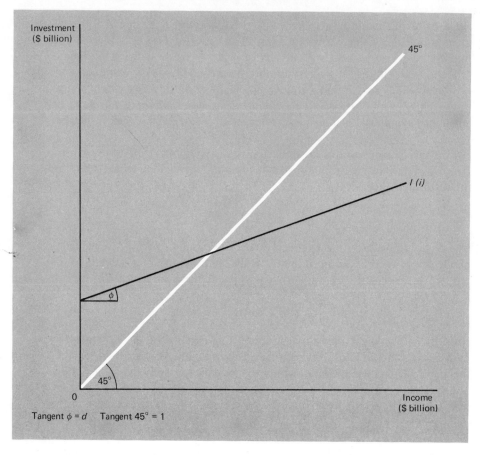

FIGURE 2-11

An Investment Function for a Stipulated Rate of Interest

tion of an increment of income invested by firms. This will be positive, and unless firms invest all of the increment of national income (an unlikely event), it will be less than 1.

If the rate of interest were to fall, we would expect the constant term in the investment function to increase (since the effect of the interest rate is negative), shifting the investment function upward. In fact, we can conceive of a *family* of parallel investment functions, each associated with a different rate of interest but having the same slope. Such a family of investment functions is shown in Figure 2-12. As the interest rate rises from i_1 to i_4, the investment function shifts downward, indicating the inverse relationship between investment and the rate of interest. The lowest in-

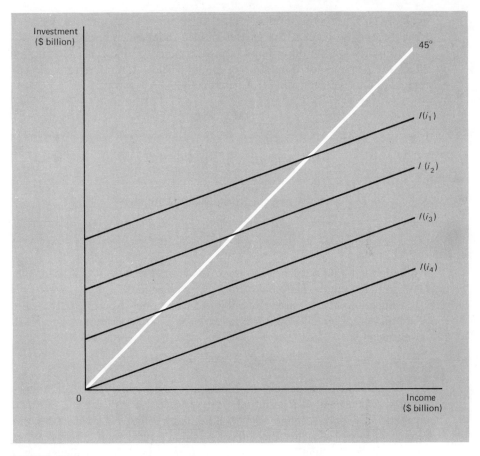

FIGURE 2-12

A Family of Investment Functions
Associated with Different Rates of Interest

terest rate, i_1, is associated with the highest investment function in the family.

THE FOREIGN SECTOR

Demand from abroad, exports, is also included in aggregate demand. Imports, or purchases of foreign goods, should be subtracted from consumption, investment, and government spending to determine domestic aggregate demand.

Factors governing export demand are complex and are linked only in an indirect way to the level of domestic income. Consequently, we shall treat them as *exogenous,* that is, determined independently of income.

Imports, on the other hand, are determined by the same factors that affect the demand for domestic goods. In particular, imports are directly related to the level of income.[11] Algebraically,

$$M = mY$$

where

$$M = \text{imports}$$
$$Y = \text{income}$$
$$m = \text{marginal propensity to import}[12]$$

and

$$0 < m < 1$$

While the marginal propensity to import is greater than 0, it will be smaller in magnitude than the marginal propensity to consume.

Since imports, M, are a function of income, net exports, X_n, will also be a function of income, even if total exports, E, are considered exogenous. Algebraically,

$$X_n = E - mY$$

Graphically, the net export function is shown in Figure 2-13. Since exports, E, are fixed at E_0, and imports, M, increase with income at a rate m, then net exports decline with income. Notice that net exports become zero at income Y_0, where the import function equals total exports. When income is greater than Y_0, the trade balance is in deficit, while at lower income levels the balance is in surplus.[13] Note that when exports are treated as fixed, the trade deficit increases as national income increases, as long as the marginal propensity to import is positive.

The Shape of the Aggregate Demand Function

We are now prepared to consider the shape of the aggregate demand function. Aggregate demand is equal to the sum of its components:

[11] Imports can also be affected by credit conditions at home, reflected in the interest rate. The impact of the domestic interest rate on import demand is likely to be small, however, and we shall ignore it in this model for simplicity. The interest rate can be introduced, however, in a more complete model, with no loss of generality.

[12] Since there is no constant term, the marginal propensity to import equals the average propensity to import. This is not necessarily true for all models.

[13] The balance of trade is not to be confused with the balance of payments, which includes financial transactions, transfers, and gold flows.

$$D = C + I + X_n + G$$

The aggregate consumption, investment, and net export functions have been specified:

$$C = a + bY$$

$$I = h + dY$$

$$X_n = E_0 - mY$$

Suppose government spending can take on any value, G_0, selected by the central authorities:

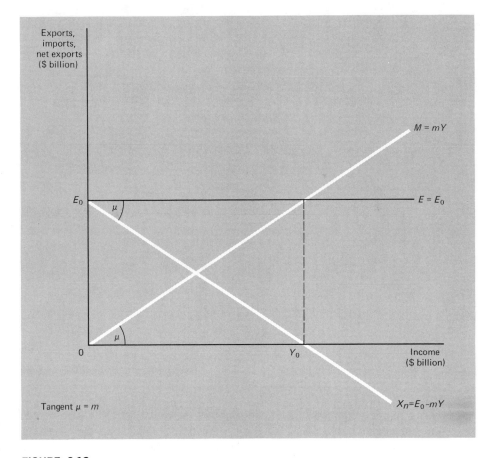

FIGURE 2-13

Net Exports as a Function of Income

$$G = G_0$$

Then,

$$D = C + I + X_n + G$$
$$= (a + bY) + (h + dY) + (E_0 - mY) + G_0$$
$$= (a + h + E_0 + G_0) + (b + d - m)Y$$

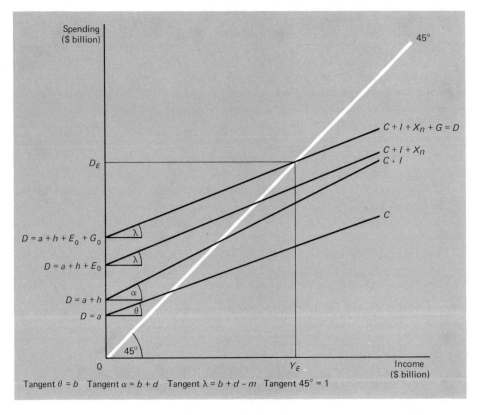

FIGURE 2-14

The Aggregate Demand Function

Using our hypothetical linear consumption and investment functions, aggregate demand is a linear function of income, intersecting the spending axis at $(a + h + E_0 + G_0)$, with a slope of $(b + d - m)$. This implies that even if income were zero, the level of spending would be $a + h + E_0 + G_0$.

For every increment of income, $b + d - m$ percent of that increment would be spent domestically.

The aggregate demand function is shown in Figure 2-14. It is the vertical sum of the consumption, investment, and net export functions and government spending.

Recall the analytical device of the 45° line. In Figure 2-14, along such a line, total spending is always equal to total income. Along the aggregate demand function, D, total spending is equal to total income, Y, only at $Y_E = D_E$ where D intersects the 45° line. There is no other income level at which spending is exactly equal to income. When income is greater than Y_E, spending is less than income, and when income is less than Y_E, spending exceeds income. The difference between income and spending at any income level is the vertical distance between the 45° line and the aggregate demand function. Only where the aggregate demand function intersects the 45° line is spending exactly equal to income or output. Only where the aggregate demand function intersects the 45° line is all output actually purchased and no orders left unfilled. At all other income levels, Say's Law is invalid.

In this chapter the aggregate supply and demand functions have been defined and analyzed. Chapter 3 will show how the macroeconomic equilibrium between aggregate supply and demand determines the level of income and employment. Once the theory of income determination is thoroughly developed, we shall see how macroeconomic policy can be used to manipulate the level of income and employment.

QUESTIONS FOR STUDY AND REVIEW

1. (a) Suppose the baker in the text example found that he could sell only 800 loaves of bread for $400. Then he would be left with an inventory of 200 loaves of bread valued at $100. How would this affect his accounts?

(b) Because he has accumulated unplanned inventory valued at $100, the baker expects that his future sales will amount to only $400 in each production period. Consequently, he decides to produce only 800 loaves of bread, valued at $400. Show how his decision to produce less bread will affect the accounts of the miller and the farmer, as well as his own.

When the value of output falls to $400, total income must also fall to $400. Be sure your revised accounts reflect the output–income identity.

2. A production function for a firm in perfect competition is shown below:

Labor Input (per hour)	Output (per hour)
0	0
1	10
2	17
3	22
4	26
5	27

(a) If the hourly wage is $1.00, derive and graph the expected total revenue function for the firm.

(b) Suppose minimum wage legislation goes into effect and the firm must now pay an hourly wage of $1.50. How will this affect the expected total revenue function of the firm? Show the new expected total revenue function in the same graph with the old one.

(c) Suppose the firm undertakes a program which trains labor to produce output more efficiently. If man-hour productivity is doubled, so that

Labor Input (per hour)	Output (per hour)
0	0
1	20
2	34
3	44
4	52
5	54

and the hourly wage is $1.50, how will this affect the firm's expected total revenue function?

3. Consider the aggregate demand function

$$D = C + I + X_n + G$$

for a hypothetical economy for which

$$C = 200 + 0.6 Y$$
$$I = 100 + 0.3 Y$$

$$X_n = E - 0.1Y$$

$$E = 150$$

$$G = 150$$

(a) Find the level of aggregate demand in this economy when total income, Y, equals total spending, D.

(b) Suppose the government increases spending by 50. What will be the effect on aggregate demand? (*Hint:* Aggregate demand will increase by *more* than 50.)

(c) Suppose the government wants to effectuate an increase in aggregate demand of 500. How much will the government need to increase its spending to achieve this goal? (*Hint:* Government spending will have to increase by *less* than 500.)

(d) It is possible that the government may wish to use monetary policy rather than fiscal policy to increase the level of aggregate demand. Suppose the interest rate is reduced and the investment function becomes

$$I = 150 + 0.3Y$$

What will be the effect on aggregate demand?

4. We have defined a consumption function which relates total consumption and total income:

$$C = a + bY$$

Household spending on some types of durable consumption goods, however, may be a function of the interest rate. Can you derive a *family* of consumption functions, each associated with a *different* rate of interest? (*Hint:* Remember how we derived the family of investment functions.)

ADDITIONAL READING

DAVIDSON, PAUL, and EUGENE SMOLENSKY, *Aggregate Supply and Demand Analysis.* New York: Harper & Row, Publishers, 1964, Chapters 9 and 10.

HANSEN, ALVIN H., *A Guide to Keynes.* New York: McGraw-Hill Book Company, Inc., 1953, Chapter 1.

KEYNES, JOHN MAYNARD, *The General Theory of Employment, Interest, and Money.* New York: Harcourt Brace Jovanovich, Inc., 1965, Chapter 3; originally published by Macmillan & Co., Ltd., 1936.

U.S. Department of Commerce, Office of Business Economics, "U.S. Income and Output," supplement to *The Survey of Current Business* (November, 1958). Washington, D.C.: U.S. Government Printing Office, 1958.

3

The Analytics
of Income Determination:
National Income
and Employment Equilibrium

Having examined the output-income identity and the aggregate supply and demand functions, we shall consider how the interaction of aggregate supply and demand determines a unique level of national income and employment. The analysis of this chapter represents the framework of Keynesian economics.

3-1   THE THEORY OF INCOME DETERMINATION

THE CONCEPT OF ECONOMIC EQUILIBRIUM

Equilibrium in economics refers to the attainment of a position from which there is no tendency to move because that position is preferred by the economic units involved. Equilibrium reflects only the preferences of economic units, households, and firms, acting independently of each other, not social or aggregate preferences. Consequently, an equilibrium position is not necessarily socially desirable. Furthermore, the preferred position will depend upon certain underlying conditions or *parameters* that represent constraints on behavior. Although they may be viewed as undesirable by the individual households or firms, these conditions are not subject to their control.

For example, recalling the analysis of aggregate supply, a firm will employ N workers on the basis of some expected total revenue—for example, $1000. These workers will produce output value at $1000. The firm's expected total revenue function, based on the assumption that the firm wishes to maximize profits at each level of sales, is shown in Figure 3-1.

The desire to hire N workers, however, is contingent upon receipts or sales actually totaling $1000. If total sales fall short of $1000, the firm will regret hiring N workers since profits will be less than they could have been, had a smaller wage cost been incurred and had less output been produced. If sales fall short of expectations, the firm will most likely revise its estimates of future sales receipts. Suppose expected total revenue is revised to $900 and the firm hires M workers. If actual sales receipts are not $900, as shown in Figure 3-1, the firm will be at its maximum profit position for that level of sales. The firm is said to be in equilibrium, given the underlying condition, or parameter, that actual sales are $900.

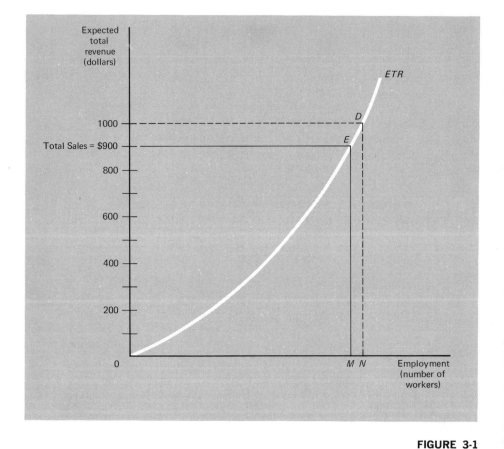

FIGURE 3-1

Equilibrium and Disequilibrium Positions for a Profit-Maximizing Firm When Total Sales Are $900

In Figure 3-1, point E on the expected total revenue function represents an equilibrium, or preferred, position for the firm when actual sales are $900. Actual total revenue is $900, and the firm maximizes profits by hiring M workers. Point D is a disequilibrium position, since expectations are not fulfilled and the firm can increase profits by reducing its labor force and moving to point E. There will be a movement from D to E, from a disequilibrium to an equilibrium position.

Suppose actual sales increase to $1000. This represents a change in the underlying conditions, or parameters, for the firm. Now the firm maximizes profits by hiring N workers, and D is the new preferred, or equilibrium, position. The examination of the various equilibrium positions associated with different underlying conditions, or parameters, is called *comparative statics*.

THE ATTAINMENT OF MACROECONOMIC EQUILIBRIUM

For the production sector, income and employment equilibrium occurs when actual revenue is equal to expected total revenue for all firms. The attainment of macroeconomic equilibrium, therefore, implies that total spending equals expected total revenue or, alternatively, that aggregate demand equals aggregate supply.

Keeping in mind the various national income identities, the macroeconomic equilibrium condition can be expressed in a number of ways. By definition, it is clear that

$$\text{Total income} \equiv \text{Value of output} \Rightarrow \text{Expected total revenue}$$

and

$$\text{Total spending} \equiv \text{Total revenue}$$

Furthermore, the firm is in a preferred, or equilibrium, position when

$$\text{Total revenue} = \text{Expected total revenue}$$

Given these relationships, the equilibrium condition can be expressed in several alternative ways:

$$\text{Expected total revenue} = \text{Total revenue}$$

or

$$\text{Expected total revenue} = \text{Total spending}$$

or

$$\text{Total income} = \text{Total spending}$$

It is important to keep in mind that all these relationships reflect essentially the same equilibrium condition; that is, the firms' expectations are realized. Keynes used the same reasoning presented here in his criticism of Say's Law. The equality between income and spending, he pointed out, is an equilibrium condition, not an identity. Furthermore, macroeconomic equilibrium could occur at less than full employment, as the expectations of firms are not necessarily realized at full employment.

The reader will recall the relationship between income and spending, the aggregate demand function. Equilibrium is attained when income is equal to spending. This is shown in Figure 3-2. Equilibrium income occurs at the point where the aggregate demand function intersects a 45° line from the origin, point P in Figure 3-2.

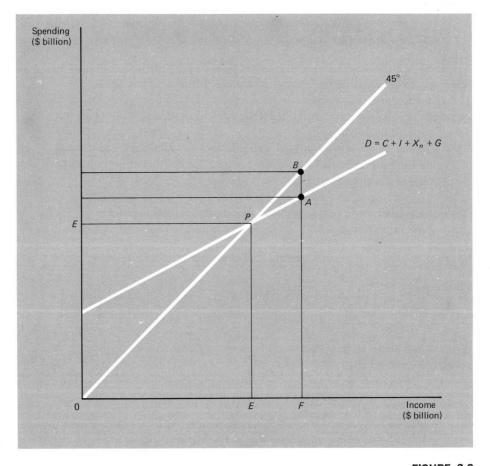

FIGURE 3-2

National Income Equilibrium

At all points on the 45° line, spending is equal to income, but only at income *E,* where the aggregate demand function, *D,* is coincident with the 45° line, will spending units decide to spend exactly *E,* in the aggregate. If income is greater than *E,* spending will fall short of income. At income *F,* for example, income exceeds spending by the amount *AB,* the vertical distance between the aggregate demand function and the 45° line at income *F.* If income is less than *E,* spending will exceed income. The difference between income and spending at any level of income is the vertical distance between the aggregate demand function and the 45° line at that income level.

If all income is not spent, all output will not be purchased and total revenue of the firm will fall short of expectations. Aggregate supply will exceed aggregate demand, and a preferred, or equilibrium, position will not have been attained. Employment and income will fall until equilibrium is reached. If, on the other hand, spending units wish to spend more than their income, in the aggregate, firms will not be able to fill all orders. Aggregate demand will exceed aggregate supply, and consequently, firms will employ more workers, thereby increasing the level of aggregate income until an equilibrium is attained. The relationship between aggregate supply and aggregate demand is shown in Figure 3-3.

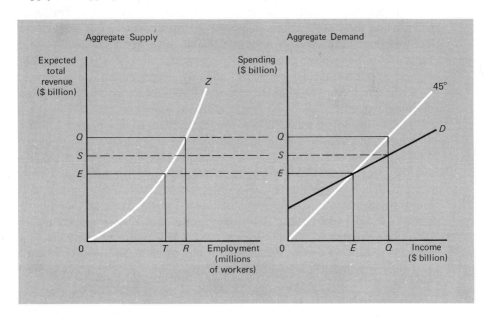

FIGURE 3-3

The Relationship Between Aggregate Demand and Aggregate Supply

Suppose firms expect total revenue to be at level Q and so employ R workers. Total output and income is Q and total spending is S. If total spending is S, total revenue is also S, since

$$\text{Total spending} \equiv \text{Total revenue}$$

Since total revenue has fallen short of expectations by SQ, the firms will revise estimates of total revenue. Employment and income will fall until income and spending reach point E and employment falls to T. At this point

$$\text{Total income} = \text{Total spending} = \text{Expected total revenue}$$

Consumers and producers have reached a preferred, or equilibrium, position from which there is no tendency to move.

3-2   THE CLASSICAL THEORY OF INCOME AND EMPLOYMENT

SAY'S LAW

Pre-Keynesian macroeconomics was based on Say's Law. The original version, attributed to the eighteenth-century economist Jean Baptiste Say, was that supply creates its own demand. In a barter economy where goods are exchanged for goods, Say's Law would always, necessarily, hold because goods would be produced only for consumption or exchange. Thus, the production or supply of goods would always be matched by an offsetting demand.

In an economy where goods can be exchanged for money, on the other hand, the possibility of holding money instead of goods is introduced. Now Say's Law can no longer be assumed to hold, but instead its validity must be demonstrated. Say's Law was reinterpreted by later economists to mean that in a free enterprise market system with flexible prices and wages, the aggregate demand for goods would equal the aggregate supply of goods at full employment. Say's Law in a money economy becomes an equilibrium condition, not an identity as it was in a barter economy, but classical economists took the position that a full-employment macroeconomic equilibrium would always result from free market forces.[1]

---

[1] This interpretation of Say's Law for a money economy is sometimes called Walras' Law. For a good, but somewhat difficult discussion see R. W. Clower, "The Keynesian Counter-Revolution: A Theoretical Appraisal," in F. H. Hahn and F. Brechling (eds.), *The Theory of Interest Rates,* Chapter 5 (New York: The Macmillan Company, 1965).

Unemployment might occur in the short run, but this was viewed as a disequilibrium situation that would eliminate itself after appropriate adjustments were made by households and firms and if prices and wages were flexible. The analysis of macroeconomic equilibrium that we have just developed was unnecessary, because it followed from classical macroeconomic theory that equilibrium would always be achieved at full employment.[2] Everyone who wanted to work would be employed because all output could always be sold, no matter how much was produced, and any amount of expected total revenue could be realized. There is no rationale for government intervention.

Say's Law was based on the assumption that all income not spent on consumption or by the government would be channeled to firms through the credit market and ultimately spent on investment. If this were true, then aggregate demand in equilibrium would always lie on the 45° line from the origin of the income-spending graph. Ignoring the foreign sector for simplicity, as shown in Figure 3-4, Say's Law implied that investment would always be equal to the gap between the $C + G$ portion of the aggregate demand function and the 45° line.

Classical macroeconomics, relying on Say's Law, was obviously not adequate for analyzing the Great Depression in which 25 percent of the industrial labor force was unemployed. Economists could not recommend appropriate government action when they were guided by a theory which said that a full-employment level of income would always be maintained, regardless of the level of government spending. Any deviation from full employment was viewed as only a short-run phenomenon which would be corrected automatically by free-market adjustments. Such a wait-and-see attitude was difficult to maintain politically as pressure from the jobless mounted. It moved Keynes to make the statement: "In the long run we are dead."

THE KEYNESIAN APPROACH

The innovation of Keynesian analysis was the notion that equilibrium between aggregate demand and aggregate supply can occur at any level of employment, not necessarily full employment. This implies that product market equilibrium might produce a state of perpetual disequilibrium in the labor market. The problem with the classical approach should be clear from the analysis which has preceded. Spending decisions and output–

---

[2] The analysis the classical economists used to demonstrate the validity of Say's Law, that is, the proposition that full employment will be achieved automatically in a market economy, is developed in Chapter 9.

employment decisions are made by different economic units with different motives. There is no reason to expect that spending units will decide to buy exactly as much as firms can produce at all levels of employment.

We have seen that consumption is a function of income. Saving is

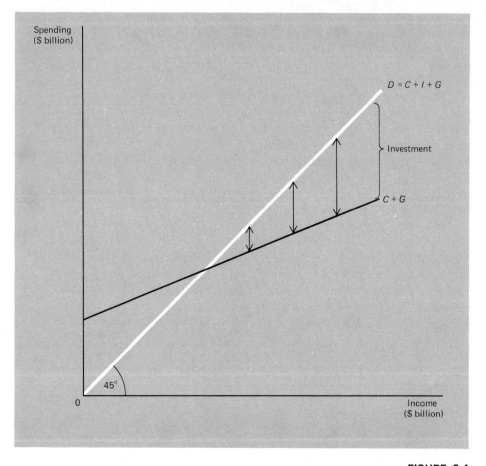

FIGURE 3-4

The Classical Aggregate Demand Function

the residual left over from income after consumption expenditures are made and taxes are paid:

$$Y = C + T + S$$

Therefore,

$$S = Y - C - T$$

The decision to save, therefore, is made by households.[3]

The decision to invest is made by business firms. As we shall see in Chapter 6, the investment decision is based upon many factors, including expected future profits, credit conditions, and the internal flow of funds. Since

$$D = C + I + X_n + G$$

then if we assume for simplicity that government finances all expenditures by taxation, so that

$$G = T$$

and assuming exports are matched by imports, so that

$$X_n = 0$$

then all income will be spent; that is,

$$Y = D$$

only if saving is equal to investment, or

$$S = I$$

However, saving and investment decisions are made by different groups of people with different motives, and there is no reason to expect that saving and investment will always be equal at all levels of income and employment. The equality between saving and investment is a precondition for national income equilibrium; that is,

$$S = I$$

and this equality may occur at any level of income, not necessarily the level associated with full employment.

---

[3] Actually much aggregate saving is done by business firms in the form of undistributed profits and capital consumption allowances. However, as we shall see in Chapter 6, these retained earnings are typically reinvested by firms. The problem occurs when saving must be channelled into investment through the credit market. Consequently, for an understanding of the issue at hand it is useful to simplify the analysis and ignore business saving that is directly invested. This is not to suggest that such saving is not important for analyzing other phenomena such as aggregate investment behavior. We shall explore that issue in Chapter 6.

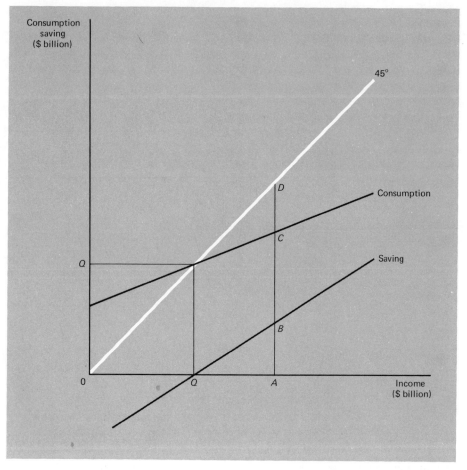

FIGURE 3-5

The Saving Function

Saving at any level of income is equal to the distance between the consumption function and a 45° line on the income-spending graph. At income A, for example, saving is AB, consumption is AC, and the difference between consumption and income is $CD = AB$. At income Q, the consumption function intersects the 45° line, consumption is equal to income, and saving is zero.

Figure 3-6 shows a Keynesian income equilibrium, ignoring the public and foreign sectors. Since investment and saving are independent linear functions of income, equilibrium occurs at a unique level of income. Equilibrium is at E, where saving is equal to investment and where the

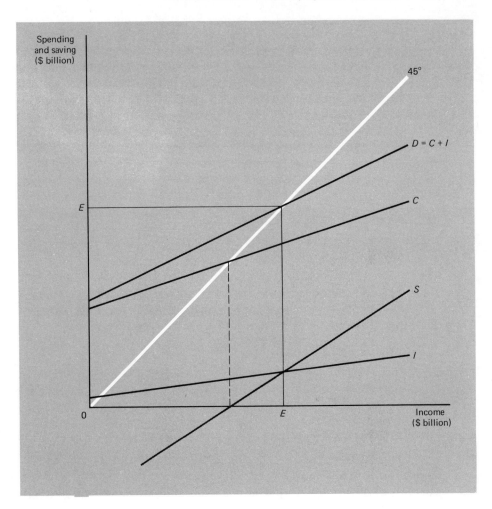

FIGURE 3-6

A Keynesian Income Equilibrium

aggregate demand function crosses the 45° line. Both investment and saving represent the distance between the consumption function and the 45° line at equilibrium.

Critics of the Keynesian approach were quick to suggest an inconsistency in his thinking. Consider the possible uses to which income can be put. It can be spent on consumption goods, C, imports, M, or taxes, T, or it can be saved, S:

$$\text{Income} \equiv C + S + T + M$$

Output produced is either consumed by households, C, foreigners, E, or government, G. Any output not consumed is invested in plant and equipment or inventories. Therefore,

$$\text{Output} \equiv C + I + E + G$$

Since

$$\text{Income} \equiv \text{Output}$$

then

$$C + S + M + T \equiv C + I + E + G$$

If the government budget is balanced, so that

$$G = T$$

and the net trade surplus is zero, so that

$$E = M$$

then investment will be identical to saving,

$$I \equiv S$$

since

$$C \equiv C$$

Does the output–income identity imply an investment–saving identity? Is Say's Law vindicated after all? Keynes pointed out that two different concepts of saving and investment are involved in the discussion.

Returning to the question of the disposition of output,

$$\text{Output} \equiv C + I + E + G$$

we recall that investment was defined as any output not purchased by households, governments, and foreigners. This is an *ex post* concept of investment and includes unplanned or unexpected inventories of goods not purchased by the spending units as well as planned inventories and capital goods. Firms will not be in equilibrium if unplanned inventory is accumulated.

On the other hand, investment in the aggregate demand function is an *ex ante* concept. *Ex ante* investment is the amount all firms plan to spend on capital goods and inventories. Only when *ex post* (actual investment) and *ex ante* (planned) investment are equal will firms be in a preferred position and hence in equilibrium.

While *ex post* investment, a residual component of output, is identical to saving, that is,

$$I_{ex\ post} \equiv S$$

ex ante investment is equal to saving only *in equilibrium*. Indeed, the equalities

$$I_{ex\ ante} = S$$

and

$$I_{ex\ ante} = I_{ex\ post}$$

are alternative statements of the macroeconomic equilibrium condition that aggregate demand be equal to aggregate supply. Thus, in answering his critics Keynes clarified the relationship between the saving–investment equality and macroeconomic equilibrium.

To summarize the results, consider the aggregate supply and demand schedules in Figure 3-7. Point *B* represents a disequilibrium level of in-

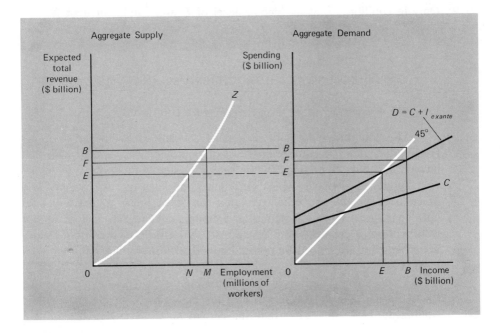

FIGURE 3-7

Aggregate Supply and Aggregate Demand

come. At income B, expected total revenue is B, the value of output is B, and employment is M. However, spending is equal to F. Since B is produced and F is purchased, then FB is unplanned inventory investment:

$$I_{ex\ post} = I_{ex\ ante} + FB$$

Now it is clear that

$$S = I_{ex\ ante} + FB$$

since saving is measured by the distance between the 45° line and the consumption function on the income–spending graph in Figure 3-7.
   Therefore,

$$I_{ex\ post} = S$$

and

$$I_{ex\ ante} \neq S$$

This analysis holds for any disequilibrium point, so that

$$I_{ex\ post} \equiv S$$

Only in equilibrium, at an income level of E and employment of N, will

$$I_{ex\ ante} = S \equiv I_{ex\ post}$$

3-3   CONCLUSIONS OF THE EQUILIBRIUM ANALYSIS

THE POSSIBILITY OF AN UNDEREMPLOYMENT EQUILIBRIUM

The equilibrium level of income is determined by the level of aggregate demand. The equilibrium level of employment associated with that income in turn is determined by the aggregate supply function.

Aggregate demand, which determines the level of employment, is a function of income and other economic variables. Since equilibrium does not occur at all levels of income and employment, everyone looking for work will not necessarily find jobs. Spending decisions of the major spending groups are not guided by considerations of the economy's full-employment goal.

Thus, Keynes, writing in the midst of the worst economic depression the world has ever known, envisioned the possibility of a macroeconomic equilibrium persisting at less than full employment:

In particular, it is an outstanding characteristic of the economic system in which we live that, whilst it is subject to severe fluctuations in respect of output and employment, it is not violently unstable. Indeed it seems capable of remaining in a chronic condition of sub-normal activity for a considerable period without any marked tendency either toward recovery or collapse. Moreover, the evidence indicates that full, or even approximately full, employment is of rare and short-lived occurrence.[4]

Suppose, for example, in Figure 3-8, full employment is at F. When F workers are employed, the value of aggregate output and income is G, and at an income level of G, aggregate supply will exceed aggregate de-

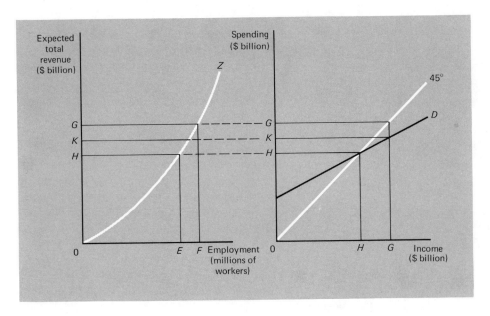

FIGURE 3-8

An Underemployment Equilibrium

mand by the amount KG. In equilibrium, firms will hire fewer than F workers to produce less output. Output and income in equilibrium will be H, and employment will be E. Consequently, EF workers will be unemployed in equilibrium; that is, EF workers will be looking for work and unable to find jobs.

Full employment in equilibrium can be achieved by an upward vertical shift of the aggregate demand schedule from D_1 to D_2 as shown in Figure

[4] John Maynard Keynes, *The General Theory of Employment, Interest, and Money* (New York: Harcourt Brace Jovanovich, Inc., 1965), pp. 249–250; originally published by Macmillan & Co., Ltd., 1936.

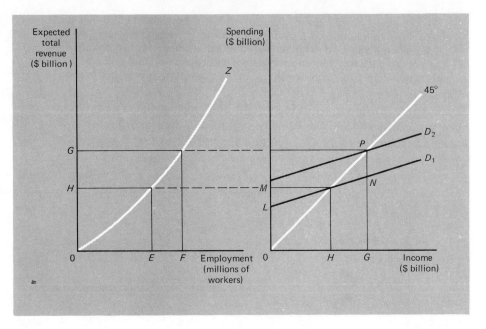

FIGURE 3-9

Attainment of a Full-Employment Equilibrium
by a Shift of the Aggregate Demand Function

3-9. An upward shift of $LM = ND$ is required to bring the economy to full employment.

What factors might cause the aggregate demand function to shift from D_1 to D_2? Recalling that

$$D = C + I + X_n + G$$

and assuming that all the spending units are at equilibrium at D_1, then the central authority can take measures to shift aggregate demand to D_2.[5]

The most obvious measure is to increase government expenditure by the amount LM. Other possibilities include

---

[5] A shift in aggregate demand can also occur as a result of changes in certain underlying conditions or parameters which we have assumed to be constant. For instance, an advance in technology might affect investment by increasing the rate of replacement for obsolete machines, thus causing the investment function to shift upward. We shall consider such possibilities in Chapter 6. However, in general, economic policy makers cannot rely upon chance events for maintaining full-employment income equilibrium.

1. reducing personal taxes, thereby causing households to increase consumption spending.
2. reducing corporate income taxes, thereby encouraging investment spending by firms.
3. reducing the interest rate, thereby stimulating both consumption and investment.
4. increasing tariffs to discourage imports and stimulate consumption of domestic goods.[6]
5. reducing taxes and the interest rate for exporters, thereby stimulating demand in the foreign sector.

UNEMPLOYMENT AS A MONETARY PHENOMENON

An important result of our analysis is the notion that income is not always equal to spending. If income and spending were identical, Say's Law would be valid, and full employment could be attained without conscious intervention by the central government.

It is a characteristic of a money economy, that is, an economy in which goods and factor services are exchanged for money rather than for goods and factor services, that units receiving income can choose not to expend their income. In a nonmoney (or barter) economy, income is received in kind, all goods produced are received as income, and

$$\text{Aggregate demand} \equiv C + I + X_n + G \equiv \text{Income} \equiv \text{Aggregate supply}$$

at all levels of income.

In a money economy we can conceive of income and output as a circular flow, as illustrated in Figure 3-10. Income earned in the form of money represents claims on goods produced. Therefore, money functions as a *store of value*. Since income earned is identical to the value of output, that is,

$$\text{Income} \equiv \text{Value of output}$$

the value of claims, or money, in the hands of spending units is exactly equal to the value of output. If all the claims are not exercised, that is, if aggregate demand is less than income, the spending loop will be smaller than the income loop and all output will not be purchased. Unplanned inventory investment will result, and firms will produce less and employ fewer people, distributing fewer claims in the form of income. The circular

---

[6] Such a policy may be unsuccessful if foreign countries respond by increasing their tariffs and discouraging your exports. It proved to be self-defeating during the depression of the 1930's.

flow shrinks until the equilibrium position has been reached. Equilibrium occurs when all claims generated in the circular flow are exercised, when the spending loop is the same size as the income loop, or in other words, when all goods produced are purchased. Government, of course, through

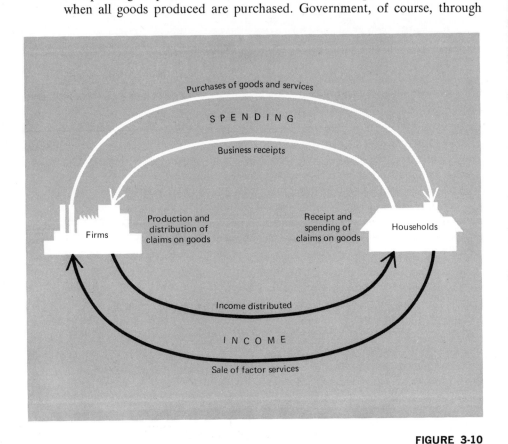

FIGURE 3-10

The Circular Flow of Income

its power not only to reduce taxes but also to increase the supply of money, or claims on goods, can prevent the spending loop from shrinking and can even cause it to expand. When the spending loop expands, firms will produce more and employ more people, distributing more claims in the form of income, and consequently, both loops of the circular flow will expand until they are of equal size.[7]

---

[7] In terms of the saving-investment analysis developed earlier, if savers hold money balances rather than channeling them into the credit market, then saving will exceed investment and the level of income will fall.

It is important to keep in mind that unemployment, except for the structural and frictional varieties, is basically a monetary phenomenon. Because money serves as a store of value, the equilibrium condition

$$Income = Spending$$

is not an identity and holds for a single value of income and employment, not necessarily at full employment. In a barter economy, on the other hand, Say's Law is an identity and equilibrium can occur at any value of income and employment, including, of course, full employment.

3-4   THE MULTIPLIER ANALYSIS

FULL EMPLOYMENT THROUGH POLICY PLANNING

Although equilibrium occurs in a money economy only at a single value of income and employment, we need not worry about being trapped in a permanent underemployment equilibrium. Keynes was overly pessimistic in *The General Theory* when he wrote of full employment as a "rare and short-lived occurrence." As long as the central government can manipulate the aggregate demand function through appropriate fiscal and monetary policies, equilibrium can be effectuated at many levels of income and employment. The ultimate objective is to design government policies that will always fill the gap between spending and income at all levels of income up to full employment. As illustrated in Figure 3-4, classical economic theory suggested that the gap between consumption spending and income will always be filled by investment. Keynes asserted that if investment does not fill the gap, it can be filled by expenditure stimulated or initiated by government action.

Under these circumstances a new kind of aggregate demand function can be envisioned. Government policies will always ensure that the gap between income and consumption spending is filled at all levels of income, up to the level of full employment. This gap can be filled in a variety of ways: by stimulating additional consumption and investment through tax and monetary policies or by increasing government expenditure.

The aggregate demand function, embodying this principle, is shown in Figure 3-11. Full-employment income is at F. By stimulating or initiating expenditures in the amount AB, government policy enables the economy to achieve its goal of full employment.

This is the principal difference between classical and Keynesian macroeconomics. The classical approach asserted that full employment could be achieved automatically through the market mechanism. Recognizing the possibility of an underemployment equilibrium resulting from the in-

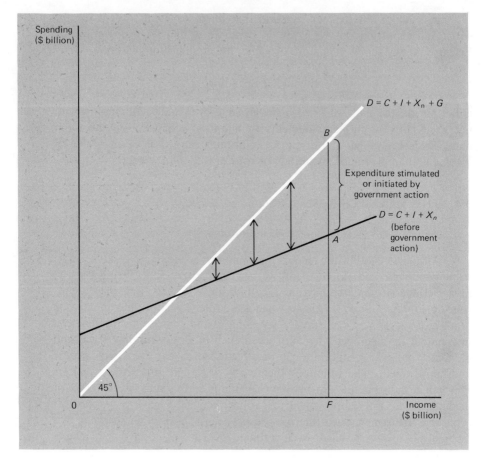

FIGURE 3-11

Aggregate Demand with Government Intervention

dependent spending decisions of households and firms and the use of money as a store of value, Keynesian theory implied an active role for government. To attain the full-employment goal, the government must manipulate the level of aggregate demand.

AUTONOMOUS AND INDUCED EXPENDITURES

There are many ways in which the government can affect the level of aggregate demand. All of these involve vertical shifts in one or more of the components of the aggregate demand function and hence of the aggregate demand function itself.

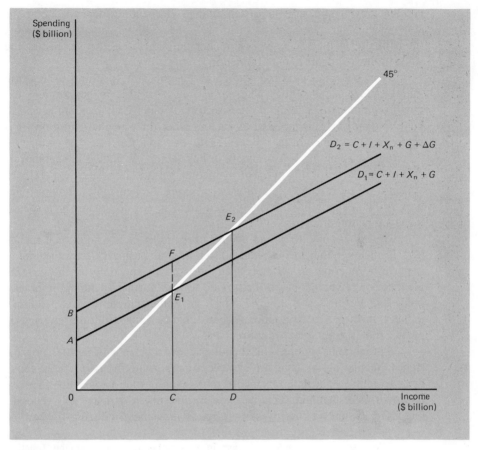

FIGURE 3-12

An Autonomous Change in Spending

Suppose the government effectuates a shift in the aggregate demand function by increasing expenditure by the amount AB, as shown in Figure 3-12. The aggregate demand function shifts from D_1 to D_2. The notation, ΔG, refers to the change in G. In this case

$$\Delta G = AB$$

How does this affect the equilibrium level of income? Notice that before the government action, income was in equilibrium at C. With the increased expenditure of $AB = E_1F$, equilibrium income increases from C to D. The change in the equilibrium level of income, CD, is greater than the initial change in spending, AB. The relationship between the change in equilibrium income and the initial change in spending depends upon the slope of the aggregate demand function. For any initial change in spending, the ultimate change in equilibrium income is greater, the steeper is the slope of the aggregate demand function.[8]

Why does the ultimate change in income and spending exceed the initial change in spending? The *autonomous* increase in government expenditure *induces* spending in other sectors. A change in spending is said to be *autonomous* if it is initiated by factors other than income variation. It is represented by a *shift* in the aggregate demand function. A change in autonomous spending can originate in any sector. A change in spending is said to be *induced* if it is initiated by income variation. Induced expenditure changes are represented by a *movement along* the aggregate demand function. A change in induced spending can occur in any sector in which spending is a function of income.

How does an autonomous change in spending induce additional spending? Remember that in both the household and business sectors spending is partly a function of income. Since autonomous spending by the government sector raises income in the private sectors, further spending by households and businesses is induced. Since an initial autonomous expenditure induces further spending, the ultimate change in equilibrium income is greater than the initial expenditure.[9]

Autonomous changes in spending can occur in any sector. For instance, technological changes in several important industries can cause firms to replace obsolete machinery more rapidly than usual, thus increasing investment demand. This increase in investment demand will generate increased income in the investment goods industries, inducing further in-

---

[8] Consider, for example, the case in which the aggregate demand function is horizontal. The change in income will exactly equal the initial change in spending. See the figure below.

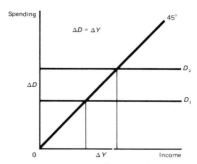

[9] For a horizontal aggregate demand function there are no induced effects since spending is not a function of income in any sector. Consequently, the total change in spending is equal to the initial change.

vestment and consumption. Now the increase in demand has spread to consumer goods industries and other investment goods industries throughout the economy, generating further increases in income and inducing still more spending.

A DYNAMIC MULTIPLIER ANALYSIS

Our model of national income equilibrium can be used to forecast the ultimate impact of an autonomous change in spending on national income. We shall ignore the foreign sector for simplicity. Suppose the consumption function in an economy is

$$C = 100 + 0.6\,Y$$

and the investment function is

$$I = 200 + 0.2\,Y$$

Table 3-1 traces the time path of income in this economy when government spending increases by $100 million.[10] The initial increase in government expenditure of $100 million generates additional income of $100 million. This added income induces additional consumption expenditure of $60 million and investment expenditure of $20 million, generating $80 million of income in addition to the $100 million generated by the government expenditure. This increased income induces even further spending. The process continues, with total expenditure increasing at a decreasing rate, until a new equilibrium is reached at a level of income $500 million greater than at the previous equilibrium. At the new equilibrium, the change in income becomes approximately zero, so that no further spending is induced. Thus, the initial increase in autonomous expenditure is multiplied five times before a new equilibrium is reached. The ratio between the total change in spending and the initial or autonomous change in spending is called the *income multiplier*. In this example, the multiplier is 5.

The process of adjustment to equilibrium is shown in Figure 3-13. With aggregate demand at D_1, the economy is at equilibrium at E_1, at an income level of C. An autonomous increase in spending shifts the aggregate demand schedule from D_1 to D_2 by the amount AB. The initial change in spending is E_1F, which is equal to AB. This spending generates additional

[10] The time path presented in this example is based on the assumption that it takes a single period for consumption and investment to respond to changes in income. Also, the possibility of a lag in output in response to changes in demand is ignored. If the response lag is different, then the time path will also be different.

income $CH = FG = E_1F = AB$. The change in income, CH, induces increased spending of the amount GI. Algebraically,

$$GI = (b + d)CH$$

where $b + d$ is the sum of the marginal propensities to consume and invest or, geometrically, the slope of the aggregate demand function. The process continues with income and spending increasing at a decreasing rate

TABLE 3-1

Time Path of Income for a Continuous Increase in Government Expenditure

Period	Increase in Government Expenditure (in millions of dollars)	+	Increase in Consumption Expenditure (in millions of dollars)	+	Increase in Investment Expenditure (in millions of dollars)	=	Total Increase in Expenditure and Income (in millions of dollars)
1	100		0		0		100
2	100		60		20		180
3	100		108		36		244
4	100		146		49		295
5	100		177		59		336
6	100		220		67		387
7	100		232		77		409
8	100		245		82		427
9	100		256		85		441
10	100		265		88		453
11	100		272		91		463
12	100		278		93		471
	—		—		—		—
	—		—		—		—
	—		—		—		—
	100		300		100		500

until the new equilibrium E_2 is reached at an income level of D. As a result of the shift in the aggregate demand function from D_1 to D_2, the total change in equilibrium income is CD. The equality $CH = AB$ is generated by the change in autonomous spending; HD is induced. The multiplier is the ratio CD/CH.

There are other ways in which the government can control aggregate demand besides varying its own expenditure. Tax and monetary policy can be employed to increase aggregate demand without increasing the size of the public sector. One important result should be clear, however.

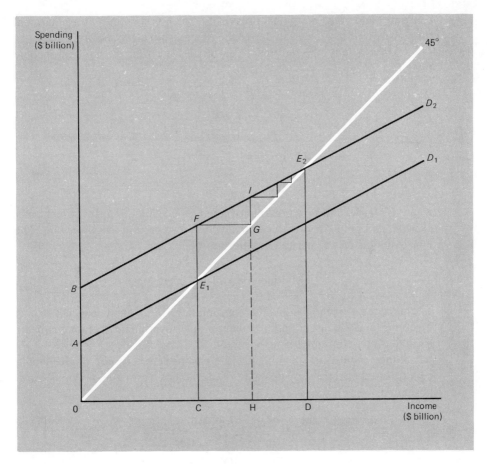

FIGURE 3-13

The Dynamics of Equilibrium Adjustment

The equilibrium level of income will change only when the aggregate demand function shifts, and shifts in the aggregate demand function occur only when there are autonomous changes in spending.

Derivation of the Multiplier

We saw on page 75–76 that, for any initial change in spending, the ultimate change in equilibrium income is greater when the slope of the aggregate demand function is steeper. Recalling that the slope of the aggregate demand function is equal to the sum of the marginal propensity to consume and the marginal propensity to invest minus the marginal propensity to import, we can derive the relationship algebraically.[11]

Algebraically, the multiplier can be derived from the national income model,

$$Y = C + I + X_n + G$$
$$C = a + bY$$
$$I = h + dY$$
$$X_n = E_0 - mY$$
$$G = G_0$$

where C, I, X_n, and G represent spending on consumption, investment, net exports, and public goods, respectively, and Y represents total income. The first equation represents the equilibrium condition:

$$\text{Total income} = \text{Total spending}$$

The next three equations are the consumption, investment, and net export functions, and the last equation indicates that government spending is being treated as predetermined, or exogenous.

Since *changes* in spending are the primary concern, the model should be expressed in terms of changes or deviations from the previous equilibrium.[12]

$$\Delta Y = \Delta C + \Delta I + \Delta X_n + \Delta G$$
$$\Delta C = \Delta a + \Delta bY = \Delta a + b \Delta Y$$
$$\Delta I = \Delta h + \Delta dY = \Delta h + d \Delta Y$$
$$\Delta X_n = \Delta E - \Delta mY = \Delta E - m \Delta Y$$
$$\Delta G = \Delta G$$

The secret in calculating multipliers is to *reduce* the aggregate demand function to its autonomous components. That is, since the multiplier reflects the total impact on income of a change in any of its autonomous components, ΔY must be expressed in terms of Δa, Δh, ΔG, and ΔE only.

Performing the appropriate substitutions,

---

[11] This section and the section to follow will develop the analysis algebraically. The reader should test his understanding by providing a graphical interpretation. The graphical analysis can be developed in the framework of Figure 3-13.

[12] These changes can be either negative or positive. An autonomous *decline* in spending of $100 will cause a multiplied *decline* in income.

$$\Delta Y = \Delta a + b\,\Delta Y + \Delta h + d\,\Delta Y + \Delta E - m\,\Delta Y + \Delta G$$

$$\Delta Y - b\,\Delta Y - d\,\Delta Y + m\,\Delta Y = \Delta a + \Delta h + \Delta E + \Delta G$$

$$\Delta Y = \frac{1}{1 - b - d + m}(\Delta a + \Delta h + \Delta E + \Delta G)$$

In this model, any change in autonomous spending, ΔD_A, will change total spending or income by

$$\Delta Y = \frac{1}{1 - b - d + m}\,\Delta D_A$$

In our previous example,

$$\Delta G = \$100 \text{ million}$$
$$b = 0.6$$
$$d = 0.2$$
$$m = 0$$

and the change in the other autonomous components, Δa, Δh, and ΔE, was zero. Consequently,

$$\frac{1}{1 - b - d + m} = \frac{1}{1 - 0.8} = 5$$

and

$$\Delta Y = \frac{\Delta G}{1 - b - d + m} = \frac{\$100 \text{ million}}{1 - 0.8} = \$500 \text{ million}$$

This is the same result we found in tracing the time path of income through all its stages. Obviously, this method of determining the multiplier is less tedious.

Suppose the foreign sector had been included in the dynamic multiplier analysis. Let us assume that the marginal propensity to import is 0.1, so that

$$M = 0.1Y$$

When import demand is induced by changes in income, the multiplier effect of an increase in spending is less than if the foreign sector had been ignored, since

$$\frac{\Delta Y}{\Delta G} = \frac{1}{1 - b - d + m} = \frac{1}{1 - 0.7} = 3.3$$

Import demand represents a "leakage" from the circular flow of income and spending which reduces the impact of changes in income on domestic spending.

The value of the multiplier will depend upon the induced components of aggregate demand. In particular, the multiplier will always equal the reciprocal of 1 minus the slope of the aggregate demand function:

$$\text{Multiplier} = \frac{1}{1 - \text{slope of } D}$$

The steeper the slope, the greater is the multiplier. This is the same result we obtained by graphical analysis.

The slope of the aggregate demand function will equal the sum of the *marginal induced effects* on expenditure. Marginal induced effects include the marginal propensity to consume, the marginal propensity to invest, and the marginal relationship between any component of spending and income. The marginal propensity to import has a negative impact on domestic spending, and, since it represents a leakage, it must be subtracted from the other marginal induced effects to estimate the overall impact of a change in income. Whether or not expenditure in a particular sector is autonomous or induced must be determined empirically. The equations in the model which describe the behavior of the various economic groups, the consumption function, investment function, and the like, will specify the values of the marginal induced components such as the marginal propensity to consume, the marginal propensity to invest, and the marginal propensity to import. In general, the degree to which expenditure is induced will vary from model to model, depending on the behavioral specification. Since the multiplier is a *forecasting* tool, it is obvious that accurate *behavioral* specification based on careful and critical analysis of empirical data is a crucial aspect of building a good forecasting model.

Complete behavioral specification of a forecasting model is also important since some components may be indirectly induced. Suppose, for example, the autonomous component of investment is a function of the rate of interest, i. The rate of interest may itself rise and fall with income. In this case an autonomous change in spending will induce a change in the interest rate which will indirectly induce a change in investment spending. Examining the complete investment model

$$I = dY - ei$$
$$i = g + fY$$

we can see that part of the "autonomous" component of I is indirectly induced. By performing the appropriate substitutions,

$$I = dY - e(g + fY)$$
$$= dY - eg - efY$$
$$= (d - ef)Y - eg$$

the reader should verify that the new multiplier is now

$$\frac{\Delta Y}{\Delta D_A} = \frac{1}{1 - b - d + ef + m}$$

where ΔD_A represents changes in autonomous components.[13] Note that the complete multiplier, taking account of the interest rate effect, is smaller than the multiplier which ignored the effect of the income change on credit conditions. As income rises in this model, tighter money discourages investment, thereby depressing demand and reducing the expansionary effect of the initial spending increase.

In addition to its usefulness as a forecasting tool, multiplier analysis is also helpful for policy planning. In the next chapter we shall see how the multiplier can be used for evaluating various fiscal and monetary programs.

QUESTIONS FOR STUDY AND REVIEW

1. Keynes had two different concepts of investment in mind in *The General Theory*. On the one hand, he said that saving is necessarily always equal to investment, while on the other, he said that the multiplier makes saving and investment equal.

Explain the difference between these two concepts of investment and, as an application, show which concept is of significance in defining equilibrium.

2. What is Say's Law? What does it mean in a barter economy? In a money economy? What are its implications for macroeconomic policy?

3. Keynes believed that, aside from structural and frictional unemployment, general unemployment is basically a characteristic of a money economy and would not occur in a barter economy. Explain Keynes' position as you think he would have justified it to a classical economist.

---

[13] An obvious restriction on the multiplier is that it does not become infinite. Furthermore, to be theoretically meaningful, it should not take on negative values. This implies that the sum of the marginal induced effects must be less than unity. This will be ensured if the marginal propensity to invest is less than the marginal propensity to save.

4. Return to the dynamic multiplier analysis in Table 3-1. Suppose the net export function is

$$X_n = 50 - 0.1\,Y$$

(a) How will this affect the time path of income in this economy?

(b) By completing the table in accordance with the new specification, show that the ultimate impact on national income of an increase in G of $100 will approach $333.

5. Consider an economy represented by the following macroeconomic model:

$$D = C + I + X_n + G$$
$$C = 200 + 0.6\,Y$$
$$I = 0.3\,Y - 15i$$
$$X_n = 50 - 0.1\,Y$$
$$G = 100$$
$$i = 4$$

(a) Find the equilibrium level of income.

(b) Calculate the multiplier.

(c) What will be the impact on national income of the following policies:

(i) increasing government spending by 25
(ii) reducing the interest rate to 3
(iii) imposing an import tariff (tax) which reduces the marginal propensity to import by 50 percent?

(d) Suppose the government undertakes policy (iii) in part (c) and foreign governments reciprocate by raising their tariffs with the result that exports are reduced by 50 percent. What will be the impact on

(i) national income,
(ii) the balance of trade (net exports)?

ADDITIONAL READING

KEYNES, J. M., OHLIN, B., and HAWTREY, R. G., *The Economic Journal,* XLVII (June, September, and December, 1937), 221–252, 423–443, 663–669.

LUTZ, FRIEDRICH A., "The Outcome of the Saving-Investment Discussion," *The Quarterly Journal of Economics,* LII (August, 1938), 588–614.

SAMUELSON, PAUL A., "The Simple Mathematics of Income Determination," in *Income, Employment, and Public Policy: Essays in Honor of Alvin Hansen,* ed. L. A. Metzler *et al.,* New York: W. W. Norton and Company, 1948.

4

Evaluating
the
Impact of Public Policy

The analysis of national income equilibrium showed that public policy for manipulating the level of aggregate income and employment will have indirect effects which must be accounted for in the formulation of policies to achieve the full-employment goal. In this chapter we shall develop a framework for analyzing the effectiveness of alternative monetary and fiscal programs in closing the gap between actual employment and full employment.

4-1 THE USE OF MULTIPLIER ANALYSIS IN EVALUATING GOVERNMENT PROGRAMS

The policy planner must consider the multiplier effects of fiscal or monetary programs. Suppose he must evaluate a variety of alternative government actions that might be used to manipulate the level of aggregate demand.

THE EXPENDITURE MULTIPLIER

Consider a variant of the original model introduced in Chapter 3:

$$Y = C + I + X_n + G$$
$$C = a + bY$$

$$I = dY - ei$$
$$X_n = E_0 - mY$$
$$G = G_0$$
$$i = i_0$$

In this formulation of the model the rate of interest, i, is a policy parameter, subject to autonomous change at the discretion of the central authority.[1]

Any change in G will shift the aggregate demand function by an amount $\Delta D_A = \Delta G$ which represents the autonomous change in spending measured along the spending (vertical) axis and will result in an ultimate change in expenditure and income of

$$\Delta Y = \frac{1}{1 - b - d + m} \Delta G$$

where

$$\frac{\Delta Y}{\Delta G} = \frac{1}{1 - b - d + m}$$

is the *expenditure multiplier*.

THE INTEREST RATE MULTIPLIER

Suppose government decided to utilize monetary instead of fiscal policy to manipulate the level of aggregate demand. What would be the change in equilibrium income associated with a given change in the interest rate, i?

Expressing the model in terms of changes, and keeping in mind that Δa, ΔE, and ΔG are all equal to zero,

$$\Delta Y = \Delta C + \Delta I + \Delta X_n$$
$$\Delta C = b \Delta Y$$
$$\Delta I = d \Delta Y - e \Delta i$$
$$\Delta X_n = -m \Delta Y$$
$$\Delta i = \Delta i$$

Making the appropriate substitutions,

---

[1] In more sophisticated treatments, the rate of interest is not viewed as a policy parameter but is determined within the context of a model of the monetary sector. In technical terms, the interest rate is most appropriately treated as endogenous, not as a predetermined variable.

$$\Delta Y = b \Delta Y + d \Delta Y - e \Delta i - m \Delta Y$$
$$\Delta Y - b \Delta Y - d \Delta Y + m \Delta Y = -e \Delta i$$

Therefore, the *interest rate multiplier* will be

$$\frac{\Delta Y}{\Delta i} = \frac{-e}{1 - b - d + m}$$

Any change in the interest rate will result in a shift of the aggregate demand schedule by the amount

$$\Delta D = \Delta I = -e \Delta i$$

and an ultimate change in the equilibrium level of income of

$$\Delta Y = \frac{-e}{1 - b - d + m} \Delta i$$

The interest rate multiplier is negative, reflecting the inverse relationship between interest rates and income. If interest rates rise in this model, other things being equal, aggregate demand will fall.[2]

THE TAX MULTIPLIER

Tax policy is a third tool with which the central government might manipulate the level of aggregate demand. Suppose the government decides to raise revenues by means of a personal income tax. What will be the effect on the equilibrium level of income when the central government varies the amount of tax it assesses?

Since individuals must pay part of their income to the government in the form of taxes, the consumption function must be altered to take this into account. Consumption is a function of *disposable income,* or income after taxes, that is,

$$C = a + b(Y - T)$$

Assuming for simplicity that all imports are consumption goods, then import demand will also be a function of disposable income, and

$$X_n = E_0 - m(Y - T)$$

[2] The empirical observation that income and interest rates often rise and fall together may be due to other components of demand changing simultaneously.

Incorporating these new relationships into the complete model,

$$Y = C + I + X_n + G$$
$$C = a + b(Y - T)$$
$$I = dY - ei$$
$$X_n = E_0 - m(Y - T)$$
$$G = G_0$$
$$i = i_0$$
$$T = T_0$$

Expressing the model in terms of changes, and assuming that Δa, ΔE, ΔG, and Δi will all be equal to 0,

$$\Delta Y = \Delta C + \Delta I + \Delta X_n$$
$$\Delta C = b\,\Delta Y - b\,\Delta T$$
$$\Delta I = d\,\Delta Y$$
$$\Delta X_n = -m\,\Delta Y + m\,\Delta T$$

Making the appropriate substitutions,

$$\Delta Y = b\,\Delta Y - b\,\Delta T + d\,\Delta Y - m\,\Delta Y + m\,\Delta T$$

Therefore, the *tax multiplier* is

$$\frac{\Delta Y}{\Delta T} = \frac{-(b - m)}{1 - b - d + m}$$

Assuming that the marginal propensity to import is greater than zero and less than the marginal propensity to consume, that is,

$$0 < m < b$$

the tax multiplier will be negative, reflecting the inverse relationship between taxes and consumption. An increase in personal income taxes will result in a shift of the aggregate demand schedule by the amount

$$\Delta D_A = \Delta C_A + \Delta X_{nA}$$
$$= -b\,\Delta T + m\,\Delta T$$
$$= -(b - m)\,\Delta T$$

and an ultimate change in the equilibrium level of income (as adjustments are made along the aggregate demand function) of

$$\Delta Y = \frac{-(b-m)}{1-b-d+m} \Delta T$$

THE BALANCED BUDGET MULTIPLIER

Since the marginal propensity to consume minus the marginal propensity to import is positive and less than unity,

$$0 < b - m < 1$$

the tax multiplier is smaller in absolute value than the expenditure multiplier, since

$$\frac{1}{1-b-d+m} > \frac{b-m}{1-b-d+m}$$

A reduction in taxes will result in a smaller increase in aggregate demand than an equal increase in government expenditure. This is because a part of the tax reduction will be saved rather than spent. An increase in government expenditure of $100 million will shift the aggregate demand schedule up by $100 million:

$$\Delta D_A = \Delta G = \$100 \text{ million}$$

A reduction in taxes of $100 million will shift the aggregate demand schedule up by $100 million multiplied by the marginal propensity to consume minus the marginal propensity to import:

$$\Delta D_A = \Delta C + \Delta X_n = -b\,\Delta T + m\,\Delta T = -(b-m)\,\Delta T$$

Since

$$0 < b - m < 1$$

the aggregate demand schedule shifts upward by a smaller amount when taxes are reduced by $100 million than when expenditures are increased by $100 million.

The conclusion that the expenditure multiplier is greater than the tax multiplier leads to an interesting question. At first glance a balanced government budget appears to be fiscally neutral. That is, if the government increases expenditures and finances them through an equal increase in taxes, one would expect there to be no change in aggregate demand.

But since the expenditure multiplier is greater than the tax multiplier, an increase in spending accompanied by an equal tax increase will have a net effect of *increasing* the level of aggregate demand. Since

$$\frac{\Delta Y}{\Delta G} = \frac{1}{1 - b - d + m}$$

and

$$\frac{\Delta Y}{\Delta T} = \frac{-(b - m)}{1 - b - d + m}$$

then assuming

$$\Delta G = \Delta T$$

$$\Delta Y = \frac{1}{1 - b - d + m} \Delta G - \frac{b - m}{1 - b - d + m} \Delta T$$

$$= \frac{1}{1 - b - d + m} \Delta G - \frac{b - m}{1 - b - d + m} \Delta G$$

$$= \frac{1 - b + m}{1 - b - d + m} \Delta G$$

The *"balanced budget" multiplier* is

$$\frac{\Delta Y}{\Delta G} = \frac{1 - b + m}{1 - b - d + m}$$

which is greater than 1. In the special case in which there is no induced effect on investment, so that

$$d = 0$$

the balanced budget multiplier is

$$\frac{\Delta Y}{\Delta G} = \frac{1 - b + m}{1 - b + m} = 1$$

and

$$\Delta Y = \Delta G = \Delta T$$

Aggregate demand will increase by the size of the government budget when the change in spending is completely financed by taxes.

It is sometimes believed that the government budget must be in deficit to have an expansionary impact on the economy. But it is clear that a *balanced* budget also has an impact on aggregate demand. In addition, the total size of the government budget is relevant in determining that impact. Thus, the net budget deficit or surplus alone is not indicative of the role of the public sector in the total demand picture. The absolute size of the budget is also important.

It is clear that a variety of alternative fiscal policies can be employed to produce a given change in the level of aggregate demand. The greater the increase in taxes that accompanies an increase in government expenditure, the greater is the increase in expenditure necessary to effectuate a given increase in aggregate demand. Theoretically, a budget change can show a surplus, that is, taxes can increase by more than expenditures, and still have an expansionary effect on aggregate demand.[3] In fact, for a budget to have no effect on aggregate demand, that is, for

$$\Delta Y = 0$$

the change in taxes must exceed the change in expenditure by a definable amount. Since

$$\Delta Y = \frac{1}{1 - b - d + m} \Delta G - \frac{b - m}{1 - b - d + m} \Delta T$$

when

$$\Delta Y = 0$$

then

$$\frac{1}{1 - b - d + m} \Delta G = \frac{b - m}{1 - b - d + m} \Delta T$$

and

$$\Delta G = (b - m) \Delta T$$

or

$$\Delta T = \frac{1}{b - m} \Delta G$$

Thus, the change in taxes must be $1/(b - m)$ times the change in expenditure for a budget change to be fiscally neutral. If

$$b - m = \tfrac{3}{4}$$

[3] To achieve a given expansionary effect on aggregate demand, government spending must increase more, the greater the proportion of it financed by taxes. Those who deplore the ever-increasing size of the public sector might note that deficit spending achieves a greater impact on income with considerably smaller increases in public spending than is necessitated if the budget is to be kept in balance.

the requisite change in taxes will be $1\frac{1}{3}$ times the change in expenditure. The smaller the marginal propensity to consume minus the marginal propensity to import, the greater is the change in taxes needed to offset the expenditures in a fiscally neutral budget.

CHANGES IN THE TAX RATE

We have assumed up to this point that taxes are a fixed amount, regardless of the level of income. Suppose income is taxed at some rate t.[4] Now the tax function becomes

$$T = tY$$

This affects the consumption function and the net export function in the following way:

$$C = a + b(Y - T)$$
$$= a + b(Y - tY)$$
$$= a + b(1 - t)Y$$

and

$$X_n = E_0 - m(Y - T)$$
$$= E_0 - m(Y - tY)$$
$$= E_0 - m(1 - t)Y$$

An income tax reduces the marginal propensity to consume and the marginal propensity to import by $(1 - t)$, where t is the marginal tax rate or the marginal propensity to tax. Suppose personal taxes are increased by 10 percentage points. If the marginal propensity to consume out of disposable income is .8, the effect of the tax would be to reduce it to $(.8 \times .9)$ or .72.

This relationship means that an income tax affects the multiplier, and the new multiplier will be[5]

$$\frac{\Delta Y}{\Delta D_A} = \frac{1}{1 - b(1 - t) - d + m(1 - t)}$$

---

[4] This assumes a proportional tax rate. A progressive rate structure could be introduced, but it would complicate the algebra. In a multiplier analysis, only the marginal tax rate is of interest anyway.

[5] A corporate income tax would affect the marginal propensity to invest similarly.

Since tax changes are now endogenous, they no longer produce changes in D_A. Instead, they affect the sensitivity of income to autonomous changes in demand produced by other policy instruments. An income tax reduces the marginal propensity to spend and hence reduces the multiplier and the sensitivity of the economy to autonomous changes in demand. That is why the income tax is sometimes called an *automatic stabilizer*.

4-2   DEFLATIONARY GAP ANALYSIS

A policy planner may approach the multiplier analysis from a different point of view from that of the forecaster. A forecaster asks the question, "What will be the ultimate impact of a particular monetary or fiscal policy on the level of aggregate demand?" The policy maker, on the other hand, will want to know, "What monetary or fiscal programs will effectuate a particular change in the level of aggregate demand?"

In Figure 4-1, income is in equilibrium at E, while full employment is at F. The difference between actual income and full-employment income is EF. The distance HG between the aggregate demand function and the 45° line at full-employment income is called the *deflationary gap*. It represents the difference between spending and income at full employment. An autonomous shift in aggregate demand by the amount of the deflationary gap, HG, will, taking into account the multiplier effects, result in an ultimate change in equilibrium income equal to EF. The deflationary gap shows the increase in autonomous spending which is necessary to bring an economy to the level of income associated with full employment.

The relationship between the deflationary gap and the difference between equilibrium and full-employment income can be derived from the multiplier analysis. Since

$$Y_F - Y_E = \Delta Y = \frac{\Delta D_A}{1 - b - d + m}$$

therefore,

$$\Delta D_A = (1 - b - d + m)(Y_F - Y_E)$$

The deflationary gap is the difference between equilibrium and full-employment income multiplied by the reciprocal of the multiplier. Obviously, the deflationary gap is smaller than the required change in income.

Suppose the economy has a deflationary gap of $200 million. With a multiplier of 5, this implies the required change in income is $1 billion. Several alternative monetary and fiscal policies will be appropriate to bring income to its full-employment level. Assume the marginal propensity to consume is 0.7, the marginal propensity to import is 0.1, and the investment function is

$$I = 0.2Y - 100i$$

Table 4-1 shows some alternative measures which can close the deflationary gap and bring the economy to a full-employment level of income. Actually, an infinite variety of policy combinations can be employed to close the deflationary gap. If the policy maker finds one measure not politically feasible, he will have a vast number of alternative choices.

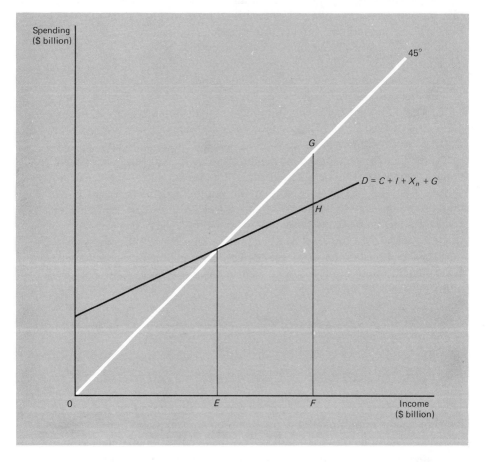

FIGURE 4-1

A Deflationary Gap

TABLE 4-1

Alternative Measures to Close
a Deflationary Gap of $200 Million

Policy	Effect on D	Actual Change in Policy Parameter
Increase in G	$\Delta D_A = \Delta G$	+$200 million
Reduction in T	$\Delta D_A = \Delta C + \Delta X_n = -(b - m)\,\Delta T$	−$332 million
	$= -0.6\,\Delta T$	
	$\Delta T = -1.66\,\Delta D_A$	
Reduction in i	$\Delta D_A = \Delta I = -e\,\Delta i$	−2 points
	$= -100\,\Delta i$	
	$\Delta i = -\frac{1}{100}\,\Delta D_A$	
Equal increase in G and T (balanced budget change)	$\Delta D_A = \Delta G + \Delta C + \Delta X_n$	+$500 million
	$= \Delta G - b\,\Delta T + m\,\Delta T$	
	$= \Delta G - (b - m)\,\Delta G$	
	$= 0.4\,\Delta G$	
	$\Delta G = 2.5\,\Delta D_A$	

4-3 PERIOD ANALYSIS OF THE MULTIPLIER

When forecasting the effect of a particular monetary or fiscal policy, the planner is generally concerned with its impact on income and employment *within some definite period of time.* Our previous examples have taken a *comparative statics* approach, examining the movement from one equilibrium to another in response to changes in the underlying conditions, policy parameters, or functional relationships. The passage of time has been ignored.

For some purposes, however, the ultimate equilibrium position of the economy may be irrelevant. In the example illustrated in Table 4-2, the sum of the marginal induced spending effects is 0.8. Notice that we have ignored the foreign sector to simplify the exposition. An increase in government expenditure of $100 million will *ultimately* cause an increase in income of $500 million. Thus, given sufficient time the total multiplier will be 5. But our time horizons are generally short. We want to know what will happen this year or next.

Suppose the central authority is considering increasing public expenditure by $100 million. A forecaster is asked to estimate the impact on total GNP within one year after the expenditure is made. He must examine the time path of income as it is moving to its new equilibrium. The forecaster will need to know not only the magnitude of the marginal induced spending effects, but also the average length of time which will pass between expenditure and income receipt and income receipt and expenditure.

Suppose that the expenditure-receipt-expenditure period is estimated to be three months. Furthermore, assume the government increases its expenditure by $100 million (per three-month period) and maintains it at that new level. Referring to Table 4-2, we can see that the level of income will be increased by $295 by the end of the year (at the end of four three-month expenditure-receipt-expenditure periods), or about $\frac{3}{5}$ of the ultimate effect of $500. Using *period analysis,* we find that after one year the multiplier is 2.95 rather than 5. The total multiplier will still be 5, however, given a sufficiently long time horizon.

TABLE 4-2

Time Path of Income for a Continuous Increase in Government Expenditure

Period	Increase in Government Expenditure (in millions of dollars)	+	Increase in Consumption Expenditure (in millions of dollars)	+	Increase in Investment Expenditure (in millions of dollars)	=	Total Increase in Expenditure and Income (in millions of dollars)
1	100		0		0		100
2	100		60		20		180
3	100		108		36		244
4	100		146		49		295
5	100		177		59		336
6	100		220		67		387
7	100		232		77		409
8	100		245		82		427
9	100		256		85		441
10	100		265		88		453
11	100		272		91		463
12	100		278		93		471
	–		–		–		–
	–		–		–		–
	100		300		100		500

Table 4-2 suggests that the multiplier can be treated as a decreasing geometric series. In period 1, $100 million in new government expenditure is paid out as income in the form of wages, profits, interest, and rent. The quantity $b + d$, or 80 percent, is spent on consumption and investment in period 2. Thus, including the autonomous increase in spending by the public sector, additional spending in period 2 is

$$\text{Spending} = \$100 \text{ million} \times (1 + 0.8)$$
$$= \$100 \text{ million} + \$80 \text{ million} = \$180 \text{ million}$$

In period 3, income is $100 million $\times (1 + 0.8)$. Additional induced expenditure is

$$\text{Induced spending} = \$100 \text{ million} \times (1 + 0.8) \times 0.8$$
$$= \$100 \text{ million} \times (0.8 + 0.8^2)$$
$$= \$80 \text{ million} + \$64 \text{ million} = \$144 \text{ million}$$

Thus, including the autonomous increase in spending by the public sector, total expenditure in period 3 is

$$\text{Spending} = \$100 \text{ million} \times (1 + 0.8 + 0.8^2)$$
$$= \$100 \text{ million} + \$80 \text{ million} + \$64 \text{ million} = \$244 \text{ million}$$

Letting

$$k = b + d$$

where k represents the sum of the marginal induced effects, and assuming $0 < k < 1$, the ultimate multiplier can be represented by the decreasing geometric series,

$$\text{Multiplier} = 1 + k + k^2 + k^3 + k^4 + \cdots = \frac{1}{1 - k}$$

At the end of any period, t,

$$\text{Multiplier} = 1 + k + k^2 + \cdots + k^{t-1}$$

If the expenditure-receipt-expenditure period is known, it is easy to calculate the multiplier for any time period. In our example,

$$\text{Multiplier} = 1 + 0.8 + 0.8^2 + 0.8^3$$
$$= 1 + 0.8 + 0.64 + 0.512$$
$$= 2.95$$

The period multiplier can be traced in Figure 4-2. A shift in the aggregate demand function from D_1 to D_2 results in an initial increase in income of $CH = E_1F = AB$. This induces spending in period 2 of GI. By the end of period 2, the increase in income is

$$CM = AB(1 + k)$$

At the end of period 3, income is

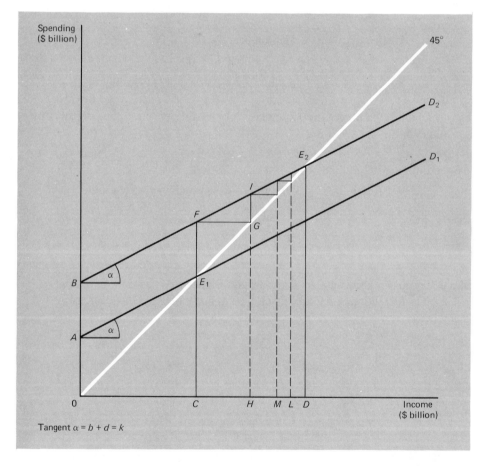

Tangent $\alpha = b + d = k$

FIGURE 4-2

The Period Multiplier

$$CL = AB(1 + k + k^2)$$

The process continues until a new equilibrium is reached at E_2, with an ultimate change in income of CD, where

$$CD = \frac{AB}{1 - k}$$

Because the multiplier is a decreasing geometric series, the largest impact of an autonomous change in spending is felt soon after it is made. In our example, 60 percent of the ultimate change in income is felt after a single year, and 85 percent is felt after two years. Consequently, although the time horizon of the policy maker is limited, he may often treat the total multiplier as an acceptable approximation to the short-term effect. For more precise forecasting, however, period analysis should be used.

PERIOD ANALYSIS AND THE DEFLATIONARY GAP

Period analysis can also be applied to the problem of closing a deflationary gap. The policy maker may wish to know, "What amount of tax reduction would be necessary to bring the economy to full employment within one year?"

We know that the deflationary gap is the difference between equilibrium and full-employment income multiplied by the reciprocal of the multiplier,

$$\Delta D_A = (1 - b - d)(Y_F - Y_E)$$
$$= (1 - k)(Y_F - Y_E)$$

where ΔD_A represents the autonomous change in spending needed to close the gap and bring the economy to full employment.

Since

$$\frac{1}{1 - k} = 1 + k + k^2 + k^3 + k^4 + \cdots$$

after four three-month periods

$$\Delta D_A = \frac{1}{1 + k + k^2 + k^3}(Y_F - Y_E)$$

In our example, $k = 0.8$, so that

$$\Delta D_A = \frac{1}{2.95}(Y_F - Y_E)$$

Since

$$\Delta D_A = \Delta C = -b\,\Delta T$$

and

$$b = 0.6$$

then

$$\Delta D_A = -0.6\,\Delta T = \frac{1}{2.95}(Y_F - Y_E)$$

Therefore,

$$\frac{Y_F - Y_E}{\Delta T} = -1.77$$

and

$$\Delta T = -\frac{1}{1.77}(Y_F - Y_E) = -0.56(Y_F - Y_E)$$

The tax reduction should be over half the desired change in equilibrium income.

Since the period multiplier is only a partial multiplier, the policy maker should keep in mind that the tax reduction will continue to have an expansionary influence in future years. If the deflationary gap is closed in the first year, it will have an inflationary effect in the future.[6] However, since the multiplier effect decreases over time, the bulk of the impact will be felt in the first year. Offsets such as a restrictive monetary policy or gradually increasing taxes might be used in the next year if the policy maker wishes to halt the expansion or inflationary trend.

4-4   THE EMPLOYMENT MULTIPLIER

We have seen that an autonomous change in spending in any sector of the economy will induce changes in spending in other sectors. The ratio of the total change in spending to the initial autonomous change in spending is the income multiplier.

In Chapter 2 we defined the aggregate supply function relating employment to expected total revenue, which in equilibrium will equal total spending. For any autonomous change in spending, there will be a corresponding change in employment. As additional changes in spending are

---

[6] If all resources are already fully employed, a further increase in the value of output, or GNP, can only reflect price increases, or inflation, not an increase in real output.

induced, additional changes in employment will occur as firms revise their sales revenue expectations. The ratio of the total change in employment, which occurs as a result of a change in autonomous spending, to the initial change in spending is the *employment multiplier*.

In Figure 4-3, the economy is in equilibrium at E_1 when the aggregate demand function is D_1. The aggregate supply function is Z. Aggregate

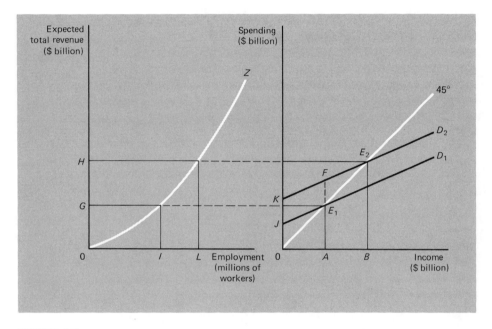

FIGURE 4-3

The Employment Multiplier

supply equals aggregate demand at an income of $0A$ and an employment level of $0I$. Consider a shift in the aggregate demand function to D_2. The initial increase in autonomous spending is $JK = E_1F$. The new equilibrium is at E_2. Aggregate supply equals aggregate demand at income $0B$ and an employment level of $0L$. The autonomous change in spending, JK, generates a total change in spending and income of $GH = AB$, and a total change in employment of IL. The income multiplier is

$$\frac{\Delta Y}{\Delta D_A} = \frac{AB}{JK} = \frac{1}{1-k}$$

where k represents the sum of the marginal induced components.

The employment multiplier is[7]

$$\frac{\Delta N}{\Delta D_A} = \frac{IL}{JK}$$

Since employment and income are related through the aggregate supply function,

$$N = f(Y)$$

where N represents employment in number of workers and Y represents the level of income, which in equilibrium is equal to spending, the employment multiplier is functionally related to the income multiplier.

Suppose

$$N = Y^\alpha$$

If the aggregate supply function is convex to the employment axis then α will be between zero and unity; that is,

$$0 < \alpha < 1$$

This implies that successively greater increments to income are required to induce firms to hire additional workers as employment increases. Once the functional relationship between employment and output is specified, the employment multiplier can be calculated.

The income multiplier is

$$\frac{\Delta Y}{\Delta D_A} = \frac{1}{1 - k}$$

where ΔD_A is the autonomous change in spending and k is the sum of the marginal induced spending effects.

Let

$$Y_2 - Y_1 = \Delta Y$$

where Y_1 is the initial equilibrium level of income and Y_2 is the new equilibrium income attained as a result of the autonomous change in spending, ΔD_A. From the aggregate supply function, the level of employment before and after the change in spending can be found:

$$N_1 = Y_1^\alpha$$

and

---

[7] Because income and employment are measured in different units, the actual value of the multiplier will depend upon the units of measurement along the axes.

$$N_2 = Y_2{}^\alpha$$

Therefore,

$$\Delta N = N_2 - N_1 = Y_2{}^\alpha - Y_1{}^\alpha$$

The employment multiplier is

$$\frac{\Delta N}{\Delta D_A} = \frac{Y_2{}^\alpha - Y_1{}^\alpha}{\Delta D_A}$$

Suppose

$$k = 0.8$$

and the initial level of income is $400 million. What would be the impact on employment of an autonomous increase in spending of $100 million? Since

$$\Delta Y = \Delta D_A \frac{1}{1-k}$$
$$= \$100 \text{ million} \times 5$$
$$= \$500 \text{ million}$$

the income multiplier is 5.

Therefore, at the new equilibrium, income, Y_2, will be $900 million.

$$Y_2 = Y_1 + \Delta Y = \$400 \text{ million} + \$500 \text{ million} = \$900 \text{ million}$$

Suppose that the functional relationship between employment and income is

$$N = Y^{1/2}$$

Then

$$\Delta N = N_2 - N_1 = Y_2{}^{1/2} - Y_1{}^{1/2}$$
$$= (900 \text{ million})^{1/2} - (400 \text{ million})^{1/2}$$
$$= 30,000 - 20,000$$
$$= 10,000$$

and

$$\frac{\Delta N}{\Delta D_A} = \frac{10,000}{100 \text{ million}} = \frac{1}{10,000}$$

The total change in employment which occurs in response to an autonomous increase in spending of $100 million is 10,000 workers. The employment multiplier is $\frac{1}{10,000}$.

A period analysis can also be introduced. Suppose the planner wishes to ascertain the impact on employment *after one year* of an autonomous increase in spending of $100 million. Expenditure is to be increased by $100 million every three months. If the expenditure-receipt-expenditure period is also three months, we know that

$$\Delta Y = \Delta D_A(1 + k + k^2 + k^3)$$
$$= \$100 \text{ million} \times (1 + 0.8 + 0.8^2 + 0.8^3)$$
$$= \$100 \text{ million} \times 2.95$$
$$= \$295 \text{ million}$$

The period multiplier is 2.95.

If income was $400 million initially, after one year the new income level will be

$$Y_2 = Y_1 + \Delta Y = \$400 \text{ million} + \$295 \text{ million} = \$695 \text{ million}$$

Since

$$N = Y^{1/2}$$

then

$$\Delta N = N_2 - N_1 = Y_2^{1/2} - Y_1^{1/2}$$
$$= (695 \text{ million})^{1/2} - (400 \text{ million})^{1/2}$$
$$= 26{,}000 - 20{,}000$$
$$= 6{,}000$$

and

$$\frac{\Delta N}{\Delta D_A} = \frac{6{,}000}{100 \text{ million}} = \frac{6}{100{,}000}$$

The change in employment after one year in response to an autonomous spending increase of $100 million is 6,000 workers. This is 60 percent of the ultimate effect. The period employment multiplier for one year is $\frac{6}{100{,}000}$.

4-5   IMPACT ON THE BALANCE OF TRADE

One goal of national economic policy is to avoid excessive balance-of-payments deficits. While we shall not consider the complete payments balance here, we can analyze the impact of fiscal and monetary policy on the trade balance. While some countries can support substantial trade deficits by accepting aid from abroad or by maintaining a surplus on capital account, others require perpetual trade surpluses to compensate for large capital outflows and unilateral transfers abroad. Nevertheless, for any country concerned with avoiding increased payments deficits, the impact of public economic policy on the trade balance must be considered.

Consider the national income model:

$$Y = C + I + X_n + G$$
$$C = a + b(Y - T)$$
$$I = dY - ei$$
$$X_n = E_0 - m(Y - T)$$
$$G = G_0$$
$$i = i_0$$

What will be the impact of an increase in government spending, G, on the trade balance, X_n? Expressing the model in terms of changes and assuming that Δa, ΔT, ΔE, and Δi will be zero,

$$\Delta Y = \Delta C + \Delta I + \Delta X_n + \Delta G$$
$$\Delta C = b\,\Delta Y$$
$$\Delta I = d\,\Delta Y$$
$$\Delta X_n = -m\,\Delta Y$$
$$\Delta G = \Delta G$$

By substitution,

$$\Delta Y = b\,\Delta Y + d\,\Delta Y - m\,\Delta Y + \Delta G$$
$$= \frac{1}{1 - b - d + m}\,\Delta G$$

and

$$\Delta X_n = -m\,\Delta Y = \frac{-m}{1 - b - d + m}\,\Delta G$$

The impact, therefore, of a change in G on the trade balance is

$$\frac{\Delta X_n}{\Delta G} = \frac{-m}{1 - b - d + m}$$

which is negative if the marginal propensity to import is positive. An increase in government spending will, other things being equal, cause imports to increase and, with exports fixed, reduce the net export surplus.

The process is seen graphically in Figure 4-4. In Figure 4-4(B), exports, E, are fixed, and imports, M, increase with income. Net exports, X_n, decline with income. In Figure 4-4 (A) when aggregate demand is D_1, national income is Y_1, and the trade balance is in surplus at X_{n1}. If demand is increased to D_2, income will be Y_2 and exports will exactly equal imports. If demand increases beyond D_2, however, the trade balance will go into deficit.

Suppose the government decides to use tax policy to influence demand. What will be the impact on the balance of trade? There are two effects.[8] First, there is a direct effect that reduces imports by the amount of the tax times the marginal propensity to import, that is

$$(\Delta X_n)_1 = \Delta E - m(\Delta Y - \Delta T)$$
$$= m\,\Delta T$$

or

$$\left(\frac{\Delta X_n}{\Delta T}\right)_1 = m$$

The second effect is the indirect effect of taxes through their multiplier effect on income, where

$$\frac{\Delta X_n}{\Delta D_A} = \frac{-m}{1 - b - d + m}$$

Solving for the initial change in demand associated with a change in taxes,

$$\Delta D_A = \Delta C + \Delta X_n = -b\,\Delta T + m\,\Delta T = -(b - m)\,\Delta T$$

Therefore, since

$$\frac{\Delta X_n}{\Delta D_A} = \frac{\Delta X_n}{-(b - m)\,\Delta T} = \frac{-m}{1 - b - d + m}$$

then

$$\left(\frac{\Delta X_n}{\Delta T}\right)_2 = \frac{m(b - m)}{1 - b - d + m}$$

[8] I am grateful to John D. Eshelman for pointing out an error in the first edition of *The Theory of Macroeconomic Policy* that omitted the first of these effects.

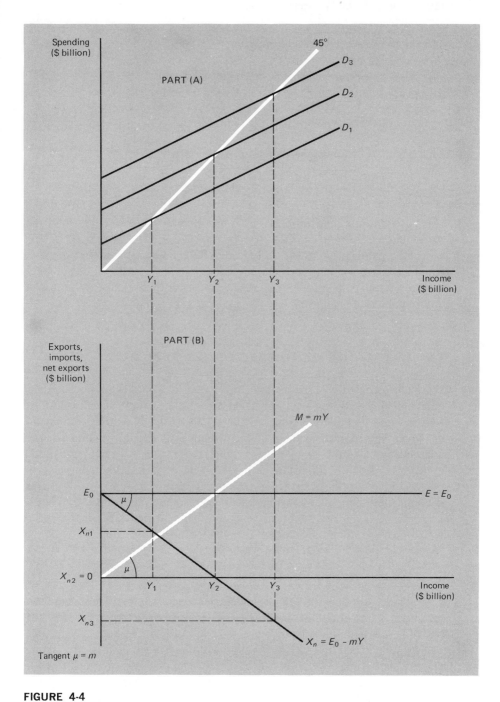

FIGURE 4-4

The Impact of a Change in Aggregate Demand
on the Balance of Trade

109

The total effect of the tax on the trade balance is

$$\frac{\Delta X}{\Delta T} = \left(\frac{\Delta X}{\Delta T}\right)_1 + \left(\frac{\Delta X}{\Delta T}\right)_2$$

$$= m + \frac{m(b - m)}{1 - b - d + m}$$

This effect will be positive and a tax increase will increase the trade surplus if

$$0 < m < b$$

that is, if the marginal propensity to import is positive and less than the marginal propensity to consume.

In general, if imports tend to rise with income and if export demand is independent of domestic economic conditions, then expansionary monetary and fiscal policies will reduce net exports and restrictive policies will improve the trade balance.

4-6 LIMITATIONS OF THE MULTIPLIER APPROACH

We have repeatedly observed that any forecasting model or policy planning model is only as good as its underlying structural specification. If all the important determinants of the components of aggregate demand are not taken into account, or if the structure of decision making at the microeconomic level changes over time, the model will not give good predictions. Equally important is the problem of lags. Although we have not considered a lag specification in this chapter, we have seen in our dynamic multiplier analysis that the way income will change over time in response to an autonomous change in demand depends on the speed with which spending units respond to changes in their income.

Tax Policy: 1964 Versus 1968

As an example of the problems one encounters by the strict application of the multiplier concept it is interesting to compare the tax cut of 1964 with the tax increase of 1968. In 1964, personal income taxes were reduced by about $10 billion with the explicit goal of stimulating employment. The mass media—newspapers and weekly news magazines—contained short courses in Keynesian economics, explaining how the multiplier effect works and encouraging consumers to spend their increased disposable income in the interests of the national economy. In a period of general optimism it was hardly necessary to encourage people to spend more. As one might expect, the short-run multiplier effect was quite high. By mid-1965, estimates of the multiplier effect of that policy alone were in the range of 2.5.

In 1968, President Johnson announced a personal income tax surcharge of 10 percent. Much publicity was given to the temporary nature of the tax increase. In an election year many politicians attempted to ward off pessimism by emphasizing the buoyancy of the economy and pointing out the possibility that rising wages might well offset the loss in disposable income associated with the tax surcharge. The inflationary expectations that developed in the early seventies were not yet felt and so people were subject to some money illusion; that is, they associated rapidly rising money wages with gains in real wages.

As might be expected under these conditions, the tax increase affected consumption hardly at all in the short run. Consumption fell by far less than a multiplier analysis based on the 1964 experience would have predicted. Since the initial autonomous change in income induced very little change in consumption spending, the multiplier effect was negligible. If anything, the tax increase only contributed to the inflation by strengthening demands for compensatory increases in wages in a tight labor market.

Later, in 1969, President Nixon undertook strong restrictive monetary and fiscal measures that eventually pushed the economy into a recession. Some observers argue that the recession would not have been as bad as it was had there not been a delayed reaction to the 1968 tax increase.[9] They claim that the problem was not in estimating the strength of the multiplier effect but only the lags involved in the dynamic adjustment process. Unfortunately, it is impossible to judge how much impact the 1968 tax surcharge actually had since the restrictive measures taken by President Nixon in 1969 produced additional autonomous changes in demand that worked in the same direction.

In any event, it is important to recognize that a multiplier is derived from an underlying structural model of the economy that changes from time to time for a variety of reasons. The expected permanency of the initial and subsequent changes in income, the degree of optimism about the future and other sources of income, the credibility and intent of the entire policy package, all influence the way spending units will

[9] Milton Friedman argues that because we are not able to specify reaction lags very well, discretionary policy measures are likely to overcompensate most of the time and hence aggravate the very macroeconomic instability they are designed to prevent. For a statement of his position see Milton Friedman, "A Monetary and Fiscal Framework for Economic Stability," *The American Economic Review,* XXXVIII (June, 1948), 245–264.

react to changes in policy instruments. Unless these are taken into account by policy planners, multiplier analysis will not be very accurate.[10]

Having developed the basic model of national income equilibrium, in Chapters 5 and 6 we shall take a closer look at the two major components of private demand: consumption and investment. This will provide the foundation for the development of a more sophisticated national income analysis in Chapters 8 and 9.

QUESTIONS FOR STUDY AND REVIEW

1. Consider an economy represented by the following macroeconomic model,

$$D = C + I + X_n + G$$
$$Z = N^2$$
$$C = 200 + 0.6(Y - T)$$
$$I = 0.3\,Y - 15i$$
$$X_n = E - 0.1(Y - T)$$
$$E = 50$$
$$G = 200$$
$$T = 100$$
$$i = 4$$

where

D = aggregate demand (in millions of dollars)

Z = aggregate supply (in millions of dollars)

Y = national income (in millions of dollars)

N = employment (in millions of workers)

and the other notation follows that of the text.

(a) Find the equilibrium level of income and employment in this economy.

(b) Calculate the government expenditure multiplier, the tax multiplier, and the interest rate multiplier. Consider the multiplier effects on income, employment, and the balance of trade.

---

[10] See Appendix A for a discussion of the multipliers obtained in econometric models of the U.S. economy.

(c) What will be the effect on income, employment, and the trade balance of the following polices:

(i) increasing government expenditure by $25 million,

(ii) increasing taxes by $25 million,

(iii) increasing simultaneously government expenditure and taxes by $50 million,

(iv) reducing the interest rate by two percentage points,

(v) reducing the interest rate by one percentage point and increasing taxes by $50 million?

2. In the economy represented in the above model, the income-expenditure-receipt period is three months.

(a) Calculate the multiplier effect *after one year* of a change in government spending, taxes, and the interest rate on income, employment, and the trade balance.

(b) What will be the effect *after one year* of the following policies on income, employment, and the trade balance:

(i) increasing government expenditure by $10 million (over the corresponding quarter of the previous year) every three months for one year,

(ii) reducing taxes by $15 million every three months for one year,

(iii) increasing simultaneously government expenditure and taxes by $50 million every three months for one year,

(iv) reducing the interest rate by two percentage points at the beginning of the year?

(c) For each policy in part (b), find the percentage of the total economic impact of the program experienced after one year.

3. Consider an economy whose structure is exactly like that of the economy represented by the model above except that investment is not a function of income. In this economy

$$I = 300 - 15i$$

(a) Find the government expenditure multiplier, the tax multiplier, and the interest rate multiplier. Consider the multiplier effects on income, employment, and the trade balance.

(b) Explain why the expenditure and tax multipliers are always lower in this economy than in the former economy, in which investment is a function of income.

4. Return to the economy represented by the model in Question 3. Suppose 10,000 workers are unemployed.

(a) What is the deflationary gap?

(b) Design three alternative fiscal and/or monetary programs that will close the deflationary gap and bring the economy to full employment.

(c) Can monetary policy *alone* close the deflationary gap? Be sure to justify your answer.

5. For the model in Question 3, suppose the government desires to increase spending, but because of serious balance of payments problems, it cannot allow the trade balance to deteriorate. If the government is willing to increase taxes, how much will they have to increase (as a percentage of the increased government spending) so that the increase in spending has no impact on the trade balance? (*Hint:* An example in the text showed the increase in taxes required to neutralize the impact of an increase in government spending on national income.)

6. Can you distinguish between a policy-planning model and a forecasting model? Why is accurate behavioral or structural specification so important in designing these models?

7. Explain why an analysis of economic policy planning is an important part of macroeconomic theory.

ADDITIONAL READING

MACHLUP, FRITZ, "Period Analysis and Multiplier Theory," *The Quarterly Journal of Economics,* LIV (November, 1939), 1–27.

MUSGRAVE, RICHARD A., *The Theory of Public Finance.* New York: McGraw-Hill Book Company, Inc., 1959, Chapter 18.

SUITS, DANIEL B., "Forecasting and Analysis with an Econometric Model," *The American Economic Review,* LII (March, 1962), 104–32.

"Tax Revision: Impact on Output and Employment," *Economic Report of the President.* Washington, D.C.: U.S. Government Printing Office, January, 1963, pp. 45–52.

5

The Theory of Consumption

In the last three chapters we developed a model of national income equilibrium. Such a model, with more accurate and complete behavioral specification, is actually used for macroeconomic forecasting and policy planning at the national level.

In Chapters 5 and 6 we shall examine some hypotheses about consumption and investment behavior. An understanding of the behavior of the economic groups in the private sector (consumers and investors) is vital to the development of a forecasting model. Even though the model-building approach to economic decision making may seem impersonal, we shall see that the economist must know a great deal about human behavior so that his quantitative relationships actually mirror real-world events.

In this chapter we are concerned with the factors which influence consumption. Chapter 6 deals with the investment decision.

5-1 THE KEYNESIAN CONSUMPTION FUNCTION

The notion that consumption is primarily a function of disposable income lies at the heart of Keynesian economics. The hypothesis is reasonable, since disposable income is the principal source by which consumption expenditures are financed. An individual cannot live beyond his means indefinitely. Keynes postulated that aggregate consumption would increase with disposable income, but that the increment to consumption would not be as great as the increment to income. In technical terms, he suggested that the *marginal propensity to consume (MPC)* would be less than 1 or algebraically,

$$\frac{\Delta C}{\Delta Y} < 1$$

Not only did he expect the *amount* of saving to increase with income, but he expected the *proportion* of income saved to increase as well. This implies that the *average propensity to consume, C/Y,* declines with income. (Note that this is not equivalent to the observation that the poor spend a higher proportion of their income than the rich. On an aggregate level, we are examining the behavior of *total* consumption as the level of national income changes.) The *a priori* reasoning behind what Keynes called "fundamental psychological laws" is somewhat tenuous. The idea seems to be that as a society becomes richer, wants become less urgent. Alternatively, it may suggest a diminishing marginal utility of consumption. While this idea may be appealing superficially, it is important to keep in mind that the alternative to consumption is saving, presumably for the purpose of future consumption. Thus, the theory actually implies that the preference for present over future consumption is weaker when the income level is higher. This hypothesis may be valid for individuals, but it is not necessarily applicable to a whole economy, particularly after national income has surpassed the subsistence level.

Nevertheless, as a first approximation it is reasonable to assume that at least part of an increment to income will be saved (or conversely, that a decline in income will be partly offset by a decrease in saving) and that the proportion of income saved rises with the general level of national income.

A consumption function such as Keynes had in mind is shown in Figure 5-1.[1] Along the 45° line which bisects the quadrant, consumption is equal to income. Consequently, the vertical distance between the consumption function and the 45° line represents saving.

As we saw in Chapter 2, Keynes' consumption function is vital to his theory of employment. Unless there is sufficient investment to offset the additional saving as income and output increase, aggregate demand will not equal aggregate supply and firms will reduce employment levels. Thus, the level of employment is determined by the level of demand.

---

[1] Keynes may have had a curvilinear relationship in mind since he suggested that the marginal propensity to consume would decline with income. A linear relationship is easier to handle algebraically, however, and does not essentially alter the conclusions of the analysis as long as the slope is less than 1.

Furthermore, since he expected saving to increase as a percentage of income in the process of economic development, Keynes believed a wealthy economy would have a particularly difficult time generating adequate aggregate demand for the maintenance of full employment. Invest-

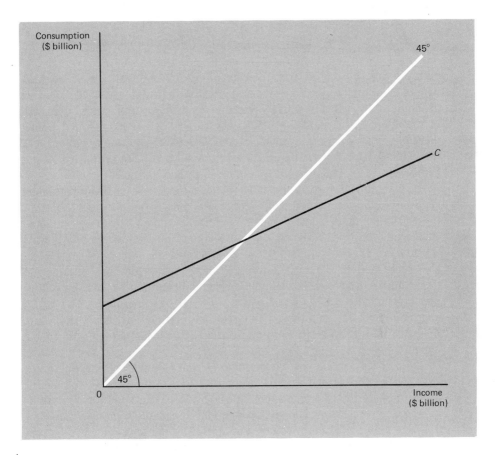

FIGURE 5-1

The Keynesian Consumption Function

ment and government spending would have to increase indefinitely relative to consumption or else the economy would experience secular stagnation as a result of economic growth.

Classical, or pre-Keynesian, economists felt that saving and investment would be equated at any level of income by movements of the interest rate. Keynes pointed out that if saving is solely a function of the interest rate, then consumption is also solely a function of the interest rate and does not depend on income—a rather unlikely hypothesis.

5-2   EMPIRICAL TESTS AND NEW HYPOTHESES

Keynes' model of income determination is theoretical in design. The behavioral relationships, such as the consumption function, are hypothetical and are not based on empirical relationships. Keynes was concerned with explaining the phenomenon of generalized unemployment in a market economy. Although his policy prescriptions were an important outgrowth of the analysis, his model was not intended to be used for actual policy planning and forecasting. It lacked complete behavioral specification, and the values of the various parameters (e.g., the *MPC*), were not estimated. Furthermore, the stability of the relationships had not been established.

Precisely because it indicated a need for active government intervention in the economy, Keynesian economics demonstrated the need for a planning model. The parameters of such a model had to be estimated empirically on the basis of data reflecting past experience. Following World War II, economists of the "new" Keynesian school began to devise such models. The consumption function was the first relationship they studied, because it is at the heart of the model and because consumption represents the largest component of GNP. Furthermore, they felt it might be the easiest and most stable relationship to specify, since consumption was believed to be primarily a function of a single variable, disposable income.

Empirical studies of consumption focus on two major questions. First, is the short-run marginal propensity to consume reasonably stable over time? This is an important consideration when multiplier analysis is used for forecasting and policy planning. Second, is there a tendency for the average propensity to consume to fall in the long run? If this were found to be the case it would imply a need for the public sector to grow faster than the private sector (or for an ever-increasing investment-output ratio in the private sector) in mature economies, unless consumers were re-educated to maintain higher levels of consumption.

APPROACHES TO ESTIMATING THE CONSUMPTION FUNCTION

A priori or deductive reasoning is useful as a first approximation in devising a theoretical model. From the *a priori* specification,

$$C = a + b(Y - T)$$

where

$$a > 0$$

and

$$0 < b < 1$$

many useful conclusions about national income equilibrium were derived in Chapters 3 and 4. However, to answer the question, "How much will demand increase next year if taxes are cut by $50 million this quarter?" we need a reliable estimate of the *MPC, b,* as well as additional information about the speed of response.

To estimate parameter values, an inductive, or *a posteriori,* approach is generally used. This method involves examination of past experience to determine if indeed a reliable relationship has existed between the variables. In the case of the consumption function, it is necessary to examine data which measure consumption and disposable income.[2]

Two sources of such data are available. First, the relationship between consumption and income can be measured for different periods of time. As income changed between 1950 and 1960, for example, how did consumption move? Such a study is called *time series analysis.*

An alternative approach is to examine the consumption of families at different levels of income. How does the consumption of a family earning $10,000 differ from that of a family earning $15,000. This is a *cross-section* or *budget study* approach.

While both use valid sources of data, the relationships found in the two analyses may differ considerably. Suppose, for example, that over a 10-year period, average disposable income rises by 50 percent. Family A earns $10,000 in the base year and $15,000 10 years later. Consider family B earning $15,000 in the base year. Would you expect the consumption of family A at the end of the 10-year period to be the same as that of family B in the base year? Probably not, for a number of reasons. Family B is likely to consume less than family A out of its $15,000 income, since in the base period family B is more affluent in relation to the general standard of living of the society than family A at the end of the period. As average income rises so does the average level of consumption, or standard of living, so that the average propensity to consume (*APC*) from $15,000 will rise over time as average income increases. Thus, while time series and cross-section studies both measure the relationship between consumption and income, they are actually examining different behavioral relationships.

---

[2] For the remainder of this chapter, the terms income and disposable income will be used interchangeably except when it is necessary to make the distinction.

The question facing a forecaster is which approach best suits his needs. He wants to know how aggregate consumption will change in response to short-run changes in disposable income. Suppose we ignore distributional problems and assume everyone is to receive a $100 transfer payment from the government. Will families adjust fully to the improved standard of living in the short run? If not, a time series analysis measuring behavior over long periods of time may not be useful in a short-run situation. A time-series study using quarterly data (data collected every three months) over a fewer number of years would be preferred. However, in the short run there are often considerable lags in consumer responsiveness to income changes. These lags are often unpredictable and difficult to estimate. Budget studies can also be useful since in the short run individuals may be subject to a *distributional illusion*. That is, they may feel their relative economic status is improved by an increase in income and indeed behave like the more affluent families of the cross section. As we shall see, budget studies and short-run time series analysis often yield similar parameter estimates. Budget studies often provide insights into the microeconomic determinants of household behavior that are useful for formulating hypotheses about aggregate behavior in macroeconomic models.

REAL VERSUS MONEY SPECIFICATIONS

In the model which we have developed, the variables were expressed in terms of their money value. We were concerned with how total money spending in the economy affects employment decisions of firms. Total money spending is comprised of consumption, investment, net exports, and government spending, all measured in money value.

Empirical studies of consumption and investment behavior typically measure the variables in *real* terms. A variable measured in real terms is deflated by a price index to abstract from price changes. This practice is based on the assumption that households and firms are not subject to a "money illusion"; that is, they take price changes into account before making decisions. Suppose money income rises by 10 percent and consumer prices rise by 10 percent simultaneously. If households are not subject to a money illusion, real consumption will be unaffected and money consumption will increase by 10 percent. If they are subject to money illusion, families will behave as if their purchasing power had increased, real consumption will rise, and money consumption will increase by more than 10 percent.

Because consumption and investment functions are generally specified in real terms for the purposes of empirical study, we shall treat them as real relationships in Chapters 5 and 6. However, to incorporate them in a model of national income equilibrium, they must be converted into money relationships by multiplying the variables measured in real terms by a price index.

If we assume for simplicity that all the variables in the relationship were originally deflated by the same price index, that is, if variations in consumer prices were about the same as for the price level in general, then the *MPC* will be the same, regardless of whether the variables are in real or money form. Denoting real variables with the subscript r, and money variables with the subscript m, then if

$$C_m = a + b Y_m$$

$$C_r = \frac{C_m}{p}$$

and

$$Y_r = \frac{Y_m}{p}$$

where p is the common price index.

$$\frac{C_m}{p} = \frac{a}{p} + \frac{b Y_m}{p}$$

or

$$C_r = \frac{a}{p} + b Y_r$$

Only the constant term, reflecting the amount of consumption which would occur independently of income variation, will change when the variables are transformed from money into real terms.

We shall return to a more detailed consideration of real versus money models in Chapter 8.

EARLY EMPIRICAL INVESTIGATIONS

One of the first attempts to study consumption behavior empirically was made by Simon Kuznets in 1946.[3] He plotted a consumption function from annual time series data covering the period 1869–1938. The consumption relationship he obtained is shown in Figure 5-2. Kuznets found that over a long period, real consumption was roughly proportional to real national income. Furthermore, the *APC* remained nearly stable, varying between 0.85 and 0.89.

[3] Simon Kuznets, *National Product Since 1869* (New York: National Bureau of Economic Research, 1946), p. 119.

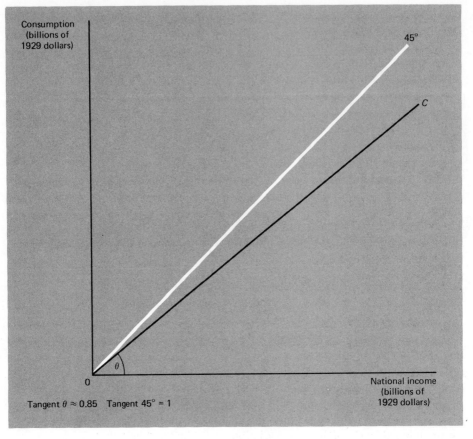

Consumption
(billions of
1929 dollars)

45°

C

0

θ

National income
(billions of
1929 dollars)

Tangent θ ≈ 0.85   Tangent 45° = 1

FIGURE 5-2

Consumption Function Estimated from Long-Period Time Series

Notice that for a linear consumption function which intersects the origin, the *APC* and the *MPC* are equal. Algebraically, the relationship is expressed as

$$C = bY$$

where *b* is both the *APC* and *MPC*. Note that *b* is a constant; it does not decline with income.

Kuznets' study supported Keynes' hypothesis that consumption is a stable function of income and that the *MPC* is less than 1. However, the idea that the *APC* and perhaps the *MPC* decline with income did not receive empirical support. Thus, while the stability of the consumption function was supported by this study, the secular stagnation thesis was not.

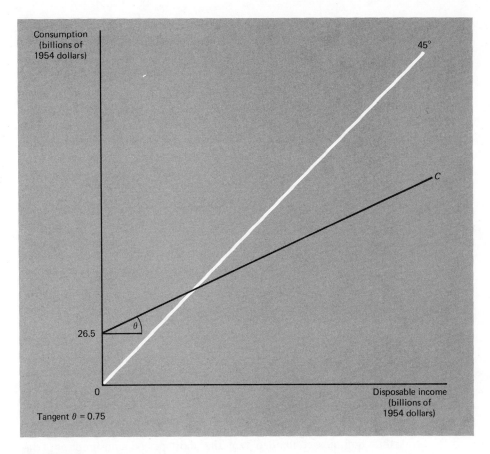

FIGURE 5-3

Consumption Function Estimated
from Short-Period Time Series Data

Although Kuznets' study was primarily intended to be descriptive of historical consumption behavior, other economists were concerned with actually forecasting postwar consumer demand. They decided to estimate the consumption function using quarterly time series data collected over a relatively short period, 1929–1941.[4] The consumption function they obtained is shown in Figure 5-3. The function has a positive intercept of $26.5 billion and a slope of 0.75 when the variables are measured in 1954 dollars and the independent variable is disposable income. Algebraically, this is expressed as

[4] Gardner Ackley, *Macroeconomic Theory* (New York: The Macmillan Company, 1961), p. 226.

$$C = 26.5 + 0.75Y$$

Since the MPC is smaller than for the Kuznets' consumption function, this implies that the short-run multiplier is smaller than the long-run multiplier. If Kuznets had used disposable income rather than national income in his relationship, the long-run MPC and the multiplier would have been even greater. It is reasonable to expect the short-run MPC to be smaller than the long-run MPC, considering that it takes time for a family to adjust its consumption behavior to a new, higher level of income.

The consumption relationship derived from short-run time series generally supported Keynes' *a priori* reasoning about consumption behavior. The APC declines with income and the MPC is less than 1. There is no tendency for the MPC to decline with income, however.

Economists using the short-period consumption function to estimate postwar consumption grossly underestimated the level of postwar demand for consumption goods. The MPC turned out to be considerably higher than 0.75. This is not surprising since they were using a relationship reflecting behavior during a severe depression to predict consumption following a wartime boom. As income increased after the war, consumption increased by a greater proportion than in the prewar experience due to a general feeling of optimism as well as the availability of liquid assets accumulated during the wartime rationing which could be used to satisfy the "pent-up" demand.

The following question then arose: "Should we use long- or short-period data to estimate our forecasting model?" Furthermore, "Is there a theoretical reconciliation of the two approaches?"

Arthur Smithies contended that the short-period consumption relationship is basically nonproportional, as shown in Figure 5-3, but that the function has shifted up over time, as shown in Figure 5-4.[5] The C_S are short-period consumption functions, estimated at different periods of time. The line C_L is a long-period consumption function such as Kuznets found. It is obtained from points on different short-period consumption functions. Thus, Smithies argued, the forecasters of postwar consumption demand failed to recognize that the short-period consumption function was likely to shift upward after the war, reflecting an increase in the APC at all levels of income.

Smithies did not provide a complete structural explanation for why the consumption function shifts upward over time. He attributed much of the shift to increases in the standard of living as median family incomes increased. But, if the magnitude of shifts in the function over time are ran-

[5] Arthur Smithies, "Forcasting Postwar Demand," *Econometrica,* XII (January, 1945), 1–14.

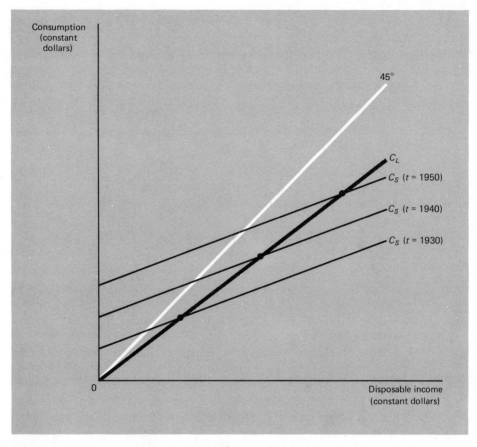

FIGURE 5-4

Shifts in the Short-Period Consumption Function

dom or arbitrary, his theory does not explain why the long-run relationship is almost exactly proportional.

Smithies estimated a relationship which took the passage of time into account. Algebraically, he found

$$C = a + bY + ct$$

where t is the year in which the variables are observed. If c is positive, then as t increases, consumption will increase, even in the absence of increases in disposable income. The exact relationship Smithies found is

$$C = 76.58 + 0.76Y + 1.15(t - 1922)$$

This is a per capita relationship. It implies that in 1922, autonomous per capita consumption (in 1929 prices) was $76.58 and increased by $1.15 every year thereafter. The *MPC* from disposable income is 0.76.

THE RELATIVE INCOME HYPOTHESIS

Despite the lack of structural theory in Keynes' *a priori* hypotheses about aggregate consumption, empirical (or *a posteriori*) evidence has tended to substantiate his view, at least in part.

James Duesenberry, one of Smithies' students, formulated a more complete *a priori* explanation for the observed discrepancy between long- and short-period consumption behavior.[6] Furthermore, he performed cross-section budget studies of income and consumption that lent support to his hypotheses about aggregate behavior. The consumption function derived from cross-section data (collected for a single time period from various income groups) appears similar to the short-period time series relationship shown in Figure 5-3. It has a positive intercept on the consumption axis and an *MPC* less than 1 and less than that of the long period found by Kuznets. Duesenberry's theory was designed to explain the discrepancy between the cross-section and short-period time series consumption functions on the one hand and the long-period relationship on the other.

Unlike Smithies, Duesenberry suggested that the most basic consumption relationship was long run and proportional. That is, since saving is undertaken primarily for the purpose of future consumption, there is no reason to expect saving to increase as a percentage of income as income rises. This is equivalent to saying that time preference is independent of the level of income.

Duesenberry's explanation of cross-section behavior is based on his idea that consumption patterns are principally social. People's tastes are so interdependent that an individual's consumption pattern may be more influenced by the income and consumption of his friends than by his own income. An individual earning $10,000 will consume more if he lives in a rich neighborhood than in a poor one. Thus, lower-income families attempting to keep up with the Joneses will spend a higher proportion of their income than high-income families. Duesenberry labeled this phenomenon the *demonstration effect*. As individuals come into contact with superior goods, the impulse to increase their own consumption will become more intense. This hypothesis has also been used to explain why the average propensity to save (*APS*) is relatively low in developing countries.

---

[6] James S. Duesenberry, *Income, Saving, and the Theory of Consumer Behavior* (Cambridge, Mass.: Harvard University Press, 1949). Chapter 3 is especially interesting. Also see James S. Duesenberry, "Income-Consumption Relations and their Implications," in *Income, Employment, and Public Policy: Essays in Honor of Alvin H. Hansen* (New York: W. W. Norton and Company, 1948), pp. 54–81.

For the economy as a whole, families with below-average income will have a higher *APC* than higher-income families. This explains why the *APC* declines with income in budget studies. As *median* (or average) family income increases with economic growth, however, there is no reason to expect the average *APC* to decline. Instead, on the average all families enjoy an increased standard of living. This explains the proportionality of the long-period consumption function.

From what he observed about the consumption behavior of households in budget studies, Duesenberry formulated an explanation for the observed nonproportional function derived from short-period time series data. If consumption is influenced by the "demonstration effect" of the goods others enjoy, then it also must be influenced by the "own-demonstration effect" of goods previously enjoyed. That is, consumption patterns must be influenced by past living standards, particularly in the short run. Thus, if disposable income declines in the short run, families attempt to maintain their old living standards and the *APC* rises. On the other hand, when disposable income rises, families do not adjust fully to the new income level, and although consumption increases, they are still tied to their old living standard to some extent. Consequently, the *APC* falls. Duesenberry labels this tendency for families to maintain living standards in periods of temporary declines in income the *rachet effect*.

He formulates the short-period consumption function as

$$\frac{C_t}{Y_t} = b_1 - b_2 \frac{Y_t}{Y_{pp}}$$

where the subscript t refers to the time period at which the variable is measured and Y_{pp} refers to previous peak income.

This relationship states that the *APC* declines as the ratio between current income, Y_t, and previous peak income, Y_{pp}, rises. The *MPC* will be somewhat less than b_1 and depends upon how widely income is varying. Thus, the multiplier to be applied to a small change in income will be greater than that to be applied to a larger variation when a forecast of total spending is required.

For the period 1929–1940, Duesenberry found the relationship between real consumption and real disposable income to be

$$\frac{C_t}{Y_t} = 1.196 - 0.25 \frac{Y_t}{Y_{pp}}$$

or

$$C_t = 1.196 Y_t - 0.25 \frac{Y_t^2}{Y_{pp}}$$

During that period, for instance, if current real income were equal to its previous peak, the *APC* would have been 0.946:

$$APC = 1.196 - 0.25 = 0.946$$

If current income were 5 percent above its previous peak, the *APC* would have fallen to 0.934:

$$APC = 1.196 - 0.25\tfrac{105}{100} = 0.934$$

THE PERMANENT INCOME HYPOTHESIS

Another explanation of the inconsistency of the short- and long-period data has been provided by Milton Friedman.[7] Like Duesenberry, Friedman argues that the consumption function is essentially proportional; that is, there is no tendency for the proportion of income saved to increase at higher income levels. He contends, however, that households do not adapt their consumption behavior to current income alone, but to the general level of their resources over extended periods of time. Income measured on a quarterly or even yearly basis, he argues, is not necessarily a good measure of the variable which influences consumers' behavior.

Consider the example of seven men, each earning $100 per week and each paid on a different day of the week. Suppose we collect budget data for these men on a daily basis. On each day, one man will have income of $100, and the others will have no income. If they distribute their consumption expenditures fairly uniformly over the week, we will find that the *APC* falls drastically with income (from infinity to something less than 1).[8] Friedman argues correctly that these results tell us nothing meaningful about consumption behavior but merely reflect the use of inappropriate measures of income and consumption. If we had measured income and consumption on a weekly basis, our results would have been more interesting.

Friedman contends that a three-month period (generally used for short-run time series data) or even a year may be inappropriate. Households make their budget plans on the basis of a more permanent measure of income. He argues that consumption, in the aggregate, will be proportional to permanent income at all income levels.[9] The difficulty in testing Friedman's hypothesis is, of course, that permanent income cannot be measured directly.

[7] Milton Friedman, *A Theory of the Consumption Function* (Princeton, N.J.: Princeton University Press, 1957).

[8] This example is taken from *ibid.*, Chapter 9.

[9] Friedman defines *permanent income* rather tautologically as that income to which households adapt their consumption behavior.

Friedman argues that individuals do not know their permanent income any more than the forecaster does. Therefore, they base their consumption behavior on their past income, as well as on current income. Friedman estimates permanent income by a weighted average of current and past measured income with exponentially decreasing weights. His consumption relationship is

$$C_t = KY_p = 0.9\,Y_p$$

and

$$Y_p = 0.33\,Y_t + 0.22\,Y_{t-1} + 0.15\,Y_{t-2} + \cdots$$

where Y_p is permanent income, Y_{t-i} is income measured i periods before t, and K is the marginal and average propensity to consume out of permanent income.

This expression for Y_p represents a weighted average of past and present values of Y with the weights declining in a geometric progression with coefficient $\frac{2}{3}$; that is,

$$Y_p = 0.33 \sum_{i=0}^{\infty} (\tfrac{2}{3})^i Y_{t-i} = 0.33(\tfrac{2}{3})^0 Y_t + 0.33(\tfrac{2}{3})^1 Y_{t-1}$$
$$+ 0.33(\tfrac{2}{3})^2 Y_{t-2} + \cdots + 0.33(\tfrac{2}{3})^\infty Y_{t-\infty}$$

Notice that since

$$C_t = KY_p = 0.33K[Y_t + \tfrac{2}{3}Y_{t-1} + (\tfrac{2}{3})^2 Y_{t-2} + \cdots + (\tfrac{2}{3})^\infty Y_{t-\infty}]$$

then

$$\tfrac{2}{3}C_{t-1} = 0.33K[\tfrac{2}{3}Y_{t-1} + (\tfrac{2}{3})^2 Y_{t-2} + \cdots + (\tfrac{2}{3})^\infty Y_{t-\infty}]$$

Subtracting,

$$C_t - \tfrac{2}{3}C_{t-1} = 0.33KY_t$$

Therefore, since

$$K = 0.9$$

Friedman's consumption function can be written as

$$C_t = 0.297\,Y_t + \tfrac{2}{3}C_{t-1}$$

For purposes of statistical estimation, this formulation is preferred to the earlier one, since it involves only two explanatory variables, present income and past consumption. The earlier expression required knowledge of past income over a very long period.

The alternative formulation of Friedman's permanent income hypothesis states that if consumption is a function of past income, it is also a function of past consumption. Thus, consumption is a function of past consumption as well as current income. Mathematically, this is strikingly similar to the Duesenberry model, although the *a priori* basis for the hypothesis is somewhat different. Because past consumption influences present consumption, the *APC* will rise in response to short-run declines in income and will fall when income rises in the short run. This explains the observed nonproportionality of the short-run consumption function. In the long run, permanent and measured income are equivalent, so that the long-run *APC* from measured income is approximately constant. To the extent that current changes in disposable income are considered temporary, the *MPC* and hence the multiplier will be smaller than for income changes expected to be permanent. According to the permanent income hypothesis, for instance, an increase in personal income taxes that is expected to be temporary will have less impact on consumption spending than a permanent increase.

Friedman's hypothesis is also consistent with cross-section behavior. He contends that families with an above-average income will, on the average, have a positive, transitory (nonpermanent) component to their income. Families with a lower-than-average income will, on the average, have a negative transitory component. Furthermore, the higher the level of income, the greater is the transitory component of income, on the average, for that income group. This accounts for the observed tendency of the *APC* to decline with income and for the *MPC* to be lower than for the long-run time series relationship.

IMPLICATIONS FOR MULTIPLIER ANALYSIS

In Friedman's view the permanent income hypothesis renders multiplier analysis virtually useless for forecasting and policy planning. The short-run *MPC* out of any change in income will depend on the extent to which that change is viewed as permanent. He defines any income change not viewed as permanent as *transitory,* and argues that the *MPC* out of transitory income is zero.[10] The *MPC* out of permanent income is a constant, *K*. Therefore, the *MPC*, *b*, out of the change in measured income, *Y*, is

$$b = K \frac{\Delta Y_p}{\Delta Y}$$

[10] This follows from his definition of permanent income as that income to which households adapt their consumption.

where $\dfrac{\Delta Y_p}{\Delta Y}$ is the proportion of the income change viewed as permanent. If all the income change is considered transitory, it will have no induced effect on consumption.

Since forecasters have no way of knowing how much of an actual income change households will consider permanent, they cannot estimate the MPC or the multiplier with an acceptable margin of error. Friedman's hypothesis is certainly consistent with the experience of tax policy in 1964 and 1968. The MPC from the temporary surcharge of 1968 was much less than the MPC from the tax cut of 1964 that was expected to be permanent.

Friedman argues against discretionary monetary and fiscal policy on a number of grounds. In this case, if households and firms do not know whether policy changes that affect their incomes will be permanent (and all discretionary policy is subject to this type of uncertainty), the induced impact on their spending cannot be reliably predicted and will render multiplier forecasts unreliable.

THE LIFE-CYCLE HYPOTHESIS

A variant of the permanent income hypothesis is based on the idea that the consumer wishes to allocate his resources to enable him to maintain approximately the same level of consumption each year of his life.[11] Consumption is estimated by the formula

$$C_t = \frac{Y_t + (N - T)Y_p + A_t}{L_t}$$

where

$$Y_t = \text{current income}$$

$$Y_p = \text{permanent income}$$

$$L_t = \text{number of years of life remaining}$$

$$N - T = \text{earning years remaining}$$

$$A_t = \text{nonearning assets}$$

This theory is similar to the permanent income hypothesis in that consumption is based on a long-run measure of household resources. In

[11] Albert Ando and Franco Modigliani, "The 'Life Cycle' Hypothesis of Saving," *The American Economic Review*, LIII (March, 1963), 55–84.

this model, however, the *MPC* out of permanent income will vary with age and family size. Furthermore, households accumulate assets, or wealth, that affect consumption.

Several studies have attempted to gauge the effect of changes in wealth on consumption. This effect may be important if there are sharp swings in the paper value of financial assets during periods of cyclical instability that produce destabilizing swings in consumption through wealth effects. The empirical evidence is somewhat mixed, largely because the relationship between wealth and consumption is complicated by off-setting influences that come into relative predominance at different times. But the Ando-Modigliani specification provided a model for testing the significance of wealth effects in econometric research.

Increases in wealth may increase consumption if households feel richer. However, households may also view the accumulation of wealth as an alternative to consumption (for precautionary reasons, to acquire power, or other motives), and then there would be a negative relationship between consumption and wealth. Furthermore, during an inflation the ratio of assets to income is likely to fall if a substantial amount of the assets are in fixed-value terms. During a period of rising prices, households may substitute durable consumer goods for financial assets. If changes in wealth are concentrated at the upper end of the income distribution, then the impact on consumption is also likely to be weak, because high-income families save a large proportion of their income anyway, and changes in their wealth are not likely to affect their consumption very much.

Although wealth holdings may affect consumption, the coefficient on the wealth variable in most econometric studies is either insignificant or unstable across different time-period samples. This should not necessarily be interpreted to mean that changes in wealth will not affect consumption, but only that the effect is likely to be different in different circumstances.

SIMILARITIES OF THE CONSUMPTION FUNCTIONS

All the theories we have studied are reasonable explanations of consumer behavior. Furthermore, the equations which specify the hypotheses are all more or less representative of the actual empirical evidence. In fact, all the equations boil down to the general form

$$C_t = b_1 + b_2 Y_t + b_3 C_{t-1}$$

or

$$C_t = d_1 + d_2 Y_t + d_3 C_{pp}$$

where C_{pp} is the previous peak consumption.

Graphically, the short-run relationship can be formulated in terms of a family of linear nonproportional consumption functions such as shown in Figure 5-4. While in the Smithies formulation these shift with time, in the Duesenberry model they shift with previous peak income. In the Friedman and life-cycle models they shift with the previous period's consumption. The long-run relationship is derived by connecting various points on the short-run functions as shown in Figure 5-4.

Both algebraically and graphically, the various models of consumption behavior are quite similar. This is not surprising, since they were all developed as attempts to explain the same *a posteriori* relationships. Since the theoretical basis for the various hypotheses are different, however, the policy implications may be somewhat different. In the next section we shall examine the effect of various economic policies on consumption behavior.

CONSUMER BEHAVIOR AND ECONOMIC POLICY

In our model of income determination, changes in spending initiated in the public sector induce further changes in consumption spending. This phenomenon, called the multiplier, occurs because consumption is a function of disposable income. Keynes assumed that the sole impact of public policy on consumption spending would be the effect induced by the change in disposable income. Post-Keynesian theories suggest, however, that public policy might have an impact on the *MPC* itself. Thus, the multiplier associated with any spending or tax program should be expected to vary with the exact nature of the program.

In this respect, Smithies' analysis is not very helpful. Since he attributes shifts in the short-run consumption function primarily to the passage of time, the influence of public policy on the *MPC* is unknown.

The relative income hypothesis suggests, however, that the *MPC* will be lower, the greater the magnitude of the change in disposable income, since consumption is influenced by the relationship of current income to the previous peak income. The *MPC* would also be reduced to the extent that the program increased the inequality of the income distribution, since consumption is influenced by other peoples' spending habits.

The permanent income and life-cycle hypotheses suggest that the *MPC* will be lower to the extent that the income change is viewed to be temporary. The life-cycle hypothesis includes the further notion that the

MPC will vary with the age composition of the population and with changes in the value of assets.

Consider, for example, a guaranteed annual income plan. This is essentially a transfer scheme, and if financed by taxes, would not initially affect aggregate disposable income at all. The relative income hypothesis would suggest that the program might increase the *MPC* of those income groups affected, since it (1) reduces inequality in the income distribution and (2) provides a buffer to large changes in disposable income. According to the permanent income hypothesis, the same conclusion would be reached for a different reason. A guaranteed annual income should increase the *MPC* by reducing the transitory component of income. Thus, the program could have an expansionary effect on aggregate demand, even though net aggregate disposable income was left unchanged by the initial transfer.

5-3   OTHER VARIABLES AFFECTING CONSUMPTION

Relationships which treat consumption as a function of disposable income and past consumption or income have proved to be good forecasting tools. The stability of the consumption-income relationship or "consumption function" has been demonstrated with both time series and budget study data. The introduction of other variables into the equation has provided little if any improvement in the predictions obtained, except in the case of durable consumer goods which we shall treat later in this chapter.

Nevertheless, other variables do influence consumption, particularly in periods of unstable prices. Furthermore, it is important to recognize that most research on consumption has taken the basic Keynesian postulate that consumption depends on income as the initial hypothesis to be tested. Non-Keynesian macroeconomic models—both the classical and the monetarist models—postulate different determinants of consumption altogether. Although in this text we are developing macroeconomic models in a Keynesian perspective, it is interesting to examine these other influences.

Price Expectations

If an inflationary psychology develops, price expectations are likely to influence consumption. If prices are expected to rise, people will purchase more now to avoid paying more for the same goods and services in the future. Although this phenomenon is typically associated with durable goods, during the rapid rise in food prices in 1973, there was a substantial increase in demand for home freezers as people bought and stored meat and vegetables in the expectation of rising prices. Although such consumption will not be maintained indefinitely, it is a source of short-run instability.[12]

Associated with price expectations is the phenomenon of money illusion. A consumption function estimated in real terms assumes households are not subject to money illusion or, equivalently, that inflation is fully anticipated and taken into account. Thus, during an inflation, consumption is like to increase over that predicted by a real consumption function if the actual rate of inflation is greater than the expected rate and households mistakenly view their real income as higher than it actually is.

Another way that inflation might affect consumption is if households shift their assets out of fixed-value holdings and into consumer goods. This is likely to affect consumer durables more than nondurables, as durables have a resale value and other characteristics that make them closer substitutes for financial assets than nondurables.

THE REAL BALANCE EFFECT

Despite these mechanisms by which inflation might be expected to stimulate consumption, some economists have argued that a price deflation would stimulate consumption. This is based on the idea that consumers hold both goods and money balances in some proportion that is determined by household utility functions[13] for goods and money and the relative prices of goods and money. A deflation reduces the price of goods relative to money or, equivalently, raises the real value of money balances. This real balance effect will stimulate the demand for goods, because households will want to reallocate their resources to have less money and more goods. Similarly, in an inflation the value of money balances fall relative to goods, and individuals will increase their nominal money holdings in place of goods.

This real balance effect is the cornerstone of two models. A. C. Pigou, the proponent of classical economics attacked by Keynes in the *General Theory,* argued that deflationary economic policy, by stimulating consumption, could be a remedy for unemployment. This, of course, was in direct contradiction to the Keynesian position that expansionary economic policy is the appropriate anti-recession weapon. Furthermore, as

---

[12] Once inventories of goods are accumulated, consumption spending may drop as househoulds consume their stocks of goods. This stock-adjustment process may generate a downturn. We will discuss this possibility in connection with inventory investment in Chapter 6.

[13] Holding money must give utility, or households would never choose to hold money instead of goods which give utility.

we shall see in Chapter 9, Pigou and other critics of Keynes' attack on Say's Law introduced the real balance effect as a mechanism that would insure full-employment equilibrium without government intervention.

The real balance effect is also the underlying behavioral assumption of the quantity theory of money. That is, monetary policy works because an increase in the quantity of money induces households (and firms) to exchange their money balances for goods and services.

As with the effect of wealth, attempts to demonstrate the existence of a reliable real balance effect in econometric work have had mixed results. This is undoubtedly because of the influence of price expectations (which are unknown) and other factors that offset the hypothesized negative relation between price changes and consumption. On the whole, the empirical evidence suggests that the impact of changes in liquid assets on consumption is usually negligible and that the real balance effect is at best unstable over time.[14]

From a theoretical viewpoint, the proposition that households will shift from goods into money during an inflation is not very appealing, particularly when purchases of consumption goods are being used as a hedge against inflation. In periods of price stability, however, changes in money holdings associated with changes in the money supply may serve as a proxy for changes in wealth and hence affect consumption in a similar way.

CHANGES IN THE INTEREST RATE

Classical economists believed that the interest rate would affect consumption. An increase in the interest rate was expected to stimulate saving and discourage consumption. Since interest rates and income generally move together over the cycle, it is difficult to separate their influence. Consumption rises and falls with income and interest rates, but whether rising interest rates provide some brake on consumption as income rises is uncertain.

Theoretically, rising interest rates produce a substitution effect away from consumption because they increase the opportunity cost of consumption. The income effect will depend on whether the net creditors or net debtors have a higher marginal propensity to consume out of interest payments. One important net debtor is the government. In the private sector creditors earn more interest income than debtors pay out in debt service, and so there may be some positive income effect on consumption of a rise in interest rates. Whether this income effect is greater than the negative substitution effect is an empirical question.

---

[14] For a detailed discussion of the econometric literature on the real balance effect see Don Patinkin, *Money, Interest, and Prices,* 2nd ed. (New York: Harper and Row, 1965), Appendix M.

Except in the case of durables, which are often financed by credit, the empirical evidence indicates that changes in the interest rate do not have an appreciable effect on consumption.[15] Perhaps this is due to the offsetting influence of the income and substitution effects and the predominance of other factors.

5-4   CONSUMPTION OF DURABLE GOODS

A *durable* consumer good can be defined as one which provides a flow of services over a period of time, generally in excess of a single year. These goods are much like capital goods, except that they are purchased by households for their own use rather than by firms for the purpose of producing goods and services for sale.[16] Durable consumption goods include such items as automobiles, televisions, and refrigerators.

Expenditure on durables is likely to be influenced by credit conditions, since these items are largely financed by credit. As they yield a stream of services which extends over a relatively long period of time, the initial cost of consumer durables may be great in relation to the immediate benefit to the household. Consequently, many families prefer to distribute the cost of the item over its useful life—a sort of pay-as-you-go arrangement at the household level. About 65 percent of new cars are financed by credit. By contrast, not more than 15 to 20 percent of business investment is financed externally.

The purchase of a durable consumer good can often be postponed, at least temporarily. Consequently, consumers are willing to wait for credit to ease. While consumption of durables is not as sensitive to credit conditions as residential housing (since the length of the debt obligation is considerably shorter in the former case), it is reasonable to expect that some measure of consumer credit cost and availability should be included in the consumption relationship. In most models, separate equations are used for consumption of durables and nondurables.

Despite the appeal of the *a priori* reasoning, however, present data on consumer expenditure for durables do not appear to support the hypothesis that this component of GNP is particularly sensitive to credit conditions. Using the Federal Reserve discount rate as roughly indicative

---

[15] For a contrasting view see Warren E. Weber, "The Effect of Interest Rates on Aggregate Consumption," *The American Economic Review*, LX (September, 1970), 591–600. He finds a tendency for aggregate consumption to increase with the interest rate. This may be related to the influence of durables, which we will examine in the next section.

[16] Traditionally, residential housing is categorized as an investment, even though it is purchased by households, not firms. Residential housing will be discussed in Chapter 6.

of the state of the credit market,[17] Table 5-1 shows consumption of durables to be highest in those years when interest rates are also high. This is particularly apparent when we examine the ratio of consumption of durables to consumption of nondurables. With the exception of 1970, this ratio has risen and fallen with the Federal Reserve discount rate.

TABLE 5-1

Expenditures on Durable Consumption Goods

Year	Federal Reserve Discount Rate (%)	Purchases of Durable Consumer Goods (in billions of dollars, 1958 prices)	Ratio of Durable to Nondurable Consumption Expenditures
1958	2.16	37.9	0.270
1959	3.36	43.7	0.298
1960	3.53	44.9	0.300
1961	3.00	43.9	0.287
1962	3.00	49.2	0.311
1963	3.23	53.7	0.331
1964	3.55	59.0	0.346
1965	4.04	66.6	0.373
1966	4.50	71.7	0.383
1967	4.19	72.9	0.383
1968	5.17	81.4	0.414
1969	5.87	84.9	0.422
1970	5.95	82.1	0.395

Source: U.S. Department of Commerce, Office of Business Economics. *Survey of Current Business,* 1958–1970.

How can we account for the observed insensitivity of purchases of durables to rising interest rates? The answer most likely lies in the fact that the rate of interest generally rises and falls with disposable income. Since most durable goods are luxury items to many families, these are most often purchased when the family experiences a short-run increase in disposable income. A family feeling a new sense of affluence may choose this time to replace an old washing machine or automobile. On the other hand, when disposable income falls in a recession, purchases of durables are often postponed until better times.[18] A family makes do with old, worn-out equipment.

[17] Although there is some lag between changes in the Federal Reserve's discount rate and changes in consumer credit rates, it is not too important when yearly data are used.

[18] The year in which there was an exception to the positive relationship between durables purchases and the interest rate, 1970 was a recession year. The monetary authorities maintained interest rates at a high level, despite declining real income and rising unemployment, and durables purchases receded.

We have also suggested that the purchase of durable goods may represent a hedge against inflation. That is, households may shift their assets out of fixed-value instruments and into durable consumer goods like automobiles, boats and other recreation vehicles, and major appliances. If higher interest rates reflect a credit-market adjustment to higher rates of inflation, then it is likely that rising interest rates will be associated with increasing consumption of durable goods.

This is not to say that credit conditions do not influence consumer spending on durables. Without the tightening of credit in a boom, consumption of durables could rise even faster than it has in recent experience. On the other hand, rising interest rates could lead the public to believe credit will become even tighter in the future, stimulating current expenditures. Nevertheless, a reliable durable goods consumption function must include disposable income as well as the interest rate; that is,

$$C_d = \alpha + \beta(Y - T) + \gamma i$$

where α, β, and γ are constants.

The data in Table 5-1 indicate that the *MPC* from short-run changes in disposable income is higher for consumption of durables than for consumption of nondurables. This fact, along with the theoretical considerations we have cited, suggests that consumption of durables is cyclically less stable than consumption of nondurables. It implies that monetary policy that affects consumer credit may have a potentially strong countercyclical influence if appropriately designed. However, to the extent that households use consumer durables as a hedge against inflation, access to consumer credit reduces the burden of inflation on the household sector. Consequently, restrictions on such credit in an inflation will have distributive implications that should be taken into account.

QUESTIONS FOR STUDY AND REVIEW

1. Discuss and compare the theories of consumption represented by the equations

(a) $C_t = a_1 + a_2 Y_t + a_3 C_{t-1}$

(b) $C_t = b_1 + b_2 Y_t + b_3 Y_{pp}$

(c) $C_t = c_1 + c_2 Y_t + c_3 i_t$

(d) $C_t = d_1 + d_2 Y_t + d_3 C_{t-1} + d_4 A_t$

where

C_t = aggregate consumption in period t
Y_t = aggregate disposable income in period t
Y_{pp} = previous peak income
i_t = market rate of interest in period t
A_t = financial assets held by individuals in period t

What signs should the various parameters have?

2. A theory of consumption must be consistent with the

(a) long-run stability of the APC,

(b) cyclical (short-run) variation in the APC,

(c) tendency for the APC to fall relative to income in budget study data.

How do several well-known theories of consumption reconcile these superficially incompatible observations?

3. "Current income measured on a quarterly basis is not the principal determinant of consumption spending. Consequently, the multiplier analysis is not very reliable." Discuss a model from which this statement can be derived. Do you agree with its implications for the Keynesian policy model?

4. One of the most important contributions of the Keynesian analysis was to show the effect of monetary and fiscal policy on consumption spending. Outline the effect which Keynes described. On the basis of post-Keynesian consumption theory, can you suggest any further role that public policy might play in influencing consumption behavior?

5. Consumption of durable goods is generally more volatile (varies more over the cycle) than consumption of nondurables. How do you account for this behavior?

6. The government is considering a program which would increase social security payments to the aged and provide free medical care for the aged and needy. The program is to be financed from general tax revenue and by increasing social security contributions. What effect, if any, might such a program have on aggregate consumption?

ADDITIONAL READING

ANDO, A. and F. MODIGLIANI, "The 'Life Cycle' Hypothesis of Saving," *The American Economic Review,* LIII (March, 1963), 55–84.

DUESENBERRY, J. S., "Income-Consumption Relations and Their Implications," in *Income, Employment, and Public Policy: Essays in Honor of Alvin H. Hansen.* New York: W. W. Norton and Company, 1948, pp. 54–81.

DUESENBERRY, J. S., *Income, Saving, and the Theory of Consumer Behavior.* Cambridge, Mass: Harvard University Press, 1949, Chapter 3.

FERBER, ROBERT, "Research on Household Behavior," *The American Economic Review,* LII (March, 1962), 19–54.

FRIEDMAN, MILTON, *A Theory of the Consumption Function.* Princeton, N.J.: Princeton University Press, 1957, Chapter 9.

KEYNES, JOHN MAYNARD, *The General Theory of Employment, Interest, and Money.* New York: Harcourt Brace Jovanovich, Inc., 1965, Chapters 8 and 9; originally published by Macmillan & Co., Ltd., 1936.

SUITS, DANIEL B., "The Determinants of Consumer Expenditure: A Review of Present Knowledge," in Commission on Money and Credit, *Impacts of Monetary Policy.* Englewood Cliffs, New Jersey: Prentice-Hall, Inc., 1963.

6

The Theory of Investment

While consumption represents the largest component of GNP, investment is the most difficult to forecast and analyze. In the previous chapter we saw that consumption is a fairly reliable function of disposable income. Investment expenditures, on the other hand, are influenced by a multitude of economic variables. These factors, moreover, assume varying degrees of importance in different situations, particularly in different phases of the business cycle. Investment, therefore, is not a reliable function of any one variable.

In this chapter several different theories of investment are considered. Because of the complexity of the investment decision, we shall see that no one theory is applicable all the time. In addition, we shall examine the various types of economic policy that might be used to manipulate this important component of aggregate demand.

6-1   THE ROLE OF INVESTMENT IN THE ECONOMY

Analytically the most troublesome, investment is the component of GNP of most concern to forecasters and policy planners. In recent years, private investment expenditures have represented about 15 percent of GNP in the United States. Despite its relatively small size in absolute terms, however, the *percentage fluctuations* in investment have been considerably greater than for any other component of GNP. These fluctuations in turn generate changes in GNP through the multiplier process. Since no other aggregate component of GNP fluctuates so widely, changes in investment account for much of the cyclical instability of the economy.

In addition to its role as a component of aggregate demand, investment is also the foundation for economic growth. Keynes predicted that in the long run the private sector would not generate sufficient investment to absorb saving at high levels of income. Whether or not Keynes' *secular stagnation thesis* is tenable, it is important to consider the long-run prospects for growth of investment opportunities as a society becomes increasingly affluent. Not only is long-run growth of investment requisite to maintaining full employment of a growing labor force, but such growth is also necessary if output and real income per worker is to increase.

Finally, investment, more than any other component of aggregate demand, is particularly sensitive to external influences such as wars and financial panics, both domestic and foreign. While the impact of such events on investment expenditures is difficult to predict, an understanding of the economic factors involved in the investment decision is helpful to the forecaster who must predict the way the economy will react to outside influences.

DEFINITION OF INVESTMENT

By *investment* the economist generally refers to the production of goods used to produce or sell other goods, that is, goods not directly consumed. Such goods are called *capital goods*. Some items, such as a blast furnace, a tractor, or a lathe, are obviously capital goods. Other items, such as automobiles and buildings, are less easily categorized.

There are three major types of expenditures which are included in Gross Private Domestic Investment as defined in the national accounts. These are expenditures on new plant and equipment, net inventory accumulation, and new residential housing construction. So-called theories of investment are primarily concerned with explaining investment in new plant and equipment. The determinants of investment in inventories and residential housing are different and will be treated at the end of this chapter.

PROBLEMS ASSOCIATED WITH THE INVESTMENT DECISION

The analysis of the investment decision, that is, the determinants of capital goods purchases by the private sector, must incorporate the notion that capital goods are basically productive factor inputs. Because capital goods are used solely as inputs into the production or sale or other goods, they have no value of their own apart from the value of the final product.

Like all productive factors, the demand for capital goods is a *derived demand.*

Let us consider for a moment the motives which determine how much of any factor of production a firm will wish to employ (i.e., the demand for that factor). If the firm is maximizing profits, it will employ a factor as long as its marginal contribution to the total product, that is, the *marginal revenue product,* exceeds its marginal cost. Algebraically, the firm will demand additional units of a factor as long as

$$MP_f \times MR_p > P_f$$

where

MP_f = marginal product of the factor
MR_p = marginal revenue from sale of the good
P_f = price of the factor

If the marginal revenue product of the factor is declining as more of the factor is utilized, as shown in Figure 6-1,[1] the firm will hire additional units of the factor until the marginal revenue product is equal to the factor price, or

$$MP_f \times MR_p = P_f$$

In Figure 6-1, when the price of the factor is P_{f1}, F_1 units will be employed. When the price falls to P_{f2}, employment will increase to F_2. If the marginal revenue product schedule ($MP_f \times MR_p$), is negatively sloped, changes in employment are inversely related to changes in the price of the factor; that is, as the factor price falls more will be demanded, and conversely, as the factor price rises less will be demanded.

In this model, the firm is expected to estimate the demand for the final product (to determine MR_p), the marginal productivity of the factor, and the factor price. The problem is particularly complicated when the factor of production is a capital good.

Consider the case of a corner grocer who must decide how many clerks to keep on the floor on any one day. He must take into account only those influences which will affect the volume of business on that day, including his own advertising and that of his competitors, the season of the year, the particular day of the week, and so forth. If he becomes short-handed, he presumably has a reserve of labor that he can call upon with little notice. He can even man a checkout counter himself. Further-

[1] A sufficient condition for a negatively sloped marginal revenue product schedule is diminishing returns to the factor and a negatively sloped product demand curve.

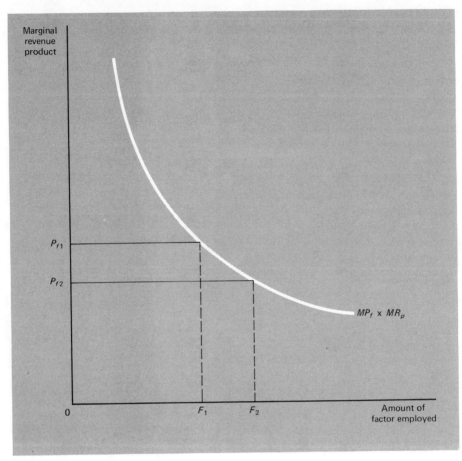

FIGURE 6-1

The Demand for a Factor of Production

more, the payoff derived from having extra help on a particular day should be realized immediately (unless the grocer has overestimated the marginal revenue product), so that provision for the payment of the extra wages is internally generated through an increase in the day's receipts.

The decision to purchase a piece of capital equipment (e.g., a new building) is more complex than deciding how many clerks to have on the floor on a particular day. Generally, considerable time elapses between the purchase of the capital equipment and the realization of the proceeds derived from sale of the output. Not only does the process of producing or delivering the capital good take time, but capital equipment is generally durable, capable of producing output over an extended period of time. Consequently, the firm must estimate such things as the following:

1. The demand for the final good produced over an extended period of time. This becomes increasingly complex if the firm itself produces capital goods or is in a highly competitive market.
2. Not only the cost of capital, but the cost of labor and other inputs over the relevant period.
3. The possibility of technological change which would make the capital good obsolete before the end of its useful life.

Furthermore, the notion of a marginal product is somewhat ambiguous for a factor of production that yields a "stream" of product returns over time, particularly when the return stream is not uniform over time.

Because the proceeds derived from the use of capital goods are realized over a long period of time, the initial cost generally exceeds the immediate return. Consequently, they must be financed by some source other than their own revenue.

Thus, the durability of capital equipment provides two unique features to the investment decision. The firm must make long-term estimates of certain economic and technological market conditions. In addition, it must make some provision for financing the expenditures other than through the extra revenue generated by the new capital equipment itself.

APPROACHES TO THE THEORY OF INVESTMENT

In this chapter we shall consider three major investment theories.[2] The classical approach, emphasizing the rate of return on investment projects, was taken by Keynes in *The General Theory*.[3] One post-Keynesian school has emphasized the relationship of capital stock to output. Another has focused upon the sources of finance for firms undertaking investment in capital goods.

6-2   THE CLASSICAL APPROACH: MARGINAL EFFICIENCY
       OF CAPITAL

A rational investor weighs the potential or expected returns from a project against its cost. As a rule of thumb, he will purchase a capital good if he expects the return to exceed the cost. While all theories of

---

[2] These theories are primarily concerned with investment in plant and equipment.

[3] This is not to be confused with the so-called "classical" macroeconomics in general, which Keynes *attacked* in *The General Theory*.

investment recognize this general principle, there is disagreement concerning how the investor estimates his potential returns and costs.

In the classical approach, the market rate of interest is the cost of investment. If the project must be financed by borrowed funds, the investor must pay interest. If, on the other hand, the investor has his own funds available, he must consider the possibility of using his money to purchase a financial asset (e.g., a bond which yields interest). The return on the bond is the *opportunity cost* of using his own money to purchase the capital good. By so doing, he foregoes the potential interest earnings on the bond, and hence, the market rate of interest again represents the cost of investment, even if borrowed funds are not used to finance it.

It is recognized, of course, that different financial assets yield different rates of interest. If, however, this is a reflection of differences in risk, then we can simply view the difference between the actual rate of return on a bond and some "prime" interest rate on a riskless asset as the return to the purchaser of the bond for bearing the risk. Assuming that an individual prefers a promise of $100 with certainty to $100 with some chance of default, only part of the return on a risky bond represents the return to the lender for loaning his funds; the rest is a premium to induce him to purchase the risky asset instead of a safe one. Consequently, only the rate of interest on a riskless bond represents the true cost of a dollar used for investment; higher interest rates reflect risk, which involves a cost of a different type.

If the cost of a dollar used to purchase a capital good is the market rate of interest, what is the return? Suppose a company is considering the purchase of a new machine which costs $1000. If the firm expects output to increase by 100 units per year as a result of using the new equipment, and if the output sells for $1 per unit, then the rate of return on the investment will be 10 percent. That is, the annual return will be $100/$1000 = 0.10 = 10 percent. The firm will purchase the machine if the market rate of interest is less than 10 percent.

Most investment projects do not generate a constant income stream over time. It may take some time for the machine to be delivered after it is ordered. This is particularly true in the case of buildings and expensive, specialized equipment. Here a cost might be incurred with no immediate return. When a machine is new, it takes time for the labor force to learn to use it most efficiently. Finally, as the machine wears out it becomes less productive. Most capital goods do not last forever and generally become obsolete and need to be replaced. While the money used to purchase the item can earn interest indefinitely in the financial market (assuming that money can always be reinvested if a bond falls due), the earning stream of a capital good is definitely limited. Hence, the concept of a single "rate of return" *in perpetuity* is usually not applicable to a real capital investment.

Suppose a machine which costs $1000 yields a return of $200 in the first year, $500 in the second, $400 in the third, $100 in the fourth, and then wears out. How does a potential investor decide whether or not to buy the machine? He must ask the question, "How does this income stream compare with the yield on a bond costing $1000 and paying the market rate of interest in perpetuity?" Suppose the market rate of interest is 5 percent. The alternatives are shown in Table 6-1 and graphically in Figure 6-2.

TABLE 6-1

Return on Capital Good Versus Return on Financial Asset Each Costing $1000

Year	Revenue Gained from Use of Machine (dollars)	Interest Yield from Bond (dollars)
1	200	50
2	500	50
3	400	50
4	100	50
5	0	50

The difficulty stems from the fact that if the return stream of the investment project is not uniform over time, as in the case of the bond, a yearly average rate of return is difficult to compute. Of course, if the return were all realized in one year, computing the return would be a relatively simple matter.

Consider the following example: Suppose the present cost of a project is $100 and this project is expected to return $110 next year, after which no further returns are expected. Since

$$r = \frac{\$110 - \$100}{\$100}$$

or

$$\$100(1 + r) = \$110$$

the rate of return, r, can be computed by the formula

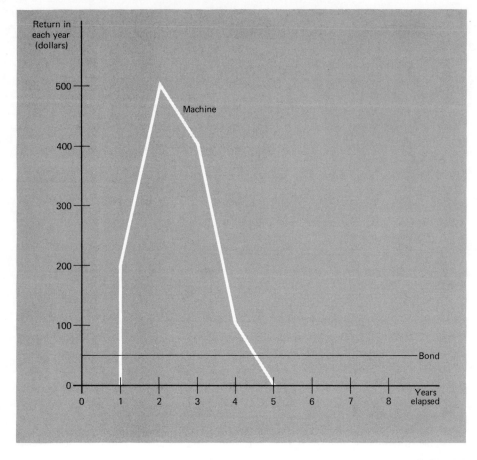

FIGURE 6-2

Payoff Stream on a Capital Good Versus the Return on a Financial Asset Shown as a Function of Time

$$1 + r = \frac{\$110}{\$100}$$

$$\$100 = \frac{\$110}{1 + r}$$

or

$$C = \frac{R}{1 + r}$$

where C is the cost and R is the return. In this case

$$r = 0.10 = 10 \text{ percent}$$

If i is the market rate of interest, then P, derived from the formula

$$P = \frac{R}{1 + i}$$

is called the *present value* of the asset.[4] If r exceeds i, the rate of return exceeds the market rate of interest, and the present value of the project will exceed its cost. The converse is also true.[5]

Since financial assets earn compound interest, an investment project must earn a compound return to be equally attractive. This applies to projects with a return stream which exceeds one year. One hundred dollars loaned at 5 percent will be worth $105 in one year:

$$\$100 + (\$100 \times 0.05) = \$105$$

or

$$\$100(1 + 0.05) = \$105$$

In two years it will be worth, not $110, but $110.25, since

$$\$100 + (\$100 \times 0.05) + (\$105 \times 0.05) = \$110.25$$

or

$$\$100(1 + 0.05)^2 = \$110.25$$

The present value of $110.25 to be paid after two years is $100, or

[4] The term *present value* derives from the fact that an asset yielding R dollars after one year is worth exactly as much as a financial asset costing P dollars this year if i is the market rate of interest.

[5] The proof is as follows:

$$C = \frac{R}{1 + r}$$

$$P = \frac{R}{1 + i}$$

If

$$r > i$$

then,

$$1 + r > 1 + i$$

and since

$$R = R$$

$$P > C$$

$$\$100 = \frac{\$110.25}{(1 + 0.05)^2}$$

Algebraically,

$$P = \frac{R_2}{(1 + 0.05)^2}$$

where R_2 is the return expected after two years.

Let the symbol R_i refer to a return expected after i years. Then the formula for the present value of an asset yielding a return stream over n years is

$$P = \frac{R_1}{1 + i} + \frac{R_2}{(1 + i)^2} + \frac{R_3}{(1 + i)^3} + \cdots + \frac{R_n}{(1 + i)^n}$$

If the cost C is known, the compound rate of return, r, can be computed by the formula

$$C = \frac{R_1}{1 + r} + \frac{R_2}{(1 + r)^2} + \frac{R_3}{(1 + r)^3} + \cdots + \frac{R_n}{(1 + r)^n}$$

Keynes called the compound rate of return on an investment project the *marginal efficiency of capital* (*MEC*).[6] As in the previous example, if the present value exceeds the cost, then the compound rate of return on an asset, or the *MEC*, exceeds the market rate of interest.

Returning to our earlier problem, the firm can compute the *MEC* for the machine whose lifetime earnings are shown in Table 6-1 by the formula

$$\$1000 = \frac{\$200}{1 + r} + \frac{\$500}{(1 + r)^2} + \frac{\$400}{(1 + r)^3} + \frac{\$100}{(1 + r)^4}$$

This equation can best be solved by trial and error. In this case

$$r \approx 8 \text{ percent}$$

[6] Some economists distinguish the *marginal efficiency of capital,* a rate of return on capital, from the *marginal efficiency of investment,* a rate of return on investment, where investment is a change in the capital stock. Although the marginal efficiency of investment is technically the appropriate concept for an aggregate investment demand schedule, it can be derived from the marginal efficiency of capital. Since MEI is marginal to MEC, it can be shown that if MEC decreases with the capital stock then MEI is a decreasing function of investment. For a derivation of the MEI see Abba Lerner, *Economics of Control* (New York: Macmillan, 1944), Chapter 25. We shall use the MEC concept for simplicity to refer to the compound rate of return on either capital or investment that is derived from the present value formula.

Since the market rate of interest is 5 percent, the machine should be purchased because the return exceeds the cost. Equivalently, since the market rate of interest is known, the firm can compute the present value of the return stream and compare it with the known cost of the machine.

The present value formula is

$$P = \frac{\$200}{1 + 0.05} + \frac{\$500}{(1 + 0.05)^2} + \frac{\$400}{(1 + 0.05)^3} + \frac{\$100}{(1 + 0.05)^4}$$

so that

$$P = \$1081$$

Since the present value exceeds the cost of $1000, the machine is worth more than a bond costing $1000 yielding the market rate of interest in perpetuity.[7]

THE MARGINAL EFFICIENCY OF CAPITAL SCHEDULE

At any one time there is a large number of potential investment projects open to the firms in the economy. Let us assume that for each project the *MEC* is known. Starting with the project or projects yielding the highest *MEC*, we can add the dollar volume of investment projects available at successively lower rates of return. The function relating the *MEC* to the dollar volume of aggregate investment is called the *MEC schedule.*

For the economy as a whole, since each investment project will be small relative to the total, the *MEC* schedule can be represented as a smooth function, as shown in Figure 6-3. As investment increases, successively less profitable projects are undertaken. Consequently, the *MEC* schedule will be negatively sloped.

If all projects are undertaken whose *MEC* exceeds the market rate of interest, then the level of aggregate investment can be determined from the *MEC* schedule if the interest rate is known.[8] In Figure 6-4, when the interest rate is i_0, investment will be I_0. If the interest rate falls to i_1, investment will increase to I_1. Thus, changes in investment will be inversely related to changes in the market rate of interest.

Shortly after the publication of *The General Theory,* a series of interviews with businessmen indicated that changes in the interest rate had a minimal effect on their decision to invest. In fact, in the depths of the depression, interest rates were quite low while investment fell to nearly zero. More recent experience has shown that investment and interest rates

[7] The present value of such a bond is, of course, equal to its cost.
[8] Note that this is not a theory of interest. The interest rate must be known.

generally move together over the cycle rather than inversely, as the theory suggests. This tends to support the skepticism with which many economists have viewed the classical approach to investment theory. The solution is apparent when time is introduced into the analysis. The *MEC*

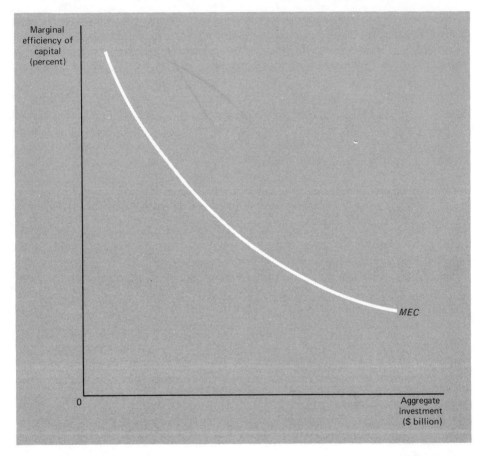

FIGURE 6-3

The MEC Schedule

schedule is constructed for a single level of aggregate demand. Thus, it is static with respect to time. If, over time, aggregate demand increases, expected returns $(R_1, R_2, \ldots, R_n)$ are likely to increase too. Since the *MEC* is the compound rate of return on an investment project, then if expected returns increase, the *MEC* will rise as well. Thus, the *MEC* schedule generally shifts up and down with aggregate demand as well as with expected changes in aggregate demand. If the authorities are under-taking a countercyclical monetary policy, then interest rates will also be moving with income. As shown in Figure 6-5, even though the "in-stantaneous" MEC schedules are all negatively sloped, investment can

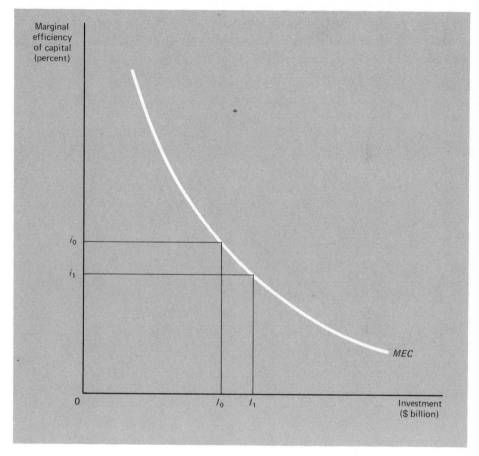

FIGURE 6-4

Determination of the Level of Investment

actually increase with interest rates if income is also increasing at the same time.[9]

Thus, as income increases from Y_0 to Y_2, the MEC schedule shifts

---

[9] In other words, the partial derivative, $\partial I/\partial i < 0$, may be negative when income is held constant while the total derivative, $dI/di > 0$, may exceed zero when income changes are taken into account.

upward and to the right. Even if the interest rate rises from i_0 to i_2, investment will increase from I_0 to I_2 as the economy moves along the expansion path E. These changes in investment are induced by income. Note, however, that the induced effect on investment of the rise in

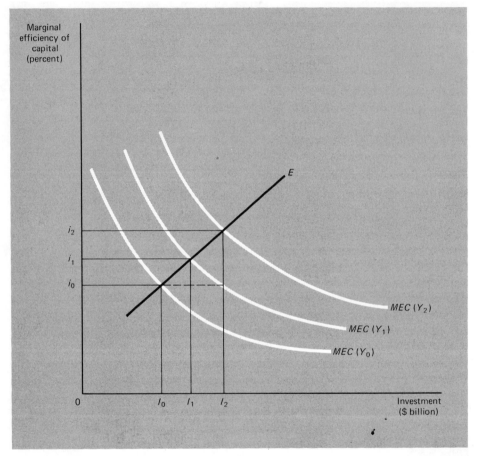

FIGURE 6-5

Shifts in the MEC Schedule

income would have been considerably greater had the rising interest rate not provided a brake. If the interest rate had remained at i_0 when income rose to Y_1, investment would have been I_2 rather than I_1.

This theory, taking into account the effect of aggregate demand on the *MEC* schedule, is the basis for the investment equation in our earlier

model in which investment is treated as a function of both income and
the rate of interest; that is,

$$I = f(Y, i)$$
$$I = g + dY + ei$$

where d is a positive constant and e is a negative constant.

Since the *MEC* depends upon expectations about future demand,
investment can be influenced by a wave of optimism or pessimism about
the future. The "announcement effect" of a proposed tax increase, for
instance, could cause producers to expect a decline in demand, the *MEC*
schedule to shift leftward, and the level of investment to fall, thereby
reducing aggregate demand through the multiplier. Thus, the proposed tax
increase could effectively reduce the level of aggregate demand even if
the policy were never enacted.

When shifts in the *MEC* schedule are induced by changes in income
or expected changes in income, investment may appear to be insensitive
to credit conditions. The two post-Keynesian theories of investment which
follow may provide additional insight into the observed insensitivity of
aggregate investment to changes in the interest rate.

6-3   THE ACCELERATOR MODEL

While the classical approach to the demand for capital goods emphasizes
the rate of return on investment projects, accelerator models are concerned with the relationship between the capital stock and output. As
we shall see, accelerator models represent a substantial departure from
the Keynesian theory of income determination. The concept of equilibrium
yields to a dynamic theory of economic activity which lays the foundation for a theory of business cycles.

The accelerator theory of investment is based on the hypothesis that
for the firm there is an optimal relationship between the level of output,
q, and the capital stock, K. This relationship may be expressed algebraically as

$$\frac{K}{q} = \hat{\beta}$$

or

$$K = \hat{\beta}q$$

where $\hat{\beta}$ represents the desired capital-output ratio. Furthermore, it is
assumed that if output is to be increased, the firm will desire to increase

its capital stock proportionately, so as to maintain the capital–output ratio at $\hat{\beta}^{10}$; that is,

$$\Delta K = \hat{\beta} \, \Delta q$$

where Δ refers to a change in the variable. (Notice that since the change in output can also be negative, the equation implies that a reduction in output will be followed by a proportional reduction in the capital stock.)

Remember that investment, I, is nothing more than a change in the capital stock, so that

$$\Delta K = I$$

and, therefore,

$$I = \hat{\beta} \, \Delta q$$

That is, investment, or the demand for capital goods, will be proportional to changes in output. Assuming for simplicity that prices do not change, the accelerator model suggests that investment is a function of changes in national income or GNP. The distinction between this theory and the one described previously is that here investment is induced by a *change* in income, while in the former it was induced by the *level* of income. Algebraically, the accelerator is expressed as

$$I = \hat{\beta} \, \Delta pq = \hat{\beta} \, \Delta Y$$

Excluding the public sector, we know that a constant level of GNP can be maintained only if investment stays constant. Yet the accelerator theory would conclude that positive net investment can be maintained only if GNP is growing. (If GNP were constant, then

$$\Delta Y = 0$$

and investment would also be zero.) Consequently, the accelerator theory rejects the possibility of a static national income equilibrium for a more dynamic approach to national income determination. In Chapter 13 we shall examine in some detail models in which national income moves over time, never reaching a static equilibrium in the Keynesian sense.

Apart from its dynamic implications, the accelerator theory is use-

---

[10] With constant returns to scale and a homogenous production function this implies the labor force will also be increased proportionately. This will be the case if the wage-interest rate ratio is unchanged. Even if there is some change in this ratio, it is still likely that an increase in output will require *some* increment to both the capital stock and the labor force. The assumption of proportionality is not necessary to the model and is convenient as a first approximation.

ful in explaining the observation that a static economy, one in which output is not growing rapidly, is generally considered to be in a state of quasi-recession. As the growth of output tapers off, investment may actually decline even though the cycle is still technically in an upswing. The decline in investment may eventually generate a downturn due to the induced effects of the multiplier.

LIMITATIONS TO THE ACCELERATOR

Undeniably, firms will adjust their capital stock as aggregate demand changes. However, the accelerator equation in its simple form is not a good description of investment behavior. In fact, if investment were as responsive to changes in national income as the model suggests, the economy would be subject to extreme fluctuations in GNP. Remember that changes in investment are multiplied due to the induced components of GNP. These changes in GNP would in turn, through the accelerator, produce further changes in investment. (We shall consider this process of multiplier–accelerator interaction further in Chapter 14.) In fact, it is unlikely that the changes in capital stock would be proportional to changes in demand for a number of reasons.

The model assumes that the firm can adjust its capital stock to achieve the optimal capital–output ratio in a very short time. However, generally some time elapses between the decision to invest and the acquisition of capital goods. Furthermore, because of the long-term nature of capital investment, the firm will not act strictly on the basis of immediate past experience (as the model implies) but will examine experience over a longer period of time and perhaps will act on the basis of expectations about the future. Hence, the mere *announcement* of a planned government policy (e.g., an increase in armaments spending) may affect current investment demand even before the spending program is actually put into effect. Both the lag in the implementation of the investment decision and the tendency of firms to take a long-run view of past and future changes in demand before adjusting capital stock reduce fluctuations in investment demand and add stability to the model.

The model assumes that the firm will act symmetrically in response to both increases and declines in output or demand. In fact, a firm might increase its capital stock when demand increases, but be unable or unwilling to disinvest as quickly when demand declines. Disinvestment takes place as the firm fails to replace worn-out or obsolete equipment. Since the wearing-out process takes time, the speed at which a firm can disinvest is much more limited than the speed at which it can accumulate capital. Furthermore, if a firm expects the decline in demand to be short lived, it may continue to replace or maintain its equipment even though it has excess capacity. In a recovery period, the existence of excess capacity would preclude new investment by the firm, even if demand were increasing rapidly.[11] Thus, it is likely that the accelerator model would be most applicable to an economy during a boom period in which demand had been increasing for some time, and less applicable in a recession or in the early phases of a recovery. Since the model allows for no autonomous investment (independent of changes in income), it is incapable of explaining why there is generally some positive investment even when income is not increasing.

Not only does the accelerator theory fail to explain investment in all but boom periods, it may actually understate investment even during periods of high demand, due to the fact that it attempts to explain aggregate investment based on a model of a single firm's behavior. In fact, aggregate income may remain constant, so that

$$\Delta Y = 0$$

but output in different firms may be increasing or decreasing. If there is some asymmetry to the response of investment to increases and declines in output, investment in those firms experiencing positive changes in demand will not be matched by proportional disinvestment by firms experiencing negative changes in demand. Consequently, even though there is no change in aggregate demand, aggregate investment induced by income changes should be positive (even excluding the possibility of autonomous investment). No matter what the change in aggregate demand, it is likely that growing firms invest more than declining firms disinvest in response to output changes; hence, the aggregate accelerator equation will tend to understate even that investment which is induced by output changes at the level of the firm.

Finally, the accelerator theory completely avoids consideration of the cost of capital. In fact, it assumes the firm has unlimited funds to carry out its capital expansion program. If funds are limited or if the cost of capital is very high, the firm may reduce its capital–output ratio, and consequently, capital accumulation will not be proportional to increases in output, even in the upswing.

The accelerator theory is not a realistic explanation of aggregate investment in recessions or early recovery periods. While it is most likely applicable in boom periods, the theory should be modified to take into account the lags in response as well as the effect of the rising cost of capital in boom periods. Nevertheless, since capital is a productive factor input,

---

[11] An accelerator model that takes excess capacity into account is called a *flexible accelerator*. We develop a flexible accelerator model of investment in Chapter 14.

it is important to recognize that additions to capital stock will be made as output is increasing. There is no reason to expect capacity-expanding investment to take place as long as output remains constant. If investment is at least partly "change-induced," we would expect to see investment declining as the growth of demand tapers off in a boom. A "level-induced" theory would not be able to explain this phenomenon.

Both the classical and accelerator theories of investment assume that firms have unlimited access to funds at some constant cost or rate of interest. Although the accelerator model seems to ignore the possibility of prohibitively high capital costs in boom periods, the classical approach views changes in capital costs over the cycle as the most important stabilizer of investment. While the accelerator theory suggests that expenditure or tax policy which generates changes in aggregate demand should be used to manipulate investment and through it aggregate demand, the classical approach puts more reliance on monetary policy.

Both theories ignore the possibility that the cost of capital to a firm at any given stage of the business cycle may itself be a function of the amount of investment the firm is undertaking. A third school of thought emphasizes the role of the cost of capital in the investment decision.

6-4   THE COST OF CAPITAL

A rational businessman will undertake investment expenditure if the rate of return or *MEC* exceeds its cost. Until now we have assumed that the market rate of interest represents the cost of capital to the firm and that this cost is invariant to the amount of investment in which the firm is engaged.

The *cost-of-capital schedule* relates the cost of capital to the level of investment. We have assumed that this schedule is infinitely elastic (horizontal) with respect to investment at the market rate of interest. Experience tells us, however, that for the typical firm the cost of capital rises as more and more funds are required for investment spending. To see why this is so, let us consider the sources of finance capital, that is, money available to the firm for capital expenditures.

The cheapest source of funds is *retained earnings,* that is, depreciation allowances and undistributed profits after taxes. Most firms consider the cost of using these funds to be very low, at least in the short run. True, there is an opportunity cost to consider; the firm could use the funds to buy bonds or purchase equity in some other business. However, apart from the possibility of running afoul of antitrust laws (a very real problem in some cases), most managers prefer not to turn their enterprise into a financial management concern. "If I wanted to manage a financial portfolio," says one top executive of a manufacturing corporation, "I would have gone into the banking business. Here our major concern is products." A second possibility is the distribution of unused earnings to stockholders. This is unappealing, however, in view of the lack of identity between ownership and management in most large enterprises. As a rule of thumb, most managers prefer to keep a fairly stable dividend payout ratio, which averages roughly one-third of total corporate profits. Thus, the cost to the corporation of finance capital coming from retained earnings is near zero.

Empirically, about 85 percent of private, nonfarm, nonfinancial investment is financed from retained earnings. As shown in Table 6-2,

TABLE 6-2

Relation of Internal Funds to Purchases of Physical Assets by Nonfarm, Nonfinancial Corporate Business, 1957–1972 (in billions of dollars)

Year	(1) Internal Funds*	(2) Nonresidential Fixed Investment	(3) Purchases of Physical Assets†	(4) (1)/(2)	(5) (1)/(3)
1957	30.6	33.4	34.7	0.916	0.882
1958	29.5	28.4	27.3	1.039	1.081
1959	35.0	31.1	36.9	1.125	0.949
1960	34.4	34.9	39.2	0.986	0.878
1961	35.6	33.2	37.0	1.072	0.962
1962	41.8	37.0	44.7	1.130	0.935
1963	43.0	38.6	53.5	1.137	0.940
1964	50.5	44.0	53.5	1.148	0.944
1965	56.6	53.2	64.9	1.064	0.872
1966	61.1	63.0	79.8	0.970	0.766
1967	61.5	64.9	74.1	0.948	0.830
1968	61.7	67.4	75.0	0.915	0.823
1969	60.7	75.6	83.7	0.803	0.725
1970	59.4	78.3	84.0	0.759	0.707
1971	69.9	81.2	86.7	0.861	0.806
1972	77.5	88.4	100.7	0.877	0.770

* Internal funds include undistributed profits, corporate inventory valuation adjustment, and capital consumption allowances.
† Purchases of physical assets includes nonresidential fixed investment, residential investment, and inventory change.
Source: Board of Governors of the Federal Reserve System, *Federal Reserve Bulletin,* 1957–1968.

investment in plant and equipment (column 2) is generally within 15 percent of retained earnings for the economy as a whole. Notice that, even in the quasi-recession periods 1958–1959 and 1961–1962, investment did not fall drastically below the level of retained earnings. This sug-

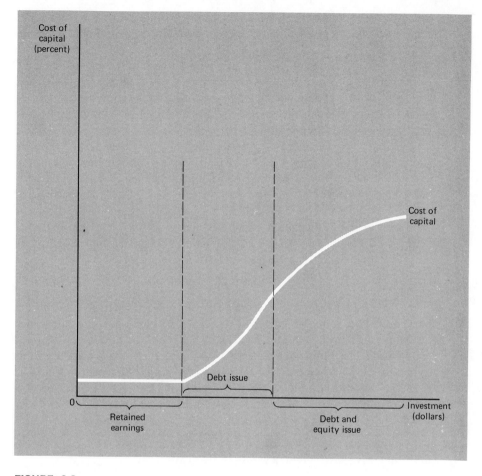

FIGURE 6-6

A Cost-of-Capital Schedule

gests that the latter provides a floor or cushion to the accelerator, or demand forces acting to inhibit the level of investment.[12]

It may be profitable, particularly in boom periods, to seek external financing for investment projects when internal sources are exhausted. A firm may issue *bonds* or debt instruments. While a limited amount of debt may be marketable at or near the market rate of interest, the bond price

[12] The figures in Table 6-2 suggest a slight downward trend in internal financing since the mid-sixties. This may reflect a change in the way the credit market functions, at least for the corporate sector, and an increase in the influence of financial corporations over nonfinancial corporations.

will fall, or alternatively, the effective interest rate will rise as the firm's debt–equity ratio or *leverage* rises. As the firm borrows additional funds for investment projects, its fixed obligations to pay interest on its debt rise as a percentage of its equity. Not only will increasing leverage affect bond prices, but it also will drive down the price of the firm's common and preferred stock.[13] These effects must be considered part of the cost of the bond issue. In general, the marginal cost of funds raised by a bond issue rises as more funds are required.

A third source of funds is from sale of *equity,* that is, the issue of additional common or preferred stock. This may be undesirable for a number of reasons and is generally considered to be the most costly. Duesenberry contends that "if current earnings can be regarded as bearing any relation to the earnings expected in the future by the management, the yield cost of equity finance is usually of the order of 7 to 10 percent for large firms. To this must be added flotation costs plus any reduction in the value of existing shares resulting from the issue. The differential is further increased by the differential tax treatment of bond and equity finance." [14]

The cost of capital to the firm will vary according to its source, and how much is required. Figure 6-6 shows a cost-of-capital schedule which takes into account the various sources of finance capital. When investment is financed from retained earnings, the cost of capital is perceived by firms to be fairly low. When external financing is required, the cost of debt issue rises rapidly with leverage. Once the cost of debt reaches the cost of issuing equity, the cost-of-capital schedule becomes flatter.

6-5 A GENERAL THEORY OF INVESTMENT

The classical and accelerator approaches emphasize the role of demand for capital goods. In the classical model, the level of income influences investment demand through its impact on expected profits. The accelerator theory views investment as changes in productive capacity which will vary with changes in income. The corporate finance school is concerned with the role of retained earnings in determining the level of investment. A study of investment behavior by John Meyer, Edwin Kuh, and Robert Glauber has

---

[13] In the limiting case, in which the bond yield is exactly equal to the *MEC,* all the return from an investment project will go to the bondholders and none to the holders of preferred or common stock. Since investment always requires some risk, the total risk is borne by the stockholders with no expectation of gain. This will make the stock less desirable than before the project was undertaken.

[14] J. S. Duesenberry, *Business Cycles and Economic Growth* (New York: McGraw-Hill Book Company, Inc., 1958), p. 95.

shown neither theory to be applicable all the time.[15] Their results indicate that the need for capacity expansion and other demand-generating forces are most important in explaining business investment during boom periods of economic activity. In recessions and the early stages of recovery, however, investment spending rarely falls far below the level of retained earnings.[16]

Consider a typical *MEC* schedule. This tells us the amount of investment desired or, alternatively, the demand for investment funds at any given rate of return. In Figure 6-7 we have superimposed a set of *MEC* schedules on a cost-of-capital schedule. The intersection of these curves represents equilibrium in the market for investment funds.

As aggregate demand increases, the *MEC* schedule shifts upward from *MEC* (Y_1) to *MEC* (Y_3). Because of the rising cost of capital, investment does not increase as rapidly as a pure demand-oriented theory would suggest. Suppose, however, demand becomes so slack that the *MEC* schedule shifts to the left of *MEC* (Y_1). In the short-run view, investment should decline proportionately. However, Meyer and Kuh found that firms take a longer view than this short-run model would suggest. In fact, firms will generally spend most of their retained earnings in recessions on technological improvements to reduce costs and advertising campaigns to increase their market share. While the distribution of spending among firms producing capital equipment may be different from that of a boom period when firms are primarily investing in capacity expansion, the overall level of investment will not fall as much as might be indicated by a simple short-run model.

Another reason why the accelerator model fails to provide an adequate explanation of investment behavior in a recession is the asymmetry of investment and disinvestment. When demand falls, firms simply permit facilities to lie idle; there is generally no mechanism for rapid disinvestment. As explained earlier, the accelerator theory is a poor description of behavior in recessions, even in the absence of financial considerations.

POLICY IMPLICATIONS

Traditionally, monetary policy (i.e., changes in the market rate of interest) was viewed as the appropriate instrument for manipulating the level of investment. This practice was supported by the classical theory of

---

[15] The original study, J. Meyer and E. Kuh, *The Investment Decision* (Cambridge, Mass.: Harvard University Press, 1956) was updated by J. Meyer and R. Glauber, *Investment Decisions, Economic Forecasting and Public Policy* (Boston: Harvard Business School, 1964).

[16] Of course, profits and hence retained earnings tend to be lowest in periods of slack activity, so that investment spending may fall concomitantly.

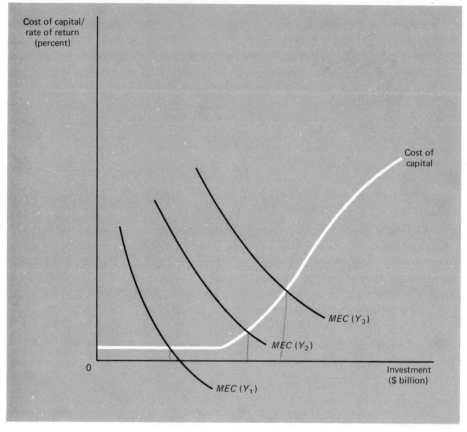

Cost of capital/
rate of return
(percent)

Cost of
capital

$MEC(Y_3)$

$MEC(Y_2)$

0

Investment
($ billion)

$MEC(Y_1)$

FIGURE 6-7

The Market for Investment Funds (Short Run)

investment. But recent developments in the theory of investment indicate
that monetary policy might be the least effective of all the macroeconomic
policy instruments.[17] In the analysis represented by Figure 6-7, the market
rate of interest plays only a small role in determining the cost of capital to
a firm. The principal effect of rising interest rates would probably be to
reduce the elasticity (increase the steepness) of the second phase of the
schedule. This would serve to brake investment, once internal sources had

[17] For a discussion of the empirical evidence see Jean Crockett *et al.*, "The
Impact of Monetary Stringency on Business Investment," *Survey of Current Business*
(August, 1967), 10–26; and E. Kuh and J. Meyer, "Investment, Liquidity, and
Monetary Policy," in Commission on Money and Credit, *Impacts of Monetary
Policy* (Englewood Cliffs, New Jersey: Prentice-Hall, Inc., 1963).

been exhausted. Conversely, an easing of credit would increase the elasticity (flatten) the second phase of the curve. This would have no effect in a recession if firms were financing all investment strictly from internal sources. Thus, monetary policy would most likely be more useful in dampening a boom than in stimulating investment in a recession.

A more effective policy instrument would control the internal sources of funds. The impact of a change in internal sources of funds on investment

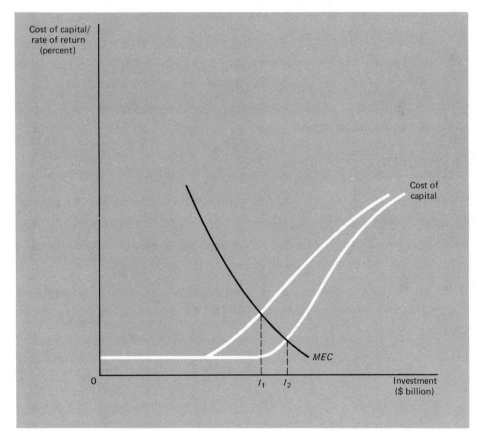

FIGURE 6-8

The Impact of a Change in Internal Funds on Investment

is shown in Figure 6-8. A reduction in corporate taxes in a recession, for instance, could stimulate investment if firms are taking a long-run view and investing all of their retained earnings in research and development and cost-reducing improvements. This policy may have the additional advantage of preventing rapid price increases as the level of economic activity recovers. In a boom, an increase in corporate taxes would shift the cost of capital curve to the left, as shown in Figure 6-8, discouraging marginal projects. In our example, investment falls from I_2 to I_1 as the cost-of-capital schedule shifts to the left. Our present system of corporate taxation, based on income, does have this stabilizing feature built in. Since the tax is based on income, receipts rise in booms and decline in recessions. Discretionary changes in corporate tax rates and depreciation allowances, however, would be an even more powerful tool for manipulating investment and, through it, aggregate demand.

Investment expenditures are also induced by the level of and changes in the level of aggregate demand. Consequently, tax and expenditure policy, through their effect on aggregate demand and the *MEC* schedule, will strongly influence the level of investment. Whenever the government is using these measures to influence aggregate demand, the indirect, induced effects on investment must be taken into account. Again, the importance of complete specification of the forecasting and policy-planning model is apparent.

6-6   INVENTORY INVESTMENT

While the accelerator model is too simplistic to provide an adequate explanation of plant and equipment investment, it is useful as a theory of inventory investment. Generally, a firm will wish to hold fixed a certain ratio between its inventory and its sales. This ratio will vary among firms depending upon such factors as how fast the stock turns over, distance from suppliers, and so forth, but in the aggregate and in the short run, the desired inventory–sales ratio can be treated as approximately constant.

Then,

$$\hat{\pi} = \frac{H}{R}$$

where

$$H = \text{inventories}$$

$$R = \text{sales}$$

$$\hat{\pi} = \text{desired inventory-sales ratio}$$

Inventory investment, I_i, or the net change in inventories will then be proportional to the *change* in sales, or

$$I_i = \Delta H = \mathring{r} \, \Delta R$$

Since the change in sales, ΔR, is equal to the change in aggregate demand, ΔY, then inventory investment will be induced by changes in aggregate demand; that is,

$$I_i = \mathring{r} \, \Delta Y$$

The limitations in applying the accelerator approach to investment in plant and equipment which we discussed earlier are largely inapplicable to inventory investment. Unlike plant and equipment, inventories can be accumulated and sold (disinvested) rapidly. Initial outlays which are large in relation to current revenue are not required to finance them, and they can be liquidated quickly if necessary.

The empirical evidence bears out the theoretical approach. Although net inventory investment is a small component of total investment (generally less than 10 percent), it is by far the most volatile. In fact, some recent observers have attributed much of the cyclical activity in the U.S. economy since the Korean conflict to the multiplier–accelerator interaction associated with inventory investment.[18]

6-7 INVESTMENT IN RESIDENTIAL HOUSING

Of the three major components of investment, residential housing is the most likely to be sensitive to conditions in the credit market. Because the commodity in question is very durable and expensive and because it is generally purchased by households without sufficient "internal" resources to incur the entire cost at one time, residential housing is generally financed by mortgages.[19] Except in the case of very large building corporations, even the building contractor finances his expenses in the mortgage market.

Not only are most homes financed by credit, but potential home buyers are quite sensitive to credit market conditions. Because the purchase of a home involves a long-term commitment (a 20- or 30-year mortgage is standard) and because the purchase of a home, unlike other consumption goods, can be postponed for months and even years if necessary, the home

---

[18] In a model simulating the U.S. economy in the recession of 1957–1959, Duesenberry, Eckstein, and Fromm found the change in inventory investment accounted for as much as 62 percent of the change in GNP. See James Duesenberry, Otto Eckstein, and Gary Fromm, "A Simulation of the United States Economy in Recession," *Econometrica,* XXVIII (October, 1960), 749–809.

[19] A mortgage is a promissory note secured by real estate.

buyer will generally wait to purchase his dwelling until credit conditions are favorable. This is particularly true if there is uncertainty about the future or if interest rates are expected to fall. The decision to purchase a home is less likely to be affected by short-run changes in disposable income. Because of the long-term commitment, the decision is probably more closely related to the buyer's dollar view of his *permanent income* (see Chapter 5).

In a study of residential housing during the 1950's, Guttentag found housing starts to be quite sensitive to credit conditions, moving inversely with disposable income.[20] (This is because interest rates and disposable income move together over the cycle.) Thus, he contends, residential housing is the one component of investment which adds stability to the economy since it moves inversely with the general business cycle. In 1966, there was a sharp drop in private nonfarm housing starts, from 1.473 million in 1965 to 1.165 million. At the same time, FHA mortgage yields rose from 5.46 percent to 6.29 percent. Mortgage yields continued to climb throughout the decade. While residential housing starts began to recover slowly, they had not reached their 1965 level by 1968.

In the recession of 1969–70 and in 1973, tight credit conditions again felt their strongest impact in the housing market. Since there are many social issues (other than macroeconomic stability) associated with the provision of an adequate supply of housing, economists in the early seventies began to question the desirability of relying on the countercyclical sensitivity of housing for stabilization, since it is the housing sector that feels the brunt of the credit squeeze.[21] Furthermore, since residential housing is such a small part of total aggregate demand (normally about 5 percent) it is not a powerful automatic stabilizer. It is, however, one of the first industries to feel the pinch of a credit squeeze. Localized structural unemployment may result, and pressure for an easier money policy is often strong from the powerful interests in this sector.

QUESTIONS FOR STUDY AND REVIEW

1. Suppose you are evaluating some projects which require certain investments (I) this year and which are expected to earn returns (R) next year. There are no returns in later years. The projects are the following:

20 J. M. Guttentag, "The Short Cycle in Residential Construction," *The American Economic Review*, LI (June, 1961), 275–298. For additional evidence of the sensitivity of the housing market to monetary policy see Jean Crockett *et al.*, *op. cit.*, and William E. Gibson, "Protecting Homebuilding from Restrictive Credit Conditions," *Brookings Papers on Economic Activity* (1973:3), 647–699.

21 Gibson, *op. cit.*

Project	I	R
A	$ 400	$ 420
B	500	530
C	600	780
D	800	1200
E	1000	1400

The market rate of interest is 10 percent.

(a) Which projects ought to be undertaken?

(b) Compare projects D and E by computing the *MEC*. If they are mutually exclusive, which ought to be undertaken?

(c) There are also some interactions among the projects. If A is undertaken, the return on C becomes $750; if B is undertaken, the return on E becomes $1500; and if both A and B are undertaken, the return on D becomes $1300. There are no other interactions and there is no change in any of the costs. If C, D, and E are mutually exclusive, which projects ought to be undertaken?

2. Investment has always been the most difficult component of GNP to forecast and analyze.

(a) How do you account for the difficulty?

(b) Why do economists attach such importance to this part of the macroeconomic model?

3. The corporate finance theory of investment can be combined with the accelerator theory to provide a complete explanation of business investment.

(a) How do the considerations introduced by the corporate finance school alter the conclusions of the pure accelerator theory?

(b) How would you design an empirical test to determine which of the theories provide the *best* explanation of business investment on the basis of time series data *alone?*

4. The classical theory of investment suggests that monetary policy is the appropriate policy instrument for influencing the general level of investment. Discuss the analysis from which this conclusion is derived. Then, on the basis of what you know about post-Keynesian investment theory and empirical findings, argue *against* this position.

5. It has been suggested that inventory cycles have accounted for most of the instability in the U.S. economy in recent years. Why should investment in inventories be any less stable than investment in plant and equipment and residential housing?

6. Can you explain the observed tendency for investment in residential housing to move inversely with the other components of gross private domestic investment over the cycle?

ADDITIONAL READING

CLARK, J. M., "Business Acceleration and the Law of Demand," *The Journal of Political Economy*, XXV (March, 1917), 217–235.

DUESENBERRY, J. S., *Business Cycles and Economic Growth*. New York: McGraw-Hill Book Company, Inc., 1958, Chapters 3–7.

DUESENBERRY, J. S., O. ECKSTEIN, and G. FROMM, "A Simulation of the United States Economy in Recession," *Econometrica*, XXVIII (October, 1960), 749–809.

GIBSON, WILLIAM E., "Protecting Homebuilding from Restrictive Credit Conditions," *Brookings Papers on Economic Activity* (1973:3), 647–699.

GUTTENTAG, J. M., "The Short Cycle in Residential Construction," *The American Economic Review*, LI (June, 1961), 275–298.

KEYNES, J. M., *The General Theory of Employment, Interest, and Money*. New York: Harcourt Brace Jovanovich, Inc., 1965, Chapters 11 and 12; originally published by Macmillan & Co., Ltd., 1936.

KUH, EDWIN, and MEYER, JOHN, "Investment, Liquidity, and Monetary Policy," in Commission on Money and Credit. *Impacts of Monetary Policy*. Englewood Cliffs, New Jersey: Prentice-Hall, Inc., 1963.

MEYER, J., and E. KUH, *The Investment Decision*. Cambridge, Mass: Harvard University Press, 1956, Chapters 2 and 12.

7

The Theory of Interest
and
Monetary Policy

Since both consumption and investment are influenced by credit conditions, a model of income determination would not be complete without a theory of interest. In particular, we shall be concerned with how actions of the monetary authorities who control the money supply affect the interest rate.[1]

Ever since Keynes described the relationship between the rate of interest and the level of income, economists have questioned the efficacy of monetary policy both as an antirecession weapon as well as a means for combating inflation. Although Keynes himself was pessimistic about the usefulness of monetary policy in recession, in recent years political considerations and institutional factors have made monetary policy the most flexible of our economic policy instruments, and in the United States it has been central to anti-inflation programs. A careful study of the factors determining the rate of interest must precede a more general analysis of the use of monetary policy to achieve the various macroeconomic goals.

7-1 THEORIES OF INTEREST RATE DETERMINATION: KEYNES AND THE CLASSICS COMPARED

A salient feature of Keynesian economics is its usefulness as a policy model. As we shall see, a theory of interest can be approached from many

[1] There are many perspectives from which one can view the theory of interest and money, and monetary theory encompasses much more than simply the re-

angles. The advantage of the Keynesian treatment is that it clearly demonstrates the link between monetary policy (changes in the money suppl$_y$) and the rate of interest.

Traditionally, interest has been viewed as the price a borrower pays for the use of money. If the borrower provides the lender with a promissory note, or bond, the interest rate is the difference between the face value of the bond and the amount actually borrowed (expressed as a percentage of the face value). Thus, interest may be viewed either as the cost of issuing the bond or, alternatively, the price paid for the use of money.

Classical economists viewed interest as the price which clears the bond market. Since the supply of bonds should decline as the interest rate (or cost) increases, while the demand for bonds should increase with the interest rate (or return), an equilibrium rate of interest would be achieved where the supply of bonds, B_S, is equal to the demand for bonds, B_D, as shown in Figure 7-1.

If the rate of interest were to exceed i_e, the demand for bonds would exceed the supply (i.e., lenders would wish to lend more than borrowers wished to borrow), and the rate of interest would be bid down. If the interest rate were below i_e, borrowers would not find sufficient funds available at that rate and would be forced to pay a higher rate. An equilibrium in which borrowers could obtain exactly the amount they wished to borrow would be achieved at i_e. At this rate of interest, all bonds offered would be sold, and the bond market would be cleared.

While this approach to the determination of the interest rate is theoretically valid, it is not particularly useful from a policy point of view, since the link between monetary policy and the interest rate is not clearly established. Moreover, it was the bond market approach to interest theory which led the classical economists to the erroneous conclusion that the rate of interest equilibrates saving and investment. If, indeed, all investment not financed directly from saving is financed from bond sales,[2] and if all saving not directly invested is used to purchase bonds, then equilibrium in the bond market would ensure the equality of saving and investment. That is, if

$$I \equiv B_S$$

and

---

lationship between the money supply and the interest rate. Unfortunately, as a comprehensive treatment is beyond the scope of this book, we will develop only enough monetary theory to round out the Keynesian model. For a good eclectic treatment of monetary theory see Harry G. Johnson, *Macroeconomics and Monetary Theory* (Chicago: Aldine Publishing Company, 1972).

[2] Corporate profit, of course, is a type of saving, and hence, internally financed investment is financed directly from saving.

$$S \equiv B_D$$

then

$$B_S = B_D$$

implies that

$$I = S$$

Since the interest rate is the mechanism by which the bond market is cleared, then implicitly, the interest rate also equates saving and investment, regardless of the level of income. Fluctuations in the rate of interest produce the saving-investment equality required for national income and employment equilibrium at full employment, as long as the bond market is cleared. Such reasoning was the basis of Say's Law, the idea that a full-employment level of income could always be achieved by the automatic operation of market forces.

Keynes recognized the validity of the bond market, or *loanable funds,* approach to interest theory, but pointed out that the extension of the

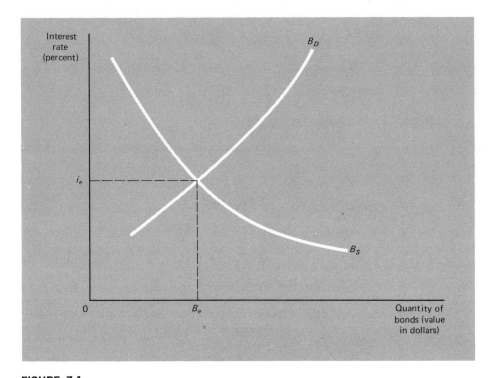

FIGURE 7-1

Equilibrium Rate of Interest Determined in the Bond Market

analysis to the so-called saving-investment market involved a fundamental fallacy. It is not necessarily true that all saving will be either directly invested or placed in the bond market, and hence, the equality

$$B_D = B_S$$

does not ensure that

$$S = I$$

Keynes pointed out that in the absence of an interest rate, a person would hold his savings in the most liquid form. To induce him to part with liquidity, a premium or rate of interest must be paid. The less liquid the bond, other things being equal, the greater is the rate of interest which the borrower must pay. Money is the most liquid of all assets. This *portfolio* approach to interest theory is useful in explaining the structure of interest rates on bonds of different periods of maturity. For the Keynesian model, it is important in explaining the pure rate of interest on a riskless bond, traded in a market. Such a bond has the greatest liquidity of any asset except cash. The interest rate on such a bond will be determined in the market where people choose between holding their assets (savings) in the form of money or in interest-bearing securities. Hence, it is determined by the demand for money and the money supply. If the demand for money increases as the interest rate (or price of money) falls, then conversely, the interest rate must fall to induce people to hold more money. Increases in the money supply must be accompanied by a decline in the rate of interest if the money market is to be cleared.

In Figure 7-2, the money demand function, M_D, is downward sloping, reflecting the inverse relationship between the demand for money and the interest rate. As the money supply increases from M_{S1} to M_{S2}, the interest rate must fall from i_1 to i_2 to induce individuals to hold the increment to the money supply in money balances and hence to maintain equilibrium in the money market.

With his *liquidity preference* theory of interest, Keynes pinpointed the relationship between changes in the money supply and the interest rate. Furthermore, he isolated the fallacy which resulted in adherence to Say's Law in classical macroeconomics.

The portfolio approach demonstrates that the demand for bonds is not identical to saving. In fact, the demand for bonds consists of saving[3] minus the net change in money holdings. Algebraically,

$$B_D = S - (\Delta H - \Delta M) = S - \Delta H + \Delta M$$

---

[3] Saving and investment are a part of the income *flow*. *Savings* is the *stock* of accumulated saving.

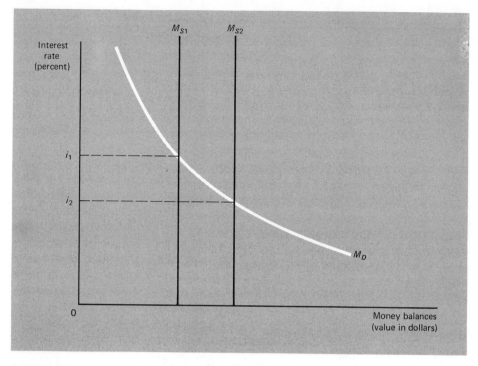

FIGURE 7-2

Equilibrium Rate of Interest Determined in the Money Market

where

$$B_D = \text{demand for bonds}$$
$$S = \text{saving}$$
$$H = \text{cash balances held}$$
$$M = \text{money supply}$$

The supply of bonds is equal to investment (not financed directly out of saving); that is,

$$B_S = I$$

Now consider the implications for equilibrium in the various markets. Suppose the interest rate adjusts so as to clear the bond market; that is,

$$B_S = B_D$$

This implies that

$$I = S - \Delta H + \Delta M$$

or

$$I - S = \Delta M - \Delta H$$

Only if the money market is cleared, that is, if

$$\Delta M = \Delta H$$

will a national income equilibrium be achieved; that is,

$$I = S$$

Equilibrium in the bond market does not ensure a national income equilibrium as the classical economists believed. While fluctuations in the interest rate may serve to clear the bond market, they do not necessarily ensure that saving will be equal to investment. As Keynes pointed out, the saving-investment equality will only be achieved by fluctuations in the level of income.

The portfolio approach underscores another interesting relationship between the various markets. Consider the basic relationships.

$$I = B_S$$
$$S = B_D + \Delta H - \Delta M$$

Suppose the economy is in macroeconomic equilibrium, so that

$$S = I$$

Then,

$$B_D + \Delta H - \Delta M = B_S$$

or

$$\Delta H - \Delta M = B_S - B_D$$

If the interest rate has adjusted so that the bond market is in equilibrium, that is, if

$$B_S = B_D$$

then the money market must also be in equilibrium:

$$\Delta H = \Delta M$$

The reverse is also the case. If a national income equilibrium is attained, then the interest rate that clears the money market will also clear the bond market. In equilibrium, the *liquidity preference* (money market) and *loanable funds* (bond market) approaches produce equivalent results. The choice between the two is hence one of methodological preference rather than theoretical validity.[4]

The liquidity preference approach which incorporates the relationship between money supply and the interest rate has more to recommend it methodologically. Incorporation of the money supply, a policy parameter, into the theoretical discussion will facilitate the adaptation of the model into a policy-planning framework. In addition, a theory which views the interest rate as the price paid for the use of money avoids the possibility of the fallacious misunderstanding that the interest rate equilibrates saving and investment.

The liquidity preference theory of interest is not without imperfections. However, before examining its faults, it will be useful to consider the liquidity preference theory in some detail. After an examination of the determinants of the demand for money and money supply, we shall consider the question of the efficacy of monetary policy in achieving the macroeconomic goals.

7-2   THE DEMAND FOR MONEY

Keynes observed that people are willing to forego interest income when they hold their assets in the form of money rather than as interest-bearing securities. Consequently, there must be some utility attached to money which would explain an individual's preference for liquidity. Keynes suggested three distinct motives for holding money balances: Individuals require money for transactions, and to meet unexpected contingencies. In addition, money may be temporarily preferred as an asset when the price of interest-bearing assets is expected to fall.

THE TRANSACTIONS DEMAND

Individuals require money balances in the form of cash and demand deposits to make day-to-day transactions. If a person expects to make $500 in transactions in a month, spread about evenly over the month, and if he is paid $500 at the beginning of the month, his average cash balance would be $250.

Several factors influence the amount of cash balances held for transactions purposes. The transactions demand for cash increases with total

---

[4] The different disequilibrium implications of the two approaches might affect one's choice between them.

expenditures. Suppose expenditures increase by $100. Again, assuming they are distributed uniformly over the period, then average money balances will increase by $50. Therefore,

$$\Delta M = \frac{\Delta E}{2}$$

where ΔM is change in money balances and ΔE is change in expenditures.

Not only do individuals hold cash balances for transactions purposes, but so do firms and government. Therefore, the demand for transactions balances can be expressed as a function not only of household expenditures, but of total aggregate demand or income; that is,

$$M_1 = l_{11}C + l_{12}I + l_{13}G = l_1(C + I + G) = l_1 Y$$

where M_1 is the *transactions demand for money,* l_{11}, l_{12}, and l_{13} are the proportions of C, I, and G respectively which are held by individuals, firms, and government in the form of money balances, and l_1 is the proportion of national income held by these groups in the form of money balances.

Institutional factors also influence the demand for money. If individuals are paid more frequently, the demand for transactions balances is reduced. In the previous example, a man who spends $500 uniformly over the month and who is paid biweekly will hold an average cash balance of $125 as compared with $250 if paid every month. Even though his expenditures remain the same, the demand for money is reduced by one-half because the pay period is shortened.

The use of credit cards reduces the transactions demand for money. If individuals pay most of their bills at the beginning of the month and the individuals are also paid then, there will be no reason to hold large transactions balances during the month. The practice of tax withholding precludes the need for accumulating balances for tax payments. Institutional influences in the United States have served to reduce the fraction of aggregate expenditure held by individuals in the form of cash balances.

Industrial organization plays a role in determining the demand for transactions balances by firms. In particular, vertical integration will reduce the requirement for cash in transactions between firms. An integrated company will simply record a transaction as a bookkeeping entry with no actual transfer of cash.

The rate of interest may also affect the demand for transactions balances. The higher the rate of interest, the more profitable it becomes to enter the bond market for short periods of time. However, the typical individual is paid at intervals not exceeding one month. At the same time, it is unlikely that he is sophisticated enough in financial practice to deal in that market in which he can realize interest income for periods shorter than a month.[5] Even at high rates of interest, the average individual will probably not enter the bond market with his transaction balances.[6] This may not be true of a large corporation, however, which may invest balances it is holding to meet an order which it expects six weeks in the future. In this case, transactions demand for money may decline as interest rates rise.[7]

THE PRECAUTIONARY DEMAND

Individuals and firms hold money balances in excess of their transactions needs to meet unexpected contingencies. Suppose, because of a clerical error, a paycheck is delayed. The man's family still must eat and make other necessary expenditures. It would not be prudent for him to allow his checking account balance to fall to zero on the day before payday. Instead, it would be advisable to keep some buffer cash in reserve as a precaution.

The amount of such precautionary balances held depends largely upon the level of transactions or income. Indeed, as a rule of thumb, an individual or firm may hold adequate precautionary balances to meet expenditures for a certain period of time, say, one week. Therefore, both precautionary and transactions balances can be viewed as a function of income, or algebraically,

$$M_1 + M_2 = l_1 Y + l_2 Y = (l_1 + l_2) Y = l Y$$

where M_2 is precautionary balances and l_2 is the fraction of income held in precautionary balances.

The proportion of income held in the form of precautionary balances will vary with the amount of uncertainty associated with receipts and expenditures. This suggests that the percentage of income held in precautionary balances may rise in times of recession. Also, the availability of so-called "near-moneys" may encourage individuals to convert precautionary balances into interest-bearing securities, particularly if interest rates are high.

---

[5] Conventional sources generally require that the asset be held for at least a month before the holder is eligible to receive interest.

[6] In this connection, it is important not to confuse transactions balances with savings which are not destined to be spent within the pay period.

[7] For a further discussion of this point see J. Tobin, "The Interest Elasticity of the Transactions Demand for Cash," *Review of Economics and Statistics,* XXXVIII (August, 1956), 241–247, and W. J. Baumol, "The Transactions Demand for Cash: An Inventory Theoretic Approach," *Quarterly Journal of Economics,* LXVI (November, 1952), 545–556.

Both the transactions and the precautionary demand for money are directly related to income and, to a lesser extent, inversely related to the rate of interest. Figure 7-3 shows a family of money demand functions each for a different level of income. As income increases, M_D shifts right-

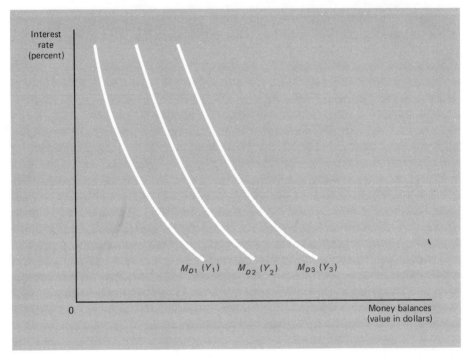

FIGURE 7-3

The Transactions and Precautionary Demand for Money

ward, from M_{D1} to M_{D3}. For any rate of interest, the demand for money will be greater the higher the level of income. For any level of income, the demand for money will increase slightly as the interest rate falls.

THE SPECULATIVE DEMAND

An individual who wishes to maximize the return on his portfolio investment will not purchase bonds if he expects their price to fall. Thus, he may find it most profitable temporarily to hold money rather than bonds as an asset, even though the former bears no interest, if the expected capital loss associated with a decline in the bond price exceeds the interest income he will forego by holding his assets in the form of money.

For example, suppose an individual purchases a bond for $100 with a 5 percent coupon interest rate. If, after a year, the bond is worth only $90 and he receives $5 in interest, the net gain from holding the bond is −$5. Since there is no loss associated with holding cash, the latter is a preferable asset.

The market value of a bond with a fixed-coupon rate varies inversely with the market rate of interest. If the market rate of interest is 5 percent, a bond with a fixed-coupon rate of $5 is worth $100 in the bond market. Suppose the market rate of interest increases to 10 percent. Unless the bond yields the market rate of interest, there will be no buyers for it in the bond market. For the relationship between the bond price and the coupon premium of $5 to reflect the market rate of interest, 10 percent, the price of the bond must fall to $50. Thus, an individual will prefer to hold money rather than bonds, if he expects the market rate of interest to rise, thereby producing a decline in the market value of the bond which is greater than the original yield. In this case, the expected gain associated with buying a bond is −$45 (the decline in the bond price, −$50, plus the $5 coupon), if interest rates are expected to rise from 5 percent to 10 percent.

The demand for money balances as a hedge against capital losses in the face of rising interest rates is what Keynes called the *speculative demand for money*. Keynes reasoned that, at very high interest rates, most people expect interest rates to fall (bond prices to rise), and consequently, the speculative demand for money is very low. Most people will prefer to hold bonds, since there is little risk of capital loss. At successively lower rates of interest, however, fewer people anticipate interest rates to fall still further and some expect them to rise. Those expecting rising interest rates (falling bond prices) liquidate their bond holdings in the expectation of capital losses and increase their money balances. At very low rates of interest, no one expects the rate of interest to fall, and everyone expects it to rise; consequently, any new additions to asset holdings are in the form of money balances.

Keynes labeled the phenomenon of a virtually infinite demand for money at very low interest rates the *liquidity trap*.[8] In this range, all increments to the money supply are "trapped" in speculative balances. Since these funds are not used to purchase bonds, the interest rate will be unaffected by increases in the money supply. A schedule of the speculative demand for money as suggested by Keynes is shown in Figure 7-4. The schedule becomes flatter as the interest rate falls and more people hold money as a hedge against the anticipated decline in bond prices.

---

[8] By similar reasoning, it can be argued that at high interest rates the demand for bonds is infinite. We shall consider the implications of this possibility in the discussion of monetary policy.

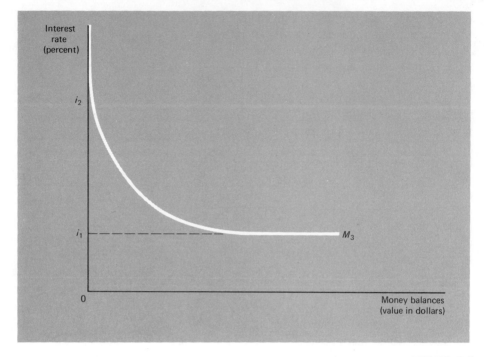

FIGURE 7-4

The Speculative Demand for Money

Algebraically, the speculative demand, M_3, can be expressed as

$$M_3 = \frac{Z}{i} \qquad \text{for } i_2 > i > i_1$$

$$M_3 = 0 \qquad \text{for } i \geq i_2$$

$$M_3 = \infty \qquad \text{for } i = i_1$$

where Z is a constant.

The liquidity preference theory of interest is based on expectations. The rate at which the demand for money may become infinitely elastic depends upon what individuals expect "normal" rates to be. In periods in which interest rates range between 2 percent and 4 percent for as long as 10 years, a 1.5 percent rate of interest may represent the lower limit. If rates are uniformly higher, the money demand schedule may flatten at higher rates. In periods of greatly fluctuating rates, there may be no rate considered "normal," and consequently, there may be no liquidity trap. In fact, Keynes himself doubted that the liquidity preference function would actually flatten out in practice except in "very abnormal circumstances." [9]

In some cases, falling interest rates may be associated with a decline in the demand for money if rates are expected to fall still farther. The reverse may also be true in the case of rising interest rates. Such behavior would result in highly unstable bond markets. Since the monetary authorities, through open market operations, are responsible for controlling bond prices (interest rates), the situation is unlikely to develop unless the authorities are expected to allow interest rates to move outside of their "normal" range.

THE DEMAND FOR MONEY

The demand for money varies directly with income and inversely with the market rate of interest. Demand for transactions and precautionary purposes increases with income. The demand for speculative balances increases as interest rates fall. Algebraically, the demand for money is the sum of the transactions, precautionary, and speculative demands,

$$M_D = M_1 + M_2 + M_3 = lY + \frac{Z}{i} \qquad \text{for } i_2 > i > i_1$$

$$= M_1 + M_2 + M_3 = lY \qquad \text{for } i \geq i_2$$

$$= M_1 + M_2 + M_3 = \infty. \qquad \text{for } i = i_1$$

The money demand schedule for a given level of income can be represented as a function of the rate of interest as shown in Figure 7-5. The distance $0M_Y$ represents the transactions and precautionary demands at the specified income level. If the demand for transactions and precautionary balances were inversely related to the interest rate, the total money demand schedule would be flatter than the speculative demand schedule over the nonhorizontal portion.

Notice that the sensitivity of the demand for money to changes in the interest rate occurs only for a discrete range of interest rates, in this case between i_1 and i_2. Above i_2 the demand for money depends only on income, and changes in the interest rate will not affect it. At i_1 the demand for money is infinite, and reductions in the interest rate below i_1 can have no further stimulating effect on the demand for money.

As shown in Figure 7-6, the demand for money as a function of the interest rate can also be represented as a family of liquidity preference

[9] J. M. Keynes, *The General Theory of Employment, Interest, and Money,* (New York: Harcourt Brace Jovanovich, Inc., 1965), p. 207. Originally published by Macmillan & Co., Ltd., 1936.

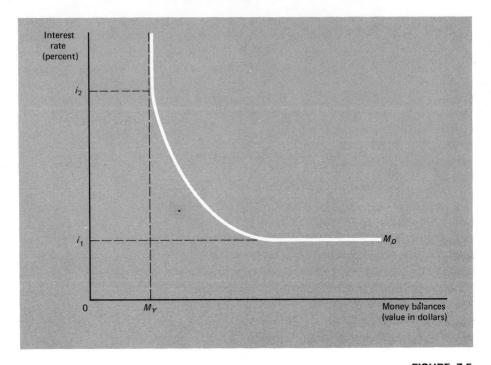

FIGURE 7-5

The Demand for Money for a Specified Level of Income

schedules, one for each level of income. At successively higher income levels, the transactions and precautionary demands increase so the liquidity preference schedule shifts to the right. For interest rates above i_1, the demand for money increases as the level of income increases. Notice, however, that at the interest rate i_1, the demand for money balances becomes infinite, regardless of the level of income. This corresponds with the algebraic statement presented above.

CHANGES IN THE PRICE LEVEL

The demand for money balances will increase and decrease in proportion to changes in the price level. If prices increase by 5 percent, the amount of money required to purchase the same goods and services also increases by 5 percent, and the demand for transactions and precautionary balances increases proportionately.[10] Thus, interest rates will increase if

[10] In a chronic inflation, the percentage of expenditures held in money balances may fall since individuals will be anxious to exchange money which is decreasing in value for goods as rapidly as possible. This phenomenon is not likely to occur when price changes are slight.

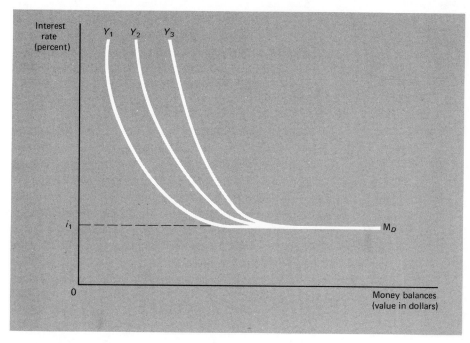

FIGURE 7-6

A Family of Liquidity Preference Schedules
Associated with Different Income Levels

the money supply remains fixed. If the variables in the model are measured in money terms, price changes are reflected in the money income variable. In such a model, M_1 and M_2 can be treated as a function of money income which reflects the effect of price changes as well as changes in real expenditures. Since bonds have a fixed-money value, price changes will not affect the relative desirability of bonds and money, but they may cause individuals to convert speculative money holdings into real property, such as gold, jewelry, and real estate, as well as paper equity such as common stock. Since bonds have a fixed value in terms of money, however, they will not be any more attractive than money in inflationary times, and bond prices will most likely fall simultaneously with the shift from money and bond holdings into real assets. Thus, even though the speculative demand for money is likely to decline in periods of chronic inflation, interest rates will also rise. A rise in the money rate of interest during an inflation does not necessarily reflect an increase in the real rate. Suppose a bond yields 10 percent. If prices are expected to increase by 4 percent before the premium is due, the real yield on the bond is only 6 percent.

If inflation persists and the money supply remains fixed, money rates of interest will rise, causing speculators to revise their expectations concerning the floor below which bond yields will not fall. This will shift the liquidity preference function (in money terms) upward, with the liquidity trap located at a higher money rate of interest. If, however, speculators are subject to a "money illusion," they may not revise their expectations about the normal range of interest rates, and the liquidity preference function will not shift with changes in the price level.

THE QUANTITY THEORY OF MONEY

Pre-Keynesian economists ignored the speculative demand for money. The so-called *quantity theory of money* (which has several versions) implied a strict proportionality between the demand for money and money income.

The quantity theory is based on the recognition of an identity between the value of all transactions in the economy, on the one hand, and the money supply multiplied by its velocity of circulation, on the other. The quantity theory identity

$$MV \equiv pT$$

where M is money in circulation, V is velocity, p is the price level, and T is transactions, allows V to vary with the transactions requirements of the economy, so that the quantity equation is always true.

Suppose transactions are proportional to real income or spending, y, so that

$$T = \lambda y$$

and

$$MV \equiv pT \equiv \lambda py \equiv \lambda Y$$

where Y is money income. Defining V', the *income velocity* of circulation, as

$$V' = \frac{V}{\lambda}$$

the quantity theory identity can be written

$$MV' \equiv Y$$

Quantity theorists hypothesized that V' is a constant that reflects certain institutional transaction practices—the use of credit cards, the length of pay periods, and the like—that exist in an economy. The relation between M and Y was assumed to be stable in much the same way that

Keynesians view the multiplier relationship between autonomous changes in demand and income change as stable. With V' postulated to be constant, the quantity theory equation is no longer an identity (since V' cannot vary to make it always true), but instead is a hypothesized functional relationship, the stability of which must be demonstrated.

The quantity theory equation can be put in another form, called the *Cambridge equation*. Letting

$$K = \frac{1}{V'}$$

the Cambridge equation

$$M = KY$$

becomes a money demand function. Notice that it is derived directly from

$$MV' = Y$$

or

$$MV = pT$$

the quantity theory of money equation.

The Cambridge equation incorporates the Keynesian transactions and precautionary demands, but not the speculative demand for money. Put in another way, the only thing Keynes added to the pre-Keynesian theory of the demand for money was the speculative demand.[11] We shall see, however, that the introduction of speculative demand had major implications for monetary policy. In particular, by emphasizing the role of the interest rate in the demand for money, Keynes turned attention away from the money supply as the principal instrument of monetary policy and focused instead on changes in the interest rate that resulted from changes in the money supply.

7-3   MONETARY POLICY AND THE MONEY SUPPLY

Given the demand for money transactions, precautionary, and speculative purposes, the monetary authorities can manipulate the interest rate by changing the money supply.[12] The Federal Reserve can increase the money

---

[11] Keynes did, however, introduce some interesting new behavioral propositions that underlie the relation between income and the demand for money.

[12] Keynesian models generally treat the money supply as subject to the discretion of the monetary authorities. Thus, the liquidity preference theory of the demand for money is combined with an assumption of an exogenous money supply to determine the conditions for money market equilibrium. Some economists argue

supply by buying bonds on the open market, lowering the discount rate at which commercial banks can borrow from the Federal Reserve banks, or reducing reserve requirements for member banks.

An increase in the money supply will have the effect of reducing the interest rate, except in the liquidity trap, as shown in Figure 7-7. As the money supply increases from M_{SA} to M_{SB} to M_{SC}, the interest rate falls from i_A to i_B to i_1 as individuals and firms convert some of the additional balances into bonds, driving bond prices up. At an interest rate of i_1, however, increases in the money supply will not cause interest rates to fall farther. In the liquidity trap, bond prices are so high that everyone prefers to hold the additional money in speculative balances rather than enter the bond market, since they expect bond prices to fall. If the money supply is increased from M_{SC} to M_{SD}, the interest rate will remain fixed at i_1.

Notice that the higher the rate of interest, the greater is the change in the interest rate associated with a given change in the money supply. Thus, monetary policy is likely to be most effective at higher interest rates. At very low rates of interest, changes in the money supply are less effective in controlling the interest rate, and in the liquidity trap, monetary policy cannot influence the interest rate at all.

CHANGES IN THE DEMAND FOR MONEY

The monetary authorities must consider certain factors which might affect the demand for money. These include price level changes, increased use of credit cards (reducing transactions demand), and increased national health and retirement insurance coverage. Suppose an increase in the price level results in an increased demand for money.[13] Figure 7-8 shows the effect on the market rate of interest. As the money demand schedule shifts rightward from M_D to M'_D, the market rate of interest rises from i to i', when the money supply is M_{SA}. If the monetary authorities were interested in maintaining a stable interest rate in the face of inflationary pressure, they would have to increase the money supply from M_{SA} to M_{SB}, which intersects M'_D at i.[14]

---

that the money supply cannot be controlled by the monetary authorities and instead is responsive to changes in money demand through fractional reserve banking practices and financial intermediaries. For a discussion of the theory of an endogenous money supply see Harry G. Johnson, *op. cit.*, pp. 135–47. For our purposes, we shall assume that monetary authorities have sufficient control over the money supply to offset any built-in tendency for it to expand and contract with the liquidity demands of the public, if they desire. This is not to say that a theory of monetary management should not take endogenous influences on the money supply into account.

[13] In cases of runaway inflation, the demand for money might actually weaken, as people transfer out of fixed-value and into real-value assets.

[14] The increased money supply may stimulate aggregate demand, causing national income and the demand for transactions balances to rise. This will cause the

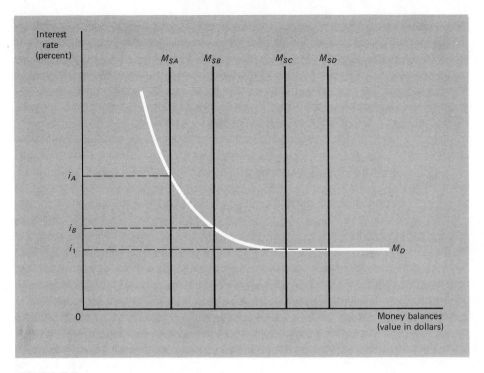

FIGURE 7-7

Determination of the Interest Rate
for a Specified Level of Income

MONETARY POLICY AND THE QUANTITY THEORY

If there were no speculative demand for money, changes in the
money supply would have no effect on the interest rate, but instead would
generate changes in money income directly. If the demand for money is
proportional to income, that is

$$M = KY$$

the implication is that there is some optimal amount of money balances
households and firms wish to hold in relation to spending. If the money
supply increases, spending units find they have too much money relative
to goods and reallocate their resources by exchanging some of the money
for goods until they have regained the desired relationship between goods

money demand schedule to shift again. Thus, to maintain the interest rate at i, the
monetary authorities would be forced to increase the money supply again, feeding continuous inflation. Undoubtedly, in such a situation the policy of maintaining the interest rate at i would be called into question.

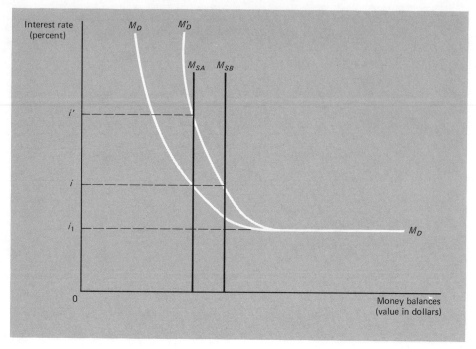

FIGURE 7-8

An Increase in the Demand for Money

and money balances.[15] This is the *real balance effect* we introduced in Chapter 5.[16]

The effect of an increase in the money supply when there is no speculative demand for money is shown in Figure 7-9. If the money supply increases from M_1 to M_2, income rises from Y_1 to Y_2 or

$$\Delta Y = V' \Delta M$$

Since the increase in money will not be held in speculative balances, it must be held in transactions balances that will only increase if income increases. The mechanism by which income rises as a result of the increased money supply is the real balance effect. The interest rate is un-

[15] Since the classical economists believed in Say's Law, the amount of goods and services available is fixed at the full-employment level. Thus, the effect of a change in the money supply was felt through price level changes.

[16] For a discussion of the behavioral (microeconomic) foundations of the real balance effect see Don Patinkin, *Money, Interest, and Prices,* 2nd ed. (New York: Harper and Row, 1965), Chapter 2.

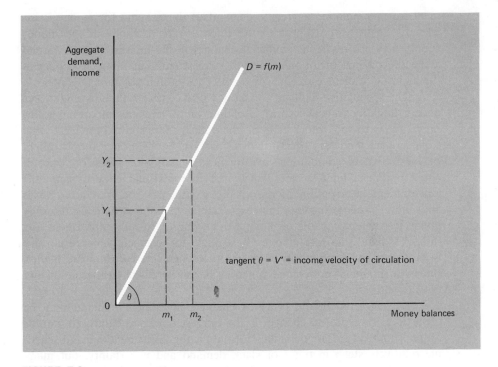

FIGURE 7-9
Effect of a Change in the Money Supply
With No Speculative Demand for Money

affected because it does not enter into the process that equilibrates the
demand and supply of money.[17]

7-4   LIMITATIONS TO THE EFFECTIVENESS
OF MONETARY POLICY

In a Keynesian model incorporating the speculative demand for money,
two major factors limit the effectiveness of monetary policy as an instru-

[17] Quantity theorists would allow for some short-run interest rate changes as
a result of a monetary operation, since the way the money supply is changed—
open market operations, discount rate policy, etc.—affects the interest rate. However, it is the real balance effect, not the stimulus from the interest rate, that causes
product-market demand to rise. In the long run, interest rates reflect the preference
for present over future consumption and investment opportunities and are determined by the equilibrium between saving and investment. We will explore this
monetarist model again in Chapter 9.

ment for manipulating aggregate demand. If the demand for money is extremely elastic with respect to the interest rate, changes in the money supply may not result in significant changes in the interest rate. A second and quite distinct factor inhibiting the effectiveness of monetary policy is the inelasticity of investment with respect to the interest rate.

The speculative demand for money in Keynesian analysis might produce a liquidity trap at low rates of interest. There are important policy implications to this rather esoteric theoretical innovation. It suggests that expansionary monetary policy, that is, increases in the money supply, might be ineffective in stimulating investment demand in a recession since it could not push interest rates below the marginal efficiency of capital.[18] Government intervention in the spending stream through reduced taxes and, more directly, through increased public spending would be the only policy instrument capable of moving the economy to full employment. On the other hand, the rate of interest is likely to be much more responsive to monetary management in boom periods when interest rates are higher, since the liquidity preference function becomes much steeper at higher rates of interest.

As suggested in the previous chapter, investment demand may be inelastic with respect to changes in the interest rate, particularly in periods of inadequate aggregate demand. Not only is the investment demand schedule relatively steep in times of slack demand and uncertainty, but many firms find internal sources of funds adequate to finance investment at this time. Furthermore, in a slump they are often actually faced with excess capacity, so there is no incentive to undertake new investment.

In boom periods, as well, accelerator effects which stimulate investment may outweigh considerations of capital cost, again weakening the impact of a tight money policy on investment. In boom periods, however, restrictive monetary policy may be particularly effective in limiting demand in those sectors in which external financing is the rule and accelerator influences are weaker. In particular, the housing industry and certain consumer durables industries might face a cutback in demand, as sources of finance dry up or become prohibitively expensive.

Milton Friedman, a noted monetary economist, has suggested an additional factor which not only limits the effectiveness of discretionary monetary policy but also implies that it may actually make things worse. Friedman argues that the lag between discretionary changes in the money supply by the Federal Reserve and their influence on spending is so great that the overall effect may be destabilizing. For instance, the Fed may

---

[18] Theoretically, the idea of the liquidity trap was not a real innovation, since the classical economists had implicitly recognized an interest rate floor of zero. At zero or negative rates of interest, everyone would prefer money to bonds, and hence, the demand for money balances would be infinitely great.

decide to increase the money supply when the unemployment rate rises, but by the time interest rates have time to adjust downward and have the desired (if any) effect on aggregate demand, the economy might well be on its way to an inflationary boom (due presumably to a faster-acting fiscal policy package). Thus the increased money supply may serve to add fuel to the inflation. Friedman proposes a system whereby the money supply is automatically changed as the level of GNP changes.[19] This would at least eliminate the lag in the recognition and decision-making process.

7-5   EVALUATION OF THE LIQUIDITY PREFERENCE THEORY OF INTEREST

Perhaps the most important contribution of the liquidity preference theory of interest is that it provides a framework for an analysis of monetary management. Classical economists, by focusing on the bond market, had viewed money as something of a "veil" which determined the absolute level of prices, but which had no influence on real variables in the economy. By showing the link between the money supply and the interest rate, Keynes demonstrated that money is more than a veil. By affecting the interest rate, in the Keynesian model, the money supply influences the level of investment and, through the multiplier, national income.

By introducing the notion of the liquidity trap, Keynes made a strong theoretical point for increased reliance on fiscal policy as an antirecession weapon. However, there is little historical evidence to support the premise that the demand for money becomes infinite at low rates of interest. It is ironic that Keynes did not place more emphasis on the interest elasticity of investment demand. Empirical findings indicate that interest inelasticity of investment demand is a far more serious limitation to monetary policy in a recession than the speculative demand for money. Nevertheless, Keynes' misgivings about the effectiveness of monetary policy represented an important milestone in the history of economic thought and policy.

QUESTIONS FOR STUDY AND REVIEW

1. Assume the following functional relationships:

$$C = 20 + .75(Y - T)$$
$$I = .25Y - 10i$$

---

[19] See Milton Friedman, "A Monetary and Fiscal Framework for Economic Stability," *The American Economic Review,* XXXVIII (June, 1948), 245–264.

$$M_1 + M_2 = .25\,Y$$

$$M_3 = \frac{30}{i} \quad \text{for } i > 2$$

$$= \infty \quad \text{for } i \leq 2$$

$$T = .33\,Y$$

$$G = 300$$

$$M = 300$$

The notation follows that in the text.

(a) What is the equilibrium level of income?

(b) If full-employment income is 1500, can it be reached by monetary policy alone?

(c) Show how fiscal policy might be used to bring the economy to full employment.

2. How might a decline in the transactions demand for money affect national income and employment? How would it affect the general level of prices? What policy measures would serve to neutralize these effects?

3. The argument that Keynes' theory of interest was not significantly different from the bond market theory has been defended and denied. State your position in this controversy, with some argument on *both* sides of the question.

4. Keynes made a strong case for the use of fiscal policy as a weapon to stimulate a sluggish economy. Outline the arguments on which this case was made.

5. Show how Keynes' theory of interest and money provides a planning model for monetary management. What behavioral parameters need specification?

ADDITIONAL READING

Bronfenbrenner, Martin, and Thomas Mayer, "Liquidity Functions in the American Economy," *Econometrica,* XXVIII (October, 1960), 810–834.

Friedman, Milton, "A Monetary and Fiscal Framework for Economic Stability," *The American Economic Review,* XXXVIII (June, 1948), 245–264.

Hansen, Alvin, *A Guide to Keynes.* Book Four. New York: McGraw-Hill Book Company, Inc., 1953, Chapter 6.

JOHNSON, HARRY G., *Macroeconomics and Monetary Theory*. Chicago: Aldine Publishing Company, 1972.

KEYNES, J. M., *The General Theory of Employment, Interest, and Money*. New York: Harcourt Brace Jovanovich, Inc., 1965, Chapters 13, 14, and 15; originally published by Macmillan & Co., Ltd., 1936.

PIGOU, A. C., "The Value of Money," *The Quarterly Journal of Economics* XXXII (November, 1917), 38–65.

8

The Complete Model

We have seen that conditions in the money market will affect aggregate demand through the rate of interest. But the demand for money also depends on the level of aggregate demand. A complete model of income determination must take into account the interrelationship between aggregate product-market demand and the financial market.

Aggregate demand and conditions in the money market are closely interrelated, and as a consequence, fiscal and monetary policy may interact in important ways. A study of the complete macroeconomic model will serve to emphasize the importance of coordination of the various monetary and fiscal measures undertaken to attain the goals of full employment, price stability, payments equilibrium, and growth.

8-1 THE VARIABLES OF THE MODEL

If the model is to be used for policy planning, it is necessary to establish links between the policy variables—government spending, taxes, and money supply—and the target variables—employment, price level, and GNP. As the model explains how these target variables are determined, however, other important indicators of economic conditions can be derived. These include the rate of interest, the level of real wages, and the distribution of the net private product between consumption and investment.

Treating the so-called "policy parameters" as exogenous, or pre-

199

determined, does not imply that the public authorities have complete discretionary control over all policy instruments. In fact, it is likely that public expenditures, taxes, and money supply are themselves dependent in part on economic conditions in the private sector. The scope of this particular model, however, is to show how public policy decisions affect the various target variables and, implicitly, how public policy can be used to effectuate desired changes or to attain certain goals. Consequently, policy instruments are treated as exogenous; the model is designed to show how changes in these instruments produce changes in the endogenous variables of the system.

REAL VERSUS MONEY MODELS

The variables in an economic model can be expressed in *real* or in *money* terms. If a variable is expressed in real terms, it is deflated by a price index so as to abstract from price level changes. For example, if GNP were to rise from $500 billion to $600 billion while prices increased by 10 percent, then the *money* increase in GNP would be $100 billion while the *real* increase would be $45 billion. The real increase is calculated as follows: For a 10 percent increase in prices from the base year, the price deflator is 110 (100 for the base year plus 10 percent of 100), so that when GNP rises to $600 billion, *real* GNP is

$$\frac{\$600 \text{ billion}}{110} \times 100 = \$545 \text{ billion}$$

Thus, the *real* change in GNP is $45 billion. The money change in GNP measures the change in the value of goods and services produced. The real change measures the change in output when valued at the prices of the base period.

In *The General Theory*, Keynes converts money variables into real variables by using a *wage unit deflator*, an index of average wages, rather than a price deflator. This practice has two major advantages. First, when a money variable is expressed in constant wage units (rather than constant money units), the variable is directly tied to the level of employment. If the proportion of national income earned in the form of wages is constant, then national income in wage units, Y, is proportional to the level of employment, N, since if

$$\lambda Y = wN$$

where λ represents the percent of national income earned as wages, and w is the wage unit deflator, then

$$\frac{Y}{w} = \frac{1}{\lambda} N$$

Income in wage units will only increase if employment increases or if the relative share of national income earned in nonwage form decreases. A second advantage of using wage units is that changes in average wages will tend to be uniform with respect to capital goods and consumer goods industries if labor is mobile between them. On the other hand, price level changes may vary considerably between capital and consumer goods industries, often necessitating the use of separate price deflators for the in-investment and consumption sectors. A difficulty with the wage unit approach is that changes in the distribution of income between wage and non-wage sources must be taken into account explicitly.

If money variables are deflated by a price index, a measure of output (real income) is obtained. If money variables are deflated by a wage index, a measure of employment is obtained. Wages and prices are related to each other through the marginal productivity of labor, since

$$w = p \times MP$$

With the wage unit fixed, an increase in aggregate demand and employment implies an increase in prices, since the marginal productivity of labor will generally fall as more workers are employed with a fixed capital stock. Thus, output measured in constant dollars will not increase as rapidly as output measured in wage units. This is equivalent to saying that output will not increase as fast as employment, or alternatively, that there are diminishing returns to labor with a fixed capital stock.

Pre-Keynesian macroeconomic models were developed in real terms. The practice may be attributable to the classical belief that money is a veil which has no impact on real variables. In a Keynesian system, however, in which the quantity of money in circulation has an important relationship to the value of the real variables, this justification for abstracting from money no longer applies.

Some economists continue to construct models in real terms, even though their models are essentially Keynesian in the sense that they recognize the impact of the money supply on the real variables. This is generally done because of the assumption that spending units make their decisions in terms of the real values of income, interest rates, and the like. In most cases it is assumed that spending units are not subject to "money illusion"; that is, they take price changes into account before making their spending decisions. Thus, real consumption is essentially a function of real income. If prices and income were to increase by 10 percent, then after a lag, consumption expenditures would also increase by 10 percent.

Although the behavioral relationships of the model may be correctly specified in terms of real variables, it is a mistake to examine the complete Keynesian system in real terms. Changes in the real variables of the system will always have an impact on the price level through the aggregate supply function. These price level changes in turn affect the real value of the money supply and hence the rate of interest, investment, and real income. For instance, consider an increase in government spending which generates an increase in employment through the multiplier. As shown in Figure 8-1,

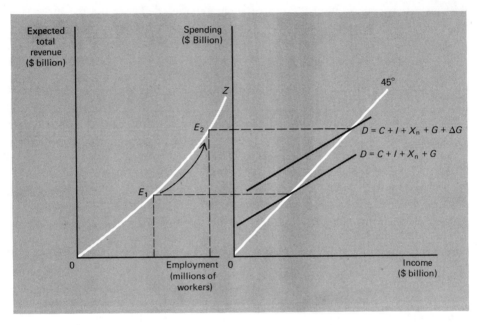

FIGURE 8-1

Impact of an Increase in Government Spending

with a fixed money wage, prices will increase as the economy moves along the aggregate supply function from E_1 to E_2, and the marginal productivity of labor declines. The price increase has the impact of increasing the transactions demand for money proportionally and raising the real rate of interest. Unless the monetary authorities increase the money supply in proportion to the price increase, the employment multiplier will be smaller than that predicted by an analysis of the real system alone. Thus, abstraction from the price changes generally associated with changes in employment ignores the impact of these changes on the value of transactions balances and hence on the rest of the system. There are important feedbacks which are ignored when variables are measured in real terms. In this case the increase in government spending must be combined with expansionary monetary policy (increased money supply) if the full impact of the multiplier is to be felt.

Converting consumption, investment, and money demand functions from real into money terms implies no loss of generality, even though the relationships which we examined in Chapters 5, 6, and 7 were essentially real in the sense that they implied no "money illusion." Empirical studies of consumption and investment behavior generally work with variables deflated by a price or wage index. However, these can easily be converted into money terms by multiplying the deflated variables by the deflator. Thus, if real consumption, C_r, is obtained by dividing the money value of consumption, C_m, by a price index,

$$C_r = \frac{C_m}{p}$$

then money consumption can be found by multiplying real consumption by the price index; that is,

$$C_m = C_r p$$

If all variables in the relationship have been deflated by the same index, then the relationship, except for constant terms, will be the same regardless of whether the variables are in real or money form.

Converting behavioral relationships into money form has the additional advantage that money illusion can be taken into account whenever it occurs. Money illusion implies that individuals react to money changes in economic variables, such as income and wages, independent of price level changes. An example of money illusion in the Keynesian system is the liquidity trap. The demand for money becomes infinite at some low rate of interest. But this floor below which the interest rate is not expected to fall and hence will not fall is presumably (according to the standard analysis) independent of the rate of change of the price level. Speculators have a money illusion if they believe that the interest rate will not fall below 2 percent even if the general price level is falling. Money interest rates will be lower in periods of falling prices than when prices are rising if the real rate remains unchanged.

In conclusion, the complete Keynesian model can be developed in either real or money terms. By abstracting from price level changes, however, we fail to account for the effect of changing levels of employment on the price level and, hence, on the real value of the money supply. The simple model developed in Chapters 2, 3, and 4 was presented in money terms. The analysis that follows will be based upon that framework.

It should be noted that while a model which involves money relationships may be most useful for policy planning and forecasting, we are often interested in separating price changes from real changes in national income aggregates. While real increases in GNP may be desirable, since they represent increases in real goods and services, price level increases are not, since they represent changes in the value of money. In fact, whether or not the government should stimulate GNP will often depend upon how much of the increase will be pure price inflation. In Chapters 10, 11, and 12 we shall consider the process of inflation and analyze the problem of

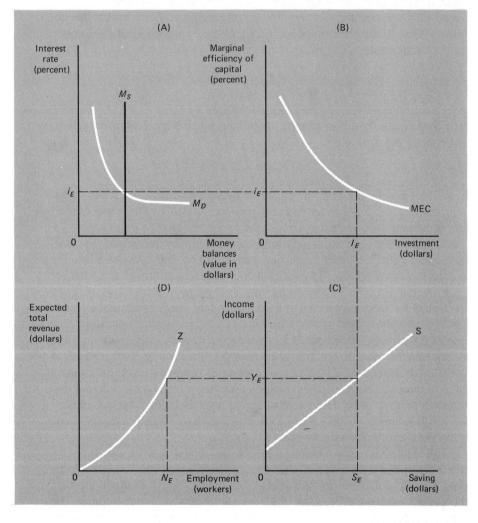

FIGURE 8-2

A Recursive Keynesian System

how to maintain high levels of employment without encountering inflation. However, the problem of inflation cannot be solved by abstracting from price level changes in the analysis. We shall see that a theory of inflation must be developed separately from the theory of income determination. There is not necessarily a one-to-one correspondence between changes in money income on the one hand and real income and price changes on the other.

8-2   THE GENERAL EQUILIBRIUM

A SIMPLE KEYNESIAN MODEL

In its simplest form, the Keynesian system of income determination can be built from the consumption or saving function, the *MEC* schedule, the liquidity preference or money demand function, and the aggregate supply function. The model is analyzed graphically in Figure 8-2. Given the money demand function and the money supply, the rate of interest is determined by the equality of money supply and demand in part A. In part B, investment is determined from the *MEC* schedule once the interest rate is known. Given the level of investment and the saving function in part C, the equilibrium level of income is found at the point on the ordinate where saving equals investment. The equilibrium level of employment is determined from the aggregate supply function in part D.

Algebraically, the model can be represented as follows:

Part A

Money demand	$M_D = \dfrac{Z}{i}$
Money supply	$M_S = M_0$
Equilibrium interest rate	$M_D = M_S \rightarrow \dfrac{Z}{i} = M_0$
	$i = \dfrac{Z}{M_0}$

Part B

Interest rate determined from part A	$i = i_0 = \dfrac{Z}{M_0}$
MEC schedule	$I = ei = \dfrac{eZ}{M_0}$

Part C

Investment determined in part B	$I = \dfrac{eZ}{M_0}$
Saving function	$S = -a + sY$
Equilibrium income	$I = S \rightarrow \dfrac{eZ}{M_0} = -a + sY$
	$Y = \dfrac{a}{s} + \dfrac{eZ}{sM_0}$

Part D

Income determined in part C	$Y = \dfrac{a}{s} + \dfrac{eZ}{sM_0}$
Aggregate supply function	$N = Y^{\alpha}$
Equilibrium employment	$N = \left[\dfrac{a}{s} + \dfrac{eZ}{sM_0} \right]^{\alpha}$

Notice that in this model, equilibrium values for the variables are determined *recursively,* or in succession. First, the rate of interest is determined in the money market. Once the rate of interest is known, investment is determined from the *MEC* schedule. Given the level of investment, equilibrium income is found from the saving function. Given the level of income, equilibrium employment is derived from the aggregate supply function.

While this approach is useful as a first approximation, it disguises some important interrelationships and feedbacks. If the transactions demand for money is taken into account, money demand is a function of the income level as well as of the rate of interest. Thus, the interest rate will depend upon the level of income as well as money supply. It is ironic that Keynes criticized the classical economists for ignoring the impact of the interest rate on the income level, because the simple Keynesian model ignored the effect of the income level on the interest rate. Furthermore, investment may depend upon the level of income and saving on the rate of interest. It is obvious that a complete macroeconomic model must account for the *interdependence* of income and the rate of interest in determining the various macroeconomic relationships.

The Extended Keynesian Model

Suppose that the demand for money is composed of both transactions and speculative demand and, hence, is a function of the level of income as well as the rate of interest. Graphically, such a money demand function is represented as a family of liquidity preference schedules shown in Figure 8-3. The higher the level of income, the greater is the demand for

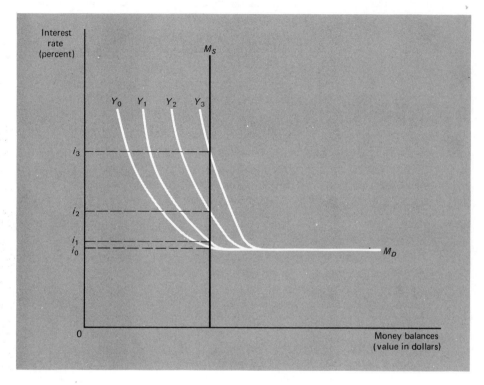

FIGURE 8-3

Money Market Equilibrium at Different Levels of Income

transactions balances and the further to the right the money demand function will lie. The equilibrium rate of interest is determined by the intersection of the money supply schedule with the money demand schedule for each level of money income. Notice that for a fixed money supply, the rate of interest required to achieve money market equilibrium is higher for higher levels of income. As income rises from Y_1 to Y_3, for instance, the interest rate will rise from i_1 to i_3 with the money supply fixed at M_S. At very low levels of income, for instance, Y_0, the transactions demand for money is very small, and the rate of interest may lie in the liquidity trap. This may be true for several different levels of income.

Consider the relationship between the level of income and the rate of interest required to clear the money market given a fixed money supply. This relationship, called the *LM* curve, is shown in Figure 8-4. The total

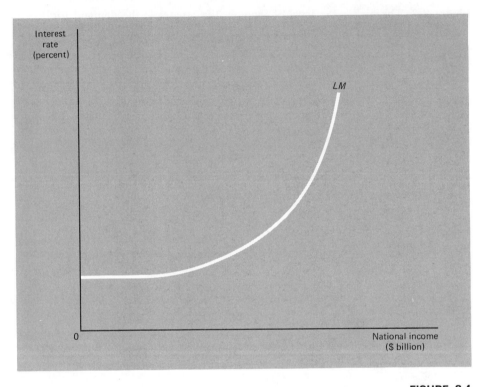

FIGURE 8-4

The LM Curve

demand for money is the sum of the transactions, precautionary, and speculative demands. At low income levels, the transactions and precautionary demand is weak; at low interest rates the speculative demand is infinite. Since the rate of interest is determined by the equilibrium between money demand and money supply, and assuming a fixed-money supply, the *LM* curve will be positively sloped with a horizontal portion to the far left, reflecting the infinite speculative demand for money in the liquidity trap. Because of the transactions demand for money, the equilibrium rate of interest rises with the level of money income, since bond prices must fall if speculative balances are to be released for transactions purposes; but due to the speculative demand for money, the interest rate will not fall below a certain level even when income is very low.

Algebraically, the *LM* function is derived as follows: The demand for transactions and speculative money balances is a function of both income and the interest rate:[1]

$$M_D = lY - ji \quad \text{for } i > i_0$$
$$M_D = \infty \quad \text{for } i = i_0$$

Setting

$$M_D = M_S$$

the *LM* equation becomes[2]

$$lY - ji = M_S \quad \text{for } i > i_0$$
$$Y = \frac{M_S}{l} + \frac{ji}{l} \quad \text{for } i > i_0$$

The *LM* curve relates money income and the rate of interest and assumes a constant money supply.

The *LM* curve shows the rate of interest consistent with financial equilibrium at different income levels. Will these same rates of interest be consistent with national income equilibrium? National income equilibrium occurs when saving is equal to investment. This equilibrium can occur at any income level, depending on the level of investment and saving. If saving and/or investment are functions of the rate of interest, then different rates of interest should be consistent with different levels of investment and saving and, hence, of income. The relationship between the rate of interest and the equilibrium level of national income is called the *IS* curve. The *IS* curve is shown in Figure 8-5. The lower the rate of interest, the greater is the level of investment, and hence, the higher is the level of national income equilibrium consistent with that rate of interest. Consequently, the *IS* curve will be negatively sloped, reflecting the inverse relationship between the rate of interest and national income equilibrium.[3]

Algebraically, the *IS* curve is derived as follows. In the most general

[1] The functional form of the speculative demand for money is changed from hyperbolic to linear to facilitate the algebra of the next section. The reader can test his understanding by formulating the graphical representation of the linear specification.

[2] If $i = i_0$, the level of income is inconsequential, since the speculative demand for money is infinite and hence consistent with money market equilibrium regardless of the level of income.

[3] See Appendix A, pp.449–452 for a more detailed discussion of the shape of the *IS* curve.

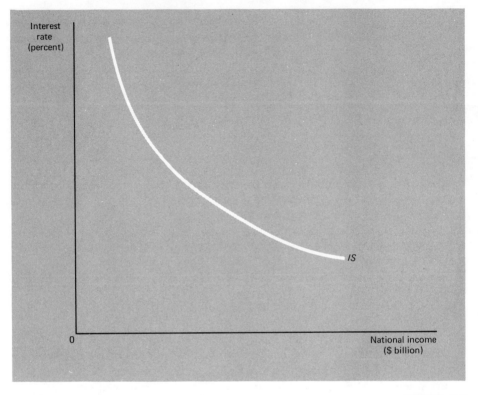

Interest
rate
(percent)

IS

0

National income
($ billion)

FIGURE 8-5

The IS Curve

formulation, saving can be a function of both income and the rate of interest:

$$S = -a + sY + wi$$

Investment is also a function of income and the rate of interest:

$$I = dY + ti$$

In equilibrium, saving is equal to investment,

$$S = I$$

or

$$-a + sY + wi = dY + ti$$

Rearranging terms, the *IS* curve becomes

$$(s - d)Y = a + (t - w)i$$

$$Y = \frac{a}{s - d} + \frac{t - w}{s - d}i$$

Since saving should increase with the rate of interest,

$$w > 0$$

and investment declines with the interest rate,

$$t < 0$$

Assuming

$$0 < s - d < 1$$

that is, the marginal propensity to save exceeds the marginal propensity to invest, then

$$\frac{t - w}{s - d} < 0$$

and the *IS* curve,

$$Y = \frac{a}{s - d} + \frac{t - w}{s - d}i$$

has a negative slope.

The rate of interest and the level of income cannot be in total equilibrium, unless both financial equilibrium (i.e., the clearing of the money market) and national income equilibrium are achieved simultaneously. If the demand for money exceeds the supply, for instance, the rate of interest will rise and national income will fall. If investment exceeds saving, the level of money income will rise and with it, the transactions demand for money and the interest rate. Only when

$$M_D = M_S$$

and

$$I = S$$

will both income and the interest rate be in equilibrium, with no tendency for either to change.

The rate of interest, i_E, and the money income level, Y_E, consistent with both financial and national income equilibrium can be found at the point of intersection of the *IS* and *LM* curves. This general equilibrium, shown in Figure 8-6, involves the simultaneous determination of the interest rate and the level of money income. In general equilibrium, the

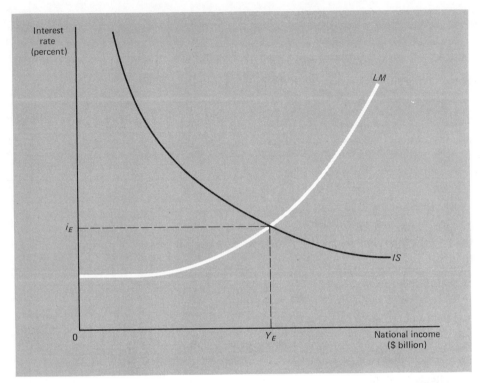

FIGURE 8-6

General Equilibrium of National Income

money market will be cleared, saving will equal investment, and there will be no tendency for income or the interest rate to change unless the equilibrium is disturbed, or *displaced,* by a shift in *IS* or *LM*.

8-3 DISPLACEMENT OF GENERAL EQUILIBRIUM

The equilibrium level of income and the interest rate will be displaced (changed) by a shift of the *IS* or *LM* curve, or both. Policies designed to manipulate the level of income and employment involve a shift in one of the curves.

SHIFTS IN THE LM CURVE

Measures which affect money supply or demand will cause the *LM* curve to shift. With more money available, a lower rate of interest will clear the money market for each income level. For a given *IS* curve, increases in the money supply will result in a lower interest rate and a higher level of money income, as shown in Figure 8-7. Suppose an increase in the money supply causes the *LM* curve to shift from LM_1 to LM_3. The interest

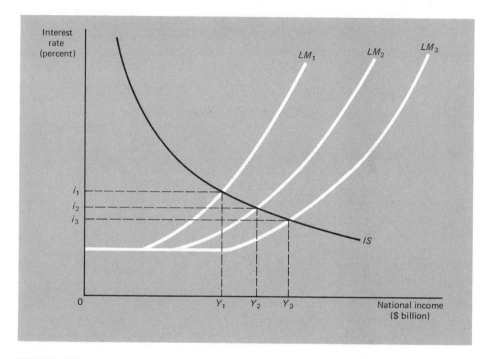

FIGURE 8-7

Impact of Shifts in the LM Curve
on General Equilibrium

rate will fall from i_1 to i_3, and the level of money income will rise from Y_1 to Y_3.

An increase in the demand for money which is due to factors other than changes in income and the interest rate will also cause the *LM* curve to shift.[4] Suppose the widespread introduction of a credit card system reduced the transactions demand for money. At each income level, the demand for money balances would fall and a lower rate of interest would be consistent with equilibrium. This would cause the *LM* curve to shift to the right, and for a given *IS* curve, the interest rate would fall and money

---

[4] Changes in money demand resulting from changes in income and interest rates are represented by *movements along* the LM curve.

income would rise as seen in Figure 8-7. Notice that the effect is the same as if the money supply had increased.

Suppose a prolonged period of tight money caused speculators to alter their expectations about future interest rates. If the structure of interest rates were expected to be generally higher than before, the *LM* curve would shift upward as shown in Figure 8-8. At any interest rate, the

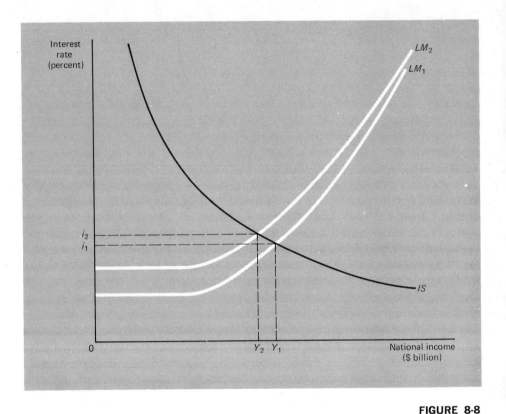

FIGURE 8-8

Impact of Changing Expectations About the Structure of Interest Rates

speculative demand for money would increase, raising the interest rate and causing a decline in the level of income. In Figure 8-8, the upward shift in the *LM* curve causes the interest rate to rise from i_1 to i_2 and the level of income to fall from Y_1 to Y_2. Notice that this same effect will occur during a price inflation if speculators are not subject to money illusion concerning the interest rate. Money interest rates may rise with no change in the speculative demand for money provided that the real rate does not increase. If prices are rising, for any given money rate of interest, the real rate will be lower and the speculative demand for money will be greater.

SHIFTS IN THE *IS* CURVE

Events which affect national income equilibrium will cause shifts in the *IS* curve. Expansionary fiscal policy, by reducing the level of investment required to offset a specified level of saving, causes any national income equilibrium to be consistent with a higher rate of interest than before. This is represented by a rightward shift in the *IS* curve as shown in Figure 8-9. For a fixed *LM* curve, national income will rise and so will the rate of interest. Suppose an increase in government spending causes the *IS* curve to shift rightward from IS_1 to IS_2, as shown in Figure 8-9. Money income will rise from Y_1 to Y_2, and the interest rate will increase from i_1 to i_2.

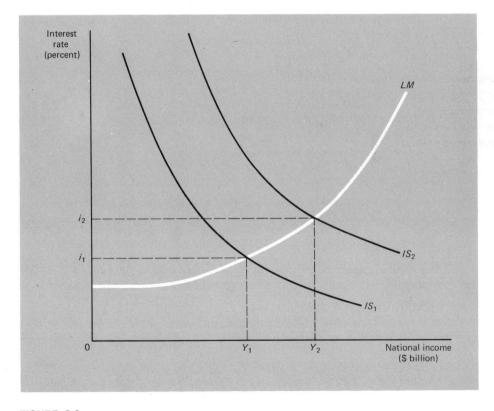

FIGURE 8-9

Impact of a Shift in the IS Curve on General Equilibrium

The *IS* curve may also shift as aggregate demand changes, even if no policy changes are undertaken. Suppose, for instance, that business confidence is undermined by rumors of a cutback in government spending. Pessimistic expectations about future demand may cause the *MEC* to decline for all levels of investment. The impact will be to reduce the level of investment associated with a given rate of interest, and the *IS* schedule will shift leftward. For a fixed *LM* curve, national income and the rate of interest will fall.

A General Equilibrium Multiplier Analysis

Let us consider the algebra of equilibrium displacement. In Chapter 3, we saw that when equilibrium is displaced by an autonomous change in public spending, the ultimate impact on income and spending is greater than the initial change. This *multiplier effect* was derived from the national income equilibrium condition that saving equal investment.

Suppose saving and investment are both functions of income and the rate of interest. Algebraically,

$$S = -a + sY + wi$$
$$I = dY + ti$$

Goverr.ment spending is set at some level, G_0.

In equilibrium,[5]

$$S = I + G$$

or

$$-a + sY + wi = dY + ti + G_0$$

$$Y = \frac{1}{s-d}[a + (t-w)i + G_0]$$

Since the interest rate is assumed to be determined independently by the monetary authorities, then when government spending increases, Δi is assumed to be zero, and

$$\frac{\Delta Y}{\Delta G} = \frac{1}{s-d}$$

[5] Note that since

$$S = Y - C$$

this is equivalent to

$$Y = C + I + G$$

Since

$$s = 1 - b$$

where s is the marginal propensity to save and b is the marginal propensity to consume,

$$\frac{\Delta Y}{\Delta G} = \frac{1}{1 - b - d}$$

which is the same multiplier which we derived in Chapter 3.

The above analysis measures the impact of a displacement of equilibrium through a shift in the IS schedule with a given interest rate. The

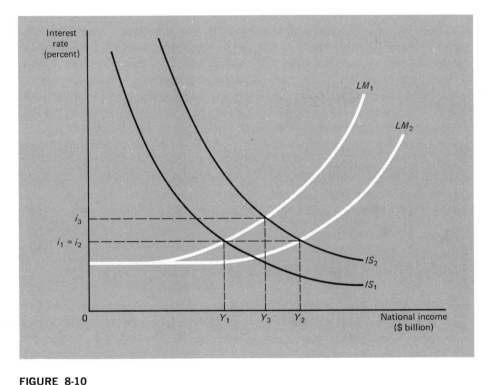

FIGURE 8-10

Shift in IS with Interest Rate Constant

change in income from Y_1 to Y_2 is shown in Figure 8-10. Essentially, we have ignored the impact of the increase in income on the demand for money and, hence, on the interest rate. If the complete model were taken into account, that is, if the money market had been examined, our analysis would have predicted a smaller change in income, from Y_1 to Y_3, as the interest rate rises with income along the function LM_1 to i_3.

Suppose we drop the assumption that the interest rate is independent of the fiscal action (increase in government spending) and is determined in the money market. Assuming the demand for money is a function of income and the interest rate[6] and that the money supply is fixed,

$$M_D = lY - ji$$
$$M_S = M_0$$

then equilibrium in the money market occurs, where

$$M_D = M_S$$

or

$$lY - ji = M_0$$

Now we have an equation which expresses the rate of interest in terms of income. It can be expressed as

$$i = \frac{l}{j} Y - \frac{M_0}{j}$$

Substituting the value of i, as determined in the money market, into the national income equation,

$$Y = \left(\frac{1}{1 - b - d}\right)[(t - w)i + G_0]$$
$$= \left(\frac{1}{1 - b - d}\right)\left[\frac{(t - w)lY}{j} + \frac{(w - t)M_0}{j} + G_0\right]$$

we can now determine the impact of an increase in government spending if the money supply is held constant and the interest rate is allowed to rise to maintain money market equilibrium as the transactions demand for money increases.

Expressing the model in terms of changes and recalling that

$$\Delta M = 0$$

then

$$\Delta Y = \left(\frac{1}{1 - b - d}\right)\left[\frac{(t - w)l}{j} \Delta Y + \Delta G\right]$$

[6] We have ignored the liquidity trap in this example.

Letting

$$\mu = \frac{(t - w)l}{j}$$

then

$$\frac{\Delta Y}{\Delta G} = \frac{1}{1 - b - d - \mu}$$

Since the signs of w, l, and j are positive, while the sign of t is negative, then the sign of μ is clearly negative. Thus, when the impact of the change in income on the transactions demand for money and the interest rate is taken into account, the size of the multiplier is reduced. The parameter μ can be called the *monetary effect* of the change in demand.

If the government undertakes an expansionary fiscal policy without increasing the money supply, interest rates will rise, discouraging investment and reducing the expansionary impact of the fiscal operation. Since we have assumed no increase in taxes, the expenditure increase must have been financed by the issue of debt, which would of course have the effect of reducing bond prices and raising interest rates. Suppose, however, the fiscal operation were accompanied by an increase in the money supply just large enough to prevent the interest rate from rising. Such a program is shown graphically in Figure 8-10. If a shift in IS from IS_1 to IS_2 is accompanied by a shift in LM from LM_1 to LM_2, then income will rise from Y_1 to Y_2 as predicted by the simple multiplier analysis in which the interest rate was assumed to be determined independently of the level of national income.

The simple multiplier analysis may be relevant to current policy planning if the monetary authorities view the rate of interest rather than the money supply as the primary policy instrument. Suppose, for example, it is determined to undertake expansionary fiscal policy and neutral monetary policy. If monetary authorities view the interest rate as the relevant policy instrument, they will increase the money supply as the expansion takes place to keep the interest rate at its previous level. If, on the other hand, the money supply is viewed as the appropriate policy instrument, the monetary authorities will not increase the money supply and will allow the rate of interest to rise. Although both types of behavior can be called neutral, the impact of the fiscal operation on national income will be greater if it is financed totally or in part by money creation rather than bond issue. Consequently, policy planners must be careful to specify what they mean by monetary neutrality before they can forecast the multiplier effect of a fiscal operation when monetary policy is neutral.

The question of whether the money supply or the interest rate should be the primary planning instrument for monetary policy has been a major source of controversy between Milton Friedman, a monetary theorist, and such neo-Keynesian economists as Walter Heller. Friedman, adhering to the quantity theory of money, argues that not only is the level of national income determined by the money supply, but also that the money supply should be the principal policy instrument for economic stabilization. Heller, on the other hand, views national income as essentially determined by aggregate demand and feels that monetary policy should essentially be effectuated by interest rate changes.[7] We shall consider Friedman's macroeconomic theory in more detail in Chapter 9.

8-4   THE IMPACT OF ALTERNATIVE ECONOMIC POLICIES

MONETARY VERSUS FISCAL POLICY

As we have seen, any change in fiscal policy will have a monetary impact since changes in income produce changes in the demand for money. In addition, changes in the money supply will affect income as changes in the rate of interest influence aggregate demand. In the preceding chapters we have suggested that the impact of monetary policy on demand is less reliable than the impact of fiscal policy. In particular, demand may be insensitive to changes in the money supply, especially in periods of recession.

Let us assume, for the moment, however, that monetary policy can be used effectively as a substitute for fiscal policy for purposes of economic stabilization. Suppose the policy maker desires to increase the level of income and employment as shown in Figure 8-11. Note that we have reversed the axes of the IS–LM diagram to make it comparable with the aggregate supply function. When the IS schedule is IS_1 and the LM schedule is LM_1, equilibrium is at Y_E with employment N_E and the rate of interest is i_E. Full employment is N_F, so the desired change in income is $Y_F - Y_E$.

The target level of income can be attained by either fiscal or monetary policy. However, while the impact on income will be the same, the effect on other variables in the system will be different. An increase in government spending sufficient to shift IS to IS_2 will achieve the target income level. If there is no increase in the money supply, the interest rate will rise to i_2. If monetary policy is used, a shift in LM to LM_2 will also produce the desired change with no change in IS. In the absence of any change in fiscal policy, the interest rate will fall to i_1.

If fiscal policy alone is used to engineer an expansion, demand in

---

[7] Heller, like most neo-Keynesians, often questions the efficacy of monetary policy of any sort and would urge more reliance on tax and expenditure policy for controlling aggregate demand.

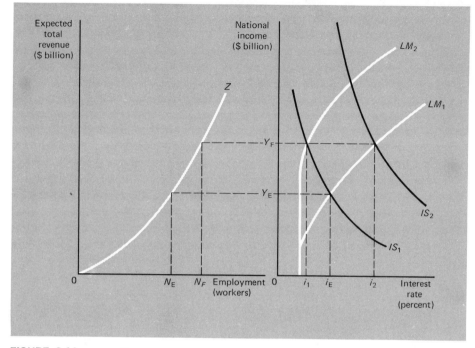

FIGURE 8-11

Use of Monetary and Fiscal Policy
to Close a Deflationary Gap

the public sector will increase. Demand in those sectors sensitive to changes in the interest rate (investment and consumption) may also rise but not as much as if the interest rate had not increased. Any increase in consumption and investment will be due to the effect induced by the change in income, but the effect will be impeded by the rising interest rate.

Because the impact of an increase in public spending is smaller when the greater proportion is financed from taxes, the change in government spending required to close any deflationary gap will be greater if financed from taxes than if financed by a bond issue or money creation. Consider the ways in which a public spending increase can be financed as shown in Table 8-1.

Closing the deflationary gap by a "balanced budget" increase in spending increases public spending at the expense of both consumption and investment, depending on the incidence of the tax. A bond issue will only restrict consumption if the latter is affected by the rise in interest rates and will have the greatest impact on investment. If financed by money creation, the smallest increase in public spending will be required to close the gap

TABLE 8-1

Methods of Financing an Increase in Government Spending
to Close a Deflationary Gap

	Required Increase in Public Spending	Increase in Consumption	Increase in Investment	Increase in Interest Rate
Tax finance				
Personal income tax	largest	smallest	largest	intermediate
Corporate income tax	largest	intermediate*	smallest	intermediate
Bond issue	intermediate	intermediate	smallest	largest
Money creation	smallest	largest	largest	smallest

* If the tax causes a reduction in dividends and hence personal income.

since there will be no increase in interest rates, and consequently, consumption and investment will rise by the greatest amount.

Monetary policy used alone can also close a deflationary gap if aggregate demand is sufficiently elastic to changes in the money supply. As shown in Figure 8-11, as LM shifts from LM_1 to LM_2, the rate of interest falls from i_E to i_1. Thus, the expansion in income is attributable to increase in investment and consumption with no increase in public spending.

If monetary and fiscal policy were combined so that the deflationary gap could be closed with no increase in interest rates, then the traditional multiplier analysis would apply. The change in income is due to an autonomous change in government spending with no initial (noninduced) changes in the other sectors. In Figure 8-12 the deflationary gap $Y_F - Y_E$ can be closed with no impact on the interest rate by an increase in IS from IS_1 to IS_2 coupled with an increase in the money supply which will shift the LM curve from LM_1 to LM_2.

We have seen that under the assumption that monetary policy can be used as effectively as fiscal policy to control aggregate demand, the policies will have different impacts on the distribution of spending among consumption, investment, and the public sector. Furthermore, the means by which a public expenditure change is financed will also affect the distribution of spending. Consequently, when deciding whether to use monetary or fiscal policy for stabilization purposes, the planner must consider not only the efficiency or reliability of his policy instruments for controlling demand, but also their distributional impact on spending in the various sectors of the economy. In general, monetary policy relies more heavily for stabilization on changes in investment than does fiscal policy. Thus, a tight money policy is more likely to cause a cutback in investment spend-

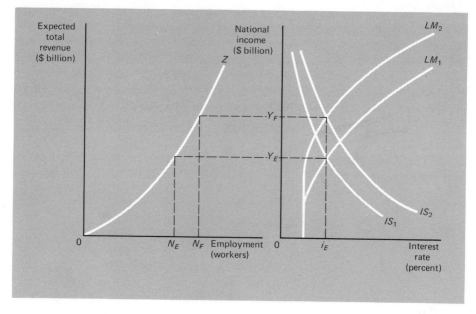

FIGURE 8-12

Closing a Deflationary Gap with No Change
in Interest Rate

ing than a personal income tax increase or a reduction in public spending.
Of course, an increase in corporate income taxes can also precipitate a
decline in investment expenditure.

EVALUATING MACROECONOMIC POLICY

Consider a simple macroeconomic model which takes into account
conditions in the money market. Such a model can be used to design alternative programs for closing a deflationary gap. Assume the following
relationships:

$$Y = C + I + G$$
$$C = 100 + 0.6Y$$
$$I = 0.2Y - 50i$$
$$M_D = 0.25Y - 30i \quad \text{for } i > 1$$
$$\quad\quad = \infty \quad\quad\quad\quad \text{for } i \leq 1$$
$$M_S = 65$$
$$G = 100$$

Substituting the consumption and investment functions into the national income identity, the *IS* curve is derived:

$$Y = C + I + G$$
$$Y = 200 + 0.8\,Y - 50i$$
$$0.2\,Y = 200 - 50i$$
$$Y = 1000 - 250i$$

The *LM* curve is found by setting money demand (M_D) equal to the money supply (M_S):

$$M_D = M_S$$
$$0.25\,Y - 30i = 65$$
$$Y = 260 + 120i \qquad \text{for } i > 1$$
$$M_D = \infty \qquad \text{for } i \leq 1$$

Assuming we are not in the liquidity trap[8] and solving the equations for the *IS* and *LM* curves simultaneously,

$$Y = 1000 - 250i$$
$$Y = 260 + 120i$$

the equilibrium level of income is found to be 500, and the interest rate is 2.

Suppose that the full-employment level of income is 600, so that the desired change in income is 100. If the money supply is held constant, what change in government spending will be required to close the deflationary gap?

Letting

$$Y = 600$$

allowing for a change in *G,* and substituting into our model, the *IS* curve becomes

$$600 = 200 + 0.8(600) - 50i + \Delta G$$
$$50i - 80 = \Delta G$$

and the *LM* curve is

---

[8] If in the solution, i is less than 1, establish the interest rate at 1 and use the *IS* equation to find Y.

$$600 = 260 + 120i$$
$$120i = 340$$
$$i = 2.83$$

Since the equilibrium rate of interest can be found from the *LM* curve when the equilibrium level of income is known, we can now determine the required change in *G* from *IS*:

$$\Delta G = 50(2.83) - 80$$
$$= 141.5 - 80$$
$$= 61.5$$

The required change in *G* could also have been found from the multiplier analysis of the preceding section. Recall that when M_s is assumed constant,

$$\frac{\Delta Y}{\Delta G} = \frac{1}{1 - b - d - \mu}$$

where μ is the "monetary effect" reflecting the impact of the increase in demand on the interest rate.

In our model

$$b = 0.6$$
$$d = 0.2$$

and

$$\mu = \frac{(t - w)l}{j}$$
$$t = -50$$
$$w = 0$$
$$l = 0.25$$
$$j = 30$$

so that

$$\mu = \frac{-50}{30}(0.25) = -0.415$$

Therefore,

$$\frac{\Delta Y}{\Delta G} = \frac{1}{1 - 0.6 - 0.2 + 0.415} = \frac{1}{0.615}$$

To induce a change in *Y* of 100,

$$\Delta G = 61.5$$

Suppose the monetary authorities decide to neutralize the impact of the fiscal operation on credit conditions and increase the money supply to hold the interest rate constant at 2 while income rises to 600. Letting M_S vary and substituting in the LM equation,

$$0.25(600) - 30(2) = 65 + \Delta M_S$$

or

$$\Delta M_S = 25$$

To find the required change in G, substitute in the IS equation:

$$600 = 200 + 0.8(600) - 50(2) + \Delta G$$

or

$$\Delta G = 20$$

Notice that

$$\frac{\Delta Y}{\Delta G} = 5$$

This result is the same as we would have obtained from the simple national income model which ignores the monetary effect. That multiplier gives

$$\frac{\Delta Y}{\Delta G} = \frac{1}{1 - b - d} = \frac{1}{1 - 0.6 - 0.2} = 5$$

Notice that in this case the change in the money supply required to neutralize the impact of the spending increase on the interest rate was greater than the spending increase itself. Thus, even if policy planners had financed the entire increase in government spending by money creation, the rate of interest would still have risen slightly, and the change in G required to close the deflationary gap would have been slightly larger.

Finally, suppose policy planners desired to achieve the target level of income using monetary policy only. From the IS curve, the required rate of interest can be found:

$$Y = 200 + 0.8Y - 50i$$
$$600 = 200 + 0.8(600) - 50i$$
$$50i = 80$$
$$i = 1.6$$

The change in M_s required to achieve this rate of interest when income is 600 can be found from the LM equation,

$$0.25\,Y - 30i = 65 + \Delta M_s$$
$$0.25(600) - 30(1.6) = 65 + \Delta M_s$$
$$\Delta M_s = 37$$

Notice that, in this particular model, the highest level of income which can be achieved using monetary policy alone is 750. Because the demand for money becomes infinite at an interest rate of 1, the interest rate cannot fall below this level no matter how great the increase in money supply. Consequently, from the IS curve,

$$0.2\,Y = 200 - 50$$
$$Y = 750$$

Now we are ready to evaluate the impact of the three policies used to effectuate an increase in income of 100 as shown in Table 8-2. Notice

TABLE 8-2

Impact of Alternative Policies for Increasing Income by 100

Policy	Impact					
	ΔY	ΔG	Δi	ΔM_s	ΔI	ΔC
Government expenditure increase (money supply unchanged)	100	61.5	+0.83	0	−21.5	60
Government expenditure increase (interest rate unchanged)	100	20	0	25	+20	60
Money supply increase (government spending unchanged)	100	0	−0.4	37	+40	60

that the greater the change in the money supply, the smaller is the proportion of the total change in income attributable to government spending and the larger is the increase in investment. Since the change in consumption is always 60 and the change in income 100, then the change in investment plus government spending must be 40. Thus, the greater the change in government spending, the smaller is the change in investment.

In this section we assumed that monetary and fiscal policy are equally effective and reliable stabilizing instruments. However, much of the controversy about the use and design of macroeconomic policy centers around the effectiveness of the various policy instruments. The discussion involves different assumptions about behavior as well as the hypothetical elasticities or slopes of the *IS* and *LM* curves with respect to interest rates and changes in GNP.

To gain further insight into the appropriate monetary-fiscal policy mix, in Chapter 9 we shall examine some alternative models of national income equilibrium.

QUESTIONS FOR STUDY AND REVIEW

1. Refer to the model on p. 223 of the text:

(a) Construct a diagram to show the equilibrium level of income.

(b) What would be the effect of increasing M_S to 125?

(c) If the full-employment level of income is 800, can it be reached in this model by increasing the money supply alone? Explain.

(d) What would be the impact of a shift in the investment demand function so that

$$I = 0.2 \ Y - 20i$$

2. How would the following events affect the equilibrium level of national income and the rate of interest:

(a) increasing the velocity of circulation,

(b) increasing corporate income taxes,

(c) increasing government spending financed by debt issue,

(d) open market purchasing by the Federal Reserve,

(e) increasing unemployment compensation financed from general tax revenues,

(f) increasing unemployment compensation financed by money creation?

3. Keynes criticized the classical economists for failing to recognize that the rate of interest is an important determinant of the level of income. Can a similar criticism be made of his model? Explain.

4. Show how the introduction of monetary considerations affect the multiplier analysis developed in Chapter 3.

5. Both the *IS* curve and the *LM* curve are derived from macroeconomic equilibrium relationships, yet neither presents a complete picture of macroeconomic equilibrium. Explain.

6. Assume that monetary policy can be used effectively as a substitute for fiscal policy for purposes of economic stabilization. Compare the effects of the two policies on consumption, saving, investment, and rate of growth.

ADDITIONAL READING

HANSEN, ALVIN H., *A Guide to Keynes.* Book 4. New York: McGraw-Hill Book Company, Inc., 1953, Chapters 7 and 9.

... ...

9

Some Models
of National Income
Determination

Having incorporated the financial sector into the Keynesian model of income determination, it is interesting to view it in the perspective of some alternative models. *The General Theory* was conceived by Keynes as a refutation of what he called classical economics. Although it had many historical antecedents this was essentially the analysis described by A. C. Pigou in his *Theory of Unemployment*. Following the publication of *The General Theory*, the Keynesian model was the subject of a lively and critical debate among the economists of the so-called classical tradition. In this chapter we shall examine the classical model and its similarities to and differences from the Keynesian model.

A more recent attack on Keynesian economics has come from a group of economists who believe that the quantity of money, rather than aggregate demand, is the essential determinant of national income. The spokesman for this group, Milton Friedman, had a particularly important influence on economic policy during the Nixon Administration. In examining the Friedman model and its relation to the Keynesian analysis, particular emphasis will be placed on the implications for economic policy.

9-1 KEYNES AND THE CLASSICS

Following the publication of *The General Theory* and after a reasonable time had been allowed for it to be absorbed and understood by the scholars of economics, it became fashionable to remark that Keynes had not said anything new, that all the Keynesian results could have been derived from the classical analysis of Pigou. No one felt this more strongly than Pigou himself, who argued that Keynes had introduced a new twist in his "liquidity trap," but that essentially the analysis was the same as his own.

In analyzing the relationship between the classical and Keynesian models, it is important to bear in mind that not only the equilibrium, but also the means by which the equilibrium is reached is important. The classical analysis begins with the assumption of full employment, based on Say's Law. It then proceeds to examine the relationship between the macroeconomic variables in this full-employment equilibrium. The Keynesian approach, on the other hand, presumes that the level of employment is determined by aggregate demand. If it can be shown that full employment will be achieved automatically (i.e., without government intervention) within the framework of a Keynesian system, one might conclude that this system is equivalent to the classical model. It is true that, in this case, the equilibrium is the same for the two models, but the sequence in which the variables adjust to equilibrium is different. Because of the differences in the adjustment process, the policy implications for a disequilibrium situation are different for the two models.

THE CLASSICAL MODEL

In the classical model, attention is focused on the labor market for determining the "real" variables in the system.[1] Assuming that the real wage will always adjust to clear the labor market, real wages and employment are simultaneously determined there.

To maximize profits, firms will hire workers until the contribution of the last worker to total revenue, his marginal value product, is just equal to the money wage, or

$$p \times MP = w$$

Equivalently, firms will hire workers until the marginal productivity of labor is equal to the real wage (the money wage divided by the product price), or

$$\frac{w}{p} = MP$$

[1] Since the classical model was always elaborated in real terms, we shall compare it with a Keynesian model developed in real terms. Alternatively, the classical model can also be developed in money terms and compared with a Keynesian model with the variables in money units. The comparison produces the same similarities and differences, regardless of how the variables are expressed. Since the analysis presented here is for comparative purposes only and not for forecasting, it is legitimate to work with the real relationships of the models.

If labor supply is also a function of the real wage, then both the demand for and supply of labor depends on the real wage. In such a market both the level of employment and real wages are simultaneously determined. Algebraically,

$$\frac{w}{p} = MP = f'(N_D) \qquad\qquad \text{demand for labor}$$

$$\frac{w}{p} = g(N_S) \qquad\qquad \text{supply of labor}$$

$$N_D = N_S \qquad\qquad \text{equilibrium condition}$$

In this three-equation model, the three variables w/p, N_S, and N_D can be determined.

The determination of employment and output in a classical model is shown graphically in Figure 9-1. In Figure 9-1(A), the level of employment and the real wage are determined in the labor market by the equilibrium between labor supply and demand. Once the level of employment is determined in the labor market, aggregate output (or real income) can be found from the production function in Figure 9-1(B).

In the classical analysis, this simple model completely describes the determination of real GNP. The level of prices and interest rates can be found by looking at monetary and financial relationships, but these do not enter into the determination of real income and employment.

The quantity theory of money is used to explain price level changes. Given the money supply, the level of money GNP or national income can be found. The quantity theory states that the money value of all transactions must exactly equal the total quantity of money in circulation multiplied by the number of times the money changes hands, or the *velocity of circulation*. Algebraically,

$$MV = pT$$

where

$$M = \text{money supply}$$
$$V = \text{velocity of circulation}$$
$$p = \text{price level}$$
$$T = \text{total transactions}$$

Assuming that transactions are proportional to real income, y,

$$T = \lambda y$$

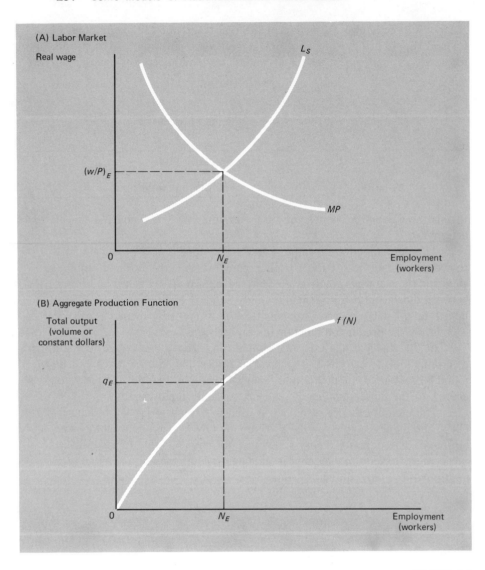

(A) Labor Market

Real wage

L_S

$(w/P)_E$

MP

0

N_E

Employment
(workers)

(B) Aggregate Production Function

Total output
(volume or
constant dollars)

$f(N)$

q_E

0

N_E

Employment
(workers)

. **FIGURE** 9-1

Determination of Aggregate Output in a Classical Model

then

$$MV = p\lambda y$$

or

$$M = KY$$

where

$$K = \frac{\lambda}{V}$$

and

$$Y = py$$

where Y is money income.

Quantity theorists assume K to be independent of changes in any of the macroeconomic variables. Since real income, y, is determined by the level of employment, then changes in the money supply, M, must result in proportional changes in the price level. While monetary policy may be useful in controlling prices, it has no impact on real GNP. Note that real GNP is also unaffected by price level changes, since it is determined by conditions in the labor market.

The rate of interest, as well as the distribution of real GNP between consumption and investment, is determined in the bond market. Investment, or the supply of bonds, is a function of the interest rate. Recalling that interest rates move inversely with bond prices, the supply of bonds increases as interest rates fall (bond prices rise) as shown in Figure 9-2. Saving, or the demand for bonds, rises with the interest rate (falls with the bond price). Equilibrium in the bond market determines not only the rate of interest, but also the levels of saving and investment, which are always brought into equality in this market.[2] Algebraically,

$S = S(i)$ saving function

$I = e(i)$ investment demand function

$S = I$ equilibrium condition

These three equations are sufficient to find the three unknowns, S, I, and i. Notice that since

$$Y = C + S$$

the equilibrium level of consumption is also determined in this market, given the level of national income.

Since the level of employment and real income are determined in the labor market, the rate of interest, saving, investment, and consumption do not have any impact at all on these variables. While the bond market may be of interest to students of finance, it has nothing to do with the analysis of income determination in the short run. Since it does determine the level

---

[2] This theory of interest is analyzed critically and in more detail in Chapter 7.

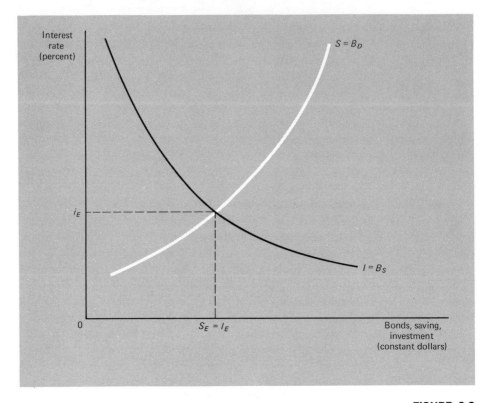

FIGURE 9-2

Bond Market Equilibrium in a Classical Model

of investment, however, the interest rate will affect the rate of growth and hence labor productivity, real wages, and output in the long run.

To summarize, the classical model may be represented algebraically in seven equations:

$$\left.\begin{array}{l} \dfrac{w}{p} = MP = f'(N) \\[2mm] \dfrac{w}{p} = g(N) \end{array}\right\} \quad \begin{array}{l}\text{labor market}\\\text{equilibrium}\end{array}$$

$$\left.\begin{array}{l} y = q(N) \\[1mm] Y = \lambda VM \end{array}\right\} \quad \begin{array}{l}\text{real income}\\\text{money income}\end{array}$$

$$\left.\begin{array}{l} S = S(i) \\[1mm] I = e(i) \\[1mm] S = I \end{array}\right\} \quad \begin{array}{l}\text{bond market}\\\text{equilibrium}\end{array}$$

Seven variables can be determined: real wages, employment, real income, money income, saving, investment, and the rate of interest. Given the identities,

$$py \equiv Y$$

and

$$Y - S \equiv C$$

the price level and consumption can also be found.

THE KEYNESIAN AND CLASSICAL MODELS COMPARED

The Keynesian model has been described in detail in Chapter 8. Table 9-1 provides a brief summary and comparison of the way in which the various macroeconomic variables and relationships are explained in the two models.

TABLE 9-1

The Classical and Keynesian Models Compared

Macroeconomic Variable or Relationship	Determination in a Classical Model	Determination in a Keynesian Model
Employment	labor market	aggregate demand
Real income or output	employment	employment
Money income	employment/money supply	aggregate demand
Prices	money supply	aggregate demand/money wage
Interest rate	bond market	money market
Saving/consumption	interest rate	income
Investment	interest rate	interest rate
$S = I$ (equilibrium)	bond market/interest rate	national income
Real wages	labor market	level of output
Best way to stimulate employment	reduce wages	increase aggregate demand

In the classical model, full employment was assured by the adjustment of wages which would clear the labor market. Since both the demand for and supply of labor are determined by the real wage, the condition for achievement of full employment (labor market equilibrium) is that real wages must be flexible in the downward direction when labor is in excess supply. Thus, in this model, attention is focused on the labor market and, in particular, wages. Policies designed to maintain full employment were essentially aimed at promoting competitive conditions in the labor market and at convincing labor that the only way full employment could be attained in a recession was for labor to accept lower wages.

The level of output was simply a function of employment. Changes in the money supply would not affect employment or real output but only the level of prices. Investment, consumption, and the real rate of interest were determined independently in the bond market. While the level of investment affected the rate of growth and, hence, the future relationship between output and employment, conditions in the bond market had no effect on employment and output in the short run.

Keynes argued that full employment was not assured by the wage-adjustment process, and that, on the contrary, employment was determined by aggregate demand rather than the reverse. He argued that negotiations between labor and management are not generally based on *real* wages, but on money wages. Real wages are determined by the marginal productivity of labor which in turn depends upon the level of employment.

Consider a period in which demand is falling, due, let us presume, to a reduction in public spending. Firms begin to lay off workers and labor in turn agrees to work for lower wages. The reaction to this by firms may be to reduce product prices, to increase sales, and conceivably, the real wage may rise. Keynes observed that

> . . . I think, that the change in real wages associated with a change in money-wages, so far from being usually in the same direction [as the classical economists assumed], is almost always in the opposite direction when money-wages are rising, that is to say, it will be found that real wages are falling; and when money wages are falling, real wages will be rising. This is because, in the short period, falling money-wages and rising real wages are each, for independent reasons, likely to accompany decreasing employment; labor being readier to accept wage-cuts when employment is falling off, yet real wages inevitably rising in the same circumstances on account of the increasing marginal return to a given capital equipment when output is diminished.[3]

Since wage bargains affect money wages rather than real wages, there is no assurance that labor-management negotiations can assure labor market equilibrium (full employment). Consider the underemployment equilibrium shown in Figure 9-3. Suppose real wages are $(w/p)'$, employ-

---

[3] J. M. Keynes, *The General Theory of Employment, Interest, and Money* (New York: Harcourt Brace Jovanovich, Inc., 1965), p. 10. Published originally by Macmillan & Co., Ltd., 1936.

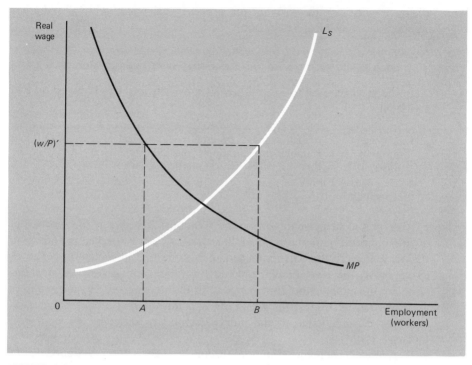

FIGURE 9-3

An Underemployment Equilibrium

ment is at A, and AB workers are unemployed. Since the real wage is determined by marginal productivity, the impact of a money wage cut will simply be a corresponding reduction in prices, with no change in the real wage and no change in the level of employment.

The only way real wages can be reduced is for the level of employment to increase, thereby reducing marginal labor productivity. Note that the sequence in which events occur is crucial. In the classical model, real wage cuts must precede increases in the level of employment, while Keynes argued that employment must increase before real wages can fall. The only way in which the level of employment can be expected to increase, in the Keynesian view, is for aggregate demand to increase. Only then will firms find it profitable to hire more workers, and only then will marginal labor productivity and real wages fall.

Since real wages, not money wages, must fall to assure labor market equilibrium, money wage cuts are neither necessary nor sufficient for full employment. The only way full employment can be attained is for aggregate demand to increase to the level required to induce firms to employ all those who wish to work. In the process, real wages will fall, whether money wages have declined or not.

EQUILIBRIUM ANALYSIS OF THE KEYNESIAN AND CLASSICAL MODELS

Classical rebuttal to *The General Theory* was essentially based on two arguments:

1. Money wage reductions will eventually cause real wages to fall and produce full employment, although the adjustment process may be different from that originally hypothesized in classical theory.
2. Downward rigidity of money wages is a principal cause of labor market disequilibrium.

A graphical presentation of the relationship between the Keynesian national income equilibrium and the classical labor market is shown in Figure 9-4. Here the Keynesian model is described in real terms. The *IS* curve shows the level of real income for which real saving and real investment are equated at different real rates of interest. The *LM* curve shows the real rates of interest for which the demand for real money balances is equal to the real value of the money supply for different levels of real income.[4]

Aggregate demand is in equilibrium in Figure 9-4(A) where the *IS* and *LM* curves intersect.[5] The demand for labor, N_E, is then found from the production function in Figure 9-4(B). The marginal productivity schedule, derived from the production function,[6] together with the labor supply function determine labor market conditions in Figure 9-4(C).

The equilibrium level of employment, N_E, represents an underemployment situation. When employment is N_E, the real wage is $(w/p)_E$. At that wage the labor supply is N_S and $(N_S - N_E)$ workers are unemployed. Suppose workers agree to accept cuts in money wages. Can full employment be achieved in this manner without any autonomous increases in aggregate demand? If so, the classical position would presumably be vindicated.

---

[4] Notice that by abstracting from price level changes for the *LM* relationship we implicitly assume that speculators are not subject to money illusion with respect to the interest rate and, therefore, that the real interest rate at which the liquidity trap occurs is independent of price level changes. In the analysis using money-valued variables, we assumed that speculators are subject to money illusion with respect to the interest rate, and therefore that the money interest rate at which the liquidity trap occurs is independent of price level changes.

These assumptions can be relaxed in either case by allowing the *LM* curve to shift perpendicular to the interest rate axis in response to price level changes.

[5] Note that the axes measuring income and the interest rate are inverted from the traditional position.

[6] Marginal productivity for any level of employment is the slope of the production function (total productivity function) there.

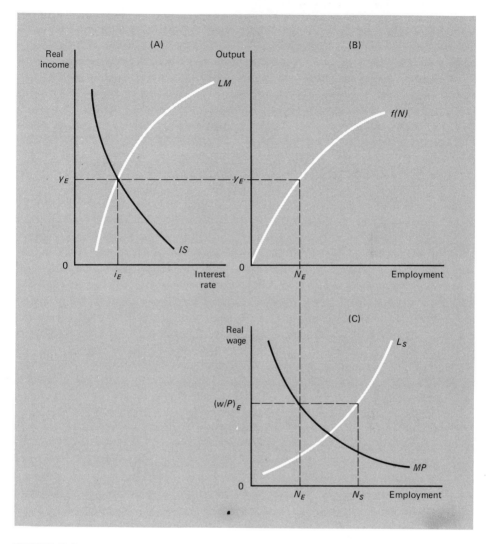

FIGURE 9-4

Equilibrium Analysis of the Keynesian and the Classical Models

If the real wage, w/p, is determined by the level of employment, N_E, then the initial impact of a decline in money wages, w, will be a reduction in prices. If the money supply is fixed, a fall in prices will cause the LM curve to shift upward,[7] as shown in Figure 9-5. The price reduction causes

---

[7] Note that the upward shift is equivalent to a rightward shift if the income and interest rate axes had not been inverted.

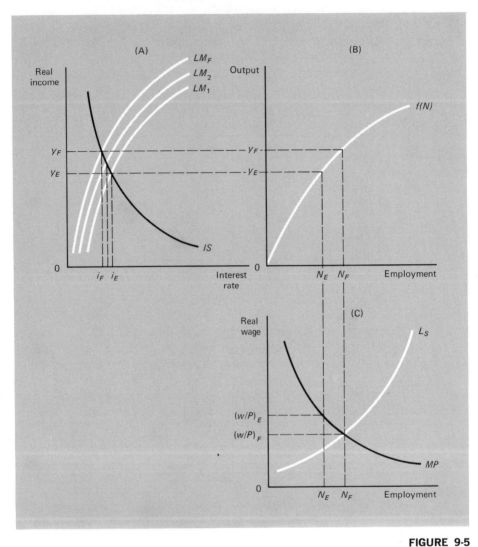

FIGURE 9-5

Impact of Money Wage Cuts on National Income Equilibrium

an increase in the real value of the money supply and a decline in the interest rate.[8] Aggregate demand increases, inducing an increase in the level of employment and a reduction in the real wage. The process continues as the money wage is bid down until full employment is attained.

[8] The effect is the same as if the money demand for money declined in a money value model. This will occur as money wages and money income fall.

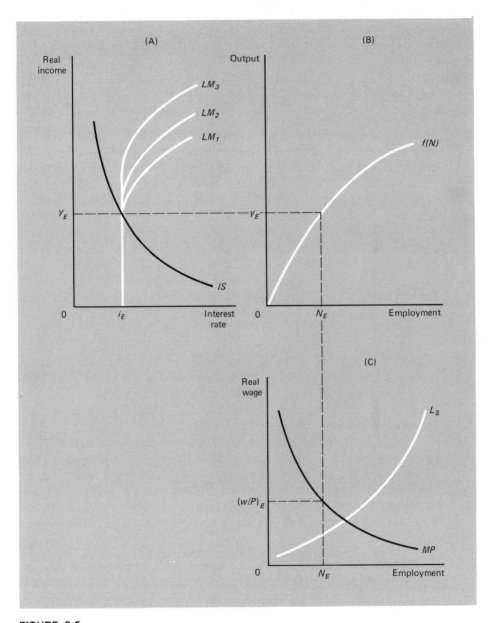

FIGURE 9-6
Impact of Money Wage Cuts in the Liquidity Trap

Viewed in a Keynesian framework, the impact of money wage cuts is exactly as described by the classical model. Money wage reductions cause real wages to decline and the level of employment to increase. Notice that if workers resist money wage cuts in the underemployment situation depicted in Figure 9-4, full employment will only be attainable by fiscal policy, which causes *IS* to shift rightward, or increases in the money supply, causing *LM* to shift upward.

The mechanism by which money wage cuts can stimulate employment is by the impact of falling prices on money market equilibrium. As prices fall, the real value of the money supply increases, causing the interest rate to fall. Thus, money wage cuts can be no more effective than expansionary monetary policy as a mechanism for stimulating employment.

Suppose interest rates fall to the level at which speculators uniformly expect bond prices to fall. When this happens, all increases in the money supply will be held as speculative balances (since no one will want to buy bonds) and the economy will be in a "liquidity trap." Increases in the real value of the money supply associated with falling prices will have no impact on the rate of interest and, hence, will have no impact on aggregate demand.[9]

In Figure 9-6, national income equilibrium is shown by the intersection of *IS* and *LM* in the vertical portion of the *LM* curve. As prices fall and *LM* shifts upward, the equilibrium level of income is unaffected. In this case, wage cuts will not affect the level of employment. The only route to full employment in this situation is to undertake expansionary fiscal policy which will shift the *IS* curve upward to the right.

Pigou, in rebutting the Keynesian position that wage cuts will not necessarily produce full employment, argued that, even in a liquidity trap, falling wages and the concomitant decline in prices would stimulate employment. He argued that as prices fell, the real value of assets with fixed-money value held by creditors would increase, causing creditors to feel wealthier and to increase their level of consumption.[10] Thus, falling prices

---

[9] If speculators are subject to a money illusion concerning the interest rate, a price deflation should result in a rightward shift of the *LM* curve (away from the income axis), causing the liquidity trap to occur at a higher real rate of interest. This is because, as prices fall, the real rate of interest corresponding to a given money rate rises. In this case a price deflation will cause speculators to sell bonds and hold more money balances at each real rate of interest, and consequently, the impact of the deflation may be to raise real interest rates and actually reduce the level of aggregate demand.

[10] Note that by this reasoning, debtors should feel poorer and their consumption should decline. Pigou argued, however, that since government is a net debtor, the private sector is a net creditor, so that the net effect of falling prices on private wealth and consumption is positive.

would cause the *IS* curve to shift rightward (as autonomous consumption increases), and income and employment would rise.

Many economists doubt that a price deflation would ever result in this *Pigou effect*. Keynes argued that workers are subject to a money illusion with respect to wages. If money wages and prices fall, workers are likely to reduce consumption, because a decline in money wages makes them feel poorer even if real wages are unchanged. In Chapter 5 we discussed other reasons why a price deflation might discourage rather than stimulate consumption of real goods and services. And the empirical evidence does not indicate a very strong or reliable effect on consumption from changes in the value of liquid assets.[11]

EVALUATION OF THE CONTROVERSY

We have seen that if wages and prices are completely flexible and if there is no liquidity trap, then money wage deflation will theoretically be sufficient to produce full employment. Money wages and real wages will move together to clear the labor market. A Keynesian underemployment equilibrium will result only if (1) workers refuse to accept money wage cuts, or (2) the economy is in the liquidity trap and the Pigou effect is inoperative.

The Keynesian position in the controversy is that the Pigovian rebuttal ignores the institutional realities of the situation. In general, there is a significant amount of money illusion in all sectors of the economy, so that individuals' actions depend more upon the money value of variables than on their real values. Furthermore, deflationary price changes may cause spending units to shift out of real-valued goods and services and into money, depressing real aggregate demand still further.

Keynes believed that workers would resist money wage cuts, even in the face of high rates of unemployment. Moreover, he argued that even if they would accept wage cuts, the mechanism by which employment would be stimulated in a classical system is through the monetary effect on the interest rate.[12] Presumably the same purpose could be served by maintaining the old level of money wages and increasing the money supply. Keynes noted that classical analysis associated increases in the money supply with inflation, but that, in an underemployment situation, inflation from this source is unlikely. If it did occur, however, it would be a tolerable price to pay for the increase in the level of employment. Furthermore, if speculators are subject to a money illusion with respect to the interest

---

[11] See, for instance, Thomas Mayer, "The Empirical Significance of the Real Balance Effect," *Quarterly Journal of Economics,* LXXIII (May, 1959), 275–291.

[12] This effect is often called the *Keynes effect.*

rate, price inflation will cause the liquidity trap to occur at a lower real rate of interest. Thus, if the price inflation is accompanied by appropriate increases in the money supply, real interest rates will fall, thereby stimulating real aggregate demand and employment even when the economy had previously been in a liquidity trap.

In view of the conclusion that, from the viewpoint of the macro-economy, wage deflation serves exactly the same function as an increase in the money supply, Keynes criticized wage deflation as an antirecession weapon on three counts:

1. Increasing the money supply is preferred to wage deflation. In the absence of money illusion, both have the same initial impact on conditions in the money market. Wage and price deflation, however, must have a depressing effect on both consumption and investment demand which will tend to shift the *IS* curve downward to the left, reducing the level of income and employment. Falling wages inhibit consumption when households are subject to money illusion. Furthermore, falling prices tend to reduce the marginal efficiency of capital for investment. Since investment requires incurring costs now for the prospect of future returns, in a deflationary economy firms invest when costs are relatively high and sell after prices have fallen.

Since an increase in the money supply will have the same impact on the interest rate without the depressing effects of a deflation, it is a better antirecession weapon than money wage cuts.

2. Ignoring the depressing impact on the *IS* curve, wage-price deflation can be no more effective than an increase in the money supply for stimulating employment. In a recession, Keynes doubted that monetary policy would effectively stimulate demand. If interest rates are already low, speculators may hold all increments to the money supply in the form of idle balances in the expectation that bond prices will fall. If they do not enter the bond market, bond prices cannot rise and interest rates will not fall. This is the liquidity trap situation depicted in Figure 9-6. Furthermore, even if the interest rate can be reduced by increasing the money supply, it may have little effect on aggregate demand. As we saw in Chapter 6, investment tends to be interest-inelastic in periods of recession.

3. It is likely that speculators will be subject to some money illusion with respect to the interest rate; that is, their expectations concerning the future course of interest rates may depend upon the prevailing money rate of interest rather than the real rate. This being the case, during a deflation money rates are below real rates of interest, and the liquidity preference function is likely to flatten out at a higher real rate of interest than when prices are stable. If prices are rising, the liquidity preference function will flatten out at lower real rates of interest. Thus, other things being equal, if speculators are subject to a money illusion, it will be easier

for the monetary authorities to effectuate a reduction in the real rate of interest during a period of stable or rising prices than during a price deflation.

IMPLICATIONS FOR ECONOMIC POLICY

While the Keynesian model, given certain assumptions, is consistent with so-called "classical propositions" (i.e., full-employment equilibrium in the absence of government intervention), the policy implications of the two approaches are quite different. Both are concerned with the question of how to remedy a situation of massive and persistent unemployment.

The classical analysis suggests that the appropriate remedy is wage deflation. Keynes argued that such a policy would reduce unemployment only in the very long run. Since an increase in the money supply will produce the same effect more quickly and less painfully, it is a preferable remedy for unemployment.

But the Keynesian model actually represented a radical new approach to macroeconomic policy in shifting attention from the labor market and wage rates to the level of aggregate demand. Since employment is determined by aggregate demand, Keynes argued, then the most effective remedy for unemployment is that which most effectively raises the level of aggregate demand. He ranked deficit spending, tax cuts, and expansionary monetary policy in that order. Deficit spending was by far, Keynes believed, the most effective way of stimulating demand and employment in a hurry. While other measures were theoretically effective, given adequate time for the appropriate adjustments to occur, the impact on employment must eventually come from demand, and consequently, the choice between them should depend on speed and efficiency and not on the necessity to vindicate traditional theories and ideologies.

9-2 MONETARY VERSUS FISCAL POLICY:
A POST-KEYNESIAN DEBATE

Keynes' economics represented an attack on the classical model of income determination and the macroeconomic policies which it espoused. In recent years, a fresh attack on Keynesian macroeconomic theory and policy has come from the monetarist school, led by Milton Friedman. While Friedman recognizes the essential Keynesian link between employment and aggregate demand, he argues that aggregate demand is itself determined by the quantity of money in circulation. Thus, an increase in government spending matched by an equal increase in taxes will have no impact on aggregate demand. Even an increase in deficit spending financed by bond sales will produce no macroeconomic stimulus.[13] As a result of this analysis, Friedman concludes that the best policy measure for stimulating employment is increasing the money supply.

The economic policy implied by Friedman's model has been the subject of considerable debate in recent years. The Nixon administration, relying heavily on monetary policy for economic stabilization, was greatly influenced by Friedman's ideas.

THE FRIEDMAN MODEL

Friedman's model of income determination is based on the quantity theory of money. In the classical model the quantity of money determined the absolute level of prices through the relationship

$$MV = pT$$

where

$$M = \text{money supply}$$
$$V = \text{velocity of circulation}$$
$$p = \text{prices}$$
$$T = \text{transactions}$$

Assuming that transactions are proportional to real income, that is,

$$T = \lambda y$$

the relationship becomes

$$MV' = py$$

where $V' = V/\lambda$ is called the income velocity of circulation.

The relationship

$$MV' = py$$

is an identity, because the money value of all transactions in the economy must exactly equal the amount of money that changes hands. A quantity theory of money, however, for it to be more than a tautology, must be based on an assumption that some of the variables in the relationship remain stable while others are varied.

In the classical model, it was assumed that both velocity, V', and real

---

[13] In the Keynesian view, of course, the effect of a "balanced budget" increase in spending or a bond-financed spending increase is expansionary. See Chapter 4.

income, y, remain fixed when the quantity of money varies. Velocity is determined by institutional factors such as the availability of alternative means of exchange (credit cards, barter relationships, etc.) and length of the pay period. Real income is determined by the level of employment. Thus, the sole effect of a change in the money supply is a proportional change in the level of prices:

$$\Delta M = \left(\frac{1}{V'} y\right) \Delta p$$

The modern quantity theory recognizes that the level of income is also a variable. In Friedman's view, however, the income velocity of circulation is a stable relationship, essentially unaffected by changes in the money supply. Friedman's position is based on the proposition that people purchase goods and services that give utility and, in addition, hold money balances.[14] If relative prices of goods and money stay the same, there is some optimal proportion in which goods and money balances are held. If the increases in the money supply result in increased money balances held by the public, individuals will exchange some of their "excess" money for goods and services, thereby increasing aggregate product-market demand. Thus, changes in the money supply must produce proportional changes in money income, or

$$\Delta Y = V' \Delta M$$

where $Y = py = $ total money income. If V' is stable with respect to changes in all macroeconomic policy instruments—government spending, taxes, interest rates, and money supply—then the only way in which aggregate demand can be increased is for the money supply to increase also[15]

---

[14] In this view, holding money must also give utility or people would never forego consumption (that gives utility) to hold money. For a discussion see Don Patinkin, *Money, Interest, and Prices*, 2nd ed. (New York: Harper and Row. 1965), Chapter 5.

[15] Friedman has developed a theory of the demand for money (the determinants of velocity) in which the interest rate plays a role. See Milton Friedman, "The Quantity Theory of Money—A Restatement," in *Studies in the Quantity Theory of Money*, ed. by Milton Friedman (Chicago: University of Chicago Press, 1956). However, the emphasis is different from the Keynesian analysis in which the interest rate was the principal determinant of the demand for money and changes in the interest rate are the main way that monetary policy affects aggregate demand. In evaluating Friedman's position on the role of the interest rate, Harry Johnson asserts that "one can draw out of Friedman's policy pronouncements an extreme quantity theory view that there is no relation between the demand for money and the rate of interest. But this is contrary to his theoretical work, in which he includes interest rates as determinants of the demand for money. But when he tests his theory empirically he finds that the demand for money is not interest elastic, even though he is careful to state that he expected it to be. With this justification of a vertical *LM* curve, Friedman is then free to advise policymakers to increase

Recall that the quantity theory relationship in the Cambridge form

$$M = \left(\frac{1}{V'}\right) Y = KY$$

where

$$K = \frac{1}{V'}$$

is a theory of the demand for money. If V' is presumed to be independent of all macroeconomic policy instruments, this is true of K as well. The demand for money balances, therefore, is independent of the interest rate and depends only on the level of income.

A graphical view of the neoquantity theory model is shown in Figure 9-7. Suppose the economy is in an underemployment equilibrium at N_E. Full employment, N_F, can be attained by increasing the money supply to M_F. Note that in this model, full employment can also be achieved by a policy of wage and price deflation with no change in the money supply, since presumably the velocity of circulation will increase (the demand for money would decrease) as the price level falls. However, since the impact of the wage deflation is the same as an increase in the money supply, the latter policy is presumably a quicker and less painful way out of a recession.

Because the validity of his theory is based on the assumption that velocity is stable, Friedman has undertaken extensive empirical studies of his position.[16] He has found, for instance, that in the period 1929–1933, U.S. monetary authorities actually reduced the money supply by one-third. "The Great Contraction," Friedman has observed, "is tragic testimony to the power of money—not as Keynes and so many of his contemporaries believed, evidence of its unimportance." [17]

Furthermore, Friedman's studies have shown that the velocity of circulation for the United States has been considerably more stable than the multiplier relationship on which the Keynesian model is based. He even goes so far as to suggest that "most of the evidence was consistent

---

money at a certain rate each year, believing that fluctuations in the *IS* curve will cause changes in interest rates, but not in employment or output." Harry G. Johnson, *Macroeconomics and Monetary Theory* (Chicago: Aldine Publishing Company, 1972), p. 122.

[16] See, for example, Milton Friedman and David Meiselman, "The Relative Stability of Monetary Velocity and the Investment Multiplier in the United States, 1897–1958," in *Stabilization Policies*, Committee on Money and Credit (Englewood Cliffs, N.J.: Prentice-Hall, Inc., 1963).

[17] Milton Friedman, *Dollars and Deficits* (Englewood Cliffs, N.J.: Prentice-Hall, Inc., 1968), p. 14.

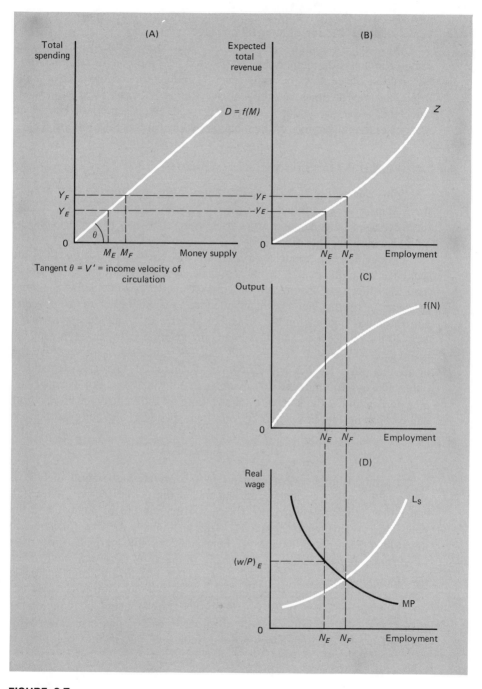

FIGURE 9-7

A Monetary Model of National Income Equilibrium

with the view that the multiplier is useless for predictive purposes except as a disguised reflection of monetary change." [18]

Although Friedman's empirical work has been strongly criticized by some economists on methodological grounds,[19] it has convinced others that his position concerning the importance of money indeed has merit. While Friedman may at times be guilty of overstating his case, most economists agree that monetary policy cannot be ignored. Even a modern Keynesian recognizes the importance of the monetary effects of fiscal operations.

KEYNESIAN AND FRIEDMAN'S MODEL COMPARED

"In one sense," Milton Friedman once remarked, "we are all Keynesians now; in another, no one is a Keynesian any longer. We all use the Keynesian language and apparatus; none of us any longer accepts the initial Keynesian conclusions." [20]

The Friedman model incorporates the Keynesian notion that the sequence of adjustment is from aggregate demand to employment rather than the other way around, as the classical model presumed. Both models concentrate on the factors which influence demand rather than on wages and the labor market for the design of policies to stimulate employment.

For both Keynes and Friedman, the relation between aggregate demand and its essential determinants can be expressed as an identity. Put in another way, Keynes and Friedman disaggregate aggregate demand in different ways for purposes of macroeconomic analysis. For Keynes, aggregate demand is the sum of total spending by different types of spending units; consumption, investment, government spending, and net exports:

$$D \equiv C + I + G + X$$

If the relationship between demand in the private sector and income is stable with respect to changes in demand in the public sector, then a link can be established between the policy instruments (fiscal policy) and the policy target (aggregate demand). The relationship between demand in the private sector and income is represented by the marginal propensity to consume and the marginal propensity to invest. If these are stable, then the multiplier (the link between fiscal policy instruments and aggregate demand) is also stable. Friedman argues that if the multiplier does not remain constant when taxes are reduced or public spending is increased, then fiscal policy is not a reliable macroeconomic policy instrument. Not only might the desired effect not be achieved, but if the multiplier is

---

[18] *Ibid.*
[19] See Harry G. Johnson, *op. cit.*, pp. 129–31.
[20] *Ibid.*, p. 15.

subject to unknown lags (e.g., as in the case of consumer reaction to a tax cut), the impact of the policy may occur at some inopportune time.

Suppose, for instance, taxes are reduced to stimulate demand. If consumers view the increase in their take-home pay as transitory rather than permanent (a possibility consistent with Friedman's *permanent income hypothesis* concerning consumption), consumption spending may not rise as much as a Keynesian model would predict. In the absence of an increase in consumption, public authorities may decide to increase government spending to close the deflationary gap. If the policy is successful, full employment may be achieved. Now suppose consumers begin to react to the tax cut and consumption spending rises. The effect will be inflationary and will involve taking measures to reduce demand. Friedman argues that the marginal propensities to consume and invest are subject to such unreliable lags that fiscal policy is apt to be destablizing and necessitate repeated on-again-off-again measures which constantly overshoot the mark.

The Friedman model views aggregate demand as identically related to the money supply and the velocity of circulation:

$$Y \equiv MV'$$

This can also be expressed as a money demand identity,

$$M \equiv KY$$

where

$$K = \frac{1}{V'}$$

Thus, he disaggregates in terms of decisions to hold money versus purchases of goods and services. If the demand for money is stable with respect to changes in the money supply, then changes in the money supply must necessarily produce changes in aggregate demand.

Keynes argued that the demand for money is a function of the rate of interest which, in turn, depends upon the money supply. Furthermore, in a recession, the money demand schedule tends to be most elastic with respect to the interest rate. In the liquidity trap, for instance, increases in the money supply are all held as idle balances so that changes in money supply have no impact whatsoever on aggregate demand.

The dispute between the followers of Keynes and Friedman boils down to the question of which is the more reliable: the relation between private demand and income or the demand for money. Keynes' position was based on *a priori*, or deductive, reasoning. Friedman, on the other hand, has provided empirical studies which, he claims, support his view.

Unfortunately, Friedman's contemporary critics base their rebuttal more on logic and rhetoric than on cold data.

Figure 9-8 shows the impact of a change in demand on GNP under alternative assumptions about the relationship between the interest rate and the demand for money. Notice that the more elastic the demand for money with respect to the interest rate, the greater is the increase in GNP associated with a given shift in the *IS* curve. For Friedman, the demand for money is independent of the interest rate, so that the *LM* curve is com-

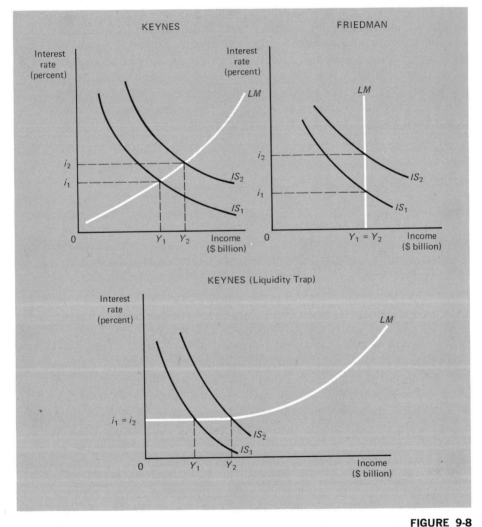

FIGURE 9-8

Impact of a Change in Demand on GNP

pletely inelastic. In this case, changes in demand represented by shifts in *IS* have no impact on GNP, despite the fact that they cause the interest rate to rise. Note that this is true even where *IS* is interest elastic.

Figure 9-9 shows the impact of a change in the money supply on GNP under alternative assumptions about the relationship between the interest rate and the demand for money. A given increase in the money supply will

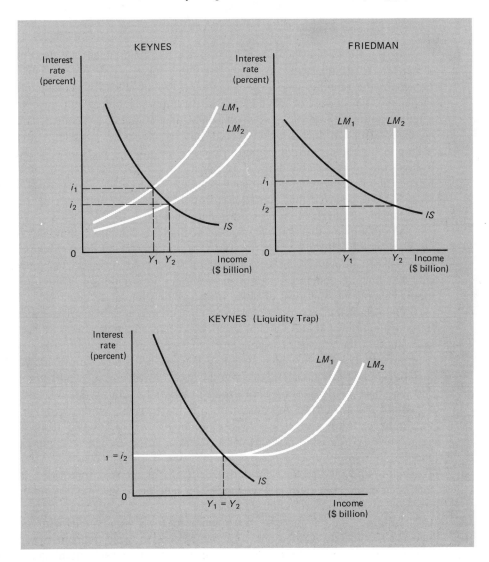

FIGURE 9-9

Impact of a Change in the Money Supply on GNP

affect GNP only if the *LM* curve rises with the interest rate, and the impact is greater the flatter the *IS* curve, that is, the more responsive total spending is to changes in the interest rate. In the Keynesian liquidity trap, increases in the money supply have no effect on GNP. If increases in the money supply result in falling interest rates, then monetary policy will be effective only if some components of aggregate demand are interest elastic.

POLICY IMPLICATIONS

In the Keynesian view, monetary policy can theoretically be used as a measure to stimulate employment, but fiscal policy is far more reliable. Except in the liquidity trap, where monetary policy would be completely ineffective, the impact of the increase in the money supply would involve a reduction in the interest rate which would then stimulate investment and aggregate demand. Such a policy would only be effective if speculators are willing to buy bonds (driving bond prices up and interest rates down) and if investors increase spending in response to the fall in interest rates. Keynes doubted the reliability of such reactions, particularly in a period of recession. He believed that an increase in public spending and tax cuts are more efficient and reliable ways to stimulate demand.

Friedman, on the other hand, argues that the demand for money is not significantly affected by the interest rate and that, if the money supply is increased, money will be exchanged for goods and services. The only way to stimulate demand is to put more money in circulation. Therefore, monetary policy is the most effective measure for stimulating demand.

Between these two positions lies a compromise which involves careful coordination of monetary and fiscal policy. In Chapter 8 we saw that in evaluating the impact of a policy of increased government spending, it is important to know how that spending increase is to be financed. If the spending increase is financed solely from taxes, a Keynesian would argue that the effect would be somewhat expansionary, since consumption spending would not fall by the full amount of the tax increase. With the money supply fixed, interest rates would rise, reducing the speculative demand for money and releasing money for transactions purposes. However, rising interest rates would tend to depress interest-elastic components of demand. Friedman, who ignores the speculative demand for money, argues that in such a case, income could not rise unless an increase in the money supply provided for increased transactions balances.

Suppose the tax increase were financed by a bond issue with no increase in the supply of money. In the Keynesian view demand would increase more than by tax financing since presumably consumption spending would not fall. As bond prices fall due to the bond issue, funds are released from speculative balances to satisfy transactions demand. Again,

Friedman would argue that such a measure would have no impact on GNP, if the money supply were not increased.

Only if the increase in spending were financed by money creation would both Keynes and Friedman predict an expansionary effect. For Keynes, the impact on GNP would be greater than by using tax finance or debt creation since new transactions balances are available without having to release funds from speculative balances. Consequently, interest rates would not necessarily rise.

Generally, fiscal and monetary policy is coordinated so that an increase in public spending is accompanied by some increase in the money supply. If expansionary measures are called for, it is unlikely that the monetary authorities will permit interest rates to rise very much. Because of this coordination, it is difficult to determine whether the expansion is due to the increased spending or the increased money supply. Indeed, this phenomenon has provided fuel for the fires of both camps.

In fact, under these circumstances, the expansion should be attributed to the interaction of fiscal and monetary policy working together. Walter Heller, taking the Keynesian position in a debate with Milton Friedman over economic policy, aptly stated:

> The monetarists have taught us much. We are far richer for their analyses and painstaking research. But we would be far poorer, I believe, for following their policy prescription. It is high time that they stop trying to establish a single variable—money supply—as all-powerful, or nearly so, and stop striving to disestablish another variable—fiscal policy —as impotent, or nearly so. The path to progress in economic policy lies, instead, in a mutual undertaking to work out the best possible combination of fiscal, monetary, and wage-price policies—coupled with measures to speed the rise in productivity—for reconciling sustained high unemployment with reasonable price stability.[21]

QUESTIONS FOR STUDY AND REVIEW

1. A policy planner wishes to achieve full employment. These programs are available to him:

(a) wage deflation,

(b) fiscal policy,

(c) monetary policy.

Which of these would you recommend to him and why? In justifying your answer, be sure to explain why you rejected the alternatives.

---

[21] Walter Heller, in *Monetary vs. Fiscal Policy: A Dialogue,* ed. by Milton Friedman and Walter Heller (New York: W. W. Norton and Company, 1969), p. 41.

2. One of the major conclusions to be drawn from Keynesian economics is that an underemployment equilibrium can be maintained indefinitely in the private sector of an economy. Another school of thought argues that the economy cannot be in equilibrium if a major market (in this case, the labor market) is left uncleared. How (if at all) can the controversy be reconciled?

3. "Deficit spending by the federal government during a recession is not an effective means of eliminating a deflationary gap if the deficit is financed solely by the issuance of bonds." Outline the theoretical framework on which that statement is based and discuss it critically.

4. Trace, in detail, the impact on real wages of a general increase in the level of money wages.

5. Recently it has been argued that "Keynesian economics is dead," and that the Friedmanian (monetarist) position essentially represents a return to the classical tradition. Do you agree?

ADDITIONAL READING

FRIEDMAN, MILTON, *Dollars and Deficits*. Englewood Cliffs., N.J.: Prentice-Hall, Inc., 1968, Introduction.

——, and WALTER HELLER, *Monetary vs. Fiscal Policy: A Dialogue*. New York: W. W. Norton and Company, 1969.

——, "The Quantity Theory of Money—A Restatement," in *Studies in the Quantity Theory of Money*, ed. by Milton Friedman. Chicago: University of Chicago Press, 1956.

HANSEN, ALVIN H., *A Guide to Keynes*. New York: McGraw-Hill Book Company, Inc., 1953, Chapters 1 and 10.

HICKS, J. R., "Mr. Keynes and the 'Classics'; A Suggested Interpretation," *Econometrica*, V (April, 1937), 147–159.

KEYNES, JOHN MAYNARD, *The General Theory of Employment, Interest, and Money*. New York: Harcourt Brace Jovanovich, Inc., 1965, Chapters 2 and 19. Published originally by Macmillan & Co., Ltd., 1936.

MODIGLIANI, FRANCO, "Liquidity Preference and the Theory of Interest and Money," *Econometrica*, XII (January, 1944), 45–88.

PATINKIN, DON, "Price Flexibility and Full Employment," *The American Economic Review*, XXXVIII (September, 1948), 543–564.

SMITH, WARREN, "A Graphical Exposition of the Complete Keynesian System," *The Southern Economic Journal*, XXIII (October, 1965), 115–125.

10

The Theory
of
Inflation

The previous analysis has examined the relationship between the money value of national income and the traditional instruments of macroeconomic policy. But it is important to keep in mind that the policy target is not money income, but full employment and the growth of real output. If in fact real output and money GNP (or national income) always moved together in response to autonomous changes in aggregate demand, and the unemployment rate were inversely related to them, then changes in money GNP would be an indicator of how our policy instruments were affecting these targets. Indeed, the Keynesian model implicitly assumes a reliable and positive relationship between real and money income (until full employment is reached) and an inverse relation between unemployment and aggregate demand. Consequently Keynesians have traditionally seen aggregate demand as a satisfactory barometer of the macroeconomic soundness of the economy. In this view, if the economy is not at full employment, monetary and fiscal policies to increase aggregate demand will always reduce unemployment and increase real output.

While these relationships between aggregate demand and the policy targets once appeared reliable, the experience in the U.S. economy during the recession that began in the latter part of 1969 presented a real puzzle for macroeconomic policy planning. Indeed, this experience represented a serious challenge to the applicability of the Keynesian model for planning policies to reduce unemployment and control inflation, since neither the inflation rate nor the unemployment rate seemed to be very sensitive to changes in the level of aggregate demand.

As shown in Table 10-1, money GNP rose steadily over the period 1969–1972. Beginning in the third quarter of 1969, however, both real GNP and industrial production declined, and the slump continued into 1971. The rise of money GNP in this period was attributable to price in-

TABLE 10-1

Indicators of Economic Activity, 1969–1972

Quarter	GNP (current prices, in billions of dollars)	GNP (1958 prices, billions of dollars)	Industrial Production (1967 = 100)	Unem- ployment Rate	Consumer Price Index (annual rate of change)	Wholesale Price Index (annual rate of change)
1969 (1)	908.7	723.1	107.7	3.4	6.4	5.6
1969 (2)	924.8	726.7	109.2	3.4	5.6	5.2
1969 (3)	942.8	730.6	110.2	3.8	5.6	2.0
1969 (4)	952.2	729.8	108.7	3.5	6.0	6.4
1970 (1)	958.0	720.4	107.7	4.2	6.0	4.4
1970 (2)	971.7	723.2	107.5	4.8	5.6	1.2
1970 (3)	986.3	726.8	107.3	5.2	4.8	4.4
1970 (4)	989.7	718.0	103.6	5.8	5.2	0.0
1971 (1)	1023.4	731.9	105.8	6.0	2.8	5.2
1971 (2)	1043.0	737.9	107.1	5.9	4.8	4.8
1971 (3)	1056.9	742.5	106.5	6.0	2.8	2.4
1971 (4)	1078.1	754.5	107.4	6.0	2.8	3.2
1972 (1)	1109.1	766.5	110.0	5.9	3.6	4.4
1972 (2)	1139.4	783.9	113.1	5.7	2.4	5.2

Source: *Economic Report of the President* (Washington, D.C.: U.S. Government Printing Office, 1974).

creases rather than to increases in the output of goods and services as shown by the steady rise of the consumer price index and wholesale price index as real output fell. The recession of 1969–1970 was characterized by the paradoxical phenomenon of inflation and falling real output occurring simultaneously.

The unemployment rate began to rise in the third quarter of 1969 in response to the decline in real output, but as the recovery in real output began in 1971, the unemployment rate remained at the highest level it reached during the recession. By the middle of 1972, industrial production had surpassed the pre-recession level, but the unemployment rate was 5.7 percent as compared with 3.4 percent at the beginning of 1969. This suggests that even if *real* output is rising, a decline in unemployment may not occur and that restoring income to its previous level will not necessarily return the economy to the former unemployment rate.

To frame policies designed to eliminate involuntary unemployment and maintain economic growth without inflation, policymakers must be able to separate real from money changes in output and the link between price changes and output changes needs to be examined more carefully than in the past. In addition, the relationship between the unemployment rate and the level of aggregate demand should be analyzed if aggregate demand measures are to be used as the principal weapons to reduce unemployment. In this chapter, we will be concerned with the determinants of price level changes and their relationship to income and employment. In Chapter 11, we shall examine factors that affect unemployment and its relation to product market conditions that are reflected in aggregate demand. This will provide the basis for the discussion of policies to reduce unemployment and stabilize prices in Chapter 12 as well as an evaluation of the Keynesian model and its associated policy remedies for achieving our macroeconomic goals of full employment and price stability.

10-1 MEASURES OF PRICE CHANGES

In Chapter 5 we discussed how a price deflator is used to convert money demand into a measure of real demand. But one must bear in mind that given the great variety of goods and services that constitute the Gross National Product, any aggregate measure of "real" output must still be evaluated in money terms. Thus, we speak of "constant-dollar" GNP, assuming that deflation by a price index corrects "current-dollar" GNP for changes in the purchasing power of money. This would not be a problem if the value of money remained constant or if, when prices change, all prices changed by the same proportion. But when the prices of some goods change more than others, it is difficult to determine how the aggregate quantity of goods and services produced (measured in so-called constant dollars) has changed.

The mirror-image of determining real changes in output is the price index. If GNP rises from $500 billion to $690 billion, a gain of 35 percent, and prices increase by 20 percent, then real GNP is said to have increased to $575 billion, or 15 percent. Real GNP is the value of output that would have resulted had prices not risen. Thus,

$$\text{Real GNP} = \frac{\text{money GNP}}{\text{price index}} \times 100$$

or

$$\$575 \text{ billion} = \frac{\$690 \text{ billion}}{120} \times 100$$

The price index, which measures the percentage increase in prices over the base year price level (conventionally set at 100) is presumably the target at which anti-inflation policy is addressed. But while we need to have a reliable measure of price change to design anti-inflation policy, there are conceptual and practical difficulties in constructing price indices that limit their usefulness as indicators of inflation. The price indices most commonly used as measures of inflation in the United States, the Wholesale Price Index, Consumer Price Index, and GNP Deflator are not perfect measures of price change and a clear understanding of how they are constructed is essential to making an intelligent interpretation of their movements.

THEORETICAL PROBLEMS

What is meant by a price increase of 20 percent? Of course, all prices do not rise by 20 percent. Some may increase more or less and others may fall. A price index is a weighted average of price changes for many goods; the weights are determined by the importance of the goods in total spending. This means a base period must be defined and a "market-basket" of goods and services selected so that appropriate weights can be determined.

Since price indices measure changes over time, a conceptual problem arises when the pattern of demand changes or when new goods are introduced. The price index is only a measure of the change in prices of goods in the market basket, a demand pattern that was established in the base period with respect to certain types of economic units and geographic location. The Consumer Price Index (CPI), for instance, is based on spending patterns of urban wage earners and clerical workers in 1964. Whether it is a good measure of changes in living costs for a family today depends on whether spending patterns have changed over the decade and the social status and geographic location of the family in question.

Consider the two families whose expenditure patterns are shown in Table 10-2. Assuming that these represent the total expenditures of these families for each year we can compute the change in the cost of living for each family in the following way. Suppose for each family we compute the change in the cost of the goods purchased in Year 1. Letting the notation

$$\sum p^J q^K = \sum_{i=1}^{n} pi^J qi^K$$

represent the total cost of the goods purchased in year K in the prices of year J, the change in the value of the goods purchased in Year 1 can be expressed as

TABLE 10-2

Change in Living Costs for Two Hypothetical Families

Item	Price and Quantity Purchased			
	Year 1		Year 2	
	p_1	q_1	p_2	q_2
	Family A			
Television	$ 300	0	$ 300	1
Automobile	$2500	1	$3000	0
Rent (per month)	$ 200	12	$ 250	12
Milk (gallons)	$ 1	300	$ 1.25	350
Total Expenditure	$5200		$3737.50	
	Family B			
Television	$ 300	1	$ 300	0
Automobile	$2500	0	$3000	1
House Payment (per month)	$ 200	12	$ 200	12
Milk (gallons)	$ 1	500	$ 1.25	400
Total Expenditure	$3200		$5900	

$$I_1 = \frac{\sum p^2 q^1}{\sum p^1 q^1} \times 100$$

According to this formula, for Family A, the index of living costs based on the market basket of goods in the initial period is 118.6. For Family B it is 103.9, despite the fact that we have assumed they both consume the same types of goods and pay the same prices for those goods.

An index based on the market basket of goods in the initial period is called a *Laspeyres index*. Suppose we consider the change in prices of the goods purchased in Year 2, that is,

$$I_2 = \frac{\sum p^2 q^2}{\sum p^1 q^2}$$

In this case the index of living costs rises by 118.6 for Family A and 111.3 for Family B. An index based on the current market basket of goods is called a *Paasche index*. For each family, the Laspeyres and Paasche indices were computed for the same change in expenditure and prices, but the results were much different. For Family B the cost of living rose by only 3.9 percent measured by I_1 and by 11.3 percent measured by I_2. For Family A, on the other hand, the cost of living rose less on a Paasche index than on a Laspeyres.

This example, based on rather reasonable assumptions about changes in expenditure patterns over time and differences between households, demonstrates the great sensitivity of a measure of price change to the assumptions about the pattern of demand. A measure of price change for an entire economy, which must account not only for differences in spending patterns among different households (the CPI) or firms (the WPI) or between all the spending units including government and the foreign sector (the GNP deflator), but all the various goods and services available, must of necessity be an imperfect measure of price change for any single spending unit. Only a sample of items can actually be included in the index and the determination of the weights to be applied to them involves many assumptions about the relevant reference group.

Another problem in the construction of price indices is the introduction of new products after the base period and quality improvements in old products. This is particularly troublesome in the service sector in which prices are often equivalent to wage remuneration and the product cannot be identified. Wages may rise in a non-service industry such as steel with no concomitant price increase if marginal productivity rises proportionately. However, the only way a dentist can obtain a wage increase is to increase the price of his services. Presumably, the increase reflects, at least in part, an improvement in the quality of those services, but there is no way to measure this.

Paradoxically, policies undertaken by the government to control inflation also contribute to the upward bias in the price indices, generating the appearance of the very inflation those policies are designed to prevent. Since the Consumer Price Index is expected to reflect changes in the "cost of living," indirect taxes and interest rates are included in the index. When increases in indirect taxes and increases in interest rates are used as anti-inflationary measures, governments will promote an appearance of the very price increases they are trying to halt. Actually, increases in the index may not be due to increased prices of goods and services at all.

A final problem in constructing price indices is determining what the price changes actually are. While we would like to measure changes in transactions prices, that is, the prices actually paid, this is often a problem in measuring industrial prices. The Wholesale Price Index (WPI) is comprised largely of sellers' list prices and thus fails to take account of special discount offers. Some people feel the WPI overstates the rate of inflation for this reason, or at least, is less sensitive to changing economic conditions than the CPI which is based primarily on transactions prices. If changes in list prices serve to ratify prior changes in actual transactions prices, there may also be a lag built into the WPI as a measure of price change. Thus, a decline in aggregate demand may cause a decline in the actual rate of price increase that will not show up in the WPI until some time later.

STATISTICAL PRICE INDICES

The three most closely watched price indices in the U.S. are the Consumer Price Index (CPI) and Wholesale Price Index (WPI), both compiled by the Bureau of Labor Statistics, and the GNP deflator compiled by the Department of Commerce. We shall consider each of these briefly in turn.

CONSUMER PRICE INDEX

The Consumer Price Index is a measure of changing living costs for households. It is most frequently cited as a gauge of the deterioration of real wages relative to money wages. Alternatively, it can be interpreted as the compensation required to offset rising living costs for workers or individuals living on pensions, welfare, social security, alimony, or other fixed incomes. The market basket of goods used to weight price changes is based on a 1960–61 expenditure survey (which was revised in 1964) and covers about 400 items. Thus, it is a Laspeyres-type index. It is available for 56 different cities and is designed to reflect expenditure patterns of urban wage earners and clerical workers. Price estimates are based on market surveys and so presumably reflect actual transactions prices rather than list prices.

WHOLESALE PRICE INDEX

The Wholesale Price Index is a measure of price changes of commodities at all stages of production at the level of their first important commercial transaction. It is a Laspeyres index based on the 1963 Census of Manufactures where the weights are expenditures for items measured by net value of shipments of producers. Component indices are available for a wide range of industry groups and product classifications. Because of the lower stage of processing many of the items in the WPI are not affected by quality changes as are the consumer goods in the CPI. Also the WPI excludes services and retail costs so that price changes associated with qualitative changes are easier to measure.

Because of the difficulties in surveying industrial prices, price data for the WPI are generally obtained from firms who provide list price information. As we mentioned earlier this may produce a certain "stickiness" of the WPI in response to changes in the level of economic activity.

However, the WPI is generally viewed as the best measure of inflationary pressure in product markets, since it includes price movements across the entire commodity spectrum, not just for consumer goods. Food and other basic commodity prices are included in the WPI and are more heavily weighted than in the CPI.

The GNP Deflator

The GNP deflator takes into account current shifts in the components of GNP between consumption, investment, government, and the foreign sector. Each component of GNP is deflated by the appropriate subindex of the CPI or WPI. For instance, the plant and equipment component of investment would be deflated by the WPI for producers' durable equipment. When the components of GNP are deflated individually the resultant "constant dollar" GNP is divided into current dollar GNP to obtain the GNP deflator. Since account is taken of current changes in the components of GNP, the GNP deflator is a Paasche-type index. Such an index is particularly valuable in periods where there are important changes in the relative weights of the major components of GNP.

Graphical Method of Showing Price Changes

For the rest of this chapter we shall abstract from the theoretical and practical problems associated with measuring price changes. Although we will return to these considerations in Chapter 12 in our discussion of anti-inflation policy, for the present we shall assume we can identify some pure rate of price change.

An analysis of price level changes can be introduced into the macroeconomic model developed through Chapter 9 using the aggregate supply function and aggregate production function. The aggregate supply function relates the level of employment with the expected total revenue of all firms in the economy. It is the link between the labor market and the product market. That is, it relates the aggregate demand for goods and services to the aggregate demand for labor.

Expected total revenue is equal to the expected money value of output, or

$$ETR = py = g(N)$$

where p is a price index and y is the real value of output or income.

The aggregate production function relates real output to employment. If the capital stock is fixed in the short run, output will increase with employment, but at a decreasing rate, as shown in Figure 10-1. Thus,

$$y = f(N)$$

A price index can be derived by deflating (dividing) the aggregate supply function by the aggregate production function, since

$$p = \frac{py}{y} = \frac{g(N)}{f(N)}$$

Such an index shows the price level as a function of the level of employment, as shown in Figure 10-1.

Suppose for instance that

$$ETR = g(N) = N^\alpha$$

and

$$y = f(N) = N^\beta$$

then

$$p = \frac{g(N)}{f(N)} = N^{(\alpha-\beta)}$$

In Chapter 2 the general equation for the aggregate supply function was shown to be

$$py = \frac{wAP}{MP} N$$

where w is the money wage, AP is the average product of labor, and MP is the marginal product of labor.

Note that total output is equal to output per worker, AP, multiplied by the number of workers employed:

$$y = AP \times N$$

Therefore, a general form for the relation between prices and employment is

$$p = \frac{py}{y} = \frac{(wAP \times N)/MP}{AP \times N} = \frac{w}{MP}$$

The price level varies directly with the level of money wages and inversely with marginal labor productivity.[1] Notice that even if money wages are fixed, prices will rise with employment if the marginal productivity of labor

---

[1] This same condition can be derived by assuming that firms are perfect competitors, maximizing profits. It implies that price will be equal to the cost of the last unit produced. In Chapter 12, we shall consider some other, non-competitive pricing models and their implications for the price-employment relationship.

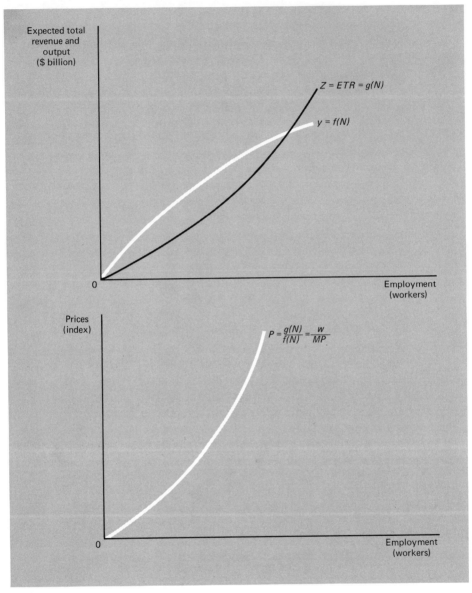

FIGURE 10-1

Graphical Method of Showing Price Level Changes

declines with employment.[2] Alternatively, prices will change in proportion to wage changes if marginal productivity remains constant. Wage increases matched by increases in marginal productivity, on the other hand, should not affect prices at all.

The price-employment relationship may be steeper or flatter than the aggregate supply function. Although the relationship between the slopes of the two functions is complicated to derive, it essentially depends upon how fast the average productivity of labor declines as employment increases. In general, the faster the rate of decrease of AP, the flatter will be the aggregate supply function with respect to the price-employment relationship.

10-2   AGGREGATE DEMAND AND THE PRICE LEVEL

In a Keynesian model, changes in both prices and employment are directly linked to aggregate demand. Shifts in aggregate demand cause the economy to move along its aggregate supply function and the associated price-employment relationship, with prices increasing as aggregate demand and employment rise. Conversely, a decline in aggregate demand presumably will reduce prices and employment will fall. This notion has influenced public policy to such a large degree that measures such as tax increases, spending cuts, and tight money are sometimes viewed as the only effective and legitimate anti-inflationary policy instruments, even though direct wage-price controls have gained some political and intellectual respectability.

It is important to bear in mind, however, that Keynesian economics was basically depression economics. Keynes pointed out that the way to increase employment is to increase aggregate demand and that decreases in demand reduce the level of employment. Since his major concern was to eliminate unemployment, his analysis did not extend in any depth to the relation between price level changes and demand. Perhaps this orientation was due to the fact that in recovering from a depression, inflation is generally not a serious problem. Furthermore, Keynes believed that a moderate amount of inflation is a healthy thing for a stagnating economy, since it stimulates investment by increasing the marginal efficiency of capital. If there is money illusion and households feel richer when money incomes rise, inflation may also be conducive to increased consumption; in the absence of money illusion consumption may still increase as a hedge against inflation.

---

[2] Diminishing marginal productivity of labor is implied by a production function in which total output increases with employment but at a decreasing rate.

Price determination in a Keynesian model is shown in Figure 10-2. The level of money income is determined simultaneously with the interest rate by the general equilibrium relationship between *IS* and *LM* as shown in Figure 10-2(A). The equilibrium level of employment associated with this level of money income is found from the aggregate supply function in Figure 10-2(B). Employment equilibrium occurs when producers' expec-

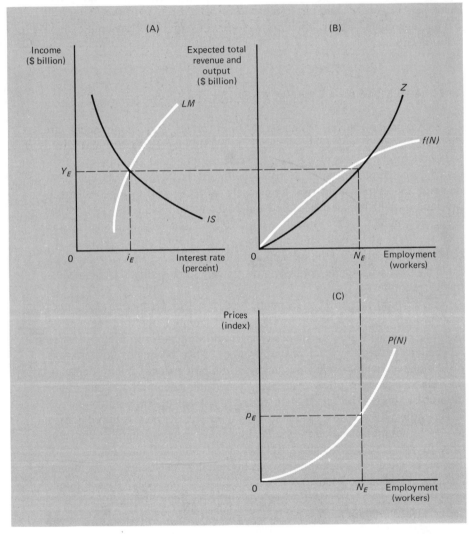

FIGURE 10-2

Price Determination in a Keynesian Model

tations concerning sales are fulfilled. Once the level of employment is known, the price level can be found from the price-employment relationship in Figure 10-2(C).

EFFECT OF CHANGES IN DEMAND ON THE PRICE LEVEL

The impact of a change in demand on the price level is determined by the shape of the aggregate supply function and the price-employment relationship. Assume, as a first approximation, that the aggregate supply function and the price-employment relationship are independent of changes in aggregate demand. In this case the impact of a shift in the IS curve from IS_1 to IS_2 is shown in Figure 10-3. Such a shift could have been initiated by an increase in government spending or a reduction in taxes. As income rises from Y_1 to Y_2, firms increase employment from N_1 to N_2 and prices rise from p_1 to p_2. Notice that the impact of a change in demand on the price level will be greater, the steeper the aggregate supply function and the price-employment relationship in the relevant region. The steeper these curves, the greater is the change in prices and the smaller is the change in employment associated with a given change in aggregate demand.

Since the price-employment relationship and the aggregate supply function incorporate the assumption that money costs of labor and other inputs are fixed, then the slope depends upon the rate at which the marginal productivity of labor changes as the level of output increases. Once full employment is attained, there can be no further increases in real output, and any increase in money GNP will have to be attributed to pure price rise.

In his discussion of inflation, Keynes assumed for simplicity that marginal labor productivity would remain constant until full employment was reached.[3] Thus, increases in demand would not produce inflation until full employment was attained, after which, all expansionary measures would be inflationary. An aggregate supply function incorporating this assumption is shown in Figure 10-4. As long as the labor force is not fully employed, increases in demand will generate increases in output and employment, with no price increases. Constant returns to labor implies constancy of both marginal and average labor productivity. Hence, for a shift in demand from IS_1 to IS_2, along the aggregate supply curve,

$$Y = \frac{wAP}{MP} N$$

[3] This assumption was inconsistent with his earlier observation that the marginal product of labor will decline as employment increases, necessitating falling real wages. Given this assumption and rigid money wages, prices will rise with employment. If money wages also rise as employment increases, the price-employment relationship is even less favorable.

output will increase in proportion to employment. Prices, determined by the relationship

$$p = \frac{w}{MP}$$

will remain constant. Once full employment is attained, however, further shifts in demand will result in price increases with no further increase in

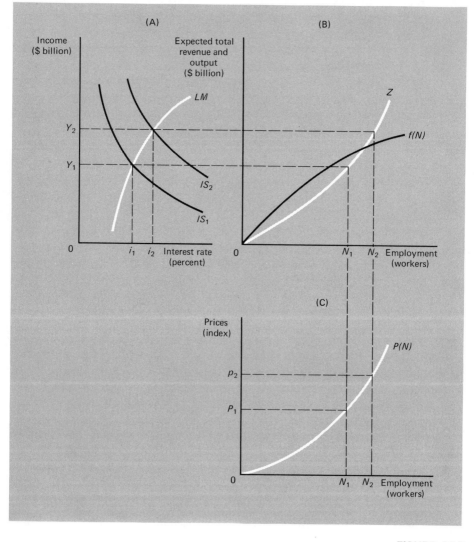

FIGURE 10-3

Impact of a Shift in the IS Curve on the Price Level

employment. The simple Keynesian model suggests, therefore, that if the labor force were not fully employed, full employment could be attained without inflation merely by increasing aggregate demand. On the other hand, it follows that the best way to stop an inflation is to reduce demand. Furthermore, demand can be reduced in such a way that full employment can be maintained once the inflation is halted.

The simple Keynesian assumption of a constant marginal labor prod-

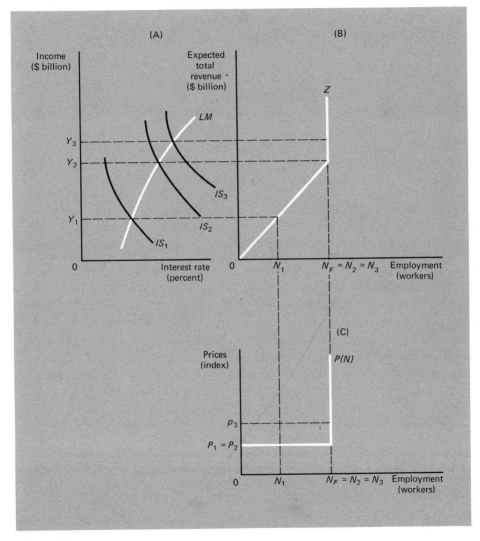

FIGURE 10-4

Price Level Changes in a Simple Keynesian Model

uct may have been an adequate approximation for describing a situation in which both the labor force and capital stock are chronically underemployed. However, as full-capacity production is achieved, marginal labor productivity begins to fall rapidly.[4] This occurs as the capital stock becomes fully utilized and as less efficient workers are drawn into the labor force. Thus, as employment increases, the price level should begin to rise with the declining marginal productivity of labor even before full employment is reached.

Because the rate of decrease in marginal labor productivity depends in part upon the amount of excess capital capacity, the shape of the price–employment relationship depends upon the size and rate of growth of the capital stock in relation to the labor force. Given the size of the capital stock in relation to the labor force in the short run, there will be some range in which the price–employment relationship becomes very steep, as in Figure 10-5. In this range, increments to the labor force can be made only at the expense of rather large price increases, and as a consequence, this range is often considered to reflect full employment of the labor force even though it may more accurately reflect full employment of the capital stock. In Figure 10-5, the price–employment relationship rises sharply before full employment, N_F, is reached. If IS is IS_1, income is Y_E, employment is N_E, and the price level is p_E. Suppose policy makers increase public spending to stimulate employment, shifting IS to IS_2. Employment will rise to N_G, but in the process, prices will rise to p_G. Substantial inflation has occurred, but full employment has not been achieved.[5]

To design policies to achieve full employment and price stability simultaneously, it would be desirable that the price–employment relationship remain relatively flat until full employment is attained, or alternatively, that marginal labor productivity be maintained at high levels. This necessitates ample capital capacity, growing at a rate consistent with the rate of labor force growth. If investment declines, it may become more difficult to achieve full employment without price inflation. Policies to increase labor mobility, to train or retrain labor, as well as policies designed to maintain an adequate rate of capital stock growth will, by maintaining high rates of labor productivity at all levels of employment below full

---

[4] Paradoxically, the rate of productivity growth may be quite rapid in a high-employment economy as firms turn to more capital-intensive production processes in the face of rising labor costs. But expanding employment in the short run may still be associated with falling marginal labor productivity (or rising unit labor costs) for the firm.

[5] The shape of the *aggregate supply function* depends upon the *ratio* between average and marginal labor productivity. Assuming average labor productivity falls more slowly than marginal labor productivity as the capital stock becomes more heavily utilized, the slope of the aggregate supply function will increase, but not as rapidly as that of the price–employment relationship.

employment, prevent the price–employment relationship from rising drastically before full employment is reached. Such policies will facilitate the achievement of the dual objective of full employment without inflation.

The simple Keynesian price–employment relationship, shown in Figure 10-4, can be viewed as an ideal situation for macroeconomic management. If the actual price–employment relationship rises drastically before full employment is attained, it will be impossible to design policies

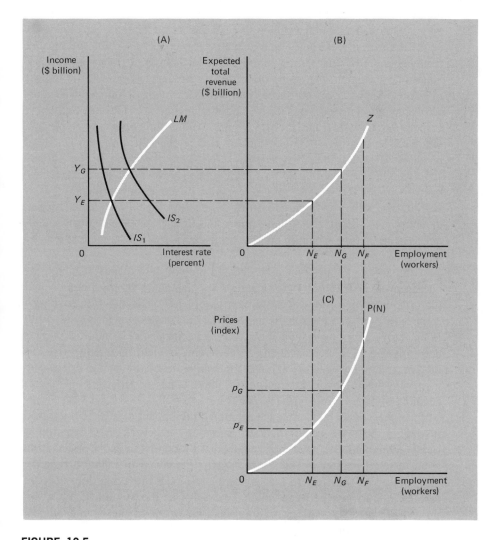

FIGURE 10-5

Price Level Changes with Declining Marginal Labor Productivity for achieving full employment and price stability simultaneously. One goal must be sacrificed if the other is to be achieved.

MONETARY VERSUS FISCAL POLICY

It is sometimes presumed that monetary policy is a more appropriate anti-inflationary weapon than fiscal policy. Perhaps because of the association of fiscal policy with Keynesian (or depression) economics, fiscal policy is considered to be more useful for effectuating changes in employment. Although monetary policy is generally more effective in slowing a boom than in stimulating demand in a recession, it does not follow that monetary policy is necessarily more effective than fiscal policy as an anti-inflationary weapon. Confining ourselves to the demand model, the impact of monetary policy on the price level works through its impact on aggregate demand. Suppose the initial national income equilibrium is at Y_1, corresponding to IS_1 and LM_1 in Figure 10-6. Employment is at N_1 and the price level at p_1. If policy makers decide that the price level should be deflated to p_2, this can be engineered by a reduction in the money supply sufficient to shift LM to LM_2. Notice, however, that the same impact on prices will result from a reduction in government spending or a tax increase which will shift IS to IS_2 when LM is at LM_1. In each case, monetary and fiscal policy have the same impact on aggregate demand, and in this model, changes in the price level are determined solely by aggregate demand.

In this model, prices can be deflated only at the expense of increasing unemployment of labor. Indeed, unless the aggregate supply function and the price–employment relationship are completely inelastic (vertical) with respect to changes in employment, a reduction in prices will always result in an increase in unemployment. Conversely, however, inflation is always accompanied by increases in the level of employment. Consequently, this model cannot be used to explain the phenomenon of rising prices and increasing unemployment which the United States experienced in the recessions of 1957–1958 and 1969–1971.

In the previous example we examined the impact of a policy designed to deflate the price level. In actual practice, however, price deflation is rarely attempted. In most cases the goal is merely to stop prices from rising. Such a policy implies a more dynamic analysis of inflation than we have presented thus far. In fact, a complete model must take into account certain interactions between all the variables in the system which affect the price level. Nevertheless, within the framework of the demand model we can analyze the following problem.

Suppose policy makers are aware that the level of aggregate demand is in the inelastic range of the aggregate supply function, as shown in

Figure 10-7, where income is Y_1. Producers are optimistic about future demand, and there is an accelerator effect to investment. Policy makers expect the projected increase in investment to push the *IS* curve to IS_2, which would cause income to rise to Y_2 and prices to increase to p_2. In the process, the level of employment would rise from N_1 to N_2.

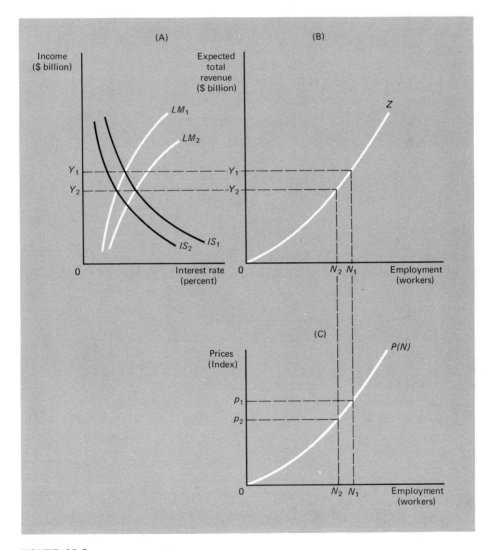

FIGURE 10-6

The Impact of Monetary and Fiscal Policy
on the Price Level (Demand Model)

Since the price–employment relationship is steep in this range, the increase in demand will produce an increase in the price level with little impact on the level of employment. Consequently, the public authorities may decide to take anti-inflationary measures. Monetary or fiscal policy

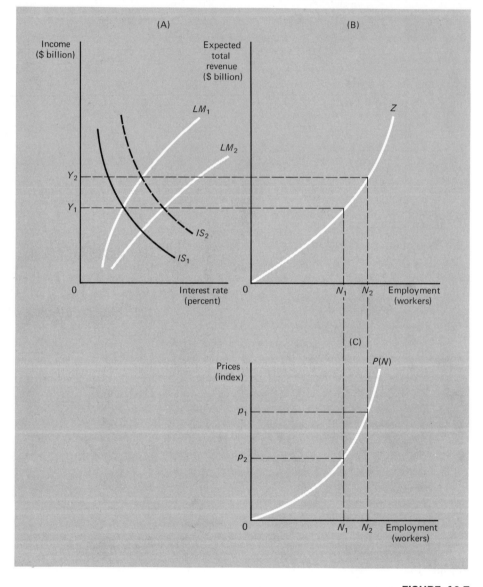

FIGURE 10-7

Anti-Inflationary Policy When Aggregate Demand Is Increasing can be used to halt the threatened price inflation. If the policy goal is to maintain prices at p_1, a reduction in public expenditure or a tax increase could counteract the effect of the increased investment on IS, thereby maintaining equilibrium at Y_1 with employment at N_1 and prices at p_1. The same effect could be achieved by a reduction in the money supply sufficient to shift the LM curve to LM_2. Equilibrium would be maintained at Y_1 with employment N_1 and prices p_1.

Notice that, by using an excess demand approach to anti-inflationary policy, price stability can be achieved only if the level of employment is not permitted to rise in the short run. The inflationary aspects of a boom cannot be dampened without also dampening the effects of the boom on output and the level of employment. The only way to stop prices from rising is to stop the other variables in the system from increasing.[6]

Thus, the problem of halting demand-induced inflation is that of effectuating a transfer of resources from one sector to another. If investment demand increases and prices are to be kept stable, the level of employment and hence of output must also be held constant. Increased investment can occur only if resources are released from consumption or the public sector. A tight money policy may dampen some types of investment so that resources are reallocated within the capital goods sector.

The Keynesian model emphasizes product market conditions, or aggregate demand, as determining the level of employment and prices. In its purest form, the theory ignores the labor market altogether, despite the rather paradoxical conclusion that price changes are tied to changes in employment.[7] Nevertheless, the relation between price changes and employment in the aggregate supply function became the theoretical basis for later empirical studies and policy debates.

10-3   AGGREGATE SUPPLY AND THE PRICE LEVEL

The modified Keynesian or aggregate demand model of inflation assumes that the aggregate supply function is stable with respect to price changes. That is, when aggregate demand changes the economy moves up or down the aggregate supply function so that an inflationary process can be reversed and a former relationship between prices and employment restored simply by reducing aggregate demand. This analysis fails to account for

[6] Of course, real output can rise at the rate of growth of productivity without producing inflation. But in the very short run, productivity gains are not likely to be substantial.

[7] It is even more curious that Keynes' analysis of unemployment also disregards the labor market, with unemployment being attributed to slack product market demand. We shall discuss this more fully in Chapter 11.

the impact of price changes on money wages which are in the aggregate supply function.[8]

Let us return to the labor market and consider the microeconomics of wage determination that we discussed in Chapter 9. As a function of the money wage, the demand for labor depends on its marginal value product, that is, the marginal product times the product price. The supply of labor depends on the real wage since it is the real wage that reflects the goods and services foregone by not working (the real opportunity cost of leisure).

Suppose that workers do not recognize that price changes affect the purchasing power of their wage. This is called "money illusion." If there is money illusion in the labor market, then the supply curve of labor is a function of the money wage as shown in Figure 10-8.

When the demand for labor is D, and employment at N_E, there is some involuntary unemployment, that is, (N_F-N_E) workers are willing to work at the prevailing wage (w_E), but cannot find jobs. Now, suppose there is an increase in demand to D'. Employment increases from N_E to N_F and prices rise from p_E to p_F along the price–employment relationship due to diminishing returns. This produces a decline in the real wage. Will workers now require a money wage higher than w_E? This depends on whether they recognize the deterioration of the real wage as a result of rising prices. If not, they are subject to "money illusion" and will view w_E, the money wage, as equivalent to the real wage. This is the assumption behind the pure aggregate demand (Keynesian) model of inflation outlined in the previous section.

If on the other hand, workers recognize the deterioration of their real wages as prices rise, they will require an increase in money wages in proportion to the price increase to induce the previous supply of labor.[9] As shown in Figure 10-9, when the demand for labor increases from D to D', prices rise along $P(N)$ from p_E to p_F, and the supply curve of labor shifts up by an amount equal to (p_F-p_E). This increases the money wage to w'_E, shifting the price-employment relationship to $P'(N)$. If aggregate demand for labor remains at D', prices will continue to rise

[8] It is ironic that Keynes criticized the classical economists for ignoring the effect of product market conditions on the labor market but failed to account for the impact of wage changes in labor market on product prices. Just as the post-Keynesian IS-LM analysis produced a general equilibrium synthesis of money market equilibrium and saving-investment equilibrium, the modern theory of inflation attempts to view price-wage determination as a general equilibrium process. In some respects, it represents a synthesis of Keynesian and classical macroeconomics.

[9] The assumption that the supply of labor would drop to zero if the perceived real wage were to fall is not necessary to the argument. Presumably, however, in the institutional context of the U.S. economy, unions are successfully able to resist erosion of money wages so the effect is the same as that shown if there is money illusion.

along $P'(N)$ to p'_F, producing another upward shift in the labor supply curve (not shown), a further leftward shift in $P'(N)$, higher prices and a continued upward movement of wages and prices.

Clearly, the interaction of wages and prices in an inflationary spiral

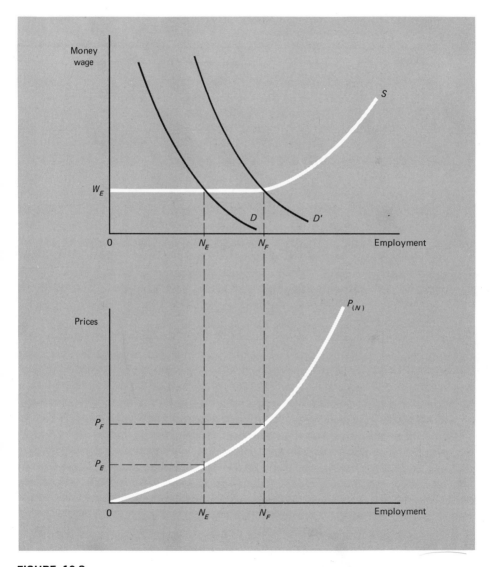

FIGURE 10-8

The Impact on Wages of an Increase in the Aggregate Demand for Labor with Money Illusion

depends on how complete is the loss of money illusion. With partial money illusion, the supply curve of labor will not shift quite so much in response to price changes. But as a psychology of inflationary expectations develops the wage-price spiral is likely to intensify. This suggests that the

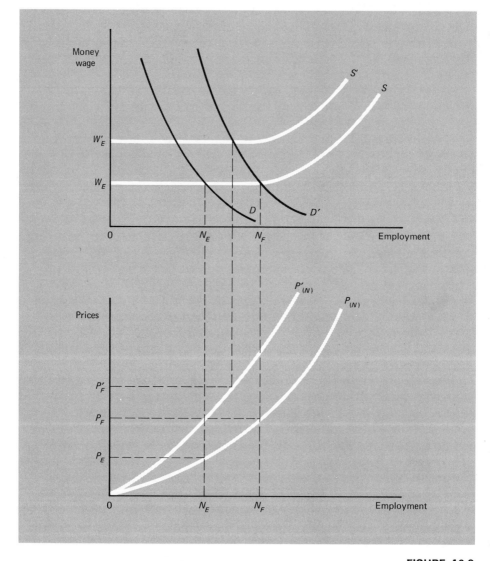

FIGURE 10-9

The Impact on Wages of an Increase in the Aggregate Demand for Labor without Money Illusion

rate of inflation might be expected to accelerate if inflation is allowed to persist too long.

There may be other reasons for money wages to rise with employment when there is involuntary unemployment. Certain segments of the labor market, that is, particular industries, skill categories, regions or demographic groups, may have no involuntary unemployment while involuntary unemployment exists elsewhere in the labor market. Then an increase in the demand for labor would cause a movement along an upward-sloping labor supply curve in the tight segments of the labor market (to the right of N_F) necessitating wage increases (either real or money, depending on the existence of money illusion) to attract additional workers. Such increases may "spill over" into the slack sectors where employed workers will seek similar gains, intensifying the unemployment problem. Of course, if the monetary and fiscal authorities attempt to increase aggregate demand in the absence of involuntary employment then wages would rise along the upward portion of the aggregate labor supply curve. In actual practice, determining whether some amount of unemployment is "voluntary" or "involuntary" is not at all straightforward. In fact, the notion of involuntary unemployment, that is, unemployed persons who would be willing to work at the prevailing wage, is currently the subject of much controversy in view of the recent rise in the so-called full-employment unemployment rate. We will examine this issue in some detail in Chapter 11.

THE WAGE-PRICE SPIRAL

Remember that the aggregate supply function and the price–employment relationship were constructed with the assumption that money wages are fixed. If, however, changes in the demand for labor cause wage changes, then these are not stable functions. That is, movements along Z and $P(N)$ will cause them to shift, and in a predictable way.

Suppose there is an increase in aggregate demand, from IS_1 to IS_2, as shown in Figure 10-10. Initially employment increases from N_1 to N_2 and prices rise from p_1 to p_2. Now suppose workers recognize the deterioration of real wages, and refuse to work for reduced real wage. Money wages will rise by the amount of the price increase so that $P(N)$ shifts from $P_1(N)$ to $P_2(N)$ and Z from Z_1 to Z_2. Since the entire increase in demand is inflationary (there was no change in real wages so real output must be unchanged), the level of employment returns to N_1 but prices remain at p_2.[10]

---

[10] Notice that if the loss of money illusion were only partial, money wages would rise by less than the price increase, Z and $P(N)$ would shift leftward by less, and employment would increase. The new level of employment would be somewhere between N_1 and N_2 and the real wage would fall.

The inflation will stop here if there is no further impact on demand.[11] However, the fiscal and monetary authorities may be forced to take expansionary action to prevent rising unemployment. Also, the Fed may increase the money supply to avoid the large increase in the interest rate associated with the inflationary spiral. In Figure 10-10, the interest rate rises from i_1 to i_2. Normally, monetary authorities will take action to prevent interest rates from skyrocketing, even if a tight money policy is being followed.

As the Fed buys bonds to support bond prices and prevent interest rates from rising, the *LM* curve will shift leftward, increasing demand and prices and perhaps triggering money wage increases and concomitant shifts in the aggregate supply function.

Other factors may tend to keep the wage-price spiral moving. If inflation and high levels of money demand remain unchecked, both consumption and investment demand may rise in expectation of further price increases. In extreme cases, a runaway inflation might ensue. However, unless expectations result in "panic spending," further increases in demand can normally be checked by restrictive monetary and fiscal policy.

A wage-price spiral cannot be held in check by restricting demand if it is reinforced by continued shifts in the aggregate supply function and price–employment relationship. If inflation produces recurrent increases in money wages, for instance, with no autonomous increases in demand, prices can be stabilized only at the expense of increases in the level of unemployment.

RIGID MONEY WAGES AND THE PRICE LEVEL

The fact that money wages tend to rise in boom periods but remain rigid in recessions builds in an inflationary bias for an economy. Suppose expected demand rises from ETR_1 to ETR_2 as shown in Figure 10-11. As the demand for labor increases (moving along Z_1) money wages increase, shifting the aggregate supply function to Z_2 and the price–employment relationship to $P_2(N)$. Expected total revenue rises to ETR_3 as wages increase, and prices rise from p_1 to p_3. Note that prices would have moved only to p'_1 if money wages had remained stable.

Suppose the shift in expected demand was only temporary, due perhaps to an expected tax cut which never materializes. Expected demand returns to ETR_1 but money wages remain rigid. Firms adjust employment along Z_2 and prices along $P_2(N)$. To maintain employment at the previous level (N_1), prices will be p'_2, higher than before.

---

[11] In Figure 10-9, the inflationary spiral continued because the demand for labor (in real terms) was maintained at D'. In this case, money demand is maintained constant at Y_2, but the demand for labor returns to N_1 as prices increase to p_2.

If demand were to increase again, a money wage increase would shift aggregate supply to Z_3, and so on, with a still higher price level associated with the old level of employment. Thus, wage rigidity means that to maintain a stable price level (i.e., to keep prices from rising with respect to a base year) the level of employment must continually fall.

From this analysis it is clear that the mere *announcement* of a tax cut or an increase in spending may set off an inflationary spiral even if the actual program is not carried out. This may be the case for a tax cut being debated for so long that it produces inflation. Obviously, a tax cut would not be desirable in the presence of a rising price level, so the plan

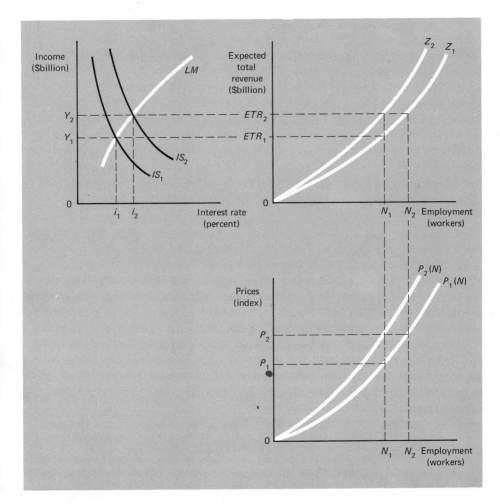

FIGURE 10-10

A Wage-Price Spiral

is abandoned. Expected demand falls, firms cut back production, but prices do not return to their old level and the unemployment rate rises.

DEMAND SHIFT INFLATION

The observation that money wages are flexible only in the upward direction has led some economists to conclude that a shift in the sectoral composition of demand will produce inflation even if there is no overall increase in aggregate demand.[12] Suppose demand increases by $100 million in the steel industry and declines by $100 million in the textile industry. As expected total revenue rises, the demand for labor in the steel industry rises, and money wage rates increase for that industry. Since money wages are downwardly rigid, there is no offsetting fall in wages in the textile industry. In fact, textile workers may press for wage increases to match increases in sectors for which demand is rising. Thus, even though the initial wage increase and concomitant price rise is in a single sector of the economy, there is a "spillover" into other sectors if all sectors compete for labor by increasing wages.

In this example, the impact of the price increase for steel is intensified by the fact that steel is a basic input in many other industries. Rising steel prices increase the cost of production for these industries, shifting the aggregate supply function leftward. It has been estimated that 40 percent of the total increase in wholesale prices over the period 1947–1958 was attributable to the increase in steel prices.[13] It is a small wonder then that steel prices have been a major target of anti-inflationary policy. One of the most dramatic tests of presidential strength in recent years was the ability of President Kennedy to force the steel industry to rescind a price increase when inflation threatened in 1962.

THE PHILLIPS CURVE

The idea that there is a relationship between money wage changes and unemployment [14] was tested empirically by A. W. Phillips in 1958.[15]

[12] This theory has been developed by C. L. Schultze, "Recent Inflation in the United States," in *Employment, Growth, and Price Levels.* Joint Economic Committee Study Paper No. 1 (Washington, D.C.: U.S. Government Printing Office, 1959).

[13] See Otto Eckstein and Gary Fromm, "Steel and the Postwar Inflation," in *Employment, Growth, and Price Levels,* Joint Economic Committee Study Paper No. 2 (Washington, D.C.: Government Printing Office, 1959).

[14] Our discussion has centered around the price–employment relationship. In Chapter 11, we will discuss problems associated with the *unemployment* concept. For the time being we can view them as mirror-images of each other.

[15] A. W. Phillips, "The Relation Between Unemployment and the Rate of Change of Money Wage Rates in the United Kingdom, 1861–1957," *Economica,* n.s. XXV (November, 1958), 283–299.

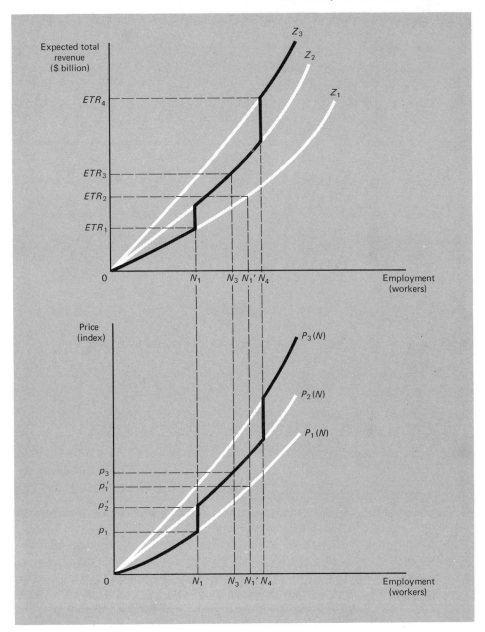

FIGURE 10-11

Rigid Money Wages and the Price Level

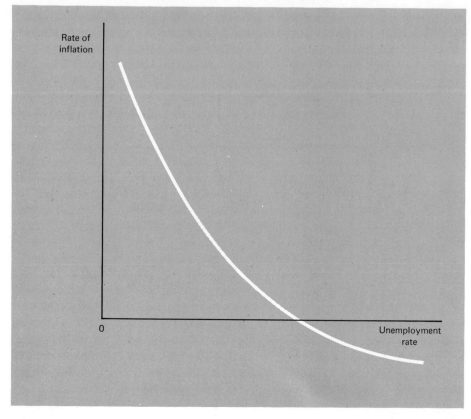

FIGURE 10-12

A Typical Phillips Curve

Phillips found a stable long-run, inverse relationship between changes in money wages and the unemployment rate, as shown in Figure 10-12. More recently, the existence of a Phillips Curve, that is a negative relation between the unemployment rate and the rate of change of money wages, has been established for the U.S. and other countries, for various time periods, both in the long-run and short-run.

From a theoretical perspective this suggests that two underlying phenomena may be at work. As employment increases, diminishing returns produce rising prices and money wages rise in response to falling real wages. In addition, structural imbalances may result in the bidding up of wages in the tight sectors of the labor market. As wages rise, prices will increase in response to the upward shifts in the aggregate supply function.

If, however, the rate of wage increase is sensitive to labor market conditions, this implies that the wage-price process is not completely dominated by the loss of money illusion. If this were the case, wage hikes could not be held in check by increasing unemployment alone—the inflationary psychology would also have to be broken.[16] The major policy implication of the Phillips curve is that there is a trade-off between inflation and unemployment—at least in the range of socially acceptable unemployment rates. Unlike the Keynesian model, full employment cannot necessarily be achieved without inflation, or conversely, some involuntary unemployment may be the cost of price stability. Furthermore, "full employment" that is, elimination of involuntary unemployment, is no longer necessarily the policy target, but stabilization policy must be defined in terms of a certain amount of involuntary unemployment associated with the highest allowable inflation rate.

Despite these differences, the results of the Phillips study, and attempts since then to estimate Phillips curves for the U.S. economy, can be viewed as the logical extension of the Keynesian model, both methodologically and from a policy perspective. We can no longer achieve full employment without inflation, but aggregate demand measures that produce rising unemployment can reduce the rate of wage increase and hence will be effective anti-inflation policy instruments.

Consider the modified Phillips curve in Figure 10-13. This is a relationship between the rate of change of prices and unemployment that takes into account the feedback of wage changes into prices.[17] But it does not take into account the possibility that price changes affect wages. Suppose we begin with stable prices and an unemployment rate of 4.5 percent. An increase in demand reduces the unemployment rate to 4 percent, but prices rise at a rate of 3 percent. The Phillips model suggests that price stability can be achieved by reducing demand to its previous level and maintaining an unemployment rate of 4.5 percent. This implies that the rate of change of money wages was unaffected by the 3 percent inflation rate and that the old level of wage change can be restored by increasing unemployment to 4.5 percent. However, if there is some absence of money illusion, wages will increase as a result of the inflation, the Phillips curve will shift rightward, and the old level of wage increase can only be restored at a higher unemployment rate.

[16] Alternatively, if workers can be convinced to accept real wage cuts as prices rise, money wage increases might be held below price increases even in the absence of money illusion.

[17] This relation also may reflect the price changes due to movements along the price–employment relationship as well as to shifts in $P(N)$ due to wage changes. It also takes into account the moderating effect of productivity gains on prices.

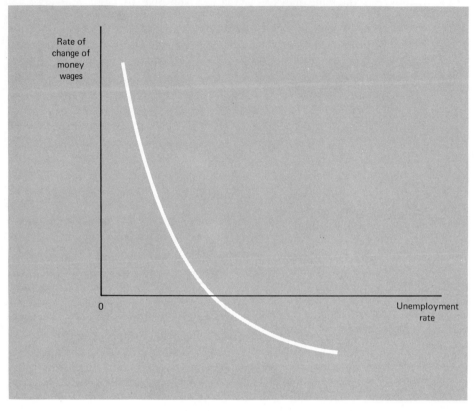

FIGURE 10-13

The Inflation-Unemployment Tradeoff in the Phillips Model
—A Modified Phillips Curve

WAGES AND THE LABOR MARKET

While the Keynesian model ignores the impact of labor market conditions on wages and hence of wages on prices, the Phillips approach emphasizes the role of labor market conditions in the inflationary process by suggesting that money wages are highly sensitive to the unemployment rate in the relevant policy range. This means that the principal way that aggregate demand affects the price level is through the labor market. Although the policy conclusions are the same, the Phillips approach shifted attention away from the Keynesian concern with product markets and returned to the neoclassical view of unemployment as a labor-market problem.

However, if we keep in mind that prices depend on wages, we must also recognize that price changes may affect the wage bargain. The Phillips model like all aggregate demand models of inflation implies money illusion on the part of workers, since the relation between money wage changes and inflation is viewed as independent of the actual rate of inflation.[18] We shall see that any theory of inflation that supports aggregate demand remedies in the presence of involuntary unemployment must rely on the assumption of at least partial money illusion in the labor market.[19]

While the assumption of money illusion may be reasonable in the early stages of an inflation, if inflation persists money illusion will gradually be lost. Suppose an inflationary psychology develops and workers begin to bargain for real, rather than money wages.

If workers refuse to accept real wage cuts, money wages are increased in proportion to prices and prices increase in proportion to wages as $P(N)$ shifts upward and the condition

$$p = \frac{w}{MP}$$

is maintained.[20] The Phillips curve becomes horizontal at the existing inflation rate. Reducing aggregate demand will increase unemployment but will not reduce the rate of inflation. To the extent that workers will accept lower real wages as unemployment increases or if some money illusion persists, inflation can be slowed down by reducing demand and producing slack labor market conditions because then money wage increases will taper off. But if there is an inflationary psychology and workers will not accept real wage cuts, aggregate demand measures cannot halt an inflationary spiral.

THE ACCELERATIONIST VIEW

One explanation for the observed insensitivity of the inflation rate to high unemployment rates in the U.S. economy is the *accelerationist*

---

[18] Phillips did find his relationship to be affected by changes in food prices that could have served as a proxy for perceived changes in the cost of living, particularly in the 19th-century England he studied. Also, the Phillips model takes into account the possibility that the wage change at some level of unemployment may have been a response to falling real wages associated with price changes, but the Phillips tradeoff is supposed to be invariant to the actual rate of inflation.

[19] If there is an attempt to increase aggregate demand when there is no involuntary unemployment, the effect will clearly be inflationary and aggregate demand remedies (that is, reducing aggregate demand) would be appropriate even in the absence of money illusion.

[20] In the longer run, wages may be allowed to rise in proportion to increases in marginal labor productivity without affecting the price–employment relationship or the aggregate supply function. This suggests that such wage increases will not be inflationary. We shall discuss this possibility in more detail in Chapter 12.

theory.[21] Accelerationists argue that the rate of inflation will have a tendency to rise with the length of the inflationary process due to a gradual loss of money illusion in the labor market. This means the inflation–unemployment tradeoff that may exist at the outset of an inflationary period shifts rightward as the inflation progresses until money illusion totally disappears and the Phillips curve becomes horizontal. If expectations accelerate (that is, workers expect next year's inflation to be worse than this year's) that curve may continually shift upward so that inflation may increase even when the unemployment rate is rising. As long as there is some money illusion in the labor market, past inflation will not be completely passed on in money wage increases and aggregate demand remedies may have some impact on money wages at the prevailing rate of inflation. But since an inflationary psychology is more likely to develop the higher the inflation rate and the longer the period of inflation, aggregate demand remedies become weaker the longer the inflation has been allowed to persist.

Accelerationists attribute the inflation during the recession of 1969–70 in the U.S. to the failure of public policy to halt the excess-demand inflation of the Vietnam War boom before an inflationary psychology developed. They argue that although the initial inflation may have come from the demand side, reducing aggregate demand could not return the economy to where it started because the Phillips curve had shifted far to the right. They advocated the use of direct price controls to break the inflationary psychology by eliminating expectations of future inflation, thereby stabilizing the Phillips curve.

Other economists argue that the post-1969 inflation was due to excess demand, but that the full employment unemployment rate had increased for other reasons. They contend that the rightward shift in the Phillips curve, that is, the worsening of the inflation–unemployment tradeoff, was due to structural and demographic changes in the labor market that were unrelated to the question of money illusion in wage bargains, but reflected a decline in the amount of involuntary unemployment associated with any official unemployment rate. We will consider this viewpoint in Chapter 11.

Autonomous Shifts in Supply

In the preceding analysis we have assumed that the initial impetus to the inflationary process came from an increase in aggregate demand.

---

[21] This should not be confused with the accelerator theory of investment in Chapter 6. They are unrelated except in name. For a more technical discussion of the accelerationist position see Robert J. Gordon, "Wage-Price Controls and the Shifting Phillips Curve," *Brookings Papers on Economic Activity* (1972:2), pp. 385–421.

However, an inflation can also be triggered by an autonomous shift in the aggregate supply function. Such a shift could come about due to an increase in money wages not associated with rising product demand but due, perhaps, to an increase in the minimum wage or increasing union power in certain sectors. Rising food prices due to shortages may also result in demands for higher money wages. Higher materials costs that result from scarcities in commodity markets or currency devaluations will also cause a shift in the aggregate supply function.

Suppose, for example, an economy relies on imports for certain industrial raw materials. A currency devaluation would raise the prices of these imports and, hence, non-labor production costs per unit of output. Thus, the price (or expected total revenue) per unit must rise if marginal or average costs enter the firm's pricing rule,[22] and the price associated with each level of employment will rise. As shown in Figure 10-14, the aggregate supply curve will shift from Z_1 to Z_2 and the price–employment relationship from $P_1(N)$ to $P_2(N)$. Unless there is an offsetting increase in demand, employment will fall from N_1 to N_2 and prices will rise from p_1 to p_2.[23]

As the unemployment rate rises, the monetary or fiscal authorities may undertake expansionary measures. A return to the previous level of employment can be achieved only if total demand rises to Y_3. This could be accomplished by fiscal measures, which would shift the IS curve to IS_2, or by an increase in the money supply which would shift the LM curve to LM_2, as shown in Figure 10-15. In either case, prices would rise to p'_1, assuming no further shifts in aggregate supply.

Suppose the monetary authorities increased the money supply and caused the LM curve to shift to LM_2, as shown in Figure 10-15. The fiscal authorities may attempt to head off the inflationary rise in prices by demand-reducing measures which cause the IS curve to fall to IS_0. Income falls to Y_0, the level of employment falls to N_0 and prices to p_0, still well above the original level, p_1, with a substantially reduced level of employment. Inflation and a rising unemployment rate appear simultaneously.

Within a Keynesian framework, the appropriate remedy is unclear. Unemployment has risen, so an increase in demand is called for. But a return to N_1 would cause the price level to increase still further to p_3, even assuming no further leftward shifts in aggregate supply due to wage in-

[22] Marginal costs enter the pricing rule for a firm maximizing profits. Average costs affect price behavior in a markup pricing model. A sales maximizer, on the other hand, does not take costs into account in determining prices.

[23] The direction of change in prices when demand is unchanged will depend upon the shape of the price–employment relationship relative to that of the aggregate demand curve. In all cases, however, the price level associated with any given level of employment will always increase when the price–employment relationship shifts upward.

creases.[24] On the other hand, a policy designed to promote price stability would call for a reduction in demand. Such a policy, however, would serve to intensify the unemployment situation, since employment at p_1 would be N_3.

Any influences which increase production costs will tend to produce this dilemma for policy planning. This is also the case if firms decide to increase their profit margins. In all cases an increase in prices is accompanied by a reduction in the level of employment (assuming no change in the level of money demand). Should public policy be expansionary, or should the level of spending be reduced? The Keynesian approach provides no clear answer because it does not deal with the phenomenon of rising prices occurring simultaneously with rising unemployment rates.

10-4   COST-PUSH VERSUS DEMAND-PULL

Theories of inflation developed in the 1950's and early 1960's emphasized the difference between "cost-push" and "demand-pull" inflation. Although it was recognized that it would sometimes be difficult to distinguish between the two types of inflation, since production costs often move in the same direction as aggregate demand, the implication was that "demand-pull" inflation could be controlled by reducing aggregate demand. Cost-push inflation, on the other hand, due to an autonomous increase in production costs, could not be eliminated by Keynesian measures without increasing unemployment. However, it was generally assumed that cost-push inflation was a once-and-for-all increase in the price level that would not produce a price spiral if other factors are held constant.[25]

We have seen, however, that once prices rise for any reason, if money illusion is lost or a psychology of inflationary expectations develops, a wage-price spiral is likely to occur. Remedies to restore price stability in such a case will depend very little on what caused the inflation to begin with. No one denies, for instance, that the inflation experienced in the U.S. economy during the late 1960's and early 1970's resulted from an excessive growth of aggregate demand and President Johnson's failure to impose price controls during the Vietnam War. However, reducing aggre-

---

[24] If such a policy is adopted, that is, if demand is increased so that employment returns to N_1, the authorities are said to have "validated" the increase in costs.

[25] See for example Martin Bronfenbrenner and F. D. Holzman, "Survey of Inflation Theory," *The American Economic Review* LIII (September, 1963), pp. 626–630 and Thomas F. Dernburg and Duncan M. McDougall, *Macroeconomics* (3rd edition) (New York: McGraw-Hill Book Company, 1968), pp. 374–375. Not only do they argue that a cost-push spiral is impossible in the absence of expansionary monetary policy, but the discussion of cost-push inflation does not even appear in the chapter on inflation; only as a special topic in a concluding chapter.

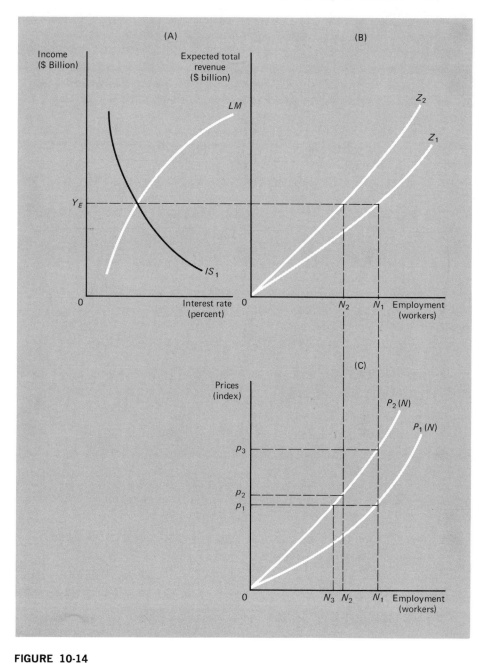

FIGURE 10-14

Impact of Increasing Production Costs
on National Income Equilibrium

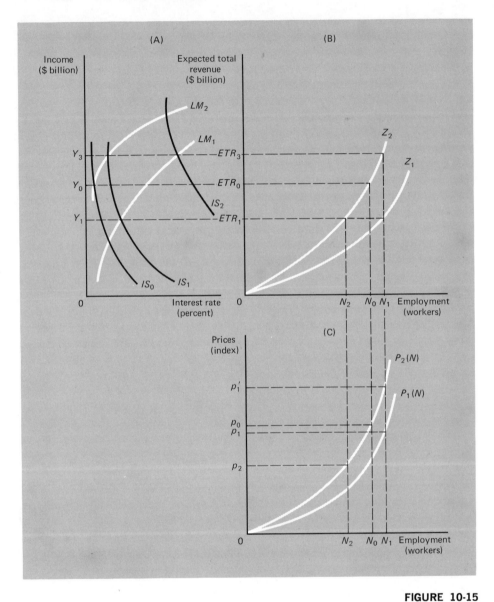

FIGURE 10-15

Attempts to Maintain the Level of Employment
After a Shift in Aggregate Supply

gate demand during the recession of 1970 had very little effect on prices and only served to exacerbate the unemployment situation. Once the psychology of inflationary expectations had developed it was impossible to return to the price–employment tradeoff experienced in the mid-1960's. Thus, the potential efficacy of Keynesian remedies for inflation is not necessarily related to the initial causes of the inflation but to what is happening to the inflation–unemployment tradeoff in the course of the inflationary process.

We have suggested that one reason for the rising unemployment cost of price stability after 1968 may have been the development of a psychology of inflationary expectations and consequent loss of money illusion in wage bargains. Another school of thought has suggested that the worsening policy tradeoff observed during the late 1960's and early 1970's was the result of structural factors in the labor market that increased the degree of labor market tightness associated with any unemployment rate. In the next chapter we shall examine this point of view in some detail. This will pave the way for a discussion of policy planning for full employment without inflation.

QUESTIONS FOR STUDY AND REVIEW

1. On the basis of the model on p. 223 of the text (referred to in Question 1 in Chapter 8) answer the questions below:

(a) If the aggregate supply function is

$$Z = N^2$$

and the aggregate production function is

$$y = \sqrt{N}$$

where

$$Z = \text{aggregate supply}$$
$$y = \text{output}$$
$$N = \text{employment}$$

find the relationship between employment and the price level.

(b) What is the equilibrium level of employment and prices?

(c) What would be the effect of increasing G to 150?

(d) Suppose the authorities desire to increase G without increasing prices. Show how price stability can be achieved by the use of monetary policy.

(e) What would be the impact of the measures taken in parts (c) and (d) on

(i) employment,

(ii) the distribution of GNP between consumption, investment, and the public sector?

(f) Can you design a policy by which the increase in G would increase the level of employment without causing a price rise?

2. President Johnson based his argument for an increase in personal income tax rates on the grounds that it would combat inflation. Discuss the theory on which the president's argument was based. Then, from your knowledge of inflation theory, argue *against* this justification for a tax increase.

3. Under what circumstances would Keynesian policy remedies be unable to ensure overall price stability in an economy? What policies might be more effective? In discussing these policies, be sure to weigh their economic, social, and political implications against the social inequities and economic problems associated with inflation.

4. Although the Phillips Curve represents a return to the classical concern with the labor market as the focal point of macroeconomic policy analysis, it is the empirical basis for the use of Keynesian policy remedies. Can you explain the apparent paradox?

5. Carefully explain the importance of money illusion for designing anti-inflation policy. What are the policy implications of the loss of money illusion?

6. Discuss some of the theoretical and practical problems associated with measuring inflation. If you were designing anti-inflation policy, which of the currently available price indices would you find the most relevant, and why?

ADDITIONAL READING

BARRETT, NANCY S. *et al., Prices and Wages in U.S. Manufacturing: A Factor Analysis.* Lexington, Mass.: D. C. Heath and Company, 1973.

COMMITTEE FOR ECONOMIC DEVELOPMENT, *High Employment Without Inflation.* New York, 1972.

ECKSTEIN, OTTO, "The Theory of the Wage-Price Process in Modern Industry," *The Review of Economic Studies,* XXXI (October, 1964), 267–286.

KEYNES, JOHN MAYNARD, *The General Theory of Employment, Interest, and Money.* New York: Harcourt Brace Jovanovich, Inc., 1965, Chapter 21. Published originally by Macmillan and Co., Ltd., 1936.

PHILLIPS, A. W., "The Relation Between Unemployment and the Rate of Change of Money Wage Rates in the United Kingdom, 1861–1957," *Economica,* n.s. XXV (November, 1958), 283–299.

PIERSON, GAIL, "The Effect of Union Strength on the U.S. 'Phillips Curve'," *The American Economic Review,* LVIII (June, 1968), 456–467.

SAMUELSON, PAUL, and ROBERT SOLOW, "Analytical Aspects of Anti-Inflation Policy," *The American Economic Review, L* (May, 1960), 177–194.

SCHULTZE, C. L., "Recent Inflation in the United States," in *Employment, Growth and Price Levels,* Joint Economic Committee Study Paper No. 1. Washington, D.C.: U.S. Government Printing Office, 1959.

WALLACE, WILLIAM H., *Measuring Price Changes.* Federal Reserve Bank of Richmond, 1970.

11

Unemployment
at Full Employment

In addition to analyzing price level changes, a second problem in applying the Keynesian model to achieve macroeconomic policy objectives has been its failure to deal effectively with certain types of unemployment. In the U.S. economy, the unemployment rate at which inflationary pressure becomes difficult to control has been increasing in recent years, making it harder and harder to justify continued use of restrictive aggregate demand measures as the major anti-inflation weapon. Furthermore, in the short run, the relationship between the unemployment rate and the level of aggregate demand is not as reliable as the Keynesian model suggests. If employment and aggregate demand are tied together through the aggregate supply function, this implies either that aggregate supply function is unstable or that the supply of labor is variable over the short run.

The traditional Keynesian model principally looks at the demand side of the labor market as the determinant of unemployment. However, other studies of unemployment have suggested that changes in the short-run supply of labor might account for the recent increases in the so-called full-employment unemployment rate. Figure 11-1 shows that the unemployment rate remained at the high level attained in the 1969–70 recession during the recovery of aggregate demand during 1971–72. Even as inflationary pressure became intense by late 1972, the unemployment rate was over 5 percent, well above the rate viewed as acceptable during the 1960's. Before we analyze the determinants of the unemployment rate at high levels of aggregate demand, we will consider the unemployment concept in more detail.

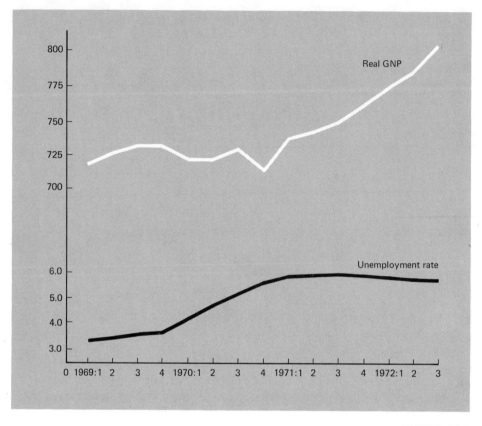

FIGURE 11-1

Aggregate Demand and the Unemployment Rate 1969:1–1972:3

Source: Real GNP is Gross National Product in billions of 1958 dollars, Department of Commerce, Bureau of Economic Analysis.

Unemployment rate (percent), Department of Labor, Bureau of Labor Statistics.

11-1 WHAT IS UNEMPLOYMENT?

Keynes was one of the first economists to make the distinction between voluntary and involuntary unemployment. Workers are said to be involuntarily unemployed if they would be willing to work for the prevailing (or slightly lower) real wage but are unable to find jobs. Keynes explicitly stated that such involuntary unemployment can be eliminated by increasing the level of aggregate demand.[1] An increase in aggregate demand,

[1] John Maynard Keynes, *The General Theory, op. cit.*, p. 26.

along the aggregate supply function, increases the demand for labor at the prevailing wage. If the level of unemployment no longer increases when aggregate demand rises, then any unemployment that persists is said to be voluntary, as jobs are presumably available at the prevailing wage.

Voluntary unemployment may consist of persons who are changing jobs, a process necessary to the efficient functioning of any real-world labor market in which the types of available jobs keep changing. Such unemployment is said to be *frictional*. Some workers may also be unemployed because they are not trained for the available jobs or do not find the available jobs suitable for other reasons. This *structural* unemployment may reflect short-run changes in the composition of product-market demand. A reduction in demand in the textile industry might be offset by an increase in demand for steel, but workers previously employed in textiles may not be able to fill the jobs in the steel industry because of such factors as differences in the geographical location of the work, skill requirements, or restrictive practices of labor unions and employers in the steel industry that discriminate against women and certain ethnic groups that have traditionally dominated the labor force in the textile industry.[2]

Although Keynes spoke of full employment in terms of the inelasticity of real output to increasing aggregate demand, from a practical policy perspective full employment can be interpreted as that level of employment beyond which increasing aggregate demand will cause an unacceptable rise in prices. Thus, the implicit assumption in the full-employment concept is that there is some relationship between aggregate demand and the rate of inflation. Furthermore, there is the recognition that there may be some involuntary unemployment, even at full employment.

WHY ARE PEOPLE UNEMPLOYED?

In making the distinction between voluntary and involuntary unemployment, Keynes was not suggesting that the worker who was unemployed for structural or frictional reasons is in any sense better off than the involuntarily unemployed worker. He intended only to distinguish between unemployment that could be eliminated by aggregate demand measures and unemployment that must be remedied through such policies as training and retraining programs, geographical relocation, and better and more rapid access to labor market information. However, when the rate of so-called voluntary unemployment, that is, the full-employment unemployment rate, is rising it may be important to make different distinc-

---

[2] This is not to suggest that the steel industry actually has followed such discriminatory practices, but is only an example of how structural unemployment might occur.

tions between types of unemployment if the welfare burden of unemployment is to be properly assessed.

Some people, for instance, may become unemployed in order to look for a better job. Such unemployment may be considered voluntary in the sense that it is undergone willingly in the hope of higher pay and better working conditions in the future. Another worker may be laid off from a job and be unable to find another one because there is no demand for someone with his experience and personal characteristics, even though the economy is technically at full employment. The first individual may be called voluntarily unemployed in the sense that he is counted in the unemployment rate but if he is able to find a better job after a reasonably short search, he poses no problem for remedial policy. The second is experiencing involuntary unemployment that calls for remedial action. From a policy perspective, it is important to distinguish between these types of voluntary and involuntary unemployment. But it is also necessary to recognize that both types may occur at full employment. That is, they cannot be eliminated by aggregate demand measures. Thus, we must distinguish between involuntary unemployment in the Keynesian sense (that is attributable to inadequate aggregate demand) and involuntary unemployment from the viewpoint of the individual (that may occur even at "full employment").

For Keynes the major welfare loss associated with unemployment was the foregone output. However, the burden of unemployment falls most heavily on those workers who experience it most often. We shall see that in the U.S. economy, the probability of being unemployed is greater for some individuals than for others. The recognition that the welfare losses from unemployment are not equally shared by different members of the labor force makes the reduction of the full-employment rate a different sort of policy issue from that envisioned by the Keynesian approach.

THE OFFICIAL UNEMPLOYMENT RATE

The official measure of unemployment in the U.S. is based on a monthly labor force survey in which people are asked about their labor force experience during the previous week. Persons who did not work during that week but were available for work and who made specific efforts to find work are counted as unemployed. The unemployment rate is the ratio of unemployed persons in the survey week to the total of employed and unemployed persons.

The provision that an individual must state that he actually looked for work to be counted as unemployed is controversial, particularly when slack labor markets have persisted for a long period of time. If people are unable to find work, they may become discouraged from further attempts to seek work. This is particularly true for women (who must often pay to have their children cared for while they seek work), young people, and other groups whose attachment to the labor force is somewhat ambiguous. It is more common for such persons to refer to periods of nonemployment as being out of the labor force than for central-age males who generally consider themselves unemployed when they are not working. Thus, the official unemployment concept may understate the number of women and young people who would like to work but who think there is no work available for them relative to similar individuals in the central-age male category. Such understatement increases during periods of high aggregate unemployment.

A special labor force survey in Sweden, for instance, showed that 10 percent of the women not in the labor force and only 1 percent of the men said they would have looked for work if they thought they could find it.[3] Thus, it appears that the discouraged-worker effect might cause an understatement of actual unemployment, that is, persons who would work at the prevailing wage if they could find a job, and that the understatement is greatest for those groups whose relation to the labor force is somewhat ambiguous for sociological and socio-economic reasons.[4]

THE COMPONENTS OF UNEMPLOYMENT

Although the Keynesian model emphasizes the unemployment rate as the best measure of foregone output, recent research into the unemployment problem has tried to assess the welfare burden for the individual who experiences unemployment. This approach has decomposed the unemployment rate into the rate of flow of individuals into new unemployment and the average duration of an unemployment spell. The unemployment rate is the product of turnover (T), defined as the weekly flow of individuals into new unemployment as a percent of the labor force, and the average duration (D), in weeks, per spell of unemployment, that is,

$$UN = T \times D$$

From a theoretical perspective, this breakdown is extremely useful for comparing and evaluating the unemployment experience of different groups or for changes over time for the entire labor force. The turnover rate can be interpreted as the probability that an individual will experience

[3] Statistiska Centralbyrån, *Arbetskraftsundersökningen.* Fall, 1969.
[4] Studies of the U.S. labor force also indicate underreporting of unemployment by women and young people. See, for instance, Richard D. Morgenstern and Nancy S. Barrett, "The Retrospective Bias in Unemployment Reporting by Sex, Race, and Age," *Journal of the American Statistical Association,* LXIX (June, 1974).

unemployment in a week. If the turnover rate is relatively high, individuals experience unemployment frequently. Duration, on the other hand, is the life expectancy of unemployment. If duration is relatively long, individuals can expect to take longer to find a job once they become unemployed. Thus, two groups with the same unemployment rates may experience unemployment in different ways.

In the example below, both groups have unemployment rates of 4 percent:

	UN (*percent*)	T (*percent*)	D (*weeks*)
Group A	4.0	.80	5
Group B	4.0	.33	12

Members of Group A experience unemployment more frequently but find jobs more rapidly than members of Group B. Individuals in B have a greater tendency to hold on to their jobs, but take more than twice as long to find a new job once they become unemployed than those in A.

Since the determinants of T and D are different, policies to reduce unemployment are likely to be different for groups A and B. For A, high turnover could be related either to job instability, reflected in a high lay-off rate, or to worker dissatisfaction with employment conditions, reflected in high quit rates. In either case, remedial action should be aimed at stabilizing or improving employment conditions. For B, on the other hand, long durations might reflect structural problems that impede the process of matching job seekers with vacancies. Appropriate policy action in this case might focus on training programs and geographical relocation.

Not only are the policy implications different according to the relative importance of turnover and duration, but the welfare implications for workers experiencing unemployment are also different. High quit rates, for instance, result in high unemployment rates for teenagers but may reflect a desire to sample the job market frequently rather than a high rate of involuntary separations. On the other hand, long durations of unemployment may not present a policy problem if the optimal search period is relatively long for certain groups. Married women, for instance, who experience relatively high unemployment rates principally because of longer average durations of unemployment, may have more specific job requirements than other groups and may be able to afford a more scrupulous search of the market while the family is supported by the husband's income. Thus, the flow approach to analyzing unemployment may shed light on the extent to which unemployment is involuntary, involuntary not in the Keynesian sense of being remediable by increasing aggregate demand but in the sense that its elimination would increase the welfare of the worker.

Although all unemployment represents a loss of potential output in the short run, we have suggested that some unemployment is undergone voluntarily and may be productive if individuals are enabled to move to jobs with higher pay and increased satisfaction. In such a case, unemployment does not necessarily present a problem for redemial policy. In the next section we shall examine the full-employment unemployment rate in more detail from this perspective.

11-2 THE FULL-EMPLOYMENT UNEMPLOYMENT RATE

In the Keynesian model, involuntary unemployment can be eliminated by raising aggregate demand. Yet in the real world we observe unemployment even when aggregate demand is so high as to put excessive inflationary pressure on prices. Furthermore, for Keynes, all involuntary unemployment is wasteful in the sense that it represents a loss of potential output and hence requires remedial policy action. In this section we shall examine the related issues of what causes unemployment in tight labor markets and how that unemployment could be eliminated through appropriate policy actions.

Consider a labor market in which the number of available, but vacant, jobs is greater than or equal to the number of jobseekers. There may be unemployment in such a labor market, but it will not be eliminated by raising aggregate demand to create new jobs as a sufficient number are already available.[6] What determines the unemployment rate in such a labor market?

Unemployment as a Turnover Problem

There are a number of reasons that individuals might leave their jobs in a full-employment labor market. First, structural or microeconomic shifts in product-market demand might cause a shift in demand for labor between industries. Suppose a liberalization of import restrictions on textiles causes a decline in demand for labor in textiles, as shown in Figure 11-2. Let this be exactly offset by an increase in the demand for labor in the steel industry. If wages in the textile industry are not downwardly flexible,

---

[6] The creation of an excess supply of vacancies may temporarily reduce unemployment if it causes wages to be bid up and compels workers to reduce the length of their unemployed search periods. We shall consider this possibility later in this section. The long-run impact of increasing aggregate demand in such a situation is purely inflationary.

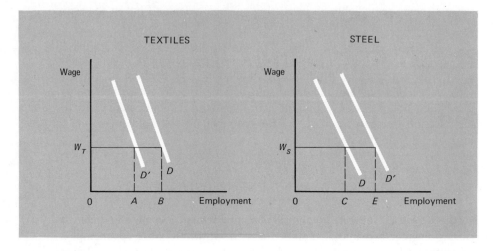

FIGURE 11-2

Interindustry Shifts in Demand and Structural Unemployment

AB workers will lose their jobs. The same number of jobs are available in the steel industry, but even in a well-organized labor market some time will elapse before job losers in textiles can be relocated in the steel industry or elsewhere in the economy.

Workers may leave their jobs for other reasons than involuntary lay-offs. Voluntary quits are notoriously high in certain low-paying occupations and among young people. Robert Hall and others have suggested that workers who do not develop career expectations or who do not believe they can benefit from attaining seniority will have no incentive to stay in employment and will frequently leave their jobs in the hope of finding higher-paying or more satisfying employment elsewhere. In low-status jobs, this effect is combined with low levels of job satisfaction and produces high "voluntary" separation rates. For young people this kind of job turnover may be beneficial, at least in the short run, in obtaining information about the suitability of different types of jobs. But for older people, particularly black males, high turnover rates may reflect a more serious problem of continual job dissatisfaction and a feeling of hopelessness about the ability to gain economic status in the long run.[7] Thus, voluntary separation from a job does not necessarily imply there is no policy problem or welfare loss.

[7] Robert E. Hall, "Why is the Unemployment Rate So High at Full Employment?" *Brookings Papers on Economic Activity* (1970:3), 369–410, and "Prospects for Shifting the Phillips Curve through Manpower Policy," *Brookings Papers on Economic Activity* (1971:3), 659–701.

Hall's analysis suggests that unemployment is not the only labor market problem faced by workers. Chronic dissatisfaction with employment conditions rather than chronic, long-run unemployment may be the major type of welfare loss experienced by some groups in the U.S. labor market. Thus, remedial measures must be focused on employment conditions as well as unemployment. Improving working conditions and removing impediments to advancement for certain labor force groups might strengthen job attachment and lower unemployment by reducing the rate of job turnover.

THE SEARCH PERIOD

Individuals may leave their jobs either voluntarily or involuntarily. Some people are able to secure a new job before leaving their old one, but many persons undergo some unemployed search in the process of changing jobs. Some labor market economists have put forward the view that the choice of a job requires a substantial amount of information and that some time must be spent by both employee and employer in job search.[8] It is unlikely that the process of gathering information about openings, interviewing, trial work periods, and the like can be accomplished while the individual holds a job. So the *search theory* approach suggests that it may be necessary and beneficial for individuals to undergo unemployed search in the process of changing jobs because it is the only way they can acquire accurate information about labor market conditions.

For any individual there are certain benefits and costs associated with unemployed search. The major cost of search is foregone earnings, which increases with the length of the search period. Other costs include child care, transportation, and communications costs which are also likely to rise with the length of the search period. Thus the marginal cost of search is likely to rise with the length of the search period, as shown in Figure 11-3. On the other hand, if the gain associated with search is related to the acquisition of information, enabling individuals to locate better-paying and more satisfying jobs, the marginal returns to continued search are likely to diminish over time, as shown on the marginal benefit curve in Figure 11-3, as more information is obtained. If continuation of search is expected to yield more favorable offers, the probability of more favorable offers forthcoming per unit of time is also likely to decrease with the length of the search period, thus contributing to a declining MB curve. The optimal search period, $t,*$ occurs where the gain from an extra day of

[8] A collection of articles representing the search theory approach is Edmund S. Phelps (ed.), *Microeconomic Foundations of Employment and Inflation Theory* (New York: W. W. Norton and Company, Inc., 1970).

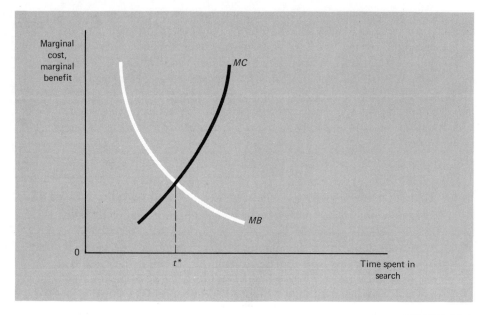

FIGURE 11-3

Determination of the Optimal Search Period

search is no greater than the additional cost incurred, that is, at the point of intersection between the MC and MB curves.

The optimal search period represents the lower limit to the actual search period for rational labor market participants. This means that even in a full-employment labor market the average duration of unemployment should be at least $t.*$ [9] Thus, for any rate of labor force turnover—due to structural changes in the demand for labor, voluntary separation because of job dissatisfaction, or other factors—the longer the optimal search period, the greater the full-employment unemployment rate.

The optimal search period will vary by the nature of the job and type of individual. The marginal cost of search is higher the higher the foregone wage, but the marginal benefit may be greater the more specialized or demanding the job requirements. For instance, search periods seem to be longer for married women (who may have less flexibility in their job re-

[9] In our example, $t*$ is defined for an individual, not for the labor force as a whole. For the entire labor force, the average optimal search period will be a weighted average of t_i* for different groups with different optimal search periods. If, for instance, women have longer optimal search periods than men, a relative increase in female labor force participation will increase the average duration of unemployment, and hence the unemployment rate, in a full-employment labor market.

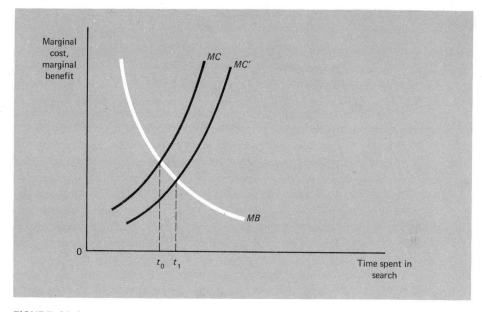

FIGURE 11-4

Impact of Unemployment Insurance
on the Optimal Search Period

quirements) and for college graduates than for other workers. On the
other hand, manpower policy might also affect the optimal search period.

The availability of unemployment insurance, for instance, will reduce
the marginal cost of search and increase the optimal search period and
the full-employment unemployment rate. In Figure 11-4, a rightward shift
of the MC curve to MC' increases the optimal search period from t_0 to t_1.
Efforts to speed the flow of information about job availabilies will work
in the opposite direction, shifting the MB curve leftward and reducing the
optimal search period and the full-employment unemployment rate. Charles
Holt has made the ingenious suggestion that the offices of the U.S. Employment Service be left open at night so that job search may be conducted
while individuals are still employed.[10]

As long as search periods are time-consuming, shifts in demand for
labor and other types of job changes will cause unemployment, even when
aggregate demand is sufficiently high to generate enough jobs for everyone
to find work. For a given search period, an increase in structural shifts in

[10] For a detailed discussion of the role of a federal employment service, see
Charles C. Holt, *The Potential Impact of the Employment Service on the Economy*
(Washington, D.C.: The Urban Institute, 1973).

demand will increase the full-employment unemployment rate. Given the amount of job turnover, variations in the full-employment unemployment rate can be attributable to changes in the optimal search period.

THE NATURAL RATE OF UNEMPLOYMENT

It is generally recognized that there is some unemployment rate at which additional pressure on aggregate demand will produce inflation without substantially reducing employment. This so-called *natural rate of unemployment* depends on the amount of structural change in the labor market, voluntary turnover, and the optimal search period.[11] Some economists attribute the inability of the U.S. economy to slow inflation without a substantial increase in unemployment to a rising natural rate of unemployment since 1968. This implies that the Phillips curve has been shifting rightward, because of either increasing job turnover or rising search periods.[12]

The term "natural rate of unemployment" is unfortunate if it is taken to mean that remedial policy action is not implied by a rising natural unemployment rate. Indeed, remedial action could be brought to bear both on rising turnover and duration of unemployment. So it must be emphasized that the natural unemployment rate concept merely refers to a type of unemployment that cannot be reduced by Keynesian, aggregate demand measures. It does not mean that no remedial measures are feasible.

Before evaluating the natural rate hypothesis and its relation to the U.S. Phillips curve, we shall turn briefly to an analysis of some empirical evidence about the unemployed at full employment.

DEMOGRAPHIC DIFFERENCES IN UNEMPLOYMENT AT FULL EMPLOYMENT

One way to evaluate the causes of unemployment at full employment is to examine the unemployment experience of different demographic groups in the labor force. In a high-employment year like 1969, for instance, the unemployment rate of blacks was twice that of whites, while the female unemployment rate was 1.7 times the male rate. Teenage men had an unemployment rate over 5 times that of the 25–44 age group.

The breakdown of the unemployment rates of demographic groups into their components of duration and turnover in Table 11-1 shows that

[11] One of the first discussions of the concept of a natural rate of unemployment is found in Milton Friedman, "The Role of Monetary Policy," *The American Economic Review*, LVIII (March, 1968), 7–11.

[12] These phenomena could be due in part to changes in the demographic composition of the labor force, since different demographic groups vary with respect to their turnover rates and average durations of unemployment.

TABLE 11-1

Duration and Turnover of Unemployment by Race, Sex, and Age in the United States, 1969

| | Whites | | | | | |
| | Males | | | Females | | |
Age	Duration (weeks)	Turnover (%) (per year)	UN * (%)	Duration (weeks)	Turnover (%) (per year)	UN * (%)
16–19	7.38	46.05	10.0	8.38	40.27	11.6
20–24	5.98	39.56	4.6	7.22	30.60	5.4
25–44	5.94	16.19	1.5	8.59	18.12	3.7
45 +	6.63	13.61	1.6	6.76	14.55	2.3
all groups	6.59	19.81	2.5	8.37	20.91	4.2
	Blacks					
16–19	8.65	83.79	21.4	78.20	78.20	27.6
20–24	6.84	53.45	8.4	11.01	61.83	12.0
25–44	6.28	32.28	3.0	8.91	32.07	5.6
45 +	6.36	26.25	2.7	7.35	21.65	3.3
all groups	7.13	37.74	5.3	9.85	37.34	7.8

* Differences between UN and the rate that can be computed from Columns 1 and 2 by the formula

$$UN_p = \frac{(1) \times (2)}{52}$$

represent the bias in reporting by the retrospective method in the Work Experience Survey. For a discussion see Richard D. Morgenstern and Nancy S. Barrett, "The Retrospective Bias in Unemployment Reporting by Sex, Race, and Age," *Journal of the American Statistical Association,* LXIX (June, 1974).

there is considerable variation in the way the unemployed experience their unemployment. Blacks and young people have relatively high unemployment rates at full employment because of high turnover rates. There is little difference in the duration of unemployment for these groups relative to central-age whites. These data support the view put forward by Hall that blacks and young people have relatively high unemployment rates because they do not stay in their jobs. The common perception of black unemployment as consisting of a "hard core" of persons out of work for a long time is not supported by these data. While there is indeed a good deal of such hard-core unemployment of blacks, the primary problem lies in the very frequent occurrence of spells of unemployment which, on the average, are not appreciably longer than for whites.

For women, on the other hand, the major reason for the relatively high unemployment rates is a longer average duration of unemployment rather than a high turnover rate.[13] From Figure 11-5 it is clear that duration increases markedly for white women of childbearing age, while it declines for all other groups at that age.

These findings indicate that women, particularly women with children, experience high unemployment rates at full employment because their average search periods are longer than those of men. Whether these longer search periods reflect longer optimal search periods due to more rigid job requirements and the ability to undergo a more leisurely search while being supported by a husband's income or whether employers are reluctant to hire women (and hire them as a last resort) because of prejudicial attitudes is not clear from these data. Cross-section studies that relate personal characteristics of unemployed individuals to the duration of their unemployment spells find no clear relation between marital status and duration and thus support the view that the longer unemployment spells experienced by females are not wholly voluntary.[14]

POLICY IMPLICATIONS

These data suggest a number of policy conclusions. First, it is clear that the labor market is highly stratified with respect to the demographic characteristics of workers, as members of different groups experience unemployment in characteristically different ways, and the burden of unemployment at full employment is very unevenly distributed. Furthermore, aggregative measures to reduce unemployment will not solve the problem for groups with high unemployment rates, even in tight labor markets.

Second, in view of the proposition that the inflation-unemployment tradeoff has worsened in recent years with the influx of secondary workers—women, blacks, young people—it is interesting to note that the reasons these groups experience high unemployment are different and so are the associated policy remedies. For blacks, for instance, remedial measures need to be aimed at a reduction in job turnover by increasing job satisfaction and improving the opportunities for career development and advancement. For young people, unemployment may not be so serious a concern

---

[13] Notice that black women suffer from both the high turnover rate associated with being black *and* the longer average duration of unemployment experienced by women.

[14] See, for instance, Nancy S. Barrett *et al.*, "Disparities in Unemployment Experience: A Cross-Section Analysis," available from the Manpower Administration, U.S. Department of Labor, 1973. For a fuller discussion of unemployment experience by demographic group see Nancy S. Barrett and Richard D. Morgenstern, "Why Do Blacks and Women Have High Unemployment Rates?" *Journal of Human Resources*, IX (Fall, 1974).

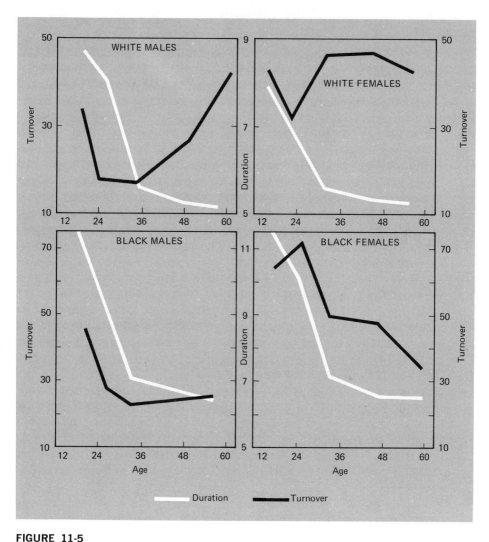

FIGURE 11-5

Age Profiles of the Components of Unemployment
by Race and Sex, 1969

if search periods continue to be reasonably short and high turnover rates
reflect efficient sampling of the market. For women, on the other hand,
policies to reduce unemployment might be most effectively focused on
measures to improve the flow of employment information to the job seeker
(thus shifting the *MB* curve leftward and reducing the optimal search

period) and in eliminating prejudicial attitudes of employers against female workers. Rising wages might also reduce female unemployment if the increased cost of search associated with higher foregone earnings reduces the optimal search period.

11-3 UNEMPLOYMENT AND INFLATION

In Chapter 10 we discussed the view that an inverse relation exists between unemployment and the rate of inflation. Econometric studies have shown that a Phillips curve, that is, an inverse statistical relationship between the rate of increase in money wages and the unemployment rate does exist for various time periods in the U.S.[15] Since wage increases (in excess of productivity gains) generate price increases, these studies establish a link between the rate of inflation and unemployment. From a policy perspective, the Phillips curve suggests that unemployment can be reduced by inflationary aggregate demand measures or, conversely, that the cost of price stability is a higher rate of unemployment. Furthermore, the Phillips curve provides the major empirical justification for using Keynesian policy remedies for both inflation and unemployment. If the Phillips curve is known, this means the feasible inflation-unemployment rate combinations are known: some target combination can be selected, and the implication is that this combination can be achieved by appropriate manipulation of the level of aggregate demand.

Although it is possible to derive a statistical Phillips curve, many economists contend that it is a highly unstable relationship. This being the case, it is important to investigate the structural mechanisms that might produce a tendency for the rate of increase of money wages to rise as unemployment falls. First, unemployment should decline if the excess demand for labor increases; partly because of a reduction in search periods as the number of vacancies exceeds the number of job seekers. The excess demand for labor should also cause an increase in the rate money wages increase as employers bid competitively for a shrinking supply of job seekers and raise wages to prevent their own workers from leaving.[16] An-

[15] See, for example, George L. Perry, *Unemployment, Money Wage Rates, and Inflation* (Cambridge, Mass.: The MIT Press, 1966) and Paul Samuelson and Robert Solow, "Analytical Aspects of Anti-Inflation Policy," *The American Economic Review*, L (May, 1960), 177–94.

[16] Holt notes that "the critical dilemma for economic policy in the United States arises because these inflationary pressures on money wages occur before full employment has been attained. This is to say, turnover, search time, market segmentation, and imbalances in the labor market prevent unemployment from reaching acceptable levels unless the level of vacancies is raised so high that inflation results. Charles C. Holt *et al.*, *Manpower Policies to Reduce Inflation and Unemployment* (Washington, D.C.: The Urban Institute, 1973), 56.

I have shown that in certain European countries this inflationary pressure

other, more institutional, explanation is that lower unemployment and tighter labor markets strengthen the power of labor unions, enabling them to negotiate inflationary wage increases in excess of increases in productivity. In both cases, of course, prices will be rising even faster than money wages, since real wages must fall as employment increases and unemployment is reduced.[17]

THE NATURAL RATE HYPOTHESIS

In Chapter 10 we considered the view that workers will demand wage increases even in slack labor markets if a psychology of inflationary expectations develops as a result of a persistent uncontrolled inflationary situation. If workers have some degree of market power through unionization and/or employers share similar inflationary expectations, it is likely that such increases will be granted. Thus, once money illusion is lost there will not be a one-to-one correspondence between wage change and the unemployment rate, and hence the Phillips curve does not exist.

Another group of economists dismisses the notion of a Phillips curve, at least for the long run, for a different reason. They argue that market forces will tend to establish the natural rate of unemployment regardless of the rate of inflation. The natural rate is determined by the normal turnover rate (which in turn depends on the amount of structural shifts in demand, job change due to dissatisfaction, desire to sample the market, and the like, which may be related to the demographic composition of the labor force), together with the optimal search period. These economists view the statistical Phillips curve as a short-run relationship that reflects a discrepancy between the actual and expected rate of inflation. Their analysis implies that if inflation is fully anticipated there is no money illusion and the Phillips curve will be vertical at the natural rate of unemployment, that is, unemployment will be at its natural rate no matter what the rate of inflation.[18]

Suppose policymakers attempt to push the unemployment rate below the natural rate by increasing aggregate demand. As the number of vacancies relative to job seekers rises, so do money wages. Job seekers, believing that they have stumbled into a fortuitous job opportunity (with imperfect

---

does not occur until unemployment is substantially lower, but the attendant welfare loss may be no less great. See Nancy S. Barrett, "The U.S. Phillips Curve and International Unemployment Rate Differentials: Comment," *The American Economic Review*, LXIV (December, 1974).

[17] This ignores the effect of productivity increases. Real wages can rise if productivity is increasing, but not by as much as the productivity gain.

[18] For a summary of this viewpoint see Edmund S. Phelps, "The New Microeconomics in Employment and Inflation Theory," in Edmund S. Phelps (ed.), *Microeconomic Foundations of Employment and Inflation Theory, op. cit.,* 1–23.

information they are unaware of the availability of higher wages elsewhere), reduce their search periods and unemployment falls. To the extent
that wage increases are unanticipated, unemployment will fall as a result
of rising money wages.[19] But since real wages must eventually fall as employment increases, price inflation will occur and workers will begin to
expect wage increases as "cost-of-living adjustments." These wage increases will be anticipated throughout the labor market so that there will
be no incentive to shorten search periods. Unemployment will return to
its natural rate as long as the rate of inflation continues as expected (presumably maintained through the mechanism described by the accelerationists).

Equivalently, a reduction in the demand for labor may cause money
wages to rise less than anticipated, causing job seekers to lengthen their
search periods in the hope of finding a better offer. The short-run effect
will be to increase the unemployment rate; but once the slower rate of
increase is anticipated, search periods will be shortened as workers will
accept lower wages more quickly, and unemployment will again return to
its natural level.

The natural rate theory views the Phillips curve as vertical, as shown
in Figure 11-6, as long as inflation is anticipated; but it admits the possibility of an inflation-unemployment tradeoff in the short run if there is a
discrepancy between actual and anticipated inflation. Because money illusion is only a temporary phenomenon, unemployment can only temporarily be above or below its natural rate and inflation can only temporarily
be a cure for unemployment. Like the accelerationist theory, the natural
rate hypothesis views any inflation-unemployment tradeoff to be the
product of money illusion; once money illusion is lost, price stability cannot be bought by increasing unemployment, nor can a reduced unemployment rate be bought by rising prices. While the policy thrusts of the two
approaches are somewhat different—the accelerationists basically interested in price controls; the natural rate economists concerned with structural policies to reduce unemployment—their views are based on similar
reasoning. Inflation can never be a cure for unemployment, and any short-
run gains can never be more than temporary. For the natural rate econo-

---

[19] Conversely, rising money wages may cause workers to leave their present
jobs to seek new ones, particularly if wages are sticky in some areas. This increased turnover into new unemployment will cause rising unemployment associated
with higher money wages and a tightening of labor market conditions. I have shown
in another connection that this phenomenon has characterized certain European
labor markets where search periods are much longer than in the United States.
In such cases tighter labor markets induce greater turnover by reducing expected
search periods. If turnover rises more than average duration of unemployment falls,
unemployment will rise. See Nancy S. Barrett, "The U.S. Phillips Curve and International Unemployment Rate Differentials: Comment," *op. cit.*

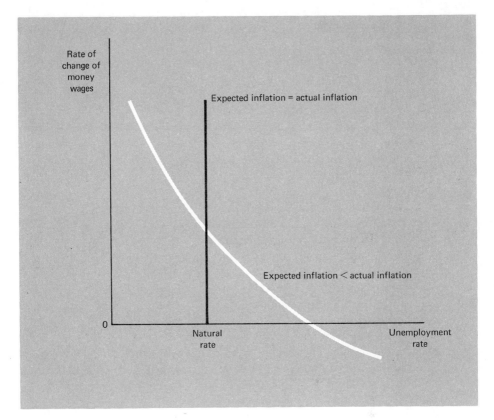

FIGURE 11-6

The Long-Run Phillips Curve Versus the Short-Run
Phillips Curve in the Natural Rate Model

mists, unemployment, in the longer run, can only be reduced by reducing
job turnover, providing better labor market information about job vacancies, and measures to improve labor mobility such as training and geographical relocation.

Is There a Phillips Curve?

The accelerationists view the unemployment rate as incidental to the
inflationary process as long as it is above the natural rate.[20] Thus, the so-

[20] Accelerationists would agree that an attempt to reduce unemployment below its natural rate contributes to the inflation. Thus, the Phillips curve becomes
horizontal only to the right of the natural rate of unemployment.

called Phillips curve is horizontal, as any rate of unemployment above the natural rate is consistent with the ongoing inflation rate, once money illusion is lost. The natural rate theorists view the inflationary process as incidental to the determination of the unemployment rate;[21] thus the Phillips curve is vertical, as the natural rate of unemployment will be established regardless of the inflation rate. For both, however, an inverse relation between inflation and unemployment will occur if inflation is unanticipated and there is money illusion in the labor market. Furthermore, for both theories expectations are formed in essentially the same way; the absence of an inflationary psychology is seen as the precondition for the effectiveness of Keynesian measures to reduce inflation and unemployment.

Some economists have taken the view that in a dynamic world with imperfect information and constantly changing conditions of product demand and labor supply, inflation and wage changes can never be fully anticipated so that some inflation-unemployment tradeoff always exists. Charles Holt argues, for instance, that the question of the stability of the tradeoff is empirical, not theoretical, since it basically depends on the extent to which lack of information, lags of wages behind price changes, and other market imperfections are institutional facts of life in the real world. In his view "the existence of a stable Phillips curve is seen to rest on the existence of frictions that cannot be ruled out simply by *a priori* arguments. The stability of the Phillips curve is an empirical matter, not one that can be settled by deductive arguments from premises that obviously are true." [22]

THE SHIFTING PHILLIPS CURVE—AN ALTERNATIVE EXPLANATION
FOR RISING UNEMPLOYMENT WITH INFLATION

Both the acceleration theory and the natural rate hypothesis have been put forward as explanations of the rather obvious inability of Keynesian policy remedies to maintain an acceptably low level of unemployment and stable prices since the late 1960's. An alternative explanation has been put forward by George Perry.[23] In his view, changes in the

---

[21] The implication of the natural rate theory is that unemployment is not effected by changes in aggregate demand in the long run, that is, if the demand for labor falls, workers will accept cuts in their real wages until the natural rate of unemployment is reestablished. This view, espoused by Friedman, among others, is essentially anti-Keynesian in the sense that it views the wage-adjustment mechanism as capable of establishing labor market equilibrium.

[22] Charles C. Holt, "How Can the Phillips Curve Be Moved to Reduce Both Inflation and Unemployment?" in Edmund S. Phelps (ed.), *Microeconomic Foundations of Employment and Inflation Theory, op. cit.,* 242.

[23] George L. Perry, "Changing Labor Markets and Inflation," *Brookings Papers on Economic Activity* (1970:3), 411–448.

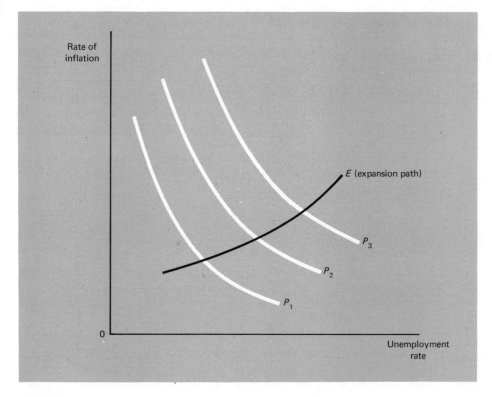

FIGURE 11-7

A Shifting Phillips Curve

demographic composition of the labor force since the late 1960's have caused the Phillips curve to shift rightward, as shown in Figure 11-7. Rising labor force participation of women and young people who have relatively high full-employment unemployment rates has raised the unemployment rate associated with any degree of labor market tightness. He attributes the inflation experienced in the U.S. economy since 1968 to an excess demand for labor. That is, labor markets have been tight even though the aggregate unemployment rate has been rising. If the Phillips curve is shifting rightward, rising unemployment rates do not necessarily mean the level of aggregate demand is too low. In an attempt to reduce unemployment to the levels of the mid-1960's, policy makers have allowed aggregate demand to rise too fast, putting inflationary pressure on prices as unemployment was reduced below its natural rate. Empirically, the economy has moved along an expansion path such as the curve E in Figure 11-7.

In Perry's view, the appropriate policy remedy is to reduce aggregate demand. Unemployment will rise, presumably to its natural rate, but the decline in inflation will be substantial, if the economy moves along P_3, as shown in Figure 11-7. To reduce unemployment, non-Keynesian remedies must be used to reduce the high unemployment rates experienced by those "secondary" demographic groups whose increased representation has raised the natural or full-employment rate. Some of these measures were discussed earlier in this chapter. Thus, Perry would view Keynesian policy as the appropriate anti-inflation instrument, rather than price controls, but he urges the sort of labor market policy espoused by the natural rate model to reduce the high unemployment rates experienced by disadvantaged demographic groups.

11-4 UNEMPLOYMENT AND ECONOMIC POLICY

Although a major contribution of Keynes was to focus on unemployment as an important problem for economic theory and policy, his model of aggregate demand turned attention away from the labor market for analyzing unemployment. Most economists are sufficiently Keynesian to recognize that unemployment, at least in short- to medium-run is exacerbated by slack product market demand. However, it is also clear that even when labor markets are tight, unemployment rates are higher than many people think is desirable. In addition, that full-employment unemployment rate seems to be still rising. Recent studies of high-employment unemployment suggest that Keynesian macroeconomic policy that focuses solely on product market demand cannot reduce the unemployment rate to socially acceptable levels.

The rapidity with which inflationary expectations have developed in recent years has substantially worsened the inflation-unemployment tradeoff even where unemployment is above the natural rate. This makes it more difficult to justify reliance on unemployment as the sole or major anti-inflation weapon.

For any of the inflation-unemployment combinations observed in recent years, say 8 percent inflation and 5 percent unemployment, economists differ over the appropriate remedy. In 1972, one position argued that aggregate demand should be increased to reduce unemployment and wage-price controls imposed to reduce inflation. Another group suggested decreasing aggregate demand to reduce inflation and using labor market policy to alleviate the unemployment situation. As Holt suggested, the choice may hinge more on empirical considerations than on theoretical ones, since both theoretical viewpoints have intuitive appeal. But clearly the Keynesian model, which can deal with inflation *or* unemployment but not both simultaneously, cannot provide the solution in a situation where both price increases and unemployment are too high. Consequently, Keynesian policy remedies must be supplemented by alternative anti-inflation measures, labor market policy, or both. In Chapter 12, we shall consider in more detail some of these non-Keynesian solutions.

QUESTIONS FOR STUDY AND REVIEW

1. How do you explain the fact that in recent years we have experienced rising unemployment simultaneously with inflation? Does this mean we can no longer rely solely on Keynesian remedies for the important macroeconomic problems?

2. What did Keynes mean by "involuntary unemployment"? What do search theorists mean by "involuntary unemployment"? Discuss the welfare implications of unemployment in the two approaches and the associated policy considerations.

3. What determines the natural rate of unemployment? What are the implications of the natural rate hypothesis for full-employment and anti-inflation policy?

4. The average rate of unemployment during periods of high product market demand is about twice as high in the U.S. as in most countries of Western Europe. Assuming that the official unemployment statistics are based on the same definitions, what are the welfare implications of this discrepancy? What do your conclusions imply about the use of the unemployment concept as an appropriate target for remedial policy action in any country?

5. Discuss the proposition that "the effectiveness of Keynesian policies to eliminate inflation and unemployment depends on the existence of at least partial money illusion in the labor market."

ADDITIONAL READING

BARRETT, NANCY S., "The U.S. Phillips Curve and International Unemployment Rate Differentials: Comment," *The American Economic Review,* LXIV (December, 1974).

FRIEDMAN, MILTON, "The Role of Monetary Policy," *The American Economic Review,* LVIII (March, 1968), 1–17.

HALL, ROBERT E., "Why is the Unemployment Rate So High at Full Employment?" *Brookings Papers on Economic Activity* (1970:3), 369–402.

HOLT, CHARLES C., *et al., The Unemployment Inflation Dilemma: A Manpower Solution.* Washington, D.C.: The Urban Institute, 1971.

PERRY, GEORGE L., "Changing Labor Markets and Inflation," *Brookings Papers on Economic Activity* (1970:3), 411–441.

PHELPS, EDMUND S., "Money-Wage Dynamics and Labor-Market Equilibrium," *Journal of Political Economy,* LXXVI (July-August, 1968). Part II.

————, "The New Microeconomics in Inflation and Employment Theory," *The American Economic Review,* LIX (May, 1969), 147–160.

STIGLER, GEORGE, "Information in the Labor Market," *Journal of Political Economy* (supplement), LXX (October, 1962), 94–105.

12

Economic Policy
and the New
Inflation

In view of the observed insensitivity of the rate of inflation to slack demand conditions and high unemployment rates since the recession of 1969, it has become fashionable to reject the Keynesian model of inflation as a description of the contemporary scene. However, because Keynesian policy remedies have retained a certain political and intellectual respectability, it is important to understand the conditions under which the model is applicable and when it breaks down as a description of reality.

The Keynesian model implied that the price level, like the level of employment, can be manipulated most effectively by policies which affect the level of aggregate demand. The idea that there is a one-to-one correspondence between the price level and the level of employment implies that the price–employment relationship and the aggregate supply function are stable with respect to changes in aggregate demand. In this view, the only source of inflation is a rising level of aggregate demand. This means that if aggregate demand is prevented from increasing, a stable price level can be maintained at any level of employment which is less than full employment. For example, it suggests that a 4 percent rate of unemployment can be maintained with no price level increases, once the appropriate level of aggregate demand is attained, by allowing demand to grow at the same rate as the labor force.

Keynes viewed the aggregate level of employment as determined by product market conditions; and his model of the inflationary process essentially ignores the labor market altogether, as it does not allow for the feedback of price increases into demands for higher money wages as real wages begin to fall. Although rising money wages would produce inflation in a Keynesian model, the mechanism by which price changes produce wage changes because of the loss of money illusion is not identified. After a brief review of the Keynesian model of inflation, we shall evaluate the related policy prescriptions. This assessment will be followed by a discussion of policy measures associated with other theories of the inflationary process.

12-1   THE STABILITY OF THE AGGREGATE SUPPLY FUNCTION AND THE PRICE-EMPLOYMENT RELATIONSHIP

The notion that inflation is caused primarily by too much demand is based on the assumption that prices rise only when the levels of real aggregate demand and employment increase. The relationship between prices and employment,

$$p = \frac{w}{MP}$$

where p is the price level, w is the money wage, and MP is the marginal productivity of labor, implies that firms will hire workers as long as the price of the product exceeds the cost of production. According to this relationship, prices will rise and fall with the level of employment if marginal labor productivity moves inversely with employment. If money wages are fixed or if they rise only when employment increases, the price–employment relationship will be positively sloped as shown in Figure 12-1.

In this case, increases in demand will cause the level of employment to increase and prices to rise. If demand falls, so will the level of employment and prices. A decrease in employment will always be accompanied by a reduction in prices, if money wages do not rise and marginal productivity increases.

Aggregate Supply and Rising Money Wages

Studies have shown, however, that money wages in the United States have increased continually since World War II, despite the fact that the unemployment rate climbed as high as 6.8 percent in 1958. Since 1969 the persistence of inflationary expectations has put upward pressure on money wages throughout periods of depressed labor market conditions. In 1960, Paul Samuelson and Robert Solow estimated that money wages would not stop increasing unless the unemployment rate rose to 8 percent and that wages would rise at a rate of 2 to 3 percent per year with 5 to 6 percent of the labor force unemployed.[1]

Experience in the seventies suggests that structural changes in the labor market have worsened the wage change–unemployment rate tradeoff.

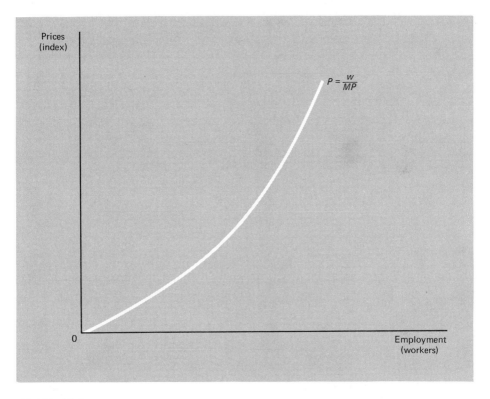

FIGURE 12-1

The Price-Employment Relationship

In 1971, when the unemployment rate was 5.9 percent, wages rose by 7.2 percent, and in 1972 a 7.7 percent wage increase was associated with an unemployment rate of 5.6 percent. Whether this worsening of the wage change–unemployment rate relationship was due to the loss of money illusion or to demographic factors, it is clear that the assumption of stable money wages in slack labor markets is not a viable description of the U.S. experience.

[1] Paul A. Samuelson and Robert M. Solow, "Analytical Aspects of Anti-Inflation Policy," *The American Economic Review,* L (May, 1960), 177–94.

Notice that rising money wages will produce upward shifts in the price–employment relationship only if they are not offset by increases in marginal productivity. If productivity is increasing by 2 to 3 percent per year, the economy could maintain price stability with a 2 to 3 percent increase in wages each year.

If, however, the unemployment rate must be maintained at a very high level to achieve this stability, the economy would have to be kept in a state of semirecession (by the standards of the 1950's and 1960's). In such an atmosphere, it is doubtful that productivity would increase at a rate of 2 to 3 percent. Indeed, reducing the level of demand may discourage the investment that is responsible for gains in labor productivity. If continual money wage increases are an institutional fact of life in the United States, then measures which encourage investment and increase productivity may be better anti-inflation remedies than those which aim to ·stop wages from rising by increasing the rate of unemployment.

This is particularly true when an inflation is already in full swing and the unemployment rate is not declining. In such a situation, the source of inflation may not be entirely an excess of demand. Suppose there is an initial increase in demand which causes the IS curve to shift from IS_1 to IS_2 as shown in Figure 12-2. With the aggregate supply function at Z_1, the initial impact is to increase employment from N_1 to N_2. Prices rise along $P_1(N)$ from p_1 to p_2. As prices rise, labor unions demand higher wages to recoup losses in real income, and since employment is rising, their bargaining position is improved. Often automatic wage increases are built into union contracts in "escalator clauses." The rise in wages will cause the price–employment relationship and the aggregate supply function to shift upward to $P_2(N)$ and Z_2 as shown in Figure 12-2. The level of employment will fall to N_0 (below the initial level, N_1), while the price level rises still further to p_0.

Although prices are rising due to an initial demand–pull situation, measures which restrict demand and discourage investment will do more harm than good. Productivity will not increase, but wages will rise anyway. In this case an easing of monetary policy or a tax stimulus to investment might have the effect of increasing investment and labor productivity—a measure which would be conducive to price stability in an economy with a persistent money wage rachet. Furthermore, such measures would increase the demand for labor in a situation in which the unemployment rate is rising simultaneously with increases in the price level.

Note that the best anti-inflationary policy in this case may look "expansionary" from a Keynesian point of view. Expansion and inflation are not always synonymous (although they sometimes are). A Keynesian might suggest that instead of increasing total demand, the current level of demand should be shifted from consumption to investment spending by means of

increasing personal income taxes and easing money or subsidizing investment. This policy might be appropriate if total demand were the only
factor involved. Consider the impact of this policy on prices, however.
Increased personal taxes would strengthen labor's argument for money

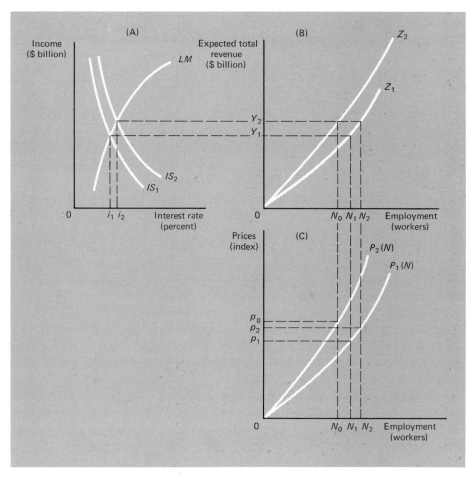

FIGURE 12-2

Impact of Rising Money Wages on the Price Level

wage increases as take-home pay is reduced. Often personal taxes are included in the cost-of-living indices which automatically escalate wages
through clauses in union contracts. Tax hikes are not a useful anti-inflation measure in periods when labor is using the "loss-in-real-income"
argument to justify wage increases.

The price–employment relationship shows the number of workers firms will employ for a given price level. Any factors which influence production costs or desired profit margins will have an impact on this relationship. We saw in Chapter 10 how a currency devaluation might produce an upward shift in the price–employment relationship for an economy which imports raw materials.

Other factors which may produce these results are the following:

1. *Increases in desired profit margins*—When demand falls, firms may try to recoup their losses in volume by increasing profit rates on the fewer units sold. This type of behavior is most likely to occur in highly concentrated industries with some degree of market power.[2]

Consider a monopoly that maximizes profits by setting marginal revenue equal to marginal cost. Such a firm will hire workers until the marginal revenue equals cost per worker, or

$$MR = \frac{w}{MP}$$

Recall that

$$MR = p \left(1 - \frac{1}{E_D} \right)$$

where E_D is elasticity of demand.[3] Therefore,

$$p = \frac{w}{MP[1 - (1/E_D)]}$$

Under these circumstances firms will attempt to increase their total profits by raising profit margins (and hence prices) if they perceive the price elasticity of demand is falling. If consumers develop inflationary expecta-

---

[2] For empirical evidence of this phenomenon see Nancy S. Barrett *et al.*, *Prices and Wages in U.S. Manufacturing* (Lexington, Mass.: D. C. Heath and Company, 1973), and Otto Eckstein and David Wyss, "Industry Price Equations," *Conference on the Econometrics of Price Determination*, Washington, D.C., 30–31 October, 1970.

[3] The derivation of this result is as follows:

$$E_D = -\frac{p}{q} \frac{\Delta q}{\Delta p}$$

$$MR = p + q \frac{\Delta p}{\Delta q} = p \left(1 - \frac{1}{E_D} \right)$$

tions about absolute prices, it is indeed likely that they will be less sensitive to price increases than during periods of general price stability, so that demand elasticity may fall, at least for certain products. In addition, purchases of durable consumer goods may be a hedge against inflation, reducing the price elasticity of demand for those products.

Other models of oligopoly pricing suggests that such firms do not maximize profits in the short run. According to one such model prices are set to establish a target rate of return on capital. Target return pricing sometimes implies raising profit margins as a response to reduced sales even if demand elasticity does not change.[4]

2. *Increases in interest rates*—Rising interest rates increase capital costs to firms and living costs to households. They may be passed on to consumers by firms in the form of higher prices and from households to firms in the form of wage increases. Although tight money has traditionally been viewed by the followers of Keynes and Friedman alike as an anti-inflationary measure, since it presumably reduces both aggregate demand and the quantity of money, it will generally cause the aggregate supply and price–employment relationships to shift upward and thus may generate the very inflation it is intended to prevent.

3. *Increases in taxes*—Tax increases raise living costs for households which may provide a justification for wage increases. In addition, many firms view increased corporate taxes as increased unit costs of production, which they pass on to consumers in the form of higher prices. Although taxes are viewed as demand inhibitors from the Keynesian viewpoint, they are also an element of production cost and, hence, play a role in the determination of prices.

4. *Increases in price of primary products*—Rising food prices almost always provide justification for money wage increases. Consumers sample the market for food frequently, and hence food price increases contribute very quickly to the development of an inflationary psychology. Since eating is a necessary and nonpostponable activity, the impact of increased food prices on perceived living costs is considerably greater than their influence on the Consumer Price Index, an influence which itself is far from negligible, since food prices have a weight of 22.4 percent in the CPI.

Primary products such as steel are inputs in many other industries, and increases in these prices represent increased production costs in secondary industry. The effect will be to shift the price–employment relationship leftward even where money wages are unchanged.

---

[4] For a discussion of the target return pricing model see Otto Eckstein and Gary Fromm, "The Price Equation," *The American Economic Review,* LVIII (December, 1968), 1164–1166.

Consequently, price increases in a limited sector of the economy, particularly in food and basic industries, will often shift the aggregate price–employment relationship upward. Since prices of basic commodities are quite sensitive to exogenous factors that determine supply—climatic conditions, political conditions in other countries that supply the materials, and so on—the need for equilibrating price increases to regulate scarcities can pose a major dilemma for anti-inflation policy. As we shall see, the food shortages and the so-called energy crisis that began in 1973 had disastrous consequences for President Nixon's anti-inflation program.[5]

THE QUANTITY OF MONEY

Some economists such as Milton Friedman argue that prices cannot rise (at least for very long) unless the quantity of money in circulation increases. If the level of GNP is determined by money supply multiplied by the velocity of circulation

$$MV = GNP$$

then increases in M will necessarily increase GNP and, hence, prices. We have examined this model in Chapter 9. Despite its limitations, it is essentially a theory of the determination of money aggregate demand or nominal GNP. It does not allow for the fact that the same level of GNP might be associated with different price levels, depending upon the level of employment and output. While it may help to explain an excess demand inflation when resources are fully employed, it is not useful in explaining why prices may rise in the face of a falling level of GNP (presumably associated with a decreasing supply of money).

A monetarist of the Chicago school like Milton Friedman would argue that cost–push inflation, that is, inflation at high levels of unemployment, is attributable to monopoly elements in product and labor markets and that the appropriate remedy is to increase competition at the microeconomic level. Monetary policy will only be an effective anti-inflation instrument to the extent that prices are responsive to market forces that generate excess supply and demand.

Monetary measures as a macroeconomic policy instrument suffer

---

[5] It is interesting to speculate whether the food and energy crises were the result of exogenous factors—the Russian wheat deal, political unrest in the Middle East, etc.—or were themselves induced by Nixon's attempts to control inflation. Undoubtedly, the fact that prices were being controlled and in some cases held below world market prices contributed to the problem.

from the same problems as any of the Keynesian remedies. In addition, tight money produces higher interest rates, raising capital costs and generating an upward shift in the price–employment relationship. In addition, it will tend to discourage investment, the source of the productivity gains required to achieve price stability in the face of the upward creep of money wages.

12-2   INFLATION AND KEYNESIAN ECONOMIC POLICY

Keynesian remedies for inflation hinge on the sensitivity of prices and wages to slack product-market and labor-market conditions. In the preceding discussion we have suggested that given the institutional structure of the U.S. economy as it has evolved since World War II, the potential for an inflationary wage–price interaction to develop in a underheated economy has increased. Undoubtedly this is due in part to bilateral monopoly elements in wage and price setting. However, in this situation the inflationary process is stimulated by measures that increase production costs, and the possibility of stagflation is presented if such measures are accompanied by reductions in aggregate demand.

Suppose unemployment is at its natural rate, say 4 percent, and a national emergency requires an increase in defense expenditure. No one would argue that such an increase would not be inflationary unless demand were reduced in other sectors. As marginal workers enter the labor force, marginal productivity will fall and money wages will be bid up. If the capital stock is fully utilized, bottlenecks will develop, again raising unit labor costs. Keynesian remedies such as tax increases and a reduction in government spending in other areas would be appropriate measures for shifting resources into the military sector with a minimum of inflation. Tight money would be less desirable since it presumably would slow down the rate of investment. Though the short-run impact of a decline in investment might be equivalent to a reduction in consumption or other spending, in the long run this impedes the growth of labor productivity which is required for price stability in an economy in which money wages are expected to rise continually.

In the situation described above, it is clear that a reduction in demand is called for. However, the amount of inflation which occurs will depend in large measure upon the way in which demand is depressed. Increased taxes and interest rates will tend to be more inflationary than direct cuts in public spending. Furthermore, as we have suggested, tight money may have long-run consequences not immediately apparent. Nevertheless, monetary policy is often the most flexible policy instrument, and a tax increase to pay for a war is likely to be more palatable to the congress than spending cuts. In an overheated economy in which the problem is essentially too much demand, any measure which inhibits spending is better than no measures at all, and tax increases and tight money would be appropriate, although they are not the best policy instruments for controlling inflation.[6]

Suppose, on the other hand, prices are increasing at a rate of 5 percent while industrial production is declining and the unemployment rate is rising. This was the case in the United States in 1969–1970 as indicated in Chapter 10. In that period, the business community was so pessimistic about future prospects that the Dow-Jones Index of industrial stock prices suffered its most severe downturn since the crash of the late 1920's. In this case the problem was obviously not excess demand. It was clearly a case of wages and profit rate rising faster than productivity as an inflationary psychology developed on the heels of the Vietnam episode. Rising prices in the primary industries meant increasing production costs in consumer goods industries, resulting in still higher prices and demands for further cost-of-living adjustments to wages. Keynesian policies designed to restrict demand not only intensified the unemployment problem, but they were designed in such a way that production costs were increased and investment discouraged.

President Nixon had inherited an inflationary situation from the Johnson Vietnam War era. Yet from early 1969, the unemployment rate was rising with the Consumer Price Index; and by the third quarter, industrial production had declined with no indication that the inflation was slowing down.

Until 1971, the anti-inflation program of the Nixon administration was essentially Keynesian, with lip service paid to the Friedman viewpoint. A temporary tax increase effected during the Johnson administration was extended. Money was tightened, credit was rationed, and the budget was balanced. With soaring interest rates, no tax relief, and a rising consumer price index, money wage increases of 10 percent and more were sought by labor unions. As prices continued to rise, Nixon's economic advisors promised to stop the inflation without increasing the rate of unemployment by using Keynesian remedies alone. They argued that any other method, such as wage guidelines, would interfere with competitive market forces and hence would be unacceptable.[7] However, by 1971 it was clear that some form of price controls was needed. Whether or not the accelerating

---

[6] Note that if the distributive consequences of the measures are considered, tax hikes and tight money, which restrict demand in the private sector, might be preferred to cutbacks in public spending. The point made here is that tax increases and tight money are likely to be more inflationary than spending cuts.

[7] See comments by A. F. Burns, economic advisor to President Nixon, in "Wages and Prices by Formula?" *Harvard Business Review* (March–April, 1965), 59.

inflation was due to monopolistic elements in the economy, the short-range problem had to be dealt with directly.[8]

There had been some experience with wage and price controls in the period 1962–1966 (in those days they were called "guideposts"), but the inflation of the early 1960's was a considerably different beast from the one faced by Nixon in 1971. In the next section we will examine some theories of wage and price control and the associated policy packages in order to understand the difference between the Kennedy-Johnson guideposts and the Nixon controls.

12-3   THE THEORY OF WAGE AND PRICE CONTROLS

The inadequacy of Keynesian anti-inflation measures has forced policymakers to turn to direct wage and price controls. But if restraining aggregate demand has been unable to control inflation without a high unemployment cost, recent experience with wage-price policy has also been disheartening. Attempts to impose wage or price controls have resulted in panic buying and withholding of supply, producing shortages, general inefficiency, uncertainty, and widespread frustration.

The bewildering variety of price control schemes unveiled in recent years may lead one to question whether the policymakers really know what they are doing. We shall see that the type of price policy one follows depends very much on the nature of the inflationary process and that the "best" price policy might not be at all desirable at some other time.

A theory of price control must be based on some underlying view of the inflationary process. We shall see, for instance, that the Nixon Phase II controls were based on different assumptions about the way inflation was transmitted than were the Kennedy-Johnson guideposts. In addition, some of the problems faced by Nixon in administering his price controls were not present in the Kennedy-Johnson era. In this section we will compare the two types of price control schemes from these perspectives.

THE KENNEDY–JOHNSON GUIDEPOSTS

The Kennedy–Johnson guideposts were based on a view of the inflationary process similar to that described by the Keynes–Phillips model.

[8] This is not to say that the inefficacy of Keynesian measures is not suggestive of undesirable structural rigidities in the U.S. economy that have reduced or eliminated the sensitivity of prices to changes in market conditions. If this is the case, economists should begin to consider alternatives for a longer-run structural reform. The possibilities, while fascinating, are unfortunately beyond the scope of this book.

With the 1958 article by Phillips providing the intellectual underpinnings,[9] the 1960's was the decade of the Phillips curve. Led by two establishment economists, Paul Samuelson and Robert Solow, who published some estimates of a U.S. Phillips curve in 1960, economists began statistical studies of the Phillips relationship from all conceivable perspectives,[10] and the Phillips curve became the basic analytical device for designing anti-inflation policy.

We have already examined the Phillips curve concept in some detail and have seen its basic consistency with the Keynesian model. Both suggest aggregate demand remedies for inflation. But in the Keynesian model inflation is attributed to excess demand in product markets that causes firms to raise prices. Phillips, on the other hand, emphasized the role of rising money wages in tight labor markets as the impetus to price increases. Prices respond to increasing labor costs, and the real culprit is found in the worker or his union, not the profiteering firm. If anything, this model strengthens the case for using unemployment as the principal anti-inflation weapon.

Money wage changes are related to the unemployment rate, but they will not be inflationary unless they cause price increases. Wage increases will shift the price–employment relationship only if they are not matched by productivity gains. If hourly wages rise by 3 percent and output per manhour also increases by 3 percent, unit labor cost will not rise and firms will not raise prices (other things equal). If wage increases are no greater than productivity increases there will be no inflation, provided of course that excess demand is not generated in the product market. An increase in product market demand would produce a rightward movement *along* the price–employment relationship, thereby generating diminishing-returns inflation.

The idea that wage increases should be limited to increases in labor productivity while at the same time aggregate demand was manipulated to keep unemployment at its natural rate was the basic idea behind the Kennedy–Johnson guideposts. This "fine-tuning" was supposed to keep the economy at full employment, without inflation, while allowing real income to rise at the rate of productivity growth. The policy was to be neutral with respect to the distribution of income between wages and

---

[9] A. W. Phillips, "The Relation Between Unemployment and the Rate of Change of Money Wage Rates in the United Kingdom, 1861–1957," *Economica*, n.s. XXV (November, 1958), 283–299.

[10] See, for example, Rattan J. Bhatia, "Unemployment and the Rate of Change of Money Earnings in the United States," *Economica*, n.s. XXVIII (August, 1961), 286–296; George Perry, *Unemployment, Money Wage Rates and Inflation* (Cambridge, Mass.: The MIT Press, 1966), Gail Pierson, "The Effect of Union Strength on the U.S. 'Phillips Curve'," *The American Economic Review*, LVIII (June, 1968), 456–467; Paul Samuelson and Robert Solow, "Analytical Aspects of Anti-Inflation Policy," *op. cit.*

profits since an increase in both wages and output per manhour of 3 percent also allows for a 3 percent increase in profits.[11]

The guideposts consisted of holding money wage increases in all industries to average annual productivity increases for the economy as a whole. If firms maximize profits and set

$$p = \frac{w}{MP}$$

and assuming that changes in marginal and average productivity are proportional, then existing price levels can be maintained in firms with average productivity increases, raised in firms with smaller productivity increases, and lowered in firms with greater than average increases.[12]

Such a policy would result in price stability if all the following four assumptions hold:

1. firms view cost per unit of output, not unit factor cost, as the relevant basis for price changes;
2. wage changes are the principal source of inflationary pressure on costs;
3. direct controls are the best way to limit wage increases;

and

4. the impetus to inflationary price increases comes from rising production costs, not demand.

But are these valid assumptions?

The first assumption is based on a model of the firm in which prices are affected by changes in marginal or average cost per unit of output. Although this may be true in competitive industries where firms follow the price-setting rule:

$$p = MC$$

or in a monopoly, sheltered from oligopolistic competition, which sets

$$MR = MC$$

it does not necessarily hold in oligopolistic markets where a firm sets prices based not only on demand and cost conditions that influence its internal

---

[11] Suppose the value of output is $100, and a 3 percent productivity gain increases it to $103. Initially let wages be $80 and profits $20. If wages rise by 3 percent they will increase to $82.40, leaving $21.60 for profits, an increase of 3 percent. The ratio of wages to profits remains 4:1.

[12] Alternatively, wage increases could be held to productivity increases on a firm-specific or industry-specific basis. Then, the market mechanism would produce shifts in labor from firms with below-average productivity increases to firms with greater increases. The theoretical effect on output and relative prices would eventually be the same in both cases.

operations but also on expectations about how its rivals will react. Some theories of oligopoly suggest that such firms use factor price changes (wages, materials costs) as "signals" for price increases in the face of uncertainty about the price policies of their rivals. Since factor price changes are generally industry-wide while changes in productivity (that link factor costs to factor costs per unit of output) are firm-specific, at least in the short run, markup pricing may be used by firms to adjust prices to longer-run changes in unit costs. Empirical studies have shown that in the manufacturing sector where oligopoly is the (statistically) predominant form of market structure, prices do respond to changes in factor costs irrespective of productivity change.[13] This means that a wage policy that holds wage increases to productivity gains but allows prices to "float" will not only be inflationary (since prices will rise by the same percent as wages) but also will allow the profit share of the increase to rise relative to that of the wage share in real terms. If the rate of inflation exactly equals the wage increase, that is, if prices are raised in proportion to money wages, the real wage share will remain constant so that all the productivity gain will go to profit. In the case cited in footnote 11, real profits will rise by $3, a gain of 15 percent.

The guideposts of the 1960's were imposed in a period when wage increases were the principal source of inflationary pressure on costs. The inflation of the early 1970's has been characterized by rising materials costs, food prices, and prices of basic resources, like energy. If such price increases are the result of actual shortages, rather than of a wage-price spiral, market forces will be put in motion to redistribute income from the industrial sector to agriculture and the extractive industries. Even when industrial productivity is rising, real incomes in the industrial sector cannot increase proportionately in the face of increasing costs of food and raw materials.

Suppose a firm produces 100 units of output at $1 per unit with a labor input of $40, materials input of $40, and profit of $20. Consider the effect of a 50 percent increase in materials costs that occurs simultaneously with a 5 percent increase in labor productivity. Output rises to 105. If wages are allowed to increase by 5 percent, labor costs will rise by $2, to $42. Materials costs are $63, assuming a 50 percent price increase and a 5 percent increase in materials requirements. If the output price is held at $1, the firm's profits will be completely eliminated. If prices are allowed to float and the firm attempts to maintain its share relative to wages, profits will increase by 5 percent to $21, the total value of the output will be $126,

---

[13] For some empirical evidence of this phenomenon see Nancy S. Barrett *et al., Prices and Wages in U.S. Manufacturing* (Lexington, Mass.: D. C. Heath and Company, 1973), and Otto Eckstein and David Wyss, "Industry Price Equations," *Conference on the Econometrics of Price Determination*, Washington, D.C., 30–31 October, 1970.

and the price per unit will increase to $1.20. If similar changes occurred economy-wide, prices would have risen by 20 percent while wages and profits would have increased by 5 percent. This would represent a decline in real industrial income of 15 percent. Although this example is exaggerated it illustrates that a wage-price policy aimed only at holding wage increases to productivity gains will not prevent price increases in the face of rising materials costs.

A third assumption implicit in the Kennedy–Johnson guideposts was that direct controls are the best way to limit wage increases. This assumes that wages are determined principally by demand conditions in the labor market and that inflationary expectations are not the source of upward pressure on wages. As we have seen, the model of inflation that most influenced policy makers in the 1960's was the modified Keynesian approach of the Phillips curve concept, in which wage changes were viewed as independent of price changes and it was assumed workers would be subject to money illusion if prices were to rise. In retrospect, such a policy may have been appropriate in the optimistic days of the early and mid-sixties. However, recent experience suggests that direct controls on wages will not be politically acceptable to labor unless they are accompanied by measures to reduce or eliminate inflationary expectations.

Finally, any scheme of wage or price controls presupposes the source of inflationary pressure to come from shifts in the aggregate supply function rather than movements along it. Although inflation may be the result of a wage-price spiral such as we have described, price increases also serve the important function of equilibrating market demand and supply. If equilibrating price increases are not permitted, shortages will occur. Again, the problem of shortages was not so serious in the 1960's as in recent experience, partly because there was no need for equilibrating increases in food and materials prices. Some observers feel, however, that a wage-price policy that allows prices to float freely is less apt to produce shortages (since equilibrating increases are theoretically permitted) than a policy of direct controls on prices. However, if equilibrating increases are needed for food and basic materials, secondary price increases and falling real incomes such as we have described are likely to trigger an inflationary spiral if an inflationary psychology develops. Thus, the conditions under which the Kennedy–Johnson guideposts were imposed were more conducive to the success of such a policy measure than were those faced by the Nixon Administration in the early 1970's.

CRITICISMS OF THE GUIDEPOSTS

Despite the fact that conditions for imposing wage-price guideposts were favorable in 1962, the Kennedy–Johnson experiment was not without its critics—not surprisingly, as it represented the first major attempt at a non-Keynesian remedy for inflation. Wage-price policy had been avoided by Eisenhower, who faced an inflationary recession; and later President Nixon turned to price controls only as a last resort. Thus, the experience with the guideposts of the sixties far from legitimatized them as a policy instrument. Consequently, it will be useful to address some of the criticisms of that early experiment.

Interference with the Market System.   A major objection to the wage-price guideposts was the contention that such a policy would interfere with the allocation of resources by the market system. Such reasoning ignores the fact that resource allocation depends upon *relative* prices and is essentially independent of the over-all price level. The guideposts would not theoretically interfere at all with relative prices. Supply price would fall in fast-growing industries, and presumably output and demand would increase in those firms. The reverse would hold for slower-growing industries. Since guideposts affect only the general price level and not relative prices, they should not interfere with the market system any more than Keynesian remedies do.

Impact on Income Distribution.   It is sometimes held that, if wages are allowed to increase by as much as productivity, all the gains will be to labor and none will be to profits. This is a specious argument. Suppose total output is 100, with labor receiving 80 percent and 20 percent going to profits. If, with the same labor force, productivity and wages both increase by 5 percent, output will rise to 105 and labor will receive an increase of $80 \times 0.05 = 4$. There will be a residual of 1, which will represent an increase in profits equal to 5 percent of 20 ($20 \times 0.05 = 1$). Thus if productivity increases by 5 percent, *both* wages and profits can be increased by 5 percent.

A more serious argument is that the wage–price guideposts do perpetuate the existing *relative* distribution of income between wages and profits. Robert Solow has provided two answers to this argument.[14] First, relative factor shares have changed very little in the United States during the experience of industrial development. Therefore, the guideposts would not weaken any inherent tendency for these to change. Furthermore, we must presume that the guideposts would not be adhered to precisely. In some years average productivity may be overestimated, in which case labor's share would increase. If productivity gains were understated, labor's relative share would decline.

We have seen that the argument is changed once we introduce the effect of rising materials costs. However, this was not an issue addressed by

---

[14] In J. P. Schultz and R. Z. Aliber, eds., *Guidelines, Informal Controls, and the Market Place* (Chicago: Chicago University Press, 1966), pp. 48–49.

critics at the time, because materials costs did not play such a dramatic role in the inflationary process. In any event, the basic argument that wage-price guideposts do not necessarily alter the relative shares of wage and profits in industrial value added is still valid, even when the effect of rising materials costs is taken into account.

Inflation Due to Increasing Profit Margins. It is sometimes argued that even if unions agreed to hold wage increases to the level of productivity gains, there is no assurance that firms would not jack up profits and raise prices.

In the competitive model, firms will set prices so that the value of the marginal product of the last worker is equal to the money wage they must pay that worker. This reasoning results in the formula

$$p \times MP = w$$

or

$$p = \frac{w}{MP}$$

on which the guideposts are based. Rational firms will raise or lower prices according to whether they have experienced lower or higher productivity increases than the national average, and the net impact on the general price level will be stabilizing. According to this theory, there can be no profits inflation.

Suppose, however, that a firm monopolizes a product market or shares the market in such a way that its selling price is affected by the amount it sells. In this case the value of the marginal product is not $p \times MP$ but $MR \times MP$, where MR is the marginal revenue, or increment of total revenue associated with the last unit sold. Marginal revenue is the change in total revenue with respect to output, or

$$MR = \frac{\Delta TR}{\Delta q} = p + q\frac{\Delta p}{\Delta q}$$

Marginal revenue is price, minus the reduction in price required to make the last sale, multiplied by all units for which the price was reduced.[15]

---

[15] Note that if a firm is a perfect competitor and can sell its entire output at a fixed price, then

$$\frac{\Delta p}{\Delta q} = 0$$

and

$$p = MR$$

Recalling the definition of demand elasticity,

$$E_D = -\frac{p}{q}\frac{\Delta q}{\Delta p}$$

and rearranging terms,

$$MR = p\left(1 - \frac{1}{E_D}\right)$$

Marginal revenue and price are related through the elasticity of demand. The greater the elasticity of demand, the smaller is the difference between marginal revenue and price.

Thus, for a monopolist, labor is hired until

$$MR \times MP = w$$

and prices are set so that

$$p = \frac{w}{MP[1 - (1/E_D)]}$$

Suppose labor unions follow the guideposts and hold wage increases to productivity increases. There will still be no tendency for prices to rise in response, since the price equation should be unaffected by equal increases in w and MP. Even though the *level* of monopoly prices may be higher than would have been the case under competitive conditions, there is no indication that price *changes* would tend to be greater. It is true that these firms will increase prices (and profit margins) in response to an expected decline in demand elasticity. Conversely, they will reduce prices if they expect demand elasticity to fall. There is no evidence, however, that the guideposts per se will affect expectations concerning demand elasticity, and consequently, inflationary price increases in response to a perceived reduction in elasticity would have occurred in the absence of guideposts.

We have seen that in some industries firms set prices in terms of factor costs rather than costs per unit of output. In such cases, firms may increase their profits at the expense of the wage share if prices are allowed to float. If, however, prices in such industries were controlled, profits could rise in proportion to wages (assuming, of course, the effect of rising materials costs is negligible). Prices are determined by the "cost-plus" rule:

$$\text{Price} = \text{Unit cost} + \text{Profit}$$

with profit set as a percentage of the cost base. Under the guideposts, if productivity were increased by 5 percent, wages and profits could also increase by 5 percent without a price increase. Thus, the problem is to design a wage–price policy that will prevent firms from raising prices in the face of rising factor costs, not to maintain relative factor shares.

Difficulty in Measuring Productivity Gains.   Critics have argued that wage–price guideposts are impossible to administer because it is not feasible to obtain an accurate estimate of average productivity gains. Provided, however, that estimates are approximately accurate, the guideposts are an effective means of controlling inflation. If, however, productivity gains are overstated, the general price level will probably rise even if unions adhere to the guidelines. On the other hand, if gains are understated, the price level will fall. In most cases guideposts based on slightly inaccurate estimates of productivity increases are better than no guideposts at all.

If there were money illusion, it would not make much difference whether or not productivity gains were accurately assessed, as wages would increase only with the estimated rise in productivity and not in response to any resulting increase in the price level. On the other hand, if price increases trigger inflationary expectations that escalate wages there should be a bias toward understating productivity gains, since the penalty for overstating them is the possibility of a wage-price spiral. However, in the likely event that firms will not reduce prices in response to falling unit labor costs, profits may gain at the expense of the wage share.

Impact on Real Wages.   In practice, it is difficult to justify the use of wage-price guideposts once an inflation is in full swing. Suppose prices are increasing by 5 percent per year, while real productivity gains are estimated to be 3 percent. If labor holds wage increases to 3 percent, this represents a *decline* in the real wage of 2 percent. How can such a decrease in real wages be justified in the face of increased productivity? Someone must be reaping the return and, labor unions argue, that someone is management.

Underlying the argument, of course, is the assumption that inflation will continue at the same rate in the future as it has in the past. This is, of course, what is meant by a psychology of inflationary expectations which develops as a result of past inflation. But real wages will decline only if inflation *continues* at a rate greater than 3 percent. Presumably, the implementation of the guideposts will eliminate the inflation so that real wages will rise by 3 percent—the same rate as the increase in money wages and the productivity increase.

However, the argument that real wages should increase by the amount of the productivity increase is a convincing one, particularly the popular version in which the price index used to compute real wage gains is taken from the past inflationary experience. Consequently, it is important to implement guideposts early in a boom period, before labor becomes accustomed to seeing wage gains frittered away by rising prices. In an inflationary situation it is difficult to convince labor that price stability will be achieved as a result of labor's own restraint.

Moral Suasion as a Policy Instrument. Some observers question the feasibility of using moral suasion or "jawboning" as a policy instrument. It is sometimes contended that those unions and management who conscientiously follow the guideposts are penalized relative to those who ignore them. J. T. Romans has observed that moral suasion works best when aimed at small groups of individuals.[16] In this way the noncompliers can be singled out and the responsibility for failure of the policy can be laid at their door. Thus, in the experience with guideposts in the Kennedy administration, only a few major, basic industries were singled out for special observation. The steel industry was of particular concern, because of the impact of steel prices on the general price level as well as the fact that the steel industry is a highly concentrated one.

It is necessary that the policy measures being imposed by moral suasion be generally popular with the public at large so that noncompliance be met with disapprobation. At the same time, the target population must be small enough that noncompliers be recognized.

EXPERIENCE WITH THE GUIDEPOSTS

Experience with wage-price guideposts as an anti-inflation measure was encouraging. Gary Fromm has estimated that for the period 1962–1966, when the guideposts were more or less in effect, they

1. reduced the annual rate of increase of average hourly earnings by about 1.25 percent,
2. reduced the rate of increase of unit labor costs by about 2 percent,
3. reduced the rate of increase of the wholesale price index by about 1.4 percent.

He also concluded that the benefit of the guideposts accrued to business more than labor.[17] These findings have been supported by other observers.[18] Despite the fact that economic expansion with wage-price guideposts in the 1962–1966 period took place with considerably less inflation than

[16] In J. T. Romans, "Moral Suasion as an Instrument of Economic Policy," *The American Economic Review*, LVI (December, 1966), 1220–1225.

[17] Gary Fromm, "The Wage-Price Issue: The Need for Guideposts," in Joint Economic Committee Hearings (Washington, D.C.: Government Printing Office, 1968), 3–7.

[18] See George W. Perry, "The Wage-Price Issue: The Need for Guideposts," in Joint Economic Committee Hearings (Washington, D.C.: U.S. Government Printing Office, 1968), 12–19.

had occurred during the less buoyant conditions of the late 1950's and late 1960's, President Nixon was reluctant to impose price controls in the early 1970's. Some of the reasons cited above were voiced by Nixon Administration economists. But a more likely reason was the fact that the inflation had been allowed to persist for so long that an inflationary psychology was rampant and clearly influencing wage negotiations. The situation became even more difficult when supply conditions in primary products markets necessitated equilibrating price increases for food and basic industrial commodities. We have seen that under these conditions, a wage-price program like that of the 1962–1966 period would not necessarily be effective. Consequently, a new type of wage-price scheme had to be devised to deal with the changed nature of the inflationary process.

12-4 ACCELERATING INFLATION AND ITS POLICY IMPLICATIONS

In Chapter 10 we discussed the accelerationist theory of inflation that has recently been offered as an explanation of the observed insensitivity of the rate of price change to slack labor and product market conditions. In this view, attempts to reduce unemployment below its natural rate will produce an initial price increase. If this price increase triggers an inflationary psychology, workers demand higher wages and prices are increased further in response. As money illusion is lost only gradually—because it takes some time for inflationary expectations to develop as a result of an initial price increase—the rate of inflation will accelerate. Since the actual rate of inflation will always be greater than the expected rate, inflation will continue to accelerate indefinitely unless inflationary expectations are somehow reduced or eliminated.

Accelerationist economists in 1970 began projecting fantastically high rates of inflation over the successive five years in the absence of direct intervention into the wage-price spiral.[19] They strongly urged the imposition of wage-price controls. However, the price control schemes suggested by the accelerationist model were conceptually different from those of the Kennedy–Johnson era, since they were based on a different model of the inflationary process.

We saw that the modified Phillips model on which the Kennedy–Johnson guidelines were based implicitly assumed that wage changes were independent of price changes and that workers were subject to money illusion. For the accelerationists, the major impetus to the inflationary process

---

[19] See, for example, Robert J. Gordon, "Wage-Price Controls and the Shifting Phillips Curve," *Brookings Papers on Economic Activity* (1972:2), 413–416.

is not exogenous wage increases, but the inflationary psychology itself. Inflation is a "vicious circle" that can be stopped only by breaking the inflationary psychology. Thus, the emphasis is on controlling consumer prices as a means of preventing inflationary wage hikes, rather than the other way around. However, like the Kennedy–Johnson guidelines, it is assumed that if wage increases are prevented there will be no feedback into wholesale prices.[20]

THE NIXON CONTROLS

The price control programs of the Nixon Administration reflected an accelerationist view of the inflationary process. Although they contained wage guidelines, the principal emphasis was on controlling prices at the consumer level. Phase II of Nixon's price control program stressed the consumer–participation aspect of price controls. Retail stores were required to list pre-control prices, and consumers were requested to report illegal price increases to a commission set up to receive such complaints. There was considerable publicity in the news media of the consumer as a price–policer. So the effectiveness of the program was presumed to depend at the outset on its credibility. The enforcement aspect of the program was much less important than the impact on the consumer psychology, and the success of Phase II was attributed by most observers to a moderation of wage increases that directly resulted in a diminution of inflationary expectations.[21]

Implications for Tax Policy.   During the period in which inflationary expectations were rampant, economists noted a general strengthening of the inflationary effect of tax policy. In the Keynesian view, a tax increase is deflationary, since it reduces aggregate consumption demand and through the multiplier process reduces national income. Loss of money illusion, however, makes workers more sensitive to changes in their real disposable income and so loss of money illusion is likely to be accompanied by a loss of tax illusion as well. This implies workers will react to higher taxes in much the same way as they react to price increases—by demanding raises in money wages. Thus, a tax increase may be a useful anti-inflation device in a period such as the early 1960's and have disastrous consequences for inflation in a period like the early 1970's. Robert Gordon, for instance, estimates that about half of the wage increase between early 1972

---

[20] We have explored the weaknesses of that assumption in the previous section. In particular, the assumption that rising materials costs will have a negligible effect on wholesale prices was the major difficulty with applying this guideposts concept in the early 1970's, when materials costs were rising rapidly.

[21] For example, see *Economic Report of the President* (Washington, D.C.: U.S. Government Printing Office, 1974), 88.

and 1973 can be explained by the very large increase in the effective
social security tax rate in the first quarter of 1973.[22]

Experience with the Nixon Price Controls. Most economists agree
that the price control policy of the Nixon Administration substantially reduced the rate of inflation between the last half of 1971 and the end of
1972. Gordon estimates that during Phases I and II (August 1971 to
January 1973), nonfarm prices rose at an annual rate that was about 2.3
percent slower than it would have been in the absence of controls. Wage
increases were about 0.6 percent lower than they would have been in the
absence of controls.[23] In this period, there seems to have been a squeeze
of profits below their "free-market" levels. This was undoubtedly due to
the emphasis on prices rather than wages as well as the lag in the forma-
tion of price expectations. In 1973, on the other hand, price increases were
greater than wage increases. Gordon estimates that the price control policy
in 1973 reduced the rate of wage increase by 1.1 percentage points.[24]
From his econometric model of wage–price interaction he concludes that
the slowdown of wage increases in 1973 was due entirely to the indirect
impact of slow price growth and that controls had no direct effect on
wages.[25] This finding was consistent with the official interpretation of the
Nixon Administration that explained moderating wage increases in terms
of the expectations of lower price changes in the future.[26]

12-5   SUPPLY-INDUCED INFLATION

Although Phase II of Nixon's price policy was reasonably successful in
slowing the rate of inflation and dampening inflationary expectations, 1973
was a year of rapid price increase. Furthermore, unlike the earlier period,
shortages developed for many commodities, resulting in panic buying and
the withholding of supply, producing more shortages and uncertainty.
Phase II worked for a while, however, and most likely would have continued to be successful had it not been prematurely abandoned and had
not the underlying inflationary process undergone a fundamental change.

Certain factors that were essentially exogenous to the inflationary
process produced substantial decreases in supply of certain food products
and raw materials. The successive currency devaluations, the corn blight,
the conflict in the Middle East, the Russian wheat deal, the Peruvian an-

[22] Robert Gordon, "The Response of Wages and Prices to the First Two
Years of Controls," *Bookings Papers on Economic Activity* (1973:3), 772.
[23] *Op. cit.* (1973), 776–777.
[24] *Ibid.*
[25] *Ibid.*
[26] *Economic Report of the President*, 1974, *op. cit.*, 88.

chovy die-off, all contributed to the problem. All of these events came at a time in which price controls were in force that prevented equilibrating increases required to relieve the pressure on demand and encourage increases in supply.[27]

THE NEED FOR EQUILIBRATING PRICE INCREASES

In addition to acting as the index of inflationary pressure, price increases serve the important function of equilibrating market demand and supply when one of them changes for some exogenous reason. The controls system was not designed to deal with a shortage situation. One might think that the need for equilibrating changes could be identified by the existence of shortages, but the answer is not simple. As a realistic price control policy must consist of uniform guidelines for all firms, at least within broad categories, the need for equilibrating changes in one area cannot always be pinpointed. The problem is aggravated if firms are suspected of deliberately withholding supply, contriving shortages in the short run in the hope of attaining a permanent increase in the control price ceiling. Such a phenomenon is, of course, a predictable reaction of firms with strong market power to the imposition of price controls. In such a case, the "contrived scarcity" would eventually force the price authorities to raise the ceiling price to alleviate the shortage situation, increasing profits for the firms in question.

Wage-price controls are based on the supposition that the basic source of inflationary pressure comes from a wage-price spiral caused by the development of inflationary expectations combined with noncompetitive price setting in relatively slack markets. But to allow equilibrating price increases for food and basic industrial commodities provides another problem for wage-price policy. Recall that such measures are also based on the assumption that the inflationary effect of costs is felt principally through wages. We have seen that if materials costs rise, firms will raise prices in the absence of wage increases; and if money illusion is absent, this will trigger a new round of inflationary expectations and demands for higher wages. Rapidly rising food prices of the magnitude experienced in 1973, an increase of about 20 percent over the previous year, also adds fuel to the inflationary psychology. Thus, some persons view price controls and commodity and food shortages as preferable to the inflationary psychology their rising prices might generate.

---

[27] An additional problem arose from setting price ceilings for internationally traded goods below world market prices. This contributed to a scarcity of certain commodities.

We have seen that price increases in the agricultural sector imply falling real incomes in the industrial sector if rising resource costs are not matched by productivity increases in industry. Even when industrial productivity is rising, real incomes in the industrial sector cannot increase proportionately in the face of increasing costs of food and raw materials. Thus, the inflationary process is set in motion by a need to redistribute income in favor of the agricultural sector and is not simply a result of a nonequilibrating wage-price spiral. Yet declining real wages and profit rates are difficult to rationalize when real GNP is rising and labor and management each instinctively view the other as the culprit who is stealthily gaining a bigger share of the pie. Historically, the farm sector has experienced a decline in its share of real income relative to the industrial sector. We have forgotten our Ricardian and Malthusian models of diminishing returns in agriculture and rising land rents relative to industrial profits. Although the current shortages of basic commodities may be only a temporary phenomenon, it is helpful to keep these models in mind.

This is not to suggest that the politics of rising food prices do not pose a problem, and they cannot be dismissed by reference to diminishing-returns models. However, in a supply-induced inflation, the situation must be evaluated in terms of a theoretical model that examines the relationship between the agricultural and industrial sectors, rather than viewing the basic distributive issue in terms of wages versus profits. An awareness of this fundamental point would facilitate a more constructive analysis of long-run sources of supply for those commodities whose shortages are most serious.

12-6 DISTRIBUTIVE ISSUES IN WAGE-PRICE POLICY

Although it is not always apparent, many of the issues associated with wage-price policy are related to the distribution of income. In Europe, wage-price controls are generally labeled "incomes-policy," in recognition that the design of such programs affects the way revenue is distributed between profits and wages as well as among workers and firms in different industries. It is often supposed that wage-price policy should be neutral with respect to relative shares. However, if market forces are at work to alter relative shares then a policy that holds shares constant will produce distortions, as needed equilibrating price changes will be prevented.

We have seen that a policy which restrains wage changes to productivity changes will be neutral with respect to the relative shares of wages and profits. A policy that permits a proportionate cost pass-through when productivity change is taken into account (assuming the price increase does not affect the quantity sold) will leave profit rates unaffected but may influence relative shares. Suppose, for instance, money wages increase by 5 percent while productivity gains are 3 percent, causing the unit labor cost to rise by 2 percent. If labor is one half of total cost, firms can raise prices by 1 percent without affecting profits. Total costs and profits have both increased by 1 percent as a result of the price increase, but wages have increased by 2 percent, thus affecting relative shares. On the other hand, if nonwage costs are increased and passed through on a percentage basis, profit rates will be unaffected but the profit-to-wage share will increase. (The relative shares of total costs and profits will remain unaffected, however.)

Although Phase II of the Nixon price control program allowed proportional cost pass-through, Phase IV restricted price increases to dollar-for-dollar cost pass-through. This means profits cannot be increased at all as a result of cost increases. Undoubtedly this restriction was due to the fact that in this period commodity price increases were widespread (as controls on commodity prices were not as strict as in Phase II), so that a proportionate pass-through rule would have favored the profit share relative to wages. In addition, real wages were feeling the pressure of rising food prices. However, there was some protection for the profit share, as the idea that some minimum rate of profit to equity be maintained was incorporated in other price rules. But dollar-for-dollar cost pass-through does represent a more extreme departure from the notion that price policy should be neutral with respect to relative factor shares, since it squeezes profits more than a proportional costs pass-through rule and the wage share almost always gains relative to the profit share.

The idea that wage-price policy should be neutral with respect to relative shares presupposes that these shares would remain unchanged in the absence of such controls. Increases in commodity and food prices, for instance, imply rising land rents and a shift in the income distribution away from the industrial sector. Other things being equal, real wages and profits should fall; and if productivity gains (the source of rising real income) are not substantial in the industrial sector, there is no reason to expect stable real wages. This means that rising money wages even if matched by productivity increases will be inflationary. Price changes may be equilibrating with regard to changes in relative shares as well as product market disequilibria, and such equilibrating changes will take place in the absence of controls. Whether profits or wages feel the bulk of the squeeze in the industrial sector will depend on which agricultural prices are rising most rapidly and how rising food prices affect the total demand for food relative to industrial commodities. In any event, it is a complicated question for which economists might come up with answers; but the desirability of the neutrality of factor shares, as well as the notion that real incomes in the industrial sector must rise as fast as productivity, can no longer be taken for granted.

One further aspect of wage-price controls may affect income distribution. If aggregate demand measures are used to reduce inflation in the absence of price controls the unemployment costs of price stability are likely to be higher than if they are combined with a controls program. By relying on measures other than unemployment to stabilize prices, wage-price policy allows tighter labor markets and higher levels of wage income than Keynesian measures. Thus, although a particular wage-price package may appear to be neutral with respect to factor shares *for the prevailing level of employment and output,* one should actually examine what would have happened to shares not only in the absence of the wage-price policy but also in the presence of a Keynesian alternative. In this light, wage-price policy is undoubtedly more favorable to the wage share than the foregoing analysis would suggest.

12-7   IS INFLATION A LABOR MARKET PROBLEM?

It is interesting that both the Kennedy–Johnson wage-price policy that tried to control wage change directly and the Nixon philosophy that attempted to influence wages by reducing inflationary expectations viewed the labor market as the major focal point of anti-inflation policy. This orientation, in part an intellectual legacy from the Phillips model, is emphasized in the discussion of the price controls program in the 1973 *Economic Report of the President.*[28]

This shift of emphasis out of the product market into the labor market is a major change from the viewpoint of the Keynesian model. Yet recent empirical work has suggested that the responsiveness of prices to wage changes and changes in materials costs is much less certain and less easy to predict than is generally assumed. It has been estimated that Phase II, for instance, had much less effect on wholesale manufacturing prices than on prices in the service sector and retail prices. Other research has shown there is much more variation across industries within manufacturing in the structure of price determination than of wage determination.[29] All this suggests that more work needs to be done to determine how firms react to changes in labor costs and materials cost. If, for instance, a price control program stipulates a cost pass-through criterion

[28] *Economic Report of the President* (Washington, D.C.: U.S. Government Printing Office, 1973), Chapter 2.
[29] Nancy S. Barrett *et al., Prices and Wages in U.S. Manufacturing, op. cit.*

but yet there are strong market forces compelling firms to use a difficult pricing rule, extra care must be taken in designing the administrative apparatus to avoid cheating. In the past, we have often assumed that firms will desire to pass through costs (and no more) and so the possibility of noncompliance has not been the subject of much study.[30]

UNEMPLOYMENT AS A REMEDY FOR INFLATION

We have seen that when an inflationary psychology develops, increasing unemployment is not necessarily a viable remedy for inflation. Although most observers would agree that high unemployment rates (or the threat of high unemployment rates) may serve to moderate labor's demand for high wages,[31] the apparent increases in the natural rate of unemployment (or, in the Perry version, rightward shifts of the Phillips curve) have made the unemployment rates required to produce this "docile worker effect" unacceptably high.

It is also agreed, however, that attempts to increase unemployment through Keynesian aggregate demand measures during an ongoing inflation would contribute fuel to the fire, even if the price increases were diagnosed as cost-induced and the unemployment were above the socially acceptable range. Consequently, manpower policy designed to reduce turnover into new unemployment and to shorten the search period becomes particularly appropriate during periods with strong inflationary expectations where Keynesian remedies are likely to intensify the problem of stabilizing prices.

THE ROLE OF MANPOWER POLICY IN INFLATION

Manpower policies such as measures to improve working conditions, the provision of more accurate and rapid information about job vacancies, elimination of discriminatory practices against certain labor force groups, retraining programs for structurally unemployed workers and for individuals

---

[30] This is not to say that there is no attempt to police noncompliance, but firms who want to raise prices more than costs are generally assumed to have been in a disequilibrium initially so that such price changes are often viewed as "equilibrating," that is, rectifying structural maladjustments.

[31] Gordon, for instance, put forward the view (with which he eventually disagreed) that in 1973, wage demands lagged behind price increases because of a "docile worker effect" that resulted from a threatened recession. If labor is convinced that the government will take restrictive monetary and fiscal measures if price controls are not successful, such behavior may be rational. In other words, lower real hourly wages are preferred to a reduction in aggregate real wages through an increase in unemployment. Robert Gordon, *op. cit.* (1973), 765–766.

re-entering the labor force after periods of inactivity, would all serve to pressure on wages, such measures would serve to reduce unemployment reduce the natural rate of unemployment. If there were aggregate demand without substantial increases in money wages. Alternatively, in periods of slack labor market demand, such measures would reduce the inflationary impact of aggregate demand measures and would render the use of Keynesian remedies for unemployment more compatible with the goal of price stability.

Thus, many economists view both wage–price controls and manpower policy as complementary to Keynesian measures in the sense that they make Keynesian economic policy more effective. They act on structural phenomena in labor and product markets that were assumed away by the Keynesian model—the loss of money illusion on the one hand and socially unacceptable rates of frictional and structural unemployment on the other. Consequently, these so-called non-Keynesian remedies should not be viewed as substitutes for Keynesian policy but should be viewed as ways to make Keynesian economics work better.

QUESTIONS FOR STUDY AND REVIEW

1. Referring to the model in Question 1 of Chapter 10, answer the following questions:

(a) Suppose the government imposed a 5 percent tax on each unit of output. What would be the impact on the price–employment relationship as well as on the equilibrium level of employment and prices?

(b) If the government wishes to impose this tax without affecting employment, what compensatory measures would be necessary? What would be the impact on the price level?

2. Consider an economy in which wage-price guidelines are in effect. How will changes in business taxes affect the distribution of total value added between wages and profits?

3. The wage-price guideposts of the Kennedy and Johnson administrations were based on a different model of the inflationary process than the Nixon price controls. Discuss the theoretical models on which the two policy packages were based and, assuming each theoretical model was an accurate description of the price process at the time, evaluate the anti-inflation impact of the two types of wage-price policy.

4. As an anti-inflation measure, wage-price guidelines have had strong advocates as well as harsh critics. What is the essential basis of the disagreement?

5. Suppose an economy is experiencing high unemployment rates

during an inflation. Discuss some policy measures that would be appropriate for reducing unemployment.

6. "Wage-price controls and manpower policy are not substitutes for Keynesian economic policy. Instead, they should be viewed as measures that make Keynesian economics work better." Discuss.

ADDITIONAL READING

BOSWORTH, BARRY, "The Current Inflation: Malign Neglect?" *Brookings Papers on Economic Activity* (1973:1), 263–283.

Economic Report of the President. Washington, D.C.: U.S. Government Printing Office, 1973. Chapter 2.

Economic Report of the President. Washington, D.C.: U.S. Government Printing Office, 1974. Chapter 3.

GORDON, ROBERT J., "The Response of Wages and Prices to the First Two Years of Controls." *Brookings Papers on Economic Activity* (1973:3), 765–779.

LEKACHMAN, ROBERT, "Inflation: Classic and Modern," in *The Age of Keynes,* by the same author (Lekachman), Chapter 10. New York: Random House, 1966.

PERRY, GEORGE L., "Wages and the Guideposts," *The American Economic Review,* LVII (September, 1967), 897–904.

POOLE, WILLIAM, "Wage–Price Controls: Where Do We Go From Here?" *Brookings Papers on Economic Activity* (1973:1), 285–299.

SAMUELSON, PAUL, "Wage–Price Guideposts and the Need for Informal Controls in a Mixed Economy," in *Full Employment, Guideposts, and Economic Stability: Rational Debate Seminars*. Washington, D.C.: U.S. Government Printing Office, 1967.

13

Economic Dynamics and the Theory of Economic Growth

Until now, our study of the theory of macroeconomic policy has consisted of an analysis of the determinants of national income equilibrium. We have been interested in the impact of changes in the various policy parameters on equilibrium income and employment or conversely, what changes in the policy parameters would be required to move to a desired equilibrium position.

Equilibrium analysis ignores the passage of time required for the system to move from one equilibrium to another. Yet the policy planner is often concerned with the immediate or short-run effects of economic policy rather than their projected ultimate impact. In Chapters 13 and 14 we shall explicitly take into account the time pattern of the target variables as they adjust to changes in economic conditions.

13-1 TIME IN ECONOMIC ANALYSIS

Equilibrium analysis is concerned with such questions as, "What will be the impact of an increase in government spending on income and employment?" Our previous examples have taken a *comparative statics* approach, examining the equilibrium income and employment before the change and comparing it with the equilibrium which would occur after the change. The process of adjustment from one equilibrium to another has been ignored.

Suppose an increase in government spending causes the *IS* curve to shift rightward from IS_1 to IS_2 as shown in Figure 13-1. Comparative statics

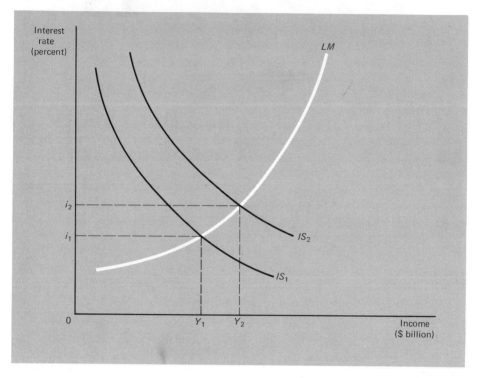

FIGURE 13-1
Comparative Statics Analysis of a Shift in the IS Curve

would project an increase in income from Y_1 to Y_2 and an increase in the interest rate from i_1 to i_2, assuming the money supply and the LM curve remain fixed.

Because the process of adjustment has been ignored, comparative statics does not tell us *when* the new equilibrium will be reached. Yet, generally, the policy planner is interested in predicting the impact of his policy within a specified period of time. A *dynamic* model explicitly takes into account the time pattern of adjustment to equilibrium.

Associated with every problem in comparative statics is a dynamic adjustment process. This association is known as the *correspondence principle*. If the dynamic adjustment process is known, then the policy planner can be told of the impact of his policy for any time period he specifies. The values of the target variables in disequilibrium may or may not be near the equilibrium values of the comparative statics model, depending upon the dynamic adjustment process.

If the values of the target values in disequilibrium approach the equilibrium values of comparative statics as the time period allowed for adjustment lengthens, then the new equilibrium is said to be *stable*. In some cases, however, the target values never reach the comparative statics equilibrium, even if a very long time period is allowed for adjustment. Then the new equilibrium is said to be *unstable*. The stability or instability of equilibrium depends upon (1) the dynamic adjustment process specified for the model and (2) the nature of the original functional relationships of the model.

EQUILIBRIUM ADJUSTMENT IN THE *IS–LM* MODEL

Consider the Keynesian model of national income determination represented by the *IS* and *LM* curves. The *IS* curve shows the interest rate that will equate saving and investment at different levels of national income. The *LM* curve shows the interest rate that will clear the money market at different levels of national income. Both the interest rate and national income will be in equilibrium (i.e., there will be no tendency for either to change) when saving equals investment and the money market is cleared simultaneously. Thus, overall equilibrium occurs where *IS* and *LM* intersect, as shown in Figure 13-1. If one curve is displaced (shifts) due to a change in one of the variables or functions which define it, then the new equilibrium can be found at the new point of intersection of the curves.

Let us consider the process of adjustment to a shift in *IS* from IS_1 to IS_2, as shown in Figure 13-2. Suppose the banking system is slow to adjust to the initial increase in demand. In case I in Figure 13-2, the initial response to the increased demand is an increase in income from Y_1 to Y_2, with no change in the interest rate, resulting in product market equilibrium with a disequilibrium in the money market. When income is Y_2 and the interest rate i_1, the demand for money will exceed the supply, and eventually the banking system will have to raise the interest rate to i_2 (assuming the money supply and the *LM* curve are fixed) which will clear the money market when income is Y_2. Now the product market must adjust to restore equilibrium in saving and investment. As the interest rate rises, investment falls and the level of income must fall until saving is reduced and equilibrium restored. In case I the process continues until eventually the new equilibrium is reached at Y_e and i_e. Notice that, in the process of adjustment, both income and the rate of interest rise and fall in a cyclical pattern with the cycles becoming of successively smaller magnitude as more time passes. Such cycles are said to be *damped*. Equilibrium in case I is *stable* because the system will eventually reach it, given adequate time for adjustment.

In case II the same dynamic adjustment process is implied, yet the new equilibrium Y_e is *unstable*. Adjustments in the product and money markets produce *explosive* cycles in income and the interest rate which

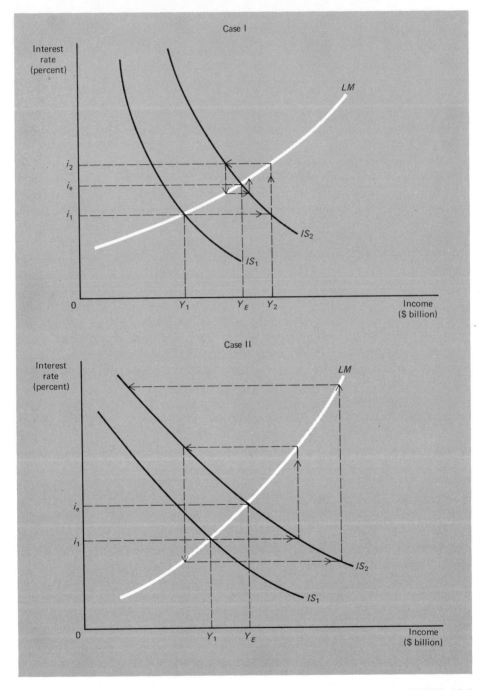

FIGURE 13-2

Dynamic Adjustment in the IS–LM Model
with a Money Market Lag

increase in magnitude with the passage of time. Notice that in case II the *LM* curve is steeper than the *IS* curves, while in case I the *LM* curve is flatter than the *IS* curves.

In general, a money market lag will result in explosive cycles and dynamic instability the less responsive the demand for money is to the interest rate and the more responsive investment demand is to the interest rate.

Suppose the policy maker asks the question, "What will be the impact of an increase in public spending?" Using a comparative statics analysis, the economist would project an increase in national income, employment, and the interest rate. A dynamic analysis must consider the adjustment process. If the banking system were slow in adjusting the interest rate to changes in economic conditions, the economist would predict that the change in spending will produce a cyclical pattern of income and employment. Whether the cycles will be damped or explosive will depend upon how sensitive the demand for money and investment spending are to changes in the interest rate and income.[1]

It is apparent that a comparative statics approach may give poor predictions if reactions to disequilibrium are not instantaneous. The immediate impact of a change in economic policy is likely to produce cyclical behavior in the target variables. Furthermore, in some cases comparative statics will not provide reliable predictions even if the planner is not concerned with the immediate impact of his policies. If an equilibrium is unstable, it will never be reached, regardless of how much time is allowed to pass.

The projection of the dynamic behavior of the economy will depend upon

1. the dynamic adjustment process, whether there are lags and where in the economy these lags occur,
2. the functional relationships in the static model, whether the *LM* curve is steeper than the *IS* curve.

NONEQUILIBRIUM MODELS

The *IS–LM* model is an equilibrium model. It has a dynamic aspect because of the behavior of the system in disequilibrium. Other macroeconomic models ignore the concept of equilibrium altogether. In these models the target variables are constantly changing over time. Consequently, the *timing* of economic policy becomes a particular concern.

Suppose the policy maker is concerned about the best time to initiate expansionary fiscal policy to ward off a potential recession. Consider the

---

[1] Note that the slopes of both the *IS* and *LM* curves depend upon the relative sensitivity of each to income and the rate of interest.

accelerator model of investment which states that investment is a function of changes in demand. The model is based on the assumption that firms must increase their capital stock to increase output. If firms try to keep a certain ratio between capital stock and sales,

$$\frac{K}{Y} = \beta$$

and since investment is equal to the net change in capital stock,

$$I = \Delta K$$

then changes in the capital stock, or investment, will be proportional to changes in demand; that is,

$$\frac{\Delta K}{\Delta Y} = \beta$$

$$I = \beta \, \Delta Y$$

The accelerator theory of investment can be incorporated into a simple Keynesian model:

$$Y = C + I$$
$$C = a + bY$$
$$I = \beta \, \Delta Y$$

Solving for income,

$$Y = a + bY + \beta \, \Delta Y$$

$$= \frac{a}{1 - b} + \frac{\beta}{1 - b} \Delta Y$$

This model is a nonequilibrium model. Applying the equilibrium concept would result in the nonsensical conclusion that in equilibrium net investment would be zero (since ΔY would be zero), and all GNP would be consumed or used for replacement investment. Note, however, that the model is useful for planning the appropriate timing of economic policy. If this model is applicable, the best time to initiate expansionary public policy is not when GNP has turned down, as an equilibrium model would suggest, but when the rate of increase in GNP declines.

In Figure 13-3 the time path of GNP is shown for an economy entering a recession. Using a Keynesian equilibrium model and ignoring the lag between policy initiation and effectiveness, the best time to undertake expansionary measures is at B, where GNP declines. The accelerator model would advise the policy maker to begin his program of expansion at A,

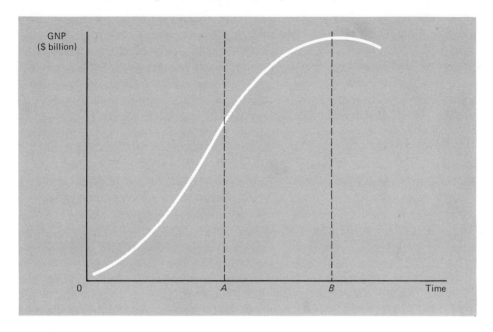

FIGURE 13-3

Optimal Timing of Anti-Recession Policy

where the rate of increase in GNP declines. When ΔY declines, even if Y is still increasing, this produces a decline in investment which will trigger the downturn in GNP through the multiplier.

In Chapter 14 we shall analyze the factors which cause nonequilibrium behavior in some detail. This behavior, often called the *business cycle,* is due primarily to factors associated with aggregate demand. We shall also consider the problem of the timing of economic policy.

THE CONCEPT OF A DYNAMIC EQUILIBRIUM

Consider an economy for which aggregate supply and aggregate demand are both increasing at the same rate over time. The increase in aggregate supply may be due to increased labor productivity due to technological change, while the increase in aggregate demand may be due to increases in investment over time. As seen in Figure 13-4, equilibrium will take place at a constant level of employment. Since aggregate demand is increasing with a constant level of employment, so must income per worker. If the economy can sustain this growth rate, it will be in a dynamic equilibrium with a fixed labor force and increasing productivity and output per head.

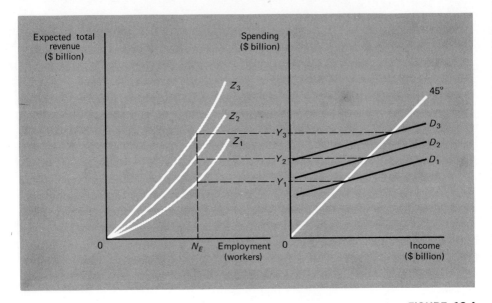

FIGURE 13-4

Dynamic Equilibrium with Economic Growth

The policy maker may ask the question, "How fast must aggregate demand grow so that full employment can be maintained in the face of a growing labor force and rising labor productivity?"

Suppose average labor productivity is rising by 3 percent and the labor force is growing by 2 percent. Then aggregate demand must grow by 5 percent in real terms to absorb the increase in productive capacity (i.e., the increased output per worker as well as an increased number of workers) for the full-employment economy.

Can the economy sustain a dynamic equilibrium in which GNP grows by 5 percent each year? This will depend upon the rate of investment. Consider a simple Keynesian model which incorporates an accelerator theory of investment:

$$Y = C + I$$
$$C = aY$$
$$I = \beta \, \Delta Y$$

Since

$$Y = C + I$$

is an equilibrium condition, an equilibrium can be found for this model, but it will not be a static equilibrium in the Keynesian sense. Instead, because investment is a function of the change in demand over time, a dynamic equilibrium can be found. This dynamic equilibrium will represent a time path of income which can be maintained indefinitely and from which there is no tendency to move, given the underlying conditions, or parameters.

Rearranging terms,

$$Y = aY + \beta \, \Delta Y$$

$$= \frac{\beta}{1 - a} \Delta Y$$

or

$$\frac{\Delta Y}{Y} = \frac{1 - a}{\beta}$$

This economy can maintain a rate of growth of aggregate demand equal to the marginal propensity to save divided by the capital–output ratio. If the capital–output ratio is 3, then the marginal propensity to save must be 15 percent if the economy is to sustain adequate demand in the private sector to keep the economy at full employment when labor productivity is rising by 3 percent and the labor force is growing by 2 percent. If the marginal propensity to save is only 10 percent, then if this model is applicable, the government will have to undertake measures to increase saving and investment to absorb the growing productive capacity of the economy.

13-2   THE THEORY OF ECONOMIC GROWTH

In the static Keynesian model, full employment could be achieved by attaining the appropriate level of aggregate demand and maintaining it indefinitely. Once time is incorporated into the analysis, however, it is clear that to maintain full employment over time, aggregate demand must grow to keep pace with the expanding productive capacity of the economy.

Productive capacity increases as the capital stock and the labor force grow over time. In the static, short-run analysis, investment is viewed as a component of aggregate demand. If the economy is at less than full employment, increases in investment are desirable, since these increases generate the demand necessary to induce firms to hire more workers. But more investment today means greater productive capacity tomorrow, since investment is synonymous with increases in the capital stock. Because of the dual character of investment, generating both aggregate demand and increased productive capacity, policies designed to reach full employment in the short run may result in serious unemployment problems in the long run.

Models of economic growth are concerned with three questions. First, how fast must an economy grow to maintain full employment of its resources as productive capacity increases? Second, will the private sector of the economy be able to sustain this growth rate in a dynamic equilibrium without government interference? And third, what public policies can aid an economy to maintain a stable growth rate over time?

HARROD–DOMAR MODELS

Roy Harrod and Evsey Domar independently developed models to describe the growth process.[2] Their analysis is essentially Keynesian in the sense that saving is assumed to be a function of income and national income equilibrium occurs when *ex ante* saving equals *ex ante* investment.

To maintain full employment of labor in the face of increasing productive capacity, the rate of growth of real aggregate demand must equal the rate of growth of the labor force plus the rate of growth of labor productivity. This growth rate is called the *natural rate of growth,*

$$G_N = n + p$$

where n is the rate of growth of labor force and p is the rate of growth of labor productivity.

Will the private sector be able to maintain such a growth rate? Suppose the productive capacity of the economy, P, is proportional to the capital stock:

$$P = \sigma K$$

Since

$$\Delta K = I$$

investment will produce proportional increases in productive capacity, or

$$I = \frac{1}{\sigma} \Delta P$$

If aggregate demand is sufficient to absorb productive capacity, firms will be in equilibrium (since in the absence of excess capacity, their sales expectations are being fulfilled), and investment will continue at the current rate. Therefore, in equilibrium,

$$\Delta P = \Delta Y$$

---

[2] See Roy Harrod, *Towards a Dynamic Economics* (London: Macmillan & Co., Ltd., 1948), and Evsey Domar, *Essays in the Theory of Economic Growth* (New York: Oxford University Press, 1957), Chapters 3–5.

Assuming a simple Keynesian model of income determination,

$$Y = C + I$$
$$C = aY$$

or

$$Y = \frac{I}{1 - a}$$

and

$$\Delta Y = \Delta I \frac{1}{1 - a}$$

This represents the relationship between changes in aggregate demand and changes in investment. Recalling the relationship between investment and changes in productive capacity,

$$I = \frac{1}{\sigma} \Delta P$$

and the equilibrium condition,

$$\Delta P = \Delta Y$$

then in equilibrium,

$$\sigma I = \Delta I \frac{1}{1 - a}$$

or

$$\frac{\Delta I}{I} = \sigma(1 - a)$$

In equilibrium, for aggregate demand to keep pace with productive capacity, investment must be growing at a rate equal to the output–capital ratio, σ, multiplied by the marginal propensity to save.[3]
Since

$$I = (1 - a)Y$$

and

$$\Delta I = (1 - a)\Delta Y$$

---

[3] Note that this result is equivalent to the analysis in the previous section in which an accelerator model of investment is incorporated into a Keynesian theory of income determination. The formulation described above follows the Domar analysis, while that of the previous section is attributable to Harrod.

then

$$\frac{\Delta I}{I} = \frac{\Delta Y}{Y} = \sigma(1 - a)$$

and income must also be growing at the same rate as investment. This growth rate is called the *warranted rate of growth.*

If the warranted rate of growth is exactly equal to the natural rate, that is, if

$$\sigma(1 - a) = n + p$$

then the economy can maintain a steady rate of growth at that rate indefinitely. Producers' expectations will be fulfilled, and the demand for labor will always equal the supply. The labor force will grow at a rate n and per capita income will rise at a rate p.

Both Harrod and Domar argued that it is unlikely that the warranted rate and natural rates will be equal since they are determined by independent factors. Consider the natural rate of growth. The rate of labor force growth is determined by demographic conditions such as the net birth rate, age structure of the population, and immigration patterns. These are presumably independent of economic conditions and the actual growth rate. The model presumes that the ratio between output and capital stock remains constant which, assuming constant returns to scale, implies that the ratio between the capital stock and labor force remains constant during the process of growth. Therefore, labor productivity will not increase unless a technological change occurs. The rate of growth of labor productivity will be equal to the rate of technological change. Although technological change may be embodied in investment and consequently may depend upon economic conditions and the actual growth rate, it is also governed by the rate of innovation which is presumed autonomous.

The warranted rate of growth depends upon the propensity to save which reflects households' preferences for present over future consumption. It also depends upon the relationship between capital stock and productivity which is essentially technological.

Because the natural rate and warranted rate of growth are determined by independent factors which are themselves not significantly influenced by the rate at which the economy is actually growing, then there is no reason to presume that they will be equal. Yet equality of the two rates is necessary to ensure a steady state of growth at an equilibrium rate.

THE INSTABILITY OF HARROD–DOMAR MODELS

For the economy to grow at a steady equilibrium rate, the warranted rate of growth must equal the natural rate,

$$G_W = G_N$$

or

$$\sigma(1 - a) = n + p$$

Only then will aggregate demand be growing at the same rate as productive capacity.

We have seen that there is no inherent tendency for these two rates to be equal, and hence, steady state growth in the private sector without government intervention is unlikely. Suppose the two rates are not equal. The time path of income is shown in Figure 13-5.

If the natural rate is greater than the warranted rate, the economy will actually grow at the warranted rate. However, the growth rate will be inadequate to absorb the natural increases in the labor force, and hence, unemployment will be an ever-increasing problem. In this case the rate of capital accumulation is lower than the rate of labor force growth, and the capital stock will be inadequate to employ the national labor force.

Suppose, on the other hand, the warranted rate exceeds the natural rate. In this case, to maintain full employment, aggregate demand must grow faster than the economy is actually able to grow. Increases in labor force and productivity are inadequate to produce the required growth of output, and consequently, the economy cannot grow at the warranted rate.

The warranted rate of growth is the rate at which aggregate demand and output must grow if productive capacity is to be fully utilized. If the growth rate, G, is less than G_W, excess capacity will result. Firms will not undertake new investment, and through the multiplier, income will fall. A downturn in income will continue, as shown in case III in Figure 12-5, until sooner or later firms will need to replace their capital stock if any positive output is to be forthcoming, investment will turn up, and the economy can grow at the warranted rate until the full-capacity ceiling is reached. This will be followed by another downturn, and fluctuations will continue indefinitely with cycles becoming increasingly more severe as the productive capacity of the economy increases.

POLICY IMPLICATIONS

Unless the warranted rate and natural rate of growth happen to be equal, the private sector cannot sustain a full-employment level of income over time. In the case where

$$G_N > G_W$$

a steady rate of growth can be maintained, but it will be insufficient to absorb the growing labor force. This situation is characteristic of less-devel-

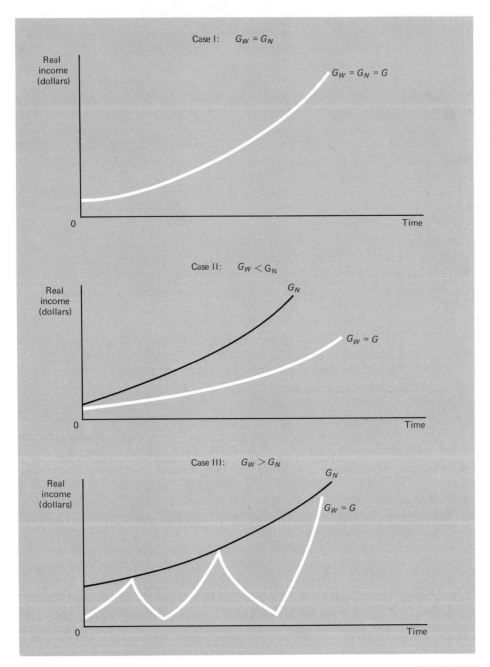

Case I: $G_W = G_N$

Real income (dollars)

$G_W = G_N = G$

0   Time

Case II: $G_W < G_N$

Real income (dollars)

G_N

$G_W = G$

0   Time

Case III: $G_W > G_N$

Real income (dollars)

G_N

$G_W = G$

0   Time

FIGURE 13-5

Time Path of Income in a Harrod–Domar Model

oped nations. In these countries the rate of growth of the industrial labor force is apt to be very great, since labor is flowing rapidly from the traditional agriculture and handicraft sectors into the modern sector. On the other hand, the warranted rate of growth is apt to be very low due to a low marginal propensity to save and a low output–capital ratio.[4]

For these economies, the growing labor force can be absorbed only by increasing the propensity to save and raising the output–capital ratio. While, theoretically, the propensity to save can be increased by tax policy, this approach may not be feasible in an economy in which the general population is living at the subsistence level. Tax policy must be aimed at upper income groups, and since these groups are generally powerful politically, such legislation may be impossible to obtain.

An alternative is to undertake measures which would raise the output–capital ratio. The average productivity of capital will depend, among other things, upon how much labor is being combined with capital in the production technology. In general, the more labor intensive the production process, the higher is the output–capital ratio, and the more labor can be absorbed for a given amount of investment. Underdeveloped countries, in recent years, have been plagued with well-meaning advisors from advanced nations who introduce them to the latest technological innovations of the advanced nations. These technologies are generally highly capital intensive. Given limited sources of investment funds, these projects cannot absorb as much of the labor force as projects using less capital and more labor.

The argument is often raised that if technology is labor intensive, labor productivity, and hence real wages, will be low relative to that of capital intensive processes. Supporters of this view ignore the fact, however, that if the capital stock is limited, fewer workers will be employed if production is capital intensive. If a major concern of economic development is to absorb labor into the modern economy, then labor intensive technologies, involving lower real wages but employing more workers, will be preferred to capital intensive processes for which labor productivity is higher but fewer workers are employed.

In advanced countries, the problem is generally that the warranted rate of growth outstrips the capacity of the economy to produce, so that

$$G_W > G_N$$

Unless the rate of technological change can be increased, then the warranted rate must be reduced if the economy is to avoid the instability inherent in this situation. Either the rate of saving must be reduced or the output–capital ratio must fall.

---

[4] Notice that the output–capital ratio is equivalent to the average productivity of capital.

Although the saving rate may be reduced by tax policy, most countries are reluctant to slow down the rate of saving and investment. Investment is presumably the source of increasing real wages which are generally a major economic goal. In addition, rising labor productivity will help to combat the inflationary trend associated with the built-in tendency for money wages to creep upward.

Increased investment will only increase labor productivity if it embodies technological change and/or if technology becomes more capital intensive. Both of these factors will also tend to bring the natural and warranted rates of growth closer together. Thus, public policy, in this situation, should be aimed at encouraging capital intensive production processes by keeping interest rates (capital costs) low. In addition, policy makers should keep in mind that very high levels of saving and investment may generate increases in productive capacity which are incompatible with full employment. Paradoxically, for mature economies a high rate of investment may not be compatible with a high growth rate if it generates recurring cycles in the level of economic activity. Instead, it will merely serve to complicate the management of macroeconomic stability for the policy maker.

NEOCLASSICAL CRITIQUE OF THE HARROD–DOMAR ANALYSIS

The Harrod–Domar analysis concludes that if a steady state growth rate can be achieved in an economy, it will be equal to the rate of increase of the labor force plus the rate of technological change. Steady state growth can only be achieved, however, in the unlikely event that this growth rate is exactly equal to the product of the marginal propensity to save and the output–capital ratio (average product of capital). The warranted rate of growth governs the actual rate which, in the typical case, will not result in a dynamic equilibrium at full employment.

Neoclassical critics of the Harrod–Domar model argue that inherent in the market mechanism there are stabilizing forces which will automatically move the economy to a steady state growth path, compatible with a dynamic full-employment equilibrium, with a growth rate equal to the natural rate of the Harrod–Domar analysis.[5]

Suppose, for instance, that

$$G_N > G_W$$

or

---

[5] See, for example, Robert Solow, "A Contribution to the Theory of Economic Growth," *The Quarterly Journal of Economics*, LXX (February, 1956), 65–94 and J. Meade, *A Neoclassical Theory of Economic Growth* (London: Unwin University Books, 1961).

$$n + p > \sigma(1 - a)$$

As growth occurs at the warranted rate, labor force unemployment becomes increasingly more serious. Workers will bid down money wages, thereby causing firms to substitute labor for capital in the production process. This will increase the output–capital ratio, raising the warranted rate of growth. The process will continue as long as there is excess supply in the labor market, until the warranted rate of growth rises to equal the natural rate. At this point, steady state growth will take place at the Harrod–Domar natural rate with all resources fully employed.

Other factors may operate to speed the adjustment process. As wages fall, if the share of national income going to profits, interest, and rent rises, the aggregate propensity to save will also increase, since the propensity to save from these sources is generally much greater than the propensity to save from wages.[6] Falling wages do not necessarily imply a decreasing share of national income going to labor, however.[7] Furthermore, increased saving will only increase the warranted rate of growth if that saving is channeled into domestic investment. In many of the less-developed countries, saving from nonwage sources is consumed or invested outside the home country.

Other factors may operate to reduce the natural rate of growth. If there is serious unemployment in the modern sector of the economy or if wages there are low, workers will tend to move more slowly out of traditional agriculture and cottage industry. If neighboring countries are experiencing more rapid rates of growth, there may be some emigration to these areas, reducing the rate of growth of the labor force and, hence, the natural rate of growth.

These same influences work in reverse in the case in which

$$G_W > G_N$$

or

$$\sigma(1 - a) > n + p$$

In such a situation, the level of investment is so great that aggregate demand must grow faster than the natural rate to keep productive capacity fully employed. As growth occurs at the warranted rate, the labor force rapidly becomes fully employed. As labor markets tighten, workers bid money wages up. If the monetary authorities do not increase interest rates proportionally, firms will substitute capital for labor in the production proc-

---

[6] This point is made by Nicholas Kaldor, "A Model of Economic Growth," *Economic Journal* (December, 1957), pp. 591–624.

[7] This depends upon the elasticity of substitution in the production function. For many countries, relative factor shares remain remarkably constant over time, even when there is considerable variation in relative factor prices.

ess, causing the output–capital ratio to fall. This process will continue until the warranted rate falls to the natural rate, at which point the economy can sustain steady state growth at the Harrod–Domar natural rate.

If investment is substantial, it is likely that the rate of technological change is also very high. This factor has been particularly important in the development of the advanced Western nations. Rapid increases in man-hour productivity have permitted high levels of investment consistent with reasonably stable growth at rates often exceeding 5 percent per year. For some countries, such as the United States, immigration has played an important role. Tight labor markets and high wages not only attract immigrants, but are generally conducive to a liberal immigration policy. Both immigration and technological change raise the natural rate of growth and reduce the disparity between the natural and warranted rates.

13-3 ECONOMIC POLICY FOR STABLE GROWTH

The neoclassical analysis of the process of growth concludes that a free-market system, with wage flexibility and labor mobility, will automatically settle into a stable pattern of steady state growth. The argument, like classical remedies for unemployment, does not consider the speed of adjustment. In particular, for a developing country wage deflation may be a slow and politically untenable solution to the problem of absorbing large segments of the population into the modern sector. In this section we shall consider how public policy can be used to speed and effectuate the process of stable, full-employment growth.

THE UNDERDEVELOPED MODEL

Developing countries are typically faced with rapid rates of labor force growth as workers move from traditional sectors of the economy. Labor productivity and technological change are also growing rapidly. On the other hand, saving is apt to be low, and any saving which does occur is often expatriated. That capital which is available is generally of foreign origin and often inefficiently utilized, so that the output–capital ratio tends to be low. These factors result in

$$G_N > G_W$$

producing a redundancy of labor and a scarcity of capital.

Neoclassical analysis would contend that wage deflation should encourage the substitution of labor for capital in production, raising the output–capital ratio. In a developing country, however, opportunities for factor substitution are often extremely limited. Working with imported capital and imported technologies, management may be tied to particular production techniques with little information about or interest in alternative methods. Furthermore, wage deflation will only encourage labor substitution if interest rates are not permitted to fall proportionally. In a developing economy, it is generally desirable to keep interest rates low, to encourage investment. In addition, wage deflation is not a politically or socially desirable measure, particularly when aspirations are high for improved living conditions.

As a consequence of all these factors, it is doubtful that wage deflation will effectively produce an increase in average capital productivity. This being the case, a conscious effort should be made to introduce labor intensive technologies and to discourage firms from using capital intensive techniques imported from abroad. Because, for these countries, technological change is also imported, care should be taken that the improvements are not merely "cost saving," but are aimed at increasing capital productivity in accordance with the relative scarcity of capital in the economy. Increasing the rate of growth of labor productivity will increase the natural rate of growth and serve only to intensify the problem of labor redundancy.

The second key to increasing the warranted rate of growth is to increase the propensity to save and to ensure that saving is channeled into domestic investment. If the privileged classes do not happen to be of an entrepreneurial bent, it is important to develop reliable channels of credit so that the saving of the wealthy *rentiers* can flow into the hands of those willing to invest. In the absence of native entrepreneurs, investment may become a function of the central government.

Finally, planners must recognize that the capacity for the modern sector to absorb labor from the traditional sector is limited by the warranted rate of growth. Consequently, it is important not to break down and disrupt traditional institutions too quickly, if problems of massive unemployment of an urban proletariat and concomitant social unrest are to be avoided.

GROWTH POLICY FOR MATURE ECONOMIES

The automatic mechanisms of the neoclassical analysis are much more likely to operate speedily and effectively in a mature economy. With high levels of investment and a high propensity to save, the desired rate of capital stock growth will be greater than the rate of labor force growth. Wages will follow their inherent tendency to rise as labor markets tighten, and if the monetary authorities do not allow interest rates to rise proportionally, firms will substitute capital for labor in production. In a mature economy, opportunities for factor substitution are much greater than in a developing one, because more technologies are available and managers are more sophisticated in their use. Furthermore, technological change will be domestically developed rather than imported, and it will tend to be of the variety which increases labor productivity, since labor is the limiting factor of production.

Consequently, the neoclassical automatic adjustment process will tend to reduce the output–capital ratio (by increasing capital intensitivity) and, hence, the warranted rate of growth, provided that the monetary authorities do not attempt to stabilize the economy by a policy of tight money. There is a danger of this, of course, because given the condition,

$$G_W > G_N$$

there will be periods of rapid growth and threatened inflation which will call for restrictive measures. Tax policy would be preferred in this case, since increased taxes would presumably reduce private saving and, hence, the warranted rate of growth.

If tight labor markets tend to produce technological change of the labor-saving type (increasing labor productivity), then the natural rate of growth will increase. Consequently, labor scarcity will tend to produce convergence of the natural and warranted growth rates and lessen the intensity of the Harrod–Domar downturn which occurs when the actual rate of growth cannot keep pace with the warranted rate.

Many mature economies are so concerned with maintaining a competitive growth rate in the world growth race that they fail to recognize their own limitations. Although, in the very short run, when there is excess productive capacity available, the actual rate of growth may be governed by the warranted rate, the growth rate of the economy is essentially limited by the natural rate. Unless technological change and the labor force are growing rapidly, high levels of saving and investment will only produce instability, and policy makers will be plagued with the necessity of managing booms and recessions of ever-increasing magnitude. An economy with an annual labor force growth rate of 2 percent and a rate of increase in labor productivity of 3 percent cannot possibly grow as fast as a country whose labor force is growing by 5 percent per year and whose labor productivity is growing by 4 percent.

Another factor tempts planners to take an overly short-sighted view of the growth process. In recovering from a recession, there is a great temptation to achieve a high rate of growth to compensate for the losses experienced in the downturn. Such a policy naturally has desirable political implications as a show of economic muscle. But while the high rates of growth can be engineered in conditions of labor market surplus, the growth rate will eventually have to slow down to the natural rate. A decline in the growth rate will cause firms to reduce their rate of investment which will, in turn, cause a further reduction in demand through the multiplier process. Such a situation may well trigger a recession.

During recovery, the economy must grow faster than the natural rate to reduce the level of unemployment. But the recovery should be carefully and cautiously engineered so that the actual rate of growth can gradually level off to the natural rate without a catastrophic reduction in the level of investment.

Mature economies have many sources of instability other than the incompatibility of the natural and warranted rates of growth. We shall consider some of these in the following chapter. However, if the potential instability inherent in the process of growth is recognized and appropriate measures are taken, the job of macroeconomic management will be much easier for the policy planner.

QUESTIONS FOR STUDY AND REVIEW

1. "The concept of equilibrium is basic to economic analysis, yet it is useless except in the context of a dynamic theory." Explain and discuss critically.

2. Suppose the monetary authorities increase the money supply, causing the *LM* curve to shift rightward.

   (a) Using a *comparative statics* approach, what will be the impact of this policy on national income, employment, and the interest rate?

   (b) Suppose there is a lag in the product market so that income does not respond immediately to changes in economic conditions. What will be the impact of the policy on national income, employment, and the interest rate?

   (c) If the money supply changes, what are the conditions for macroeconomic stability?

3. "If policy planners wait for a downturn to initiate expansionary measures, a recession cannot be avoided." Explain.

4. The Harrod–Domar model is often criticized on the grounds that its inherent instability is incompatible with the experience of growing countries. What do economists mean when they say the model is unstable? What assumptions of the model produce this instability? If the model is unrealistic, is it useless for the purposes of policy planning? Discuss critically.

5. You are an economic advisor to a country which desires to maintain a high rate of growth and full employment with a minimum of instability. The annual rate of labor force growth is 4 percent and labor productivity is growing by 3 percent. National income is $100 billion, consump-

tion is $90 billion, and the capital stock is valued at $300 billion. What advice would you give this country?

6. It is likely that a mature economy can adjust to a steady state, full-employment growth path with a minimum of government intervention in the private sector. This is not the case for a less-developed country. The latter may experience a prolonged period of labor force surplus unless a conscious effort is made to facilitate its absorption. Explain why this statement is true.

ADDITIONAL READING

BAUMOL, WILLIAM J., *Economic Dynamics*. London: Macmillan & Co., Ltd., 1970, Chapters 4 and 7.

DENNISON, EDWARD, "How to Raise the High-Employment Growth Rate by One Percentage Point," *The American Economic Review,* LII (May, 1962), 67–75.

DOMAR, EVSEY, *Essays in the Theory of Economic Growth*. New York: Oxford University Press, 1957, Chapters 3–5.

HARROD, ROY, *Toward a Dynamic Economics*. London: Macmillan & Co., Ltd., 1948.

MEADE, J., *A Neoclassical Theory of Economic Growth*. London: Unwin University Books, 1961.

SOLOW, ROBERT, "A Contribution to the Theory of Economic Growth," *The Quarterly Journal of Economics,* LXX (February, 1956), 65–94.

14

Achieving
and Maintaining
Economic Stability

The business cycle, the periodic fluctuation in the level of economic activity, has been a phenomenon common to all industrialized economies. Although these cycles vary in their intensity, they appear with remarkable regularity despite great changes in economic structure and social upheaval. In the United States, for example, the typical duration of the cycle has been about 40 months except for certain periods of severe economic and social maladjustment. In the period 1867–1966, for example, only six cycles lasted longer than four years. Two of these were associated with wars (World War II and the Korean conflict) and two with the severe depressions of the 1870's and 1930's.

Stabilization of business fluctuations is generally considered to be a major macroeconomic goal. Figure 14-1 shows the time pattern of the various phases of a cycle. Except during late recovery and at the peak, production will be below full capacity and unemployed resources represent an undesirable waste. In the later stages of the recovery, inflation may pose a threat, while the downturn is sometimes associated with financial panic and disruption of credit channels. Cyclical instability also reduces the average rate of investment, which lowers the growth rate and the rate of technological change.

To design appropriate measures to stabilize cycles, the planner must know something about their causes. Many theories have been proposed to explain economic fluctuations—from sunspots and wars to innovation and imperialism. While some of these theories are useful for explaining recovery or downturn in particular cases, most are inadequate to explain the

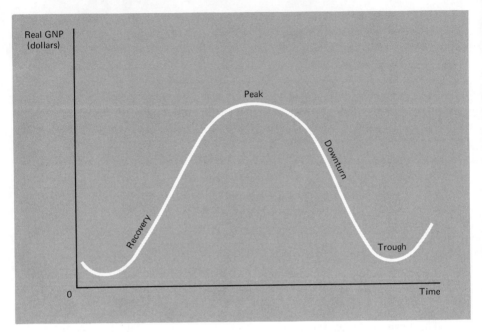

FIGURE 14-1

Phases of a Business Cycle

regularity of cycles. A theory which attributes business fluctuations to the economic consequences of war, for instance, cannot explain why cycles appear at 40-month intervals. Indeed, experience with prolonged war economies indicates that under these circumstances the recovery phase is generally longer than average.

14-1 ECONOMIC DYNAMICS AND THE BUSINESS CYCLE

Because business cycles tend to be regular and recurrent, it is likely that this behavior is inherent in the macrodynamics of an economic system, implying the need for an endogenous theory to explain them. In Chapter 13 we saw several possible sources of cyclical behavior for national income and employment. If the economy cannot sustain the warranted growth rate, investment demand will be highly unstable. Fluctuations in investment, through the multiplier, will generate even greater changes in GNP which in turn will affect employment, prices, interest rates, and wages.

Cyclical behavior may also result if reactions in some sectors are delayed or lagged. Given a lagged pattern of adjustment to equilibrium, income, employment, interest rates, and the price level will all follow a cyclical time path. As these vary, so do money and real wages, labor productivity, investment, consumption, and the growth rate.

Because reaction lags tend to produce instability, some economists argue that public policy tends to be destabilizing because of the lags involved in its execution. If this is the case, any policy designed to stabilize cycles must somehow be built into the system if it is not to do more harm than good. Proponents of this view contend that much of the instability in the U.S. economy is due to discretionary fiscal and monetary policy and argue that a comprehensive system of automatic stabilizers is required to achieve the goal of economic stability. In this section we shall examine each of these sources of instability in turn.

INVESTMENT AND THE CYCLE

Ignoring the public sector for the moment, it is clear that much of the instability of aggregate demand must come from the investment component. Consumption tends to be a rather stable function of income. Furthermore, since the average propensity to consume falls in booms and rises in recessions, consumption is a stabilizing influence over the cycle.

If export demand is highly volatile, then this component of private spending can produce cycles in domestic demand. This is generally a problem for developing countries, highly dependent on a single commodity and a small group of nations for its export market.[1] For the United States, however, in which only about 5 percent of aggregate demand comes from abroad and for which both exports and export markets are well diversified, this is not a major source of cyclical instability.[2]

Since consumption and export demand in the United States are not destabilizing influences, any study of business fluctuations in the private sector must concentrate on investment. If a portion of investment is undertaken for the sole purpose of capacity expansion, then that component of investment is likely to be highly unstable. If investment increases in proportion to changes in the level of demand, then as soon as the rate of

[1] Countries experiencing severe economic fluctuations may "export" their business cycles through the impact on demand abroad, particularly when they follow restrictive trade policies in an effort to increase the level of domestic employment. Such "beggar-my-neighbor" policies were followed by the developed countries in the 1930's with the impact of spreading the depression worldwide.

[2] This is not to suggest that conditions in the foreign sector do not have a domestic impact, even in the United States. Certainly the international rise in food and energy prices in the early seventies and the successive dollar devaluations were a major stimulus to inflation. But exports are not the principal source of business *cycles* in the United States, although they may at times be a contributing factor.

increase in output declines, investment will actually decline and, through the multiplier, the economy will be plummeted into a downturn. Notice that if investment is increasing in proportion to *changes* in output, consumption must be increasing at an *increasing* rate. If the rate of growth of consumption levels off, investment must decline.[3]

If all investment is undertaken for the purpose of capacity expansion, then net investment will fall to zero as aggregate demand declines in response to the initial decline in investment. If the interaction of the multiplier and the accelerator is the source of the cycle, then the downturn should be very swift, that is, considerably faster than the recovery. Since this is the case for most cycles, this theory has a particular appeal.

The duration of the trough and early recovery phase will depend in large measure upon the durability of the capital stock. According to the multiplier–accelerator interaction model, net investment will fall to zero in the downturn. However, assuming that the economy must maintain some positive level of consumption, eventually capital equipment will have to be replaced. The more durable the equipment, the longer the trough will last. Eventually, however, some firms begin to undertake replacement investment. This stimulates aggregate demand through the multiplier. Recovery will be slow, since many firms will have excess capacity which can be used to produce the increased output. The speed of recovery will depend upon the durability of their capital (which will determine the effective amount of excess capacity) and the initial increase in investment. In general, the longer the recession and the less durable the capital stock, the speedier is the recovery. The more homogeneous the firms with respect to capital durability, the faster will be the recovery, since once replacement investment is initiated by some firms, most other firms will find themselves with little or no effective excess capacity and all will undertake new investment in response to the initial change in demand.

Figure 14-2 shows the time path of aggregate demand in a multiplier–accelerator interaction model. The function G_N represents the natural rate of growth which is the ceiling to real income growth that causes the downturn. The function C_S is the subsistence level of consumption which must be maintained and which initiates the replacement investment that is responsible for the recovery. If the durability of equipment does not undergo a radical change and if the values of the multiplier and accelerator (the capital–output ratio) stay constant, then periodic fluctuations in economic activity should occur recurrently and with a fairly regular duration.

While the multiplier–accelerator model is useful in explaining the regularity of business cycles, it tends to explain them too well. Aggregate demand is not as unstable as this model suggests. Figure 14-3 shows the

---

[3] See Chapter 13 for an algebraic formulation of this model.

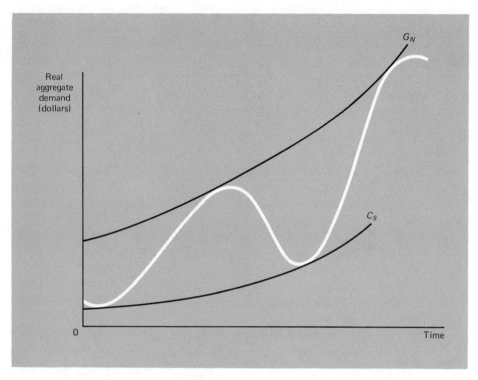

FIGURE 14-2

Time Path of Aggregate Demand in a
Multiplier–Accelerator Interaction Model

actual movement of real national income from 1957–1973. During this
period real national income actually turned down only four times, and in
only two cases, the recessions of 1960 and 1969–1970, did the downturn
last for more than two quarters. Recovery to the previous peak in all
cases (except 1969–1970) occurred within three quarters. Between 1961
and the second quarter of 1969, the rise in real national income was constant, with a slight leveling off of the *rate* of increase in late 1966 and early
1967.

National income is not as unstable as the multiplier–accelerator
model suggests for two reasons. First, investment is not governed solely
by the accelerator principle. In addition, certain factors tend to cushion
the impact of changes in investment on national income, effectively reducing the size of the multiplier.

In Chapter 6 we examined the determinants of investment in some
detail. Investment in plant and equipment, which in 1965 comprised 67.0

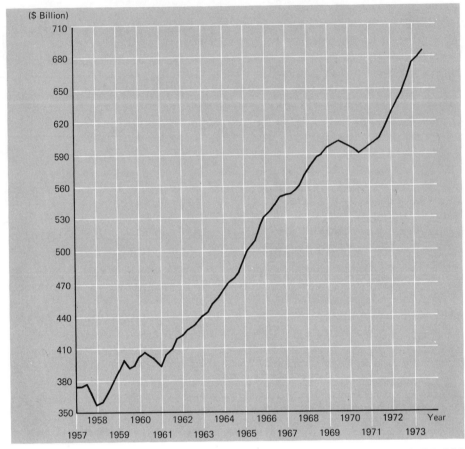

FIGURE 14-3

Time Pattern of Real National Income in the United States
1957–1973 (billions of 1958 dollars)

Source: U.S. Department of Commerce, Office of Business Economics. *Survey of Current Business* (Washington, D.C.: U.S. Government Printing Office, 1958–1974).

percent of total investment and 10.7 percent of GNP, is affected by such factors as the availability of finance capital and credit conditions. If firms are limited in booms by the availability of funds and if retained earnings provide a floor to investment, then investment will be considerably less volatile than the accelerator model would suggest. There is an additional factor which contributes to cycles in plant and equipment investment, however. The marginal efficiency of capital is based upon producers' expectations about future demand. If previous experience has conditioned businessmen to expect a 40-month cycle, then they may begin to anticipate

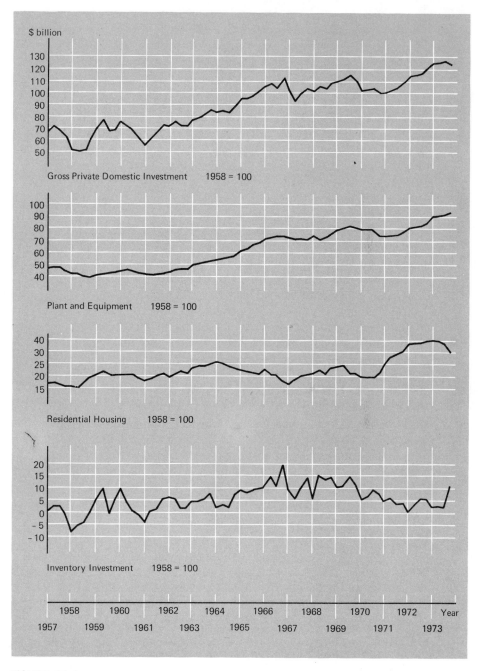

FIGURE 14-4

Time Pattern of Investment in the United States
1957–1973 (billions of 1958 dollars)

Source: U.S. Department of Commerce, Office of Business Economics. *Survey of Current Business* (Washington, D.C.: U.S. Government Printing Office, 1958–1974).

384 Achieving and Maintaining Economic Stability

turning points. For instance, they may become pessimistic after a boom has lasted for more than two years. This "anticipation effect" will actually build in the very instability they fear.

Figure 14-4 shows the time pattern of plant and equipment investment over the period 1957–1973. Performance of this component of investment has been remarkably stable with no great downturns or booms. Plant and equipment investment turned down slightly in 1958, and the downturn in late 1960 was barely perceptible. Note that the 1960 downturn *followed* rather than led the downturn in national income. In the late 1960's, plant and equipment investment began to show more instability than in the earlier period, with a decided downturn occurring in 1970. Again, the downturn followed the decline in national income.

Investment in residential housing in 1965 comprised 24.0 percent of total investment and 3.85 percent of GNP. Since investment in residential housing tends, in the short run, to be highly sensitive to credit conditions, its time pattern as seen in Figure 14-4 is actually slightly countercyclical, since interest rates tend to move in phase with the cycle. This is a stabilizing factor which reduces the volatility of total investment.

Inventory investment, which in 1965 accounted for 9.07 percent of total investment and 1.45 percent of GNP, is the most volatile component of investment. As described in Chapter 6, inventory investment is best explained by a pure accelerator model. Despite its small magnitude, some economists believe that inventory investment has accounted for most of the cyclical activity of the U.S. economy since the Korean conflict. In a model simulating the U.S. economy in the recession of 1957–1959, Duesenberry, Eckstein, and Fromm found the decline in inventory investment accounted for 62 percent of the decline in GNP.[4] Klein and Popkin, in a similar study, found that virtually all cyclical behavior in the U.S. economy since World War II could have been eliminated if inventory fluctuations were reduced by 75 percent.[5]

Although total investment is less volatile than a simple accelerator theory would suggest, it is more variable than national income, as is clear from the accompanying charts. If the multiplier analysis is correct, however, changes in investment should generate even greater changes in income.

Consider the simple multiplier of the Keynesian model,

[4] J. S. Duesenberry, Otto Eckstein, and Gary Fromm, "A Simulation of the United States Economy in Recession," *Econometrica,* XXVIII (October, 1960), 749–809.
[5] Lawrence R. Klein and Joel Popkin, "An Econometric Analysis of the Postwar Relationship Between Inventory Fluctuations and Changes in Aggregate Economic Activity," in *Inventory Fluctuations and Economic Stabilization,* paper prepared for the Joint Economic Committee (Washington, D.C.: U.S. Government Printing Office, 1961), p. 75.

$$Y = C + I$$
$$C = a + bY$$
$$I = f(i, \Delta Y, Y, \text{retained earnings, etc.})$$
$$\Delta Y = \frac{1}{1-b} \Delta I$$

In this model, the multiplier depends upon the marginal propensity to consume (*MPC*). However, note that consumption depends upon *disposable income,* while the multiplier is applied to the relationship between *national income* and investment. To find the true multiplier, we need to know not only how consumption responds to changes in disposable income, but how changes in income affect the relationship between national income and disposable income. Thus, the distribution of the various components of national income as it changes, as well as its speed of adjustment, will affect the multiplier.

Appendix B discusses in some detail the accounting differences between national and disposable income. National income measures the total value of incomes earned in the process of production, including wages, profits, interest, and rent. Disposable income measures the after-tax income of individuals. Therefore,

National income − disposable income = Corporate profits − dividends − transfer payments to individuals + personal taxes

The components of the difference between national income and disposable income operate to reduce the impact of an initial change in national income on disposable income. Corporate profits, which vary widely with the cycle, are the most important stabilizer of all. Fluctuations in this volatile component of national income are considerably greater than in national income itself, and consequently, disposable income varies far less than national income. Because firms are reluctant to vary dividend rates in response to short-run changes in profits, dividends are generally more stable than national income. Consequently, corporate profits less dividends display even more variation than corporate profits alone.

Personal taxes and transfer payments both vary with income. Both income and excise taxes rise and fall with changes in income and consumption. Transfer payments such as welfare payments and unemployment insurance rise when income falls. Both have the effect of reducing the impact of changes in national income on disposable income.

Thus, the complete national income multiplier,

$$\frac{\Delta Y}{\Delta D} = \frac{1}{1 - (b - m)(1 - t - p - z) - d - \mu}$$

where

b = marginal propensity to consume

m = marginal propensity to import

d = marginal propensity to invest (from national income)

μ = monetary effect

$t = \dfrac{\Delta T}{\Delta Y}$

T = personal taxes

$p = \dfrac{-\Delta W}{\Delta Y}$

W = transfer payments to individuals

$z = \dfrac{\Delta Z}{\Delta Y}$

Z = corporate profits less dividends (business saving)

is considerably smaller than the multiplier which ignores the difference between disposable income and national income.

The importance of "offsets" to changes in disposable income is indicated by the experience of the recession of 1961. During this period, personal income taxes offset 17.9 percent of the decline in national income and corporate income taxes offset 14.3 percent. This means that for every $100 decline in national income, individuals paid $17.90 less in personal income taxes and corporations paid $14.30 less in corporate income taxes. Unemployment insurance and welfare payments offset 6.1 percent, while excise taxes on consumer durables offset 16.1 percent.[6] These factors alone offset 54.4 percent of the decline in national income, so that disposable income declined by less than half as much as national income. Substituting into the multiplier for

$$t = 0.179 + 0.161$$

$$z = 0.143$$

$$p = 0.061$$

then

$$1 - t - p - z = 1 - 0.544 = 0.456$$

so that

$$\frac{\Delta Y}{\Delta D} = \frac{1}{1 - 0.456(b - m) - d - \mu}$$

and the impact of the marginal propensity to consume on the multiplier was reduced by over one-half.

[6] The excise tax offset in this period was unusually large due to a big decline in automobile sales in the recession.

In Chapter 5 we saw that the short-run *MPC* from disposable income is smaller than in the long run. In addition, it is likely that the speed with which income changes occur affects the *MPC* too. If income changes are rapid, they are generally viewed as transitory by households and changes in transitory income have minimal impact on consumption. Furthermore, households will attempt to maintain past living standards in the very short run. Thus, if a downturn is rapid, the *MPC* is likely to be much lower than it was in the recovery and boom phase, cushioning the impact of the downturn. In general, the national income multiplier tends to be considerably smaller in recessions than in booms. In recessions, offsets to changes in national income are greater than in booms. Furthermore, since downturns tend to be more rapid than recovery, the *MPC* tends to be lower.

THE IMPACT OF REACTION LAGS

In Chapter 13 we described how a reaction lag in the monetary sector will cause national income, employment, prices, interest rates, and the other economic variables which depend upon them to move in a cyclical pattern over time. The accelerator model of investment is also a special case of a reaction lag.

A relationship contains a reaction lag if the value of the dependent variable in period t depends upon the values of the independent variables in time $(t - n)$, where n measures the length of the lag. Denoting the time period in which the variable is measured by a subscript, the accelerator model of investment,

$$I_t = \beta \, \Delta Y_t$$

can be expressed

$$I_t = \beta(Y_t - Y_{t-1})$$

Clearly, investment today depends upon income today as well as yesterday's income.

Suppose investment depends not only upon the change in demand, but also upon the amount of capital already available. Because desired changes in the capital stock cannot take place instantaneously but require time to implement, the actual capital stock at any time may be different from the optimal level. The *flexible accelerator* model takes into account the possibility that the increased output will be produced with excess capacity capital. Denoting actual capital stock as K_t and desired capital stock as $K_t{}^*$, the model can be expressed as

$$I_t = \beta(Y_t - Y_{t-1}) - \gamma(K_t - K_t{}^*)$$
$$K_t{}^* = \beta Y_t$$

If actual capital stock is greater than the firm desires or finds necessary to produce Y_t, then investment will be lower by some proportion of the difference.[7]

Actual capital stock, however, is equal to the accumulated investment over the life of the equipment, so

$$K_t = I_{t-1} + I_{t-2} + \cdots + I_{t-n}$$

where n is the life of the equipment. Therefore,

$$I_t = f(Y_t, Y_{t-1}, I_{t-1}, I_{t-2}, \ldots, I_{t-n})$$

Investment today depends not only upon yesterday's income but also yesterday's investment.

Reaction lags are the basic source of instability in an economic system. Without these lags, the system would generally reach equilibrium instantaneously.[8] It is likely, however, that various sorts of reaction lags will exist in any economic system.

Initially, there may be a *recognition lag*. It may take some time for households, for instance, to recognize that real income has fallen. This may be followed by a *decision lag,* as households decide to readjust consumption in response to the change in income. This lag may spread over several time periods as households adjust to new standards of consumption and as they determine whether or not the decline in income is transitory or permanent. Finally, there is an *implementation lag* as households implement the decision to readjust consumption. The implementation lag may be particularly long for investment spending. Shirley Almon has estimated that the implementation lag between the decision to undertake a capital expenditure and the completion of the expenditure is about two years for most industries, with the bulk of the expenditure occurring between three and six quarters after the decision was made.[9]

DESTABILIZING LAGS IN PUBLIC POLICY

Since cyclical behavior of macroeconomic targets can be attributed to reaction lags in the various sectors of the economy, public policy may

---

[7] The flexible accelerator can also work in the opposite direction. If the capital stock is below the optimal level in period t, then investment will be greater than that projected by a simple accelerator model.

[8] The system will not reach equilibrium, even in the absence of lags if the equilibrium is unstable. See Appendix A for an example of such a possibility for macroeconomic equilibrium.

[9] Shirley Almon, "The Distributed Lag between Capital Appropriations and Expenditures," *Econometrica,* XXXIII (January, 1965), 178–196.

also be destabilizing if it is subject to lags. Some economists, such as Milton Friedman, argue that lags in discretionary stabilization policy are so long that they tend to reinforce cyclical behavior rather than stabilize it. When lags in policy initiation are combined with lags in the private sector, the problem of appropriate timing of public policy can be serious. If the composite lag is as long as two years, this requires forecasting economic behavior more than two years in advance. Not only must forecasts be made, but policy makers must be convinced that the forecasts are correct and that policy measures must be taken now to reverse these future trends.

14.2 STABILIZATION POLICY: RULES VERSUS DISCRETION

One of the most controversial aspects of macroeconomic policy is whether or not stabilization policy should rely on automatic stabilizers or whether automatic stabilizers should be supplemented by discretionary measures. Those who argue for "rules" support an overall strengthening of automatic stabilizers and reject discretionary measures as destabilizing because of lags. An extreme position is taken by Milton Friedman, who has proposed a completely automatic monetary mechanism for achieving stability. On the other side of the controversy, those who argue for "authority" contend that automatic stabilizers can never completely eliminate instability. As our understanding of macroeconomic relationships and our ability to forecast trends improves, it is foolish, they say, not to rely more heavily on discretionary policy where it is indicated. Because automatic mechanisms have traditionally been slow and unreliable, it would be unwise and impolitic to allow a recession or serious inflation to run its course with no attempt to reverse the trend by discretionary measures.

Clearly, while some discretionary control is indicated in the face of catastrophic events such as war, financial panic, or a severe depression such as occurred in the 1930's, the rules versus authority controversy has taken place within the context of economic conditions that are reasonably stable. Walter Heller once viewed the role of stabilization policy in the 1960's as that of "fine tuning." Although the unfortunate experience with stagflation and supply problems in basic commodity markets that occurred in the early seventies required policy remedies other than fiscal and monetary fine tuning (see Chapter 12), in this section we shall examine some aspects of stabilization policy in a fine-tuning context, that is, assuming no need for dramatic corrections or non-Keynesian remedies.[10]

---

[10] Even in the experience of the early seventies, some adherents of automatic stabilizers held the view that discretionary policy changes would only make things worse.

AUTOMATIC STABILIZERS

Automatic stabilizers, such as personal and corporate income taxes, excise taxes, and unemployment insurance, reduce the fluctuations in disposable income associated with changes in national income and thereby reduce the size of the multiplier. They also operate to stabilize investment, the most volatile component of GNP. These stabilizers are automatic because they are triggered by changes in the level of economic activity, usually national income. Since they are "built into" the system, no one has to decide to initiate a policy action. Because a cyclical trend must occur to activate them, the stabilizers can never be completely effective in eliminating economic fluctuations. Stabilizers can, however, significantly reduce their amplitude and duration.

In the 1960 recession we saw that automatic stabilizers offset over half the decline in national income. Furthermore, the decline in corporate taxes in this period may have provided some stimulus to investment. As indicated by the data in Figure 14-4, plant and equipment investment, which is most likely to be influenced by the availability of internal funds, remained stable despite the decline in real national income. The overall decline in investment in this recession was due to the sharp drop in inventory accumulation. Unfortunately, automatic stabilizers have little or no impact on inventory investment, which has been the major source of instability in the post-World War II economy.

In a simulation of the U.S. economy, Eilbott estimated that the stabilizers will generally offset from 35 percent to 50 percent of a decline in GNP and from 25 percent to 40 percent of the recovery.[11] In addtiion, he shows that the effectiveness of the stabilizers could be increased significantly by extending the coverage of unemployment compensation. Furthermore, he suggests that, in the absence of the stabilizers, fluctuations might be even greater than predicted by his model since psychological factors tend to reinforce swings in economic activity. On the basis of his study, Eilbott concludes that

> In general . . . the stabilizers do appear to provide, under all but unusual circumstances, a reasonably satisfactory defense against downward pressures on the economy. They do not suffer, as do discretionary policies, from problems of timing and errors of judgment, and they seem to be powerful enough (especially if the unemployment compensation system is strengthened considerably) to prevent a substantial percentage of an income decline.[12]

[11] Peter Eilbott, "The Effectiveness of Automatic Stabilizers," *The American Economic Review,* LVI (June, 1966), 450–465.
[12] *Ibid.,* p. 464.

Other economists have argued that automatic stabilizers should be strengthened by such measures as extending the system of unemployment insurance and making income taxes more progressive. The automatic stabilizers in the U.S. fiscal package were originally designed for other purposes, however, and the distributional implications of making them more responsive to income changes are not always desirable. Consequently, some observers have suggested the development of automatic fiscal and monetary policies, designed specifically as stabilization measures, and with as neutral a distributional impact as possible. This concept is known as *formula flexibility*.

One suggestion which has received serious consideration is the possibility of automatically altering tax rates in response to changes in the level of economic activity. Tax rates would rise in booms and fall in recessions in such a way that the average tax rate for the entire period would be in line with the prevailing tax schedule. One difficulty with such a program, which presents itself whenever formula flexibility is discussed, is that no one can agree on the appropriate index of economic activity to which to tie tax rate changes. Although many economists seem to favor the unemployment rate (i.e., reduce the tax rate when the unemployment rate rises above some stipulated amount and raise the tax rate when the unemployment rate falls below some different value), this would be a poor choice for stabilization purposes. The level of employment is one of the lagging variables during cyclical fluctuations, since it takes time for firms to hire and fire workers in response to changes in demand. By the time the unemployment rate rises, the economy is likely to be well into the downturn. The best time to undertake expansionary action is before the peak is actually reached, when the rate of increase in demand has begun to level off, but before the unemployment rate has increased. This is because the downturn in investment generally precedes the downturn in income. Furthermore, there is likely to be some lag in the reactions of households to the tax cut. A better, but more controversial, measure would be to tie changes in tax rates to *changes* in income, to the level of total investment or, better still, to inventory investment. Duesenberry, Eckstein, and Fromm, in their simulation of the U.S. economy in a recession, found that tying tax rate changes to changes in GNP was more effective than tying them to the unemployment rate.[13] In one case, they simulated an anti-recession policy which reduced the amount of personal income tax collected by a percentage which depended upon the deviation of GNP from its previous peak value. They found that this reduced the decline in GNP from $34 billion to $20.2 billion with consumption increasing throughout the recession.

[13] J. S. Duesenberry *et al., op. cit.* pp. 749–809.

A drawback to such a plan is that it may prematurely induce a recession psychology which may precipitate the downturn. Using the unemployment rate as an indicator of economic activity will not have this effect since the turning point will have already occurred. However, the lags involved might be so great as to be destabilizing.

DISCRETIONARY STABILIZATION POLICY

Automatic stabilizers have proved to be an effective means of shielding the U.S. economy from wide swings in economic activity. By extending their coverage and increasing their sensitivity to changes in national income as well as by designing measures with *formula flexibility,* they could presumably be made even more effective. However, because they must be triggered by income fluctuations, automatic stabilizers can never completely eliminate cyclical instability.

Discretionary measures, such as money supply changes, variations in the level of public spending, and changes in tax rates or structure, are all subject to lags of various sorts. First, there is the *recognition lag.* Cyclical indicators require interpretation, and many times different observers will disagree concerning the need for remedial action. Once the need for stabilizing action is recognized, there is the *policy initiation lag.* Planners must first decide on the appropriate remedy, and then they must convince policymakers that it should be undertaken. All discretionary policy requires political approval, and the problem is the most acute in boom periods when such measures as tax increases, spending cuts, and tight money are politically unpopular. If lags in the private sector are expected to be long, remedial action may be called for well in advance of overt indications of a change in the phase of a cycle. Thus, restrictive policies may be called for even before full employment is reached. President Johnson, for instance, requested a tax increase from Congress nearly two years before it was finally approved. By the time the measure was approved and became effective, the economy was well into the downturn and the effect was, on balance, destabilizing.

The duration of the policy initiation lag will depend upon the type of policy under consideration as well as the phase of the cycle. The most flexible instrument in all phases of the cycle tends to be monetary policy, since discretionary changes in the money supply do not require congressional approval. The least flexible instrument tends to be tax policy, since the Congress must approve all tax changes. The president has more authority on the expenditure side, particularly in the short run, so that generally there is a bias toward increasing expenditures when recession is threatened.

While tax changes have the longest policy initiation lag, they generally have a shorter *effectiveness lag* than the other discretionary measures.[14] The effectiveness lag is considerably shortened by the comprehensive tax withholding system. Recent experience, however, has shown that the effectiveness lag of a tax increase is not insignificant. The 10 percent surtax on the personal income tax imposed by the Johnson administration in 1968 had little immediate impact on consumption. One reason may have been that the tax was widely publicized as being a temporary measure, so that households considered it a transitory reduction in their income. This being the case, the *MPC* would have been negligible and the increased taxes would have been paid from savings.

The impact of a decision to reduce public spending may have a substantial effectiveness lag because it is not feasible to terminate spending programs at will. Not only would it be wasteful to halt construction of a highway or some other public works program in midstream, but it is also not politically feasible to do so.

The effectiveness lag in monetary policy is perhaps the most unreliable and difficult to estimate, particularly as an expansionary measure. This is because the link between increases in the money supply, a decline in the interest rate, and the stimulus to investment are all tenuous and unreliable.

In boom periods, discretionary policy is generally biased toward tight money since it has the shortest policy initiation lag. Since the effectiveness lag is unreliable and generally of long duration, it is difficult for planners to determine the appropriate timing. When a downturn is threatened, fiscal measures may be easier to engineer since spending increases and tax cuts are politically more desirable than their counterparts in a boom. Since the effectiveness lag is shorter for these measures, antirecession policy is easier to time and less likely to be destabilizing than restrictive policies. The timing of the Kennedy–Johnson tax cut of 1964 was considerably better than was the Johnson surtax of 1968. For the tax cut, the total recognition plus policy initiation plus effectiveness lag was less than one year.[15] For the 1968 surtax, the recognition plus policy initiation lag alone was about two years, and by 1970 (when the surtax was removed) many economists doubted that it had even had a significant effect on consumption. In fact, the major impact of the surtax may have been to feed a cost-push inflation rather than to restrict consumption as it was originally intended.

---

[14] Automatic stabilizers, of course, are subject to the same effectiveness lags as discretionary measures and may, as a consequence, be destabilizing.

[15] Some observers argue that the recognition lag for the tax cut was as long as for the subsequent increase, tracing it back to the 1962 Kennedy speech at Yale on budget deficits. But the effectiveness lag for the tax cut was undoubtedly shorter than for the increase, even if one takes the anticipation effect into account.

The timing difficulties of discretionary policies and the inadequacy of automatic stabilizers have led to various proposals for formula flexibility. An extreme position is taken by Milton Friedman, who has proposed a framework for economic stability which relies completely on an automatic monetary mechanism.[16] Friedman's proposal is in line with his belief that monetary policy is the only effective and reliable means of controlling demand. His system, he argues, being completely automatic will avoid the destabilizing lags associated with discretionary policy.

The basis of Friedman's proposal is to maintain a constant and steady rate of increase of the money supply equal to the natural rate of growth of the economy. In the absence of economic fluctuations, this would allow the rate of growth of money supply to exactly equal the growth rate of output and the transactions demand for money with full employment and stable prices.

The tax system would be progressive with income, while the level of public spending would be determined by the society's requirement for public goods. Public spending would not be used for the purpose of manipulating aggregate demand. Tax rates should be set so that at full employment there would be a slight budget deficit. This deficit would be financed by money creation and would be set so as to permit the secular increase in the money supply necessitated by the growth requirements of the economy.

The banking system would be required to hold 100 percent of its deposits as reserves. Since the sole function of the banking system would be to provide deposit facilities and check clearance, it could not make loans and, consequently, could not create money. The Fed would buy bonds from the U.S. Treasury when the government budget was in deficit and retire them when the budget was in surplus. Consequently, money would be created to meet government deficits and retired when the budget was in surplus.

Since the income tax system is designed to allow only the secular increase in the money supply at full employment, non-secular deficits and surpluses with consequent changes in the money supply will be the automatic consequences of changes in income. If income falls below the full-employment level, tax receipts will fall, the budget will go into deficit, and the money supply will be automatically increased. The reverse will occur if demand increases after full employment is achieved, since price inflation will cause money income to rise above the full-employment level, gener-

[16] Friedman's proposal is described fully in Milton Friedman, "A Monetary and Fiscal Framework for Economic Stability," *The American Economic Review,* XXXVIII (June, 1948), 245–264.

ating a budget surplus and consequent contraction of the money supply. Thus, the quantity of money is automatically determined by the needs of economic stability.

In this system, discretionary action is limited to determining the tax rates required to maintain the desired budget deficit at full employment. Since all government spending is financed either by taxes or money creation, there will be no government bonds held by the public and no open market operations. Friedman points out that debt finance is not as efficient as money creation for stimulating demand nor will debt retirement restrict demand as much as a reduction in the quantity of money.

While this proposal is internally consistent, it relies on the belief that changes in the money supply alone are adequate for controlling demand. A Keynesian would argue that the mechanism on which the program depends is the interest rate and that the interest rate may be an ineffective stabilizing instrument. Furthermore, while this proposal eliminates the recognition and initiation lags, there still may be a substantial effectiveness lag. Friedman argues that if his program is adopted the effectiveness lag may be eliminated or at least shortened, if the business community can count on automatic changes in the money supply. If they do not have to wait to see if discretionary actions will be undertaken, they will anticipate changes in monetary conditions.

An inherent weakness of the Friedman proposal is the assumption that prices will be flexible in both directions. If there is downward price rigidity, then there will not be a one-to-one correspondence between the level of money income and employment. If prices and the unemployment rate are rising simultaneously because of cost-push factors (perhaps associated with rising interest rates), the level of money income will not fall with employment, the deficit will not increase, and the automatic increase in the money supply required to stimulate the economy will not be forthcoming. Conceivably, the level of income may rise as unemployment rises, increasing the budget surplus and causing a contraction in the money supply. Not only will this reduce the level of employment still farther, but it will cause interest rates to rise, feeding the cost-push inflation. Friedman, like Keynes, views aggregate demand as the essential measure of the level of economic activity. Consequently, his remedies are more applicable to a recession than in managing a modern cost-push inflation.[17]

As with all automatic mechanisms, it is likely that the adjustment

[17] Friedman himself takes the position that his policy is equally applicable in inflation and in periods of price stability. He argues that a cost-push inflation cannot continue indefinitely without validating increases in the money supply. This presupposes, however, that money prices and wages would return to their previous levels, or else price stability would be achieved only at the cost of higher unemployment. But Friedman takes the position that unemployment will be established at its natural rate, regardless of the rate of inflation in the long run (see Chapter 11).

process implicit in the Friedman proposal would be slow and painful. If unemployment became sufficiently severe, it is conceivable that money wage rates would finally fall and with them the price level and the level of money income, setting the automatic stabilizer in motion. It is doubtful, however, that, with the principles of Keynesian economics and the appropriate fiscal remedies at their disposal, policymakers would find it politically expedient to allow a recession or prolonged inflation to drag on simply for the sake of automaticity. While discretionary measures suffer from lags and while they may overshoot the mark and hence require abrupt reversal, discretionary fine tuning by a series of successive approximations may be preferred to dependence on automatic monetary stimuli.

QUESTIONS FOR STUDY AND REVIEW

1. Consider the model

$$Y_t = C_t + I_t$$
$$C_t = aY_{t-1}$$
$$I_t = b(Y_{t-1} - Y_{t-2})$$

(a) If $a = 0.5$ and $b = 2$, trace the time path of income starting at $t = 0$ where

$$Y_0 = 100$$

and

$$Y_1 = 110$$

(b) Design a time path for government spending which would stabilize this economy at $Y = 150$.

(c) If $a = 0.8$ and $b = 3$, answer the question in part (a). Does an increase in the parameter values a and b increase or reduce the stability of the system?

(d) Suppose the investment equation is altered so that

$$I_t = b(Y_{t-1} - Y_{t-2}) - \gamma(K_t - K_t^*)$$

Find the time path of part (a), assuming

$$K_t^* = bY_t$$
$$K_0 = 250$$

and

$$\gamma = 0.5$$

How does the introduction of the capital stock variable into the investment equation affect the stability of the system?

2. Consider an economy in which the personal income tax rate is a uniform 10 percent and the corporate income tax rate is 15 percent. The MPC from disposable income is 0.8 and the marginal propensity to invest from corporate income is 0.5.

(a) Find the impact on national income of an increase in government spending of 100.

(b) Suppose the personal income tax is raised to 15 percent. Will the increase in tax revenue be sufficient to finance the expenditure increase? (*Hint:* Notice that the increased tax rate changes the value of the multiplier.)

3. Discuss and analyze the cyclical behavior of the following:

(a) consumption,

(b) corporate profits,

(c) inventory investment,

(d) plant and equipment investment,

(e) residential construction.

4. Discuss the relative merits of automatic stabilizers, formula flexibility, and discretionary fiscal and monetary policy for stabilizing business cycles. You should include in your discussion some hypothetical or historical examples.

5. Discuss and critically evaluate Milton Friedman's framework for economic stability.

6. "If federal expenditure should be held constant at the current level with no increase in tax rates, a depression is inevitable." Defend or attack the quoted proposition.

ADDITIONAL READING

BRONFENBRENNER, MARTIN, ed., *Is the Business Cycle Obsolete?* New York: John Wiley & Sons, Inc., 1969.

CLEMENT, M. O., "The Quantitative Impact of Automatic Stabilizers," *The Review of Economics and Statistics,* XLII (February, 1960), 56–61.

DUESENBERRY, J. S., O. ECKSTEIN, and G. FROMM, "A Simulation of the United States Economy in Recession," *Econometrica,* XXVIII (October, 1960), 749–809.

EILBOTT, PETER, "The Effectiveness of Automatic Stabilizers," *The American Economic Review,* LVI (June, 1966), 450–465.

FRIEDMAN, MILTON, "A Monetary and Fiscal Framework for Economic Stability," *The American Economic Review,* XXXVIII (June, 1948), 245–264.

MATTHEWS, R. C. O., *The Business Cycle.* Chicago: The University of Chicago Press, 1959.

OKUN, ARTHUR M., "The Agenda for Stabilization Policy," in *The Political Economy of Prosperity.* New York: W. W. Norton and Company, 1970.

SAMUELSON, PAUL, "Interactions Between the Multiplier Analysis and the Principle of Acceleration," *The Review of Economic Statistics,* XXI (May, 1939), 75–78.

15

The Impact
of Macroeconomic
Policy

Now that we have completed the formal analysis of models of income determination, it will be useful to review the various macroeconomic policy instruments in terms of their impact on the objectives of national economic policy discussed in Chapter 1. If public policy is to achieve full employment and economic growth with price stability and avoid excessive balance of payments deficits, that policy must be carefully designed.

As we have seen, macroeconomic policy must consist of more than simply manipulating aggregate demand, as the Keynesian model suggests. To the extent that policy targets conflict, policy must be designed to reduce the range in which the conflict occurs. Thus, if policy makers recognize an incompatibility between the goals of full employment and price stability, measures which reduce the length of search for unemployed workers and the rate of flow into new unemployment and which prevent money wages from rising as labor markets tighten may keep prices from increasing as aggregate demand and the level of employment are increased. In addition, we have seen that instruments designed to control aggregate demand may have a secondary impact on the policy objectives which may counteract the effect of the change in demand. For instance, tight money and tax increases may be used to restrict demand during an inflation, but both these policies tend to increase production costs, which may cause firms to increase prices.

When government undertakes spending programs, it must have a means of commandeering resources. How these resources are obtained—through taxes, borrowing, or money creation—will influence the policy objectives. Thus, a final analysis of the effect of economic policy must contain a discussion of the impact of federal budget operations.

In this chapter we shall consider the impact of macroeconomic policy, with particular attention paid to its secondary effects when it is designed essentially for the purpose of controlling aggregate demand.

15-1   THE PROBLEM OF CONFLICTING OBJECTIVES

In a simple Keynesian model, the way to reach full employment is to increase aggregate demand. Inflation is brought into check by reducing demand. Since the model assumes prices will remain stable until full employment is attained, there is no conflict between the goals of full employment and price stability, and both objectives can be achieved simultaneously simply by manipulating demand. In the real world, however, prices begin to rise well before full employment is reached, so that full employment is incompatible with price stability.

Two choices are open. We can remain pure Keynesians and adhere to view that controlling aggregate demand is the only legitimate sort of macroeconomic policy. In this case the policy objectives must be viewed as a trade-off; that is, we can only increase the level of employment at the cost of inflation.[1] On the other hand, we can take the position that economic policy should be designed to make Keynesian policy (demand manipulation) more effective. Thus, if public policy can reduce the rate of inflation associated with each level of employment, then increases in demand may help to achieve the full-employment goal with a minimum of inflation. In this section we shall examine several potential conflicts of objectives and consider how economic policy can be designed to reduce the range of conflict.

FULL EMPLOYMENT AND PRICE STABILITY

Prices rise with the level of employment when increases in employment are associated with rising marginal costs of production. The greatest element in these costs is marginal labor cost per unit of output. Labor costs rise as money wages increase and as marginal productivity declines. Other factors which may contribute to rising costs of production are increases in the price of materials and capital goods.

Policies which could keep production costs from rising as employment increases include the following:

[1] We have seen that in some cases Keynesian measures may not work at all, particularly for stabilizing prices during a period with sizeable inflationary expectations. In this case, the choice is between some alternative policy solution and continued instability.

1. *Wage-price controls*—If wage increases do not exceed productivity increases, unit labor costs will not rise with employment and prices should not increase unless other production costs rise. Guideposts that hold wage increases to productivity increases prevent the aggregate supply function from shifting leftward when aggregate demand changes. If inflation is allowed to persist for too long, the major impetus to wage increases may be inflationary expectations. In such a case, direct controls on consumer prices may be the most effective way of stabilizing wages and, indirectly, wholesale prices.

2. *Measures to increase labor productivity*—Given the institutional realities of an upward drift in money wages, wage-price guidelines will be difficult to enforce if labor productivity is not growing rapidly. It is particularly important to keep labor productivity from declining as the level of employment is increased. Programs to increase labor mobility, both regionally and occupationally, and other manpower measures that will improve the flow of information and reduce search periods may reduce unemployment that was originally viewed as "structural" without decreasing productivity. These programs should include retraining experience as well as aids to relocation. Improvements in the quality of the employment experience might also reduce the high rates of job turnover for certain labor force groups, eliminating a certain amount of frictional unemployment. To keep labor productivity high, it is also important not to interfere with the rate of investment and technological change. Technological change that raises labor productivity should be encouraged. Measures to increase labor productivity will also increase the potential for economic growth.

3. *Special attention to basic industries*—Wage-price guidelines and measures to improve labor productivity should be applied with particular vigor to basic industries such as steel, since prices in basic industries represent production costs for secondary industries. More problematic are price controls for industrial raw materials and energy as well as food, which are a prime source of inflationary expectations and which are often pyramided into higher wages. Although short-run solutions for shortages in these markets may necessitate equilibrating price increases (and falling real wages and industrial profits), national economic policy planners should devote increased attention to the long-run supply of strategic basic commodities such as food and industrial raw materials. Programs to ensure an adequate long-run supply should take the form of subsidies to producers rather than price supports if inflation is a major policy concern.

ECONOMIC GROWTH, FULL EMPLOYMENT, AND PRICE STABILITY

For a mature economy, the rate of economic growth consistent with full employment and price stability is limited by the rate of labor force growth and the rate of growth of labor productivity. Attempts to grow more rapidly than the productive capacity of the labor force allows will result in recurrent periods of recession (unemployment) and inflation. Increasing the rate of investment will not be consistent with noninflationary, full-employment growth unless it is accompanied by labor-saving technological change (which increases labor productivity).

Policy makers should recognize the limitations imposed by the natural rate of growth, particularly in managing an economic expansion. If recovery is too rapid, bottlenecks will appear, thereby increasing inflationary pressures. Attempts to slow down the boom may produce a contraction of the level of investment and result in a downturn.

Policies to reduce the range of conflict between the growth objective and full employment and price stability include the following:

1. *Use of monetary policy to control the warranted rate of growth*— If the warranted rate of growth is greater than the natural rate, inflation and a subsequent recession may ensue. Although public authorities may be tempted to employ a tight money policy to control the expansion, such a policy will discourage firms from substituting capital for labor as money wage rates rise. If, however, interest rates are kept from rising too rapidly, firms will be encouraged to look for more capital intensive processes, the warranted rate of growth will decline and productivity per worker and the natural rate of growth will increase.

2. *Encouraging labor-saving innovations*—The natural rate of growth, which limits the growth rate consistent with full employment and price stability, can be increased by increasing the rate of growth of labor productivity. Labor productivity can be increased by the adoption of labor-saving innovations. Such innovations are often met with opposition by labor unions on the grounds that they produce unemployment. For the economy as a whole, this is not likely to be a problem if the demand for labor is growing faster than the supply (which is equivalent to the condition that the warranted rate exceeds the natural rate of growth). However, it can be a problem in individual industries for which productivity increases are not matched by increases in demand. In this case labor must be reallocated to industries in which demand is growing more rapidly. Such reallocation may entail both retraining and geographical relocation and should be facilitated by public policy if inflation and structural unemployment are to be avoided.

FULL EMPLOYMENT, INFLATION, AND THE BALANCE OF PAYMENTS

Expansionary monetary and fiscal policy may increase the level of employment at the expense of widening the balance-of-payments deficit. Imports will rise with the level of money demand, and if exports do not increase concomitantly, the trade deficit will increase. Furthermore, if interest rates are reduced to stimulate demand, capital will go abroad where interest rates are higher.

For the United States, where the foreign sector represents a small component of demand, the conflict of objectives is not serious.[2] However, for countries such as Britain, it is often deemed necessary to maintain a state of semirecession in the domestic economy to avoid serious payments deficits.

The conflict of domestic policy objectives with that of avoiding excessive payments deficits could be eliminated by the adoption of a system of *flexible exchange rates* under which a payments deficit could not occur. If the price of each country's currency could fluctuate in response to the requirements for trade, then there would never be an excess supply of any currency, and every country would automatically experience payments equilibrium. During an expansion, as import demand increases, the supply of a country's currency would increase and its price would fall. Such an experience may be inflationary for the domestic economy, however, since it would effectively raise the price of imports in terms of the domestic currency.[3] However, measures to improve the trade balance with fixed exchange rates could also be inflationary. The policy of encouraging food exports as food prices were already rising undoubtedly contributed substantially to the so-called supply-induced inflation experienced in the U.S. economy in the early seventies.

A policy of flexible exchange rates would have to be universally adopted by many countries. Strong vested interests in the international financial community currently support the maintenance of fixed exchange rates and an international gold standard. Since flexible exchange rates are not likely to be adopted due to the opposition of these vested interests, governments must look to second-best solutions to overcome the incompatibility of their domestic economic goals and balance of payments requirements.

Such policies include

1. *Monetary policy and interest equalization tax*—The domestic government could rely on expansionary fiscal policy to stimulate investment, employment, and growth while following a tight money policy to attract

---

[2] The conflict between balance of payments objectives and national objectives may become serious if attempts to maintain international confidence in the dollar are allowed to take precedence over national economic problems. For instance, some people attribute the food shortages of the early 1970's to attempts to maintain an export surplus in the face of the declining international confidence in the dollar associated with several devaluations. This policy exacerbated the domestic inflation.

[3] For a discussion of flexible exchange rates, see Milton Friedman, "The Case for Flexible Exchange Rates," in *Essays in Positive Economics* (Chicago: The University of Chicago Press, 1953).

foreign capital and improve the balance of payments. In some cases, however, governments prefer or are required by political pressure to keep interest rates low to stimulate investment at home. When this is the case, funds may be expatriated to foreign capital markets to take advantage of higher interest rates there. Such an outflow of domestic currency will widen the balance-of-payments deficit. An *interest equalization tax* on earnings from foreign securities will reduce the actual return to holding these bonds and eliminate the gain to expatriating finance capital.

2. *Currency devaluation*—A currency devaluation by raising the domestic price of imports and reducing the foreign price of exports should discourage imports and stimulate exports, thereby reducing the trade deficit. A currency devaluation which raises import prices may be inflationary, however, particularly for a country such as Great Britain where imports are largely composed of food and primary products.[4]

A currency devaluation operates on the same principle as flexible exchange rates except that it is a one-time discretionary action in which the currency is revalued, rather than a constant and automatic realignment of exchange rates as trade conditions change. Ideally, a currency would be valued so that payments are in equilibrium at full employment. However, this ideal value depends upon the value of other currencies and upon economic conditions abroad, all of which are constantly in flux. Changes in the structure of trade also affect the optimum currency value.

3. *Trade restrictions and export subsidies*—Most economists tend to regard trade restrictions as undesirable, at least for advanced countries. By raising import prices they prevent consumers from obtaining goods from the cheapest possible source. Furthermore, most countries will follow reciprocal practices and establish comparable restrictions on imports, so that the measures are likely to be self-defeating. Their ultimate impact is merely to reduce total world trade, with goods and services being produced by high-cost domestic firms rather than by the most efficient producer. Import restrictions, by raising import prices, also are inflationary.

Export subsidies also interfere with efficient resource allocation. They permit foreigners to buy goods more cheaply than domestic purchasers. Foreigners view such practices as an unfair incursion into the domestic market and may impose import barriers which would, of course, defeat the objective of the export subsidy. If exports are primary goods, foreign manufacturers will face lower production costs than domestic producers with the result that foreigners will be able to undersell domestic manufacturers in their own markets.

---

[4] If the demand for imports is inelastic with respect to price, a devaluation may actually increase a payments deficit since the percentage increase in price will exceed the percentage reduction in quantity imported, and the value of imports will rise. If exports fall very little, the payments deficit might widen.

In the early seventies some people suggested *export* restrictions as a means of increasing the domestic supply of food and domestically produced industrial raw materials and alleviating inflationary pressure in these markets. In this case, the balance of payments objective would be explicitly sacrificed in the interest of price stability. The same objections could be raised to such a practice as for other trade restrictions. Not only would they encourage retaliation and invoke the ill-will of our trading partners, but they would distort efficient resource allocation, preventing a stimulus to supply that should be forthcoming to meet an increased world demand. Restrictions on food exports, in particular, might provoke a considerable amount of international hostility, and the ultimate effect on the international trading system might do the United States more harm than any short-run gains such a policy might produce.

15-2   CHOICE OF POLICY INSTRUMENTS

Keynesian analysis, by suggesting that policy targets can be attained solely by manipulating aggregate demand, implies that the policy variables move symmetrically with respect to negative and positive changes in policy instruments which affect aggregate demand. This is not the case for a number of reasons. First, the trade-offs between various targets do not operate in both directions. For instance, while an increase in the level of employment will produce an increase in prices, it is not likely that a reduction in employment will cause a decline in prices due to the downward rigidity of money wages. Furthermore, changes in policy instruments designed to influence demand have secondary effects which do not always act symmetrically when moving in opposite directions. Thus, a tax increase may be inflationary, while a reduction in taxes is not likely to cause a reduction in prices. Finally, there is an asymmetry in the response of various components of demand to changes in policy instruments. An increase in interest rates may discourage investment in a boom, but a reduction in interest rates may not stimulate it in a recession.

Because of this asymmetry, anti-inflation policy cannot be viewed as antirecession policy in reverse. Consequently, the appropriate choice of policy instruments will depend largely upon the state of the economy at the time the policy is designed.

ANTIRECESSION POLICY

The Keynesian model is most applicable to the design of antirecession policy. During a recession the primary objective is to increase the level of employment, real output and the growth rate. Until the expansion begins, there is little danger of serious pressure on prices from the demand side or balance-of-payments difficulties. The particular problems of managing an inflationary recession will be treated later in this section. Policy instruments for antirecession action include increases in public spending, tax cuts, and increases in the money supply. Each shall be considered in turn.

1. *Increased public spending*—Increases in public spending are the most direct and effective way to stimulate demand and the level of employment. It must be kept in mind, however, that spending increases are often irreversible. The government may involve itself in a long-term program of highway construction, for instance. If the purpose of the spending were primarily to increase the level of economic activity, presumably it would be desirable for spending to level off once full employment is reached. If there is excessive aggregate demand, the spending program should be scrapped. However, it may be difficult to justify abandoning a highway program in midstream, and consequently, the cutback in spending may have to come from consumption or investment. If government spending programs are not reversible then there will be a secular increase in the size of the public sector over the cycle if this instrument is used as an antirecession measure.

Keynes observed that it would be better

> . . . if the Treasury were to fill old bottles with banknotes, bury them at suitable depths in disused coal mines which are then filled up to the surface with town rubbish, and then leave it to private enterprise on well-tried principles of *laissez-faire* to dig the notes up again, . . . there would be no more unemployment and, with the help of the repercussions, the real income of the community, and its capital wealth also, would probably become a good deal greater than it actually is.[5]

Keynes also suggested that the ancient practice of building pyramids and cathedrals was useful in generating full employment, since these endeavors have little use-value, and as a consequence, the populace will never complain of having too many of them. Thus he argues, "Two pyramids, two masses for the dead, are twice as good as one; but not so two railways from London to York." [6]

This philosophy appears capricious in view of the chronic need for public services in today's society. Indeed, the idea that spending for the sake of spending is a good thing presents serious questions for resource allocation in a full-employment economy. What happens when the Office

[5] J. M. Keynes, *The General Theory, op. cit.*, p. 129.
[6] *Ibid.*, p. 131.

of Pyramid Construction develops such economic and political power that it wins increasingly large budgetary appropriations from the congress at the expense of education, medical care, and other socially more useful endeavors?

Even when the programs have merit, however, the use of government expenditure as a means of stimulating the economy builds in a bias toward an ever-growing public sector. This is because it is easier to increase spending in a recession than it is to reduce spending in boom periods.

2. *Tax reductions*—Tax reductions stimulate both consumption and investment spending. A cut in personal income taxes generally stimulates consumption with a very short lag. In fact, the short-run marginal propensity to consume when taxes are reduced is generally greater than the cutback in consumption when taxes are increased.

A reduction in corporate income taxes will stimulate investment and consumption (if profits are distributed to shareholders).[7] This policy is particularly useful in the recovery phase of the cycle, since it will relieve the inflationary pressure posed by capital stock bottlenecks, if the recovery is rapid. Furthermore, if technological change occurs, the natural rate of growth may be increased by this measure. Increases in labor productivity will also offset the inflationary impact of rising money wages as labor markets tighten.

If corporations view the cost of investing retained earnings as very low, then they will generally invest most of their internal funds in a recession. In this case tax reductions will be more effective in stimulating investment in a recession than monetary policy. Furthermore, as mentioned in Chapter 6, the type of investment undertaken in recessions is likely to be of the variety that improves labor productivity rather than mere capacity expansion.

Despite its favorable impact on investment, tax policy is not as reliable as expenditure policy for stimulating demand, particularly in periods of chronic depression. If the private sector is pessimistic about the future, increases in disposable personal and corporate income due to tax reductions are likely to be held as saving. Ideally, a policy of increased public expenditure will be combined with tax cuts in a severe recession. The implications of such deficit spending for the federal budget will be considered later in this chapter. Conceivably, however, in a minor recession, tax policy alone could perform the job of stimulating demand.

3. *Monetary policy*—Increases in the money supply, by causing interest rates to fall, may provide a stimulus to investment and consumption spending. Monetary policy is most likely to be effective immediately

---

[7] A reduction in corporate taxes can take the form of liberalized depreciation allowances and investment tax credit as well as a reduction in tax rates.

following a boom period in which credit has been very tight. In this case there may be a pent-up 'demand for housing and consumer durables as well as for certain types of capital equipment, and an easing of credit will facilitate purchases of these items.

In general, however, economists question the efficacy of monetary policy for stimulating the economy in the absence of expansionary fiscal policy.[8] Increases in the money supply may be ineffective in reducing interest rates to the level required to induce enough demand to trigger an expansion. This may be particularly true if money rates of interest have been relatively high in the immediate past and if speculators are subject to a money illusion with respect to the interest rate as prices stabilize in the recession. In this case it may be difficult to convince speculators that bond prices will indeed rise further, and increases in the money supply may be held in the form of speculative balances.

If there are no signs that demand will increase, investment and consumption spending may be quite inelastic to reductions in the interest rate. Any expansionary impact is likely to be restricted to particular industries in which purchases have been postponed due to tight credit conditions in the previous boom.

Clearly, however, if an expansionary fiscal policy is accompanied by an easy money policy, investment is likely to proceed more rapidly than if money is scarce. This is important during the recovery phase, particularly if money wages are rising. If capital costs are kept low, firms will substitute capital for labor, raising labor productivity. This will have the dual effect of bringing the warranted rate of growth closer to the natural rate while at the same time offsetting the inflationary pressure of rising money wages as labor markets tighten.

POLICIES FOR MANAGING AN EXPANSION

If an expansion is carefully managed, an economy can proceed along a full-employment growth path with a minimum of inflation. If the growth rate is too rapid, however, inflation will develop and measures to halt the inflation may precipitate a downturn. Furthermore, in the downturn, the inflation may persist, leaving the economy in a situation in which Keynesian economic policy is not at all helpful for achieving price stability.

While Keynesian measures (i.e., controlling the rate of growth of aggregate demand) are necessary for managing a boom, the secondary effects of these measures on the level of prices must also be considered. The use of wage-price guidelines or direct controls in an expansion will help

[8] The position of Milton Friedman is a notable exception to this viewpoint.

keep cost-push inflation in check as excess demand is controlled by the orthodox Keynesian policy instruments.

A second difficulty in designing policies for managing an expansion is that restrictive actions such as spending cuts, tax increases, tight money, and wage-price controls are bound to be unpopular and, therefore, politically difficult to implement. Because of congressional and presidential opposition, the policy initiation lag is likely to be much longer for restrictive actions than for expansionary ones, and as a consequence, the choice of policy instruments may hinge largely on the speed with which they can be adjusted.

In view of these limitations, we shall examine the available policy instruments in turn:

1. *Reductions in government spending*—Reductions in government spending are the most effective means of reducing aggregate demand. Furthermore, spending cuts do not feed a cost-push inflation as the other Keynesian policy instruments do. Government spending, however, may be difficult to curtail, particularly if on-going programs have merit from a social point of view, or if there are vested interests in their continuation. Even the Office of Pyramid Construction might argue that it would be wasteful to leave half-finished pyramids sitting around as monuments to our indecisiveness and failure to manage the economy properly.

2. *Increases in taxes*—Tax increases are less reliable than spending cuts for restricting demand, since both the magnitude and speed of the multiplier effect may depend on attitudes of households concerning their ability to recoup losses in real disposable income in the form of higher wages. In addition, they are likely to be inflationary.

Tax increases are intended to restrict consumption and investment demand. Experience has shown them to be unreliable since the impact is subject to lags of indeterminant length. If consumers have been accustomed to a long period of expansion in which real income has been steadily rising, they may view a tax increase as a temporary measure and make no immediate adjustment in their consumption. This will be particularly true if households have accumulated substantial savings during the boom. On the other hand, investment is likely to be harder hit than consumption when corporate taxes are increased, particularly if credit markets are tight.

Tax hikes will cause firms to raise prices if taxes are viewed as an element of production cost. Furthermore, tax increases are likely to stimulate demands for higher money wages by labor, again escalating costs and prices. The unfavorable impact on investment will affect the rate of growth of labor productivity which will worsen the inflationary impact of rising money wages.

Tax increases are often used as an anti-inflationary measure because they are easier to obtain from congress than spending cuts. In this case they represent a second-best solution for stabilizing demand during an expansion. Clearly, however, tax hikes should only be viewed as anti-inflationary when an inflation is being caused by excessive demand. Otherwise, they will merely feed a cost-push inflation with an undesirable effect on the level of employment.

3. *Monetary policy*—Monetary policy can be used to limit the availability of credit and raise the cost of borrowing, thus restricting investment and consumption demand.

Monetary policy is generally considered to be the most flexible policy instrument because, not requiring congressional approval, it has the shortest initiation lag. The effectiveness lag, however, is of indeterminant length, since there are so many factors which determine how firms will react to increased capital costs in a boom period.

Tight money will be most effective when investment is being externally financed or when combined with increases in corporate taxes which deplete internal funds. Credit rationing is likely to hit certain industries harder than others with well-established lines of credit or with ample internal funds, and consequently, the overall impact on investment is difficult to determine for any particular period. Experience has shown, for instance, that the housing market is typically hard-hit by restrictive monetary policy, and the social implications of this effect must be taken into account, particularly when monetary restraint is practiced over an extended period of time, as was the case in the early seventies.

A restrictive monetary policy is likely to be inflationary for two reasons. First, rising interest rates represent increased costs of production for firms. In addition, policies which restrict investment reduce the rate of growth of labor productivity which can provide an offset to the inflationary pressure of rising money wages. Tight money also nullifies the impact of rising money wages on capital substitution, so that the warranted rate of growth cannot be brought into line with the natural rate. Restated, unless productive capacity is expanding, bottlenecks will be reached early in the recovery resulting in declining labor productivity and inflation.

Since monetary policy is the easiest measure to implement when restraint is required, it is frequently employed as a means of stabilizing demand in booms. Like tax policy, it should be viewed as a second-best solution, however. Furthermore, tight money will be useful as an anti-inflationary measure only when price increases are due to excessive demand, since it tends to reinforce cost–push inflation.

4. *Wage-price policy*—Wage-price guidelines attempt to stabilize unit labor costs as money wages rise. If wage increases are proportional to increases in labor productivity, then unit labor costs will not rise and firms will not raise prices unless other costs of production increase. Since labor

cost represents the bulk of total unit cost in most industries, this policy could have a significant stabilizing influence on prices.

Wage-price guidelines represent a way to alleviate some of the inflationary pressures produced by tight money, tax increases, and a leveling off of investment. Presumably, using the guidelines, more reliance could be placed on tax policy and monetary policy for managing an expansion without the constant inflationary threat posed by these policy instruments. As a consequence, there would not be such pressure on congress and the president to cut back on-going public spending programs.

Once an inflation is allowed to develop as a result of excessive growth of aggregate demand, direct controls may have to be imposed on consumer prices to prevent the development of an inflationary psychology, loss of money illusion, and an upward pressure on money wages not directly related to the demand for labor. Such controls have a different philosophical basis from guidelines. Guideposts are designed to prevent wages from rising too rapidly as a result of increasing demand for labor. Direct price controls attempt to prevent the escalation of inflationary expectations that would render aggregate demand remedies for inflation ineffective.

HANDLING AN INFLATIONARY RECESSION

In a recession, inflation is not caused by excessive aggregate demand. Consequently, Keynesian anti-inflation measures that would reduce demand still further are not the most effective means of stabilizing prices. On the contrary, policies that affect aggregate demand should be mildly expansionary, since the recession will be characterized by a decline in real output and an increase in the unemployment rate, reflecting inadequate aggregate demand. Price policy should be directed to reducing the rising production costs that are the major impetus to price increases in conditions of slack product-market demand. Controls on consumer prices may help to break an inflationary psychology that is conducive to rising money wages. Tax cuts may also serve the purpose of mitigating the upward pressure on wages, since disposable income is thereby increased.

In addition to serving as a substitute for money wage increases, tax cuts may reduce production costs more directly when applied to business income. Reductions in both taxes and interest rates will have the dual impact of stimulating demand and reducing production costs. In a serious recession, increases in public spending may be needed, although these will not have the deflationary impact of tax and monetary policy. Furthermore, it is doubtful that a recession in which prices are rising will be severe enough to necessitate strong expansionary action, since the wage–push effect would eventually recede as the unemployment rate rises.

Policies to increase demand should be accompanied by wage-price

guidelines. Furthermore, tax policy should be designed to encourage investment. If increases in labor productivity are forthcoming, then guidelines will
be easier to implement.

When employment and the price level are moving in opposite directions, then Keynesian remedies which affect aggregate demand should be
used to attain the full-employment goal. Non-Keynesian remedies, such as
wage-price guidelines can be applied to the goal of maintaining price
stability.

THE APPROPRIATE NUMBER OF POLICY INSTRUMENTS

As demonstrated in Chapter 1, an effective policy package generally
must contain as many policy instruments as policy targets. In a simple
Keynesian model, two policy objectives—full employment and price
stability—can be achieved by judicious use of a single policy instrument for
controlling aggregate demand. This unfortunate oversimplification has
caused many people to view generalized monetary and fiscal policy as a
panacea for all the economic ills of a country.

Consider the typical case of an economy experiencing creeping inflation with less than full employment, a balance-of-payments deficit, and
an inadequate rate of growth. To achieve full employment with price
stability, balance-of-payment equilibrium, and an acceptable growth rate,
four policy instruments are generally required.

Expansionary fiscal policy would serve to increase the level of employment; however, this policy must be coupled with a policy of wage-price
guidelines to prevent prices from rising. But expansionary fiscal policy
would tend to worsen the balance-of-payments deficit, and consequently, a
tight money policy might be used to attract capital from abroad. Such a
tight money policy, however, would serve to dampen the rate of domestic
investment, to the detriment of the growth rate and full-employment goals,
and by reducing the rate of growth of labor productivity, it would render
more difficult the implementation of wage-price guidelines. Consequently,
the tight money policy would have to be accompanied by a program of
liberalized depreciation allowances or an investment tax credit to compensate for the impact on the level of domestic investment.

Not only must there be an adequate number of instruments to achieve
the policy targets, but these instruments must be effective. Thus, an easy
money policy for stimulating employment in a recession may have no impact at all on the level of investment and, consequently, should not be
counted in the set of useful policy instruments. Given that some policy instruments are not always effective and given the multiplicity and frequent inconsistency of the economic goals of a modern economy, it is important

that policy planners have as many policy instruments at their disposal as are consistent with the values and institutions of the economic system of which they are a part.

15-3   ECONOMIC POLICY AND THE FEDERAL BUDGET

There always seems to be considerable misunderstanding by the general public concerning the impact of a federal budget deficit or surplus on the economy. In addition, many people voice concern over a growing national debt arising from federal budget deficits. In this section we shall consider the relationship between the budget deficit and the level of economic activity.

BUDGET DEFICITS AND THE FULL-EMPLOYMENT SURPLUS

We have seen that the way in which a fiscal operation is financed will influence its impact on aggregate demand. Deficit spending is always more expansionary than if the spending were financed by taxes. This observation has sometimes led to the erroneous inference that when the budget is in deficit, fiscal policy is more expansionary than if the budget were balanced or in surplus.

The budget deficit is determined by federal expenditures minus receipts. Suppose a given level of discretionary expenditures and tax rates is planned for a particular period. The size of the deficit at any time will depend not only upon that planned fiscal package but also upon the level of economic activity. The lower the level of national income, the smaller are the personal and corporate tax receipts and the greater are the transfer payments such as unemployment compensation and welfare payments. Thus, for any given fiscal package, the deficit will be greater, the lower the level of economic activity.

Figure 15-1 shows the relationship between the budgetary surplus and the level of economic activity for two alternative budget packages. If national income were 95 percent of full-employment income, budget A would be balanced while budget B would show a deficit of $3 billion. Clearly, budget B would be more expansionary than budget A.

Suppose, however, the more expansionary fiscal package B causes national income to rise to 98 percent of full-employment income, while fiscal package A retards growth and causes income to fall to 94 percent of full employment. Now budget B will be balanced while budget A shows a deficit of $1 billion. Does the deficit budget A reflect a more expansionary fiscal policy than the balanced budget B? Of course not, since the deficit in

A is induced by a decline in national income, due perhaps to the fact that the fiscal package in A is not sufficiently expansionary.

A comparison of the impact of alternative budgets should be made for some specified level of income. Note that at a full-employment level of in-

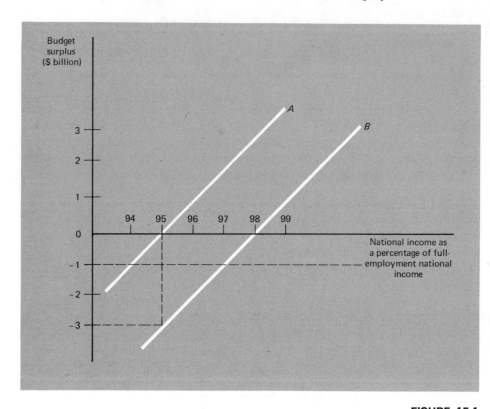

FIGURE 15-1

Budgetary Surplus and the Level of Economic Activity

come, both budgets would be in surplus. In the early sixties through the beginning of the Vietnam War buildup in 1965, the federal budget was designed to produce a surplus in the event that national income should be at the full-employment level.[9] This meant that the over-all impact of the budget represented a drag on the economy. To reach full employment, private investment would have to exceed private saving to offset the government saving represented by the budget surplus.

[9] See the *Economic Report of the President* (Washington, D.C.: U.S. Government Printing Office, January, 1964), pp. 41–43.

Recall that income earned can be consumed, saved, or paid to the government in taxes. Thus

$$Y = C + S + T$$

Ignoring the foreign sector, aggregate demand is the sum of consumption, investment, and government spending, or

$$D = C + I + G$$

National income equilibrium occurs when aggregate demand is equal to total income; that is,

$$Y = D$$

or

$$S + T = I + G$$

Rearranging terms, national income equilibrium occurs where

$$S - I = G - T$$

For equilibrium to occur at the full-employment level of income, the budget deficit, $G - T$, must be equal to the difference between private saving and private investment. If the budget is in surplus, that is, if

$$G - T < 0$$

then private investment must exceed private saving at full employment if national income equilibrium is to occur there.

Paradoxically, continuing budget deficits at less than full employment indicate that the budget is not expansionary enough. If the budget is designed to be in surplus at full employment, a budget deficit indicates that income is below full employment and a greater deficit is called for. Reducing the full-employment surplus by discretionary action would help to achieve the goal of full-employment while at the same time reducing the actual budget deficit.

As seen in Figure 15-2, the impact of the public sector on aggregate demand changed dramatically after 1965 as the full-employment budget was designed to generate a deficit from 1966 to 1969. The full-employment budget deficit reached its peak in 1968, the year in which aggregate demand pressure was so great as to generate a sizeable inflationary gap. In the seventies, the Nixon administration adopted the full-employment budget

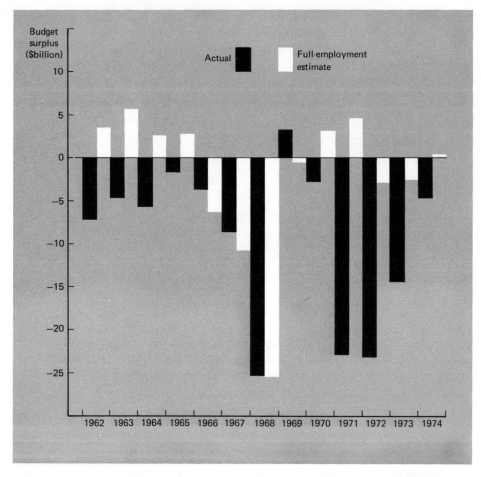

FIGURE 15-2

Actual and Full-Employment Estimates of the Federal
Budget Surplus or Deficit

Source: Department of the Treasury, Bureau of the Budget.

principle as a stabilization device.[10] As seen in Figure 15-2, the full-employment budget was brought into surplus in 1970 as an anti-inflation measure; and later government spending was increased to produce a full-employment deficit in the hope of reversing the rising unemployment rate. The use of the full-employment budget as the principal gauge of the macro-

[10] Richard M. Nixon, *The Budget Message of the President, 1974* (Washington, D.C.: U.S. Government Printing Office, 1973), p. 5.

economic impact of public sector activity (rather than the actual budget deficit or surplus) represented a significant step forward in delineating the appropriate role of the public °sector in the over-all aggregate demand picture.

THE NATIONAL DEBT

If actual budgetary surpluses do not match actual deficits over the cycle, the national debt will increase. Despite the fact that the U.S. budget is often designated to be in surplus at full employment, the budget is not cyclically balanced, being most frequently in deficit. This was true even in the early sixties when the budget was designed to produce a full-employment surplus.[11] Deficits are incurred because the economy is rarely at full employment. Figure 15-2 shows the actual budget deficits that were experienced between 1962 and 1974 in relation to the projected full-employment surplus. What will be the consequences for the national economy of piling up an ever-increasing debt, with little hope of retiring it?

It is clear that government debt is different from private debt in that governments have unlimited resources for debt service. Even if holders of government debt demand that it be retired, government can raise money through taxation to repay that debt. In an extreme circumstance, the government has the power to print money to meet its obligations. Since the government quite certainly cannot go bankrupt, it is unlikely that its debt would ever be recalled, and the only requirement or "burden" of the debt is to meet interest payments.

The public debt does not, as is sometimes believed, shift the burden of payment for today's expenditures to future generations. If there is unemployment, the government is using today's resources which would otherwise have remained unemployed today. Assuming that there is some benefit transmitted to future generations by the government spending program, the issuing of debt provides them a benefit they would not otherwise have enjoyed. Even if the economy is at full employment, deficit spending merely shifts today's resources from the private to the public sector. The burden on future generations can be measured only by the loss in private output weighed against the gain in public goods and services.

While future generations are saddled with paying interest on the debt, they are also recipients of interest payments, so that the transactions merely represent an intragenerational transfer. While this transfer represents a redistribution which may be slightly regressive with respect to income, the

---

[11] This situation is ironic since the ostensible purpose of the full-employment surplus is to retire the national debt. (See *Economic Report of the President, op. cit.,* p. 54.) Yet the fiscal drag caused by the full-employment surplus keeps the economy below full employment and the budget, on balance, in deficit.

effect is generally considered to be negligible by most economists. Only when debt is held by citizens of other nations does debt service represent a drain on the resources of future generations.

Since World War II the size of the national debt relative to GNP has declined steadily, as shown in Figure 15-3. The national debt was 24 percent greater than GNP in 1946, had dropped to about 50 percent of GNP in the early sixties, and fell to just above a third of GNP in the early seventies. Furthermore, interest payments on the debt have decreased as a percentage of national income. This means that the growth of the economy has exceeded the growth of the debt, and the tax *rate* required for debt service has declined.

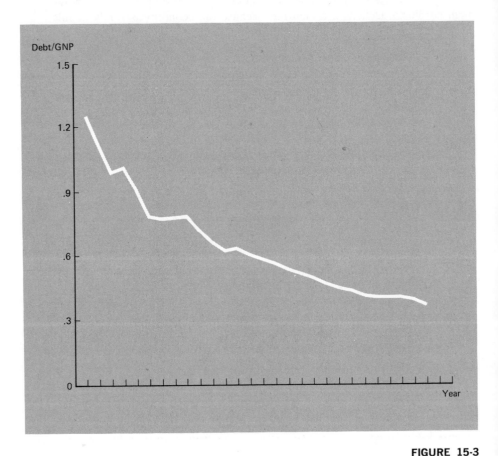

FIGURE 15-3

Ratio of National Debt to Gross National Product, 1946–1973

Source: National Debt, Department of the Treasury: Gross National Product, Department of Commerce, Bureau of Economic Analysis.

If resources are not fully employed, deficit spending utilizes resources that would not be used otherwise, and there is no burden on future generations. If resources are scarce, however, they must be drawn from other sectors of the economy. To the extent that public spending is not as socially productive as the foregone private spending, then there will be a burden on future generations. The same could be said for tax finance, however. Suppose the federal government raises corporate income taxes to finance a war. This may cause a decline in the rate of private investment and a reduction in the potential rate of growth of the capital stock. On the other hand, the war may not represent any benefit at all to future generations. The burden on future generations does not necessarily depend upon the method of finance but is represented by the cost of the war in terms of the increases in capital stock foregone because of it.

The method of finance may, however, determine the way in which resources are drawn from the private sector and, hence, may determine the extent to which future generations will be affected by an increase in public spending. If debt finance tends to draw more resources from current investment relative to current consumption than tax finance, then debt finance will affect future generations more than tax finance. Whether a "burden" is actually involved, however, depends upon the benefits accruing to future generations from the expenditure program. From the viewpoint of intergenerational equity, a program whose benefits are expected to be realized over a long time horizon should be financed like any long-term private investment project, by the issuance of long-term debt, not by current revenues.

15-4   ECONOMIC POLICY AND THE KEYNESIAN REVOLUTION

After 40 years, economic policy is still very much influenced by the ideas of Keynes, yet it is gradually abandoning some of the basic principles of Keynesian economic policy. Policy makers have come to recognize that no one model or set of rules is applicable to all situations, all the time. It is clear that our macroeconomic policy objectives cannot always be achieved merely by manipulating aggregate demand.

It took many years, a revolution in economic thought, and a chronic economic upheaval to convince society that government intervention is necessary in a free-enterprise economy. Keynes pointed out one way in which government can influence economic conditions, that is, by controlling aggregate demand. But it is a mistake to assume that controlling demand is a sufficient means of meeting all the national policy objectives. The institutional and behavioral structure of a modern economy is far more complex than that outlined in *The General Theory,* and much more work must be done if we are to understand the relationships underlying it. Furthermore, it is important to keep in mind that *The General Theory* was written 40 years ago, and the economy it described has undergone important structural changes since then. Improved specification of our macroeconomic models is a vital and challenging task. Since economic policy must be based on models of the underlying structure of the economy and of macroeconomic behavior and processes, the better the models, that is, the better we understand the economy, the more effective will be the macroeconomic policy we can design.

QUESTIONS FOR STUDY AND REVIEW

1. Keynesian economics suggests that macroecenomic policy objectives can be achieved by manipulating aggregate demand if we know enough about the structure of the economy. Do you agree? Illustrate your position with specific examples.

2. How do the traditional macroeconomic policy instruments—public spending, tax policy, and monetary policy—compare as measures for achieving full employment and growth with stable prices?

3. "Since a federal budget deficit means that the government is spending more than it receives from the private sector, the overall effect on demand must be positive. Therefore, a budget deficit means that economic policy is expansionary." Discuss.

4. "Whether the full-employment budget should be balanced or should show a surplus or deficit critically depends on the expected strength or weakness of the private sector of the economy. If the private sector is strong, a surplus might be appropriate. If not, then a deficit would be called for." Comment.

5. "A full-employment surplus in the federal budget is good, because it means we can gradually retire the federal debt and reduce the burden of our past wars for future generations." Comment on all aspects of the quoted statement.

ADDITIONAL READING

"Budget Policy, 1958–63," *Economic Report of the President*. Washington, D.C.: U.S. Government Printing Office, January, 1962, pp. 77–84.

DOMAR, EVSEY D., "The Burden of the Debt and National Income," *The American Economic Review*, XXXIV (December, 1944), 798–827.

FRIEDMAN, MILTON, "The Case for Flexible Exchange Rates," in *Essays in Positive Economics.* Chicago: The University of Chicago Press, 1953.

HELLER, WALTER W., *New Dimensions of Political Economy.* New York: W. W. Norton and Company, 1967.

MILLER, H. LAWRENCE, JR., "The New and the Old in Public Debt Theory," *The Quarterly Review of Economics and Business* (Winter, 1966), pp. 65–74.

NIXON, RICHARD M., *The Budget Message of the President, 1974.* Washington, D.C.: U.S. Government Printing Office, 1973.

OKUN, ARTHUR M., *The Political Economy of Prosperity.* New York: W. W. Norton and Company, 1969.

A

Appendix:
Economic Models
for Designing
Macroeconomic Policy

If a Keynesian model is to be used for designing macroeconomic policy, the parameters of the model must be specified numerically. Furthermore, if the model is to be used for policy planning, estimates of the required values of the policy instruments must be obtained when the targets are known. If the model is to be used for forecasting or simulation, estimates of the targets must be obtained when values of the policy instruments are known. Since the number of unknowns cannot exceed the number of equations in the model, the policy planner must select certain variables as exogenous, or predetermined. In addition, numerical values for the predetermined values must be provided.

An econometric model consists of a set of relationships formulated in algebraic terms. The parameters of the model are *estimated,* that is, specified numerically from empirical data using techniques of statistical inference. In some cases values for the predetermined variables in the model are also found inferentially; sometimes these values are known with certainty.

If such a model is consistent, it can be solved for the unknown or endogenous variables. In a forecasting model the target variables are unknown and the policy instruments are predetermined; in a policy-planning model the target variables are predetermined and the policy instruments required to effectuate these targets are unknown.

In this text we have developed a macroeconomic model in algebraic terms. Given numerical specification, we have seen how such a model can be used for policy planning and forecasting. In this appendix, we shall review the basic aspects of model building from a theoretical framework, and consider some of the techniques of statistical inference most commonly used for parameter estimation in macroeconomic models. In addition, we shall examine some of the models of the U.S. economy which have been developed in recent years for actual policy planning and forecasting. Finally, some extensions of the analysis presented in the text will be presented with particular reference to their implications for forecasting.

A-1   ELEMENTS OF A MACROECONOMIC MODEL

To solve for the endogenous variables of a model, there must be as many equations as there are unknowns. If this criterion is not met, then more equations must be added to the model or more variables must be given predetermined values.

The first step in constructing a model is *specification*. This involves determining the number of equations, the variables to be contained in each equation, the functional form of the equation, and whether or not the variables should be treated as predetermined or endogenous. Specification of a model presupposes an understanding of the system which the model describes, since it is essentially the translation of theory into mathematical form. Once the model is specified and the parameters are estimated by statistical techniques, then forecasting and policy planning on the basis of the model is relatively straightforward. It is the specification process that entails the most intimate acquaintance with the theoretical framework of the system.

EXACT VERSUS STOCHASTIC RELATIONSHIPS

The equations in a macroeconomic model can be either exact or stochastic. A *stochastic* relationship contains one or more variables whose value is not known with certainty, but which has a known probability distribution. Behavioral relationships such as the consumption function or investment function as well as technological relationships such as the aggregate production function are generally assumed to be stochastic. Thus, a consumption function may be specified as follows,

$$C_t = b_0 + b_1 Y_t + b_2 C_{t-1} + b_3 i_t + u_t$$

where

C_t = consumption in period t

Y_t = disposable income in period t

i_t = interest rate in period t

u_t = stochastic error term in period t

The stochastic error term, u_t, represents that consumption in period t not accounted for by the explanatory variables, Y_t, C_{t-1}, i_t, and the constant term, b_0, of the equation. The error term is generally assumed to have a probability distribution with a mean (expected) value of zero and a finite variance. There are several reasons for expecting some unexplained (stochastic) variation in consumption.

First, while a large part of the variation in consumption can be explained by variation in disposable income, lagged consumption, and the rate of interest, there are also other influences on consumption behavior. Since there are many such influences, they cannot all be accounted for in the model. Furthermore, taken together they should behave in a random manner, represented by the stochastic variable. The smaller the proportion of the variance in consumption which can be explained by the independent variables in the equation, the greater will be the proportion of the variance attributable to the error term.

A second reason for including a stochastic variable in behavioral equations is that human behavior often depends in part upon random influences and cannot always be explained, regardless of the number of variables included in the equation. In addition, misspecification of the functional form of the equation, that is, treating a nonlinear relationship as linear, will render an otherwise exact relationship inexact, requiring an error term to account for the difference.

Finally, random errors in measuring the dependent variable, consumption, can also be treated as a stochastic explanatory variable. Suppose the relationship

$$C = b_0 + b_1 Y$$

is exact. However, there is a random error in the data which measure consumption; that is,

$$\Gamma = C + \gamma$$

where Γ is measured consumption and γ is the measurement error. Then the equation, estimated statistically on the basis of these data, using Γ as a proxy for C, should contain a stochastic component, since

$$\Gamma = C + \gamma = b_0 + b_1 Y + \gamma$$

The error term in a stochastic relationship is assumed to have a zero mean, or expectation. This implies that it has no systematic influence on the dependent variable; that is, the most probable effect of the stochastic variable on consumption is zero.

Consider the simple relationship

$$C_t = b_0 + b_1 Y_t + u_t$$

where u_t is a random variable with zero mean. Since the most probable value of u_t is zero, that is,

$$E(u_t) = 0$$

where $E(u_t)$ is the expected value of u_t, then the most probable value of C_t is

$$E(C_t) = b_0 + b_1 Y_t + E(u_t)$$
$$= b_0 + b_1 Y_t$$

As seen in Figure A-1, the actual value of C_t may lie on either side of the line represented by the equation

$$C_t = b_0 + b_1 Y_t$$

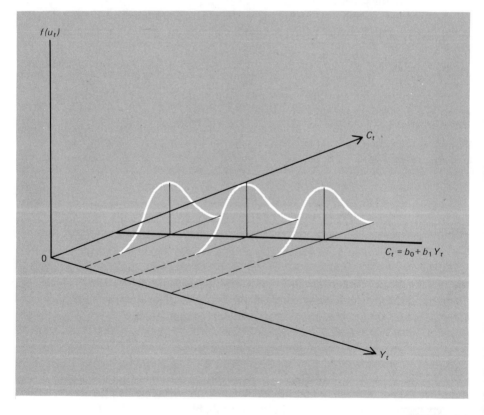

FIGURE A-1

Graphical Representation of a Linear Consumption Function with a Stochastic Error Term

In general, the larger the standard deviation of u_t, the greater the actual values of C_t will deviate from the (C_t, Y_t) line.

THE VARIABLES OF THE MODEL

Specification involves selecting the number of equations for the model, determining their functional form, and deciding whether the equations should be exact or stochastic. A second aspect of specification involves selecting the variables to be included in each equation, deciding whether they should be treated as endogenous or predetermined in each case, and selecting the appropriate statistical series for measuring them.

Since the number of endogenous variables in the model cannot exceed the number of equations, the endogenous set must be small in relation to the total number of variables which determine economic behavior. The choice of variables represents a trade-off between completeness of specification and manageability. An additional limitation to including a large number of variables is that these variables are often so closely interrelated that it is impossible to separate their influence. This interdependence of variables in economic relationships, known as *multicollinearity,* allows the model builder to explain a high proportion of the variance of the dependent variables with a few variables. It does, however, pose a problem for testing conflicting hypotheses.

Consider the problem of specifying the equation which describes investment in plant and equipment. Two explanatory variables, retained earnings and changes in sales, might be included. Suppose, however, that retained earnings tended to rise and fall with changes in sales. If the correlation between these two variables is high, presumably investment in plant and equipment could be adequately explained or predicted by either variable, and it would not be necessary to include them both in the forecasting model. On the other hand, suppose the policy planner wants to predict the impact of liberalized depreciation allowances on investment. On the basis of the data, he has no way of isolating the impact of an increase in retained earnings independent of an increase in sales. If, in the past, investment has increased with retained earnings, the effect could be due to the rise in sales which historically has accompanied an improved internal funds position. In this example, there is no way to test the accelerator hypothesis versus the cost-of-capital hypothesis for investment, since there is no independent historical experience.

Multicollinearity may occur among any of the explanatory variables, endogenous or predetermined. It is the principal factor which limits the total number of variables used in economic models.

The number of endogenous variables is limited by the number of equations in the model. The remaining variables must be predetermined.

Many variables which are treated as predetermined are not known with certainty, but are treated as such for lack of any known behavioral or technological relationships to explain them. One example of such a variable is government spending. In the absence of a theory of the process by which government spending decisions are made, this variable is generally treated by policy planners as predetermined, even though its actual value may be subject to a large degree of stochastic variation. Given the large size of the public sector, economic forecasting in the United States has been greatly hampered by the need to treat this variable as predetermined and then to estimate it by primitive techniques outside the structure of the model. Much care is given to accurate specification of the equations in the model and considerable attention is given to employing the most sophisticated techniques for estimating the parameters in the model. Yet if decisions in the public sector are unknown, the policy planner will not be able to make reliable forecasts of the target variables.

Economic forecasting with econometric models was the subject of some criticism in the last year of the Johnson administration, since the models consistently underestimated the level of demand and implied policy packages that turned out to be inflationary. The main reason for this, however, was the fact that the Administration consistently underestimated the level of public spending, particularly in the military sector. Apparently, the President's economic advisors received these low estimates and incorporated them into their forecasting models. Since there was a multiplier effect to the spending programs, the forecasts for the economy as a whole were wider of the mark than the original underestimate for the public sector.

In the seventies the forecasting record of econometric models for real variables such as constant-dollar GNP improved somewhat, with forecasting errors for real GNP in the range of 1 percent of the level of real GNP as compared with 3 percent in the late sixties. But because of the continual changes in the structure of the inflationary process and the difficulty of accounting for inflationary expectations, the models did not forecast prices and hence money values of the macroeconomic variables as well. However, because the problem lay essentially with dramatic changes in the underlying structure rather than with inability to model an essentially unchanged structure, the forecasting errors of the early seventies were not the subject of as much criticism as in the late sixties.

The reliability of a model is greatly reduced when exogenous variables are not known with certainty. Some variables, which we have treated as predetermined in this text, can be made endogenous if an appropriate theoretical relationship (equation) can be developed. Money supply, for instance, is treated as endogenous in some econometric models (see Chapter 7).

The choice of variables is often limited by the availability of data. Unless the variables in the model have been measured, the validity of the relationships cannot be established. We shall consider the problem of obtaining appropriate statistics for estimation and prediction in Appendix B. It is clear, however, that theoreticians, policy planners, and statisticians must coordinate their efforts to develop reliable econometric models.

A-2 METHODS OF STATISTICAL ESTIMATION

Once the model has been specified, the parameters of the equations must be assigned numerical values. When numerical values for the constants of the equations are estimated, then the model can be solved for the endogenous variables. The endogenous variables of an econometric model are often called "estimates," since their values are determined by estimates of the parameters of the equations as well as by the predetermined variables of the model.

The reliability of the forecasts of any model will depend upon the accuracy of the theoretical specification, the amount of nonrandom behavior in the system, the reliability of estimates of the predetermined variables, and the technique used for parameter estimation. This text has been concerned primarily with theoretical specification of macroeconomic models. To the extent that behavior is not subject to systematic influences, the science of economics fails as a method of forecasting and influencing behavior. In many cases political constraints prevent reliable estimation of predetermined variables. However, much work is left to be done in this area. Finally, we shall consider the question of techniques for parameter estimation.

Parameter estimation is one major area of concern for econometricians. In recent years, highly sophisticated techniques for estimating parameters in simultaneous equation models have been developed.[1] One rather old-fashioned technique is still widely used and is relatively easy to understand. This is the method of *least-squares regression*. Suppose the policy planner wants estimates for the parameters b_0 and b_1 in the relationship

$$C_t = b_0 + b_1 Y_t + u_t$$

[1] For a survey of the literature in this area, see J. Johnston, *Econometric Methods* (New York: McGraw Hill Book Company, Inc., 1963), Chapters 9 and 10, or Franklin M. Fisher, "Dynamic Structure and Estimation in Economy-Wide Econometric Models," in J. S. Duesenberry, G. Fromm, L. R. Klein, and E. Kuh, eds., *The Brookings Quarterly Econometric Model of the United States* (Skokie, Ill.: Rand McNally & Company, 1965), pp. 589–633.

He has a collection of data for C_t and Y_t which consists of paired values for each variable, each pair measured at some point in time. Such data can be displayed in tabular form as shown in Table A-1. The same data can be shown graphically as a scatter of points in a two-dimensional plane,

TABLE A-1

Personal Consumption Expenditures and Disposable Income,
1950–1969 (in billions of 1958 dollars)*

Year	Personal Consumption (in billions of 1958 dollars)	Disposable Income (in billions of 1958 dollars)
1950	230.5	249.6
1951	232.8	255.7
1952	239.4	263.3
1953	250.8	275.4
1954	255.7	278.3
1955	274.2	296.7
1956	281.4	309.3
1957	288.2	315.8
1958	290.1	318.8
1959	307.3	333.0
1960	316.1	340.2
1961	322.5	350.7
1962	338.4	367.3
1963	353.3	381.3
1964	373.7	407.9
1965	397.7	435.0
1966	418.1	458.9
1967	430.3	477.7
1968	452.6	497.6
1969	466.0	509.4

* Least-squares regression line: $C_t = 3.854 + 0.904 Y_t$.
Source: U.S. Department of Commerce, Office of Business Economics. *Survey of Current Business* (Washington, D.C.: U.S. Government Printing Office, 1950–1970) (issued quarterly).

as shown in Figure A-2. If the hypothesis that C_t and Y_t are linearly related has any validity, the scatter should approximate a straight line. Deviations from linearity are accounted for by the stochastic error term, u_t, in the equation.

The least-squares regression technique locates a line through the scatter such that the vertical deviations of the data points from the line are minimized. Consider such a line:

$$\hat{C}_t = b_0 + b_1 Y_t$$

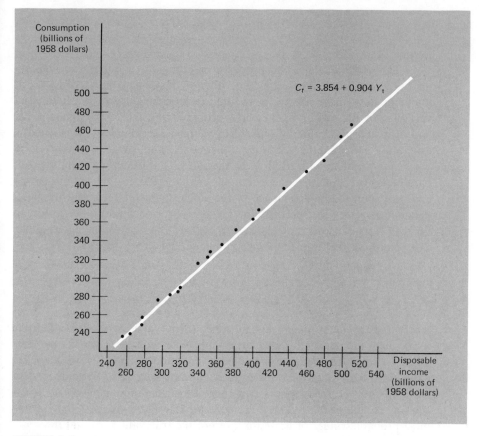

FIGURE A-2

Least Squares Regression Line Fitted to a Scatter
of Consumption and Income Data

Source: Table A-1 of this volume.

where the symbol, $\hat{\ }$, refers to an estimate of a parameter or variable.
For any value of Y_t, the corresponding estimate, $\hat{C}_t$, can be found from the
line.

Now, consider the actual value of C_t associated with Y_t. The difference between the actual and estimated values for C_t, e_t, where

$$e_t = (C_t - \hat{C}_t)$$

is the vertical distance from the regression line to the data point for the tth
observation. The least-squares technique locates $\hat{b}_0$ and $\hat{b}_1$, that is, the slope
and intercept of the line, in such a way that the value

$$\sum_{t=1}^{n} e_t^2 = \sum_{t=1}^{n} (C_t - \hat{C}_t)^2$$

is minimized.[2]

This technique has the property of minimum variance for the estimators as well as for the estimated value of the dependent variable, $\hat{C}_t$. If the error terms have a zero mean and are independent of the explanatory variables of the equation, the most probable value of the estimators, $\hat{b}_0$ and $\hat{b}_1$, is the true value, b_0 and b_1. In statistical terminology, least-squares estimators are minimum variance unbiased for the true parameter values.

One problem with using least squares as an estimating technique for parameters in simultaneous equation models is that their unbiasedness depends upon the independence of the stochastic error term and the independent variables in the equation. This property does not apply for equations in simultaneous systems as can be seen in the following example.

Consider the simple macroeconomic model

$$Y_t = C_t + I_t$$
$$C_t = b_0 + b_1 Y_t + u_t$$

where I_t is predetermined. At any time, t, the value of C_t depends upon u_t, through the consumption relationship. Note, however, that Y_t depends upon C_t, through the national income equation. Thus, the value of Y_t depends upon u_t, and the error term is not independent of the independent variable in the consumption equation. This condition causes the least-squares technique to produce biased estimates of b_0 and b_1; that is, the most probable values of $\hat{b}_0$ and $\hat{b}_1$ are not the true values, b_0 and b_1.

Several estimating techniques have been developed to overcome the bias in the ordinary least-squares (OLS) estimators produced by the interdependence of the explanatory variables and the error terms in the stochastic equations. One such technique is called *indirect least squares*. This method involves expressing the dependent variable in the equation to be estimated in terms of the exogenous variables in the model and finding OLS estimates of the parameters in these *reduced-form* equations. These will be unbiased since the independent variables are predetermined and, hence, independent of the error term in the equation. Then, the original parameters of the equation are determined from the reduced-form parameters.[3]

---

[2] The variable e_t is the actual error of estimation. The variable u_t is a theoretical error. In other words, e_t is an estimate of u_t.

[3] This is only possible if the equation is exactly identified—that is, if the number of endogenous variables in the model less one, plus the number of exogenous variables in the equation, is exactly equal to the total number of exogenous variables in the model.

Consider the model

$$Y_t = C_t + I_t$$
$$C_t = b_0 + b_1 Y_t + u_t$$

Expressing C_t in terms of the single exogenous variable in the model, I_t, the reduced-form consumption function is found to be

$$C_t = \frac{b_0}{1 - b_1} + \frac{b_1}{1 - b_1} I_t + \frac{u_t}{1 - b_1}$$

or

$$C_t = \beta_0 + \beta_1 I_t + v_t$$

where

$$\beta_0 = \frac{b_0}{1 - b_1} \tag{1}$$

$$\beta_1 = \frac{b_1}{1 - b_1} \tag{2}$$

$$v_t = \frac{u_t}{1 - b_1} \tag{3}$$

By the method of OLS, estimates of the reduced-form parameters, β_0 and β_1, can be made. Estimates of the structural parameters, b_0 and b_1, can be found from equations (1) and (2) above. Estimates of the structural parameters obtained by this method will not be unbiased for small sample sizes, although the bias disappears as the sample size grows. Furthermore, the method can be used only if it is possible to find the structural parameters from the reduced-form parameters. This implies there must be as many reduced-form parameters as structural parameters for the equation, a condition known as *identification,* and this is not true for all equations.

Other estimating techniques have been developed for equations that are not exactly identified. While most of these techniques still produce biased estimators for small sample sizes, many econometricians find them preferable to OLS because they have better large sample properties and because they tend to have a smaller sampling variance than OLS estimators.

Some econometricians have attempted to avoid the simultaneous equation bias by making their models *recursive* rather than simultaneous. A recursive model treats each equation as a step in a chain of events, with the dependent variable in the first equation becoming explanatory in the successive equations. The Duesenberry, Eckstein, and Fromm model is recursive.[4] In such a model, OLS estimators can be used.

SOURCES OF DATA

Data for estimating structural parameters can be historically generated, or they can be collected from a cross section at a single point in time. Historically generated, or *time series* data, are most commonly used for forecasting models, since the policy planner is most concerned with how behavior will change over time in response to changes in the policy instruments. If he is interested in short-run reactions, such as behavior within a three-month time frame, then quarterly data should be used to estimate the model.[5]

Sometimes, however, time series data do not provide sufficient independent variation of the explanatory variables to estimate all the parameters in the equation. Suppose, for instance, that changes in sales and internal funds of corporations have tended to vary together over time. If both variables are included in an investment equation, it is doubtful that their respective influences on investment can be separated sufficiently to provide meaningful estimates for the least-squares regression coefficients. In this case an extraneous estimate of the influence of one of the variables on investment will have to be introduced. Such an estimate can be derived from a *cross-section* study of investment behavior.

A cross-section study involves examining firms of different size within a single time frame to determine the relationship between, for instance, the level of internal funds and investment. The parameter value for the estimated relationship can then be substituted into the time series equation, with the remaining systematic (nonrandom) variation in investment being attributed to the sales variable.

Cross-section estimates should be used with caution in time series relationships, however, since behavior in the cross section may be different from behavior over time. Consider an economy in a state of semirecession. Suppose one group of firms with internal funds of $200 million invests $150 million in plant and equipment, while another with internal funds of $300 million invests $200 million. Now suppose public policy initiates a recovery, and internal funds of the first group of firms rises to $300 million.

[4] J. S. Duesenberry, O. Eckstein, and G. Fromm, "A Simulation of the United States Economy in Recession," *Econometrica,* XXVIII (October, 1960), 749–809.

[5] Data for econometric models are generally not collected for time frames shorter than three months, since a quarter is assumed to be the shortest period within which reactions to changes in economic conditions take place.

A relationship based on a cross-section estimate will predict an increase in investment of $50 million. Actually, however, investment is likely to increase much more than this if a boom is initiated and the firms decide to invest beyond the limit represented by their internal funds position. Cross-section estimates reflect microeconomic relationships that are often useful for understanding macroeconomic behavior. But it must be remembered that these estimates cannot always be incorporated directly into a model of macroeconomic behavior (see Chapter 5).

PREDICTION VERSUS STRUCTURAL ESTIMATION

Some economists argue that it is not necessary to isolate the separate influences of the explanatory variables in the model if the main interest of the policy planner is forecasting. That is, if the model predicts well, it does not really matter if we know whether changes in sales or internal funds are responsible for change in investment. Therefore, reliable estimates of the structural parameters are not important as long as all relevant explanatory variables are included in the model.

Other economists argue that structural estimation is important for forecasting. The relationships which have been numerically estimated in the model are all based on past behavior and experience. The forecaster assumes that these same relationships will hold in the future. Suppose, however, the forecaster expects a change in behavior over the period of the forecast. For example, suppose firms anticipate a sharp increase in corporate taxes which will affect their internal funds position. If internal funds are an important determinant of investment, this will certainly have an impact. Firms will discount the importance of their internal funds position for investment planning. Therefore, it is important for the forecaster to have a knowledge of structural relationships if he is to take account of anticipated changes in these relationships.

A knowledge of structural relationships is also important for policy planning. Suppose the government wishes to restrict investment. Without a knowledge of the independent effects of changes in sales and internal funds on investment it would be impossible to determine whether or not an increase in corporate taxes would be an adequate measure or whether demand would have to be restricted as well.

While forecasting might be possible in the absence of reliable structural parameter estimates, most economists agree that a knowledge of structure is helpful when historical relationships are expected to change over time. Furthermore, econometric models are used for more than forecasting. Knowledge of structure is usually important for selecting appropriate policy instruments when models are used for policy planning as well as forecasting.

A-3 ECONOMETRIC MODELS OF THE U.S. ECONOMY

Beginning in the early 1950's, economists have developed empirical models of the U.S. economy. Although these models have been principally used for forecasting, they are also used for policy planning and simulation.[6]

THE KLEIN–GOLDBERGER MODEL

The Klein–Goldberger model [7] was first estimated in 1953 and has since been expanded, respecified, and reestimated. The most up-to-date version of the model contains 20 equations and 20 endogenous variables which are listed below. The variables are expressed in the form of changes rather than absolute values. This reduces the problem of multicollinearity and improves the structural specification of the model. It will, however, increase the forecasting error in percentage terms, since changes in the policy targets are subject to a greater forecasting error than absolute values when the previous level of the variables is already known.

The equations for the Klein–Goldberger model, estimated from annual data for the period 1929–1964 (omitting 1942–1945) are given below.[8] Equations marked with an asterisk are identities and, hence, are exact. The remaining equations are stochastic, and the parameters are statistically estimated.

I. *National income identity*

*(1) $X = C_d + C_{ns} + I_p + I_h + \Delta I_i + G + F_e - F_i$

II. *Consumption*[9]

(2) $C_d - 0.7C_{d-1} = 0.230(Y - 0.7Y_{-1}) - 0.105C_{d-1} - 4.51$

(3) $C_{ns} = 0.228Y + 0.752C_{ns-1} - 1.468$

---

[6] Simulation involves solving the model for values of the target variables under alternative assumptions about structure and for various specifications of the policy programs and values for the policy parameters.

[7] L. R. Klein and A. S. Goldberger, *An Econometric Model of the United States, 1929–1952* (Amsterdam: North-Holland Publishing Company, 1955).

[8] From Michael K. Evans, *Macroeconomic Activity* (New York: Harper & Row, Publishers, 1969), pp. 498–499.

[9] Equations (2), (4), and (17) are estimated with the dependent variable in the form

$$X - \lambda X_{-1}$$

This is done to exclude capital stock variables which would be difficult to estimate statistically.

III. *Investment*

(4) $I_p - 0.951_{p-1} = 0.0656(X - W_g)_{-1} - 2.11(i_L)_{-1} - 0.590I_{p-1} + 9.329$

(5) $I_i = 0.137(X - \Delta I_i) + 0.396I_{i-1} - 24.702$

(6) $I_h = 0.0517Y - 0.0402i_{s-1} + 0.335I_{h-1} - 1.853$

IV. *Foreign sector*

(7) $F_i = 0.0284X - 10.14(p_i - p) + 0.463F_{i-1} - 0.942$

V. *Factor share equations*

(8) $RE = 0.788(P_{cb} - T_c) - 0.667(P_{cb} - T_c - RE)_{-1} - 0.148$

(9) $D = 0.0492 \sum_{i=1}^{20} P_{-1}(I_p + I_h)_{-1} + 0.0856D_u + 1.411$

*(10) $p_{cb} = pX - D - T_i - W - RI - PB$

(11) $PB = 0.0107pX + 0.898(PB)_{-1} + 0.674$

(12) $RI = 0.0623p(I_p + I_h) - 0.0230 \Delta i_L + 0.938(RI_{-1}) + 0.394$

*(13) $pY = pX - D - T_i - RE - T_c - T$

*(14) $W = whN_w$

VI. *Labor Market*

(15) $h = -0.450 \Delta w - 1.996(N_L - N_w - N_s) + 1.157$

(16) $\dfrac{W - Wg}{p} = 0.413 \left(X - \dfrac{Wg}{p} \right)$

$+ 0.282 \left(\dfrac{W - Wg}{p} \right)_{-1} - 10.607$

(17) $\left(X - \dfrac{Wg}{p} \right) - 0.95 \left(X - \dfrac{Wg}{p} \right)_{-1} = 0.364(I_p + I_h)$

$+ 3.532(N_w - N_g + N_s) - 0.95(N_w - N_g - N_s)_{-1}$

$+ 1.335(h - 0.95h_{-1}) - 6.483$

(18) $\Delta w = -1.697(N_L - N_w - N_s) + 1.116(\Delta p)_{-1} + 0.184$

VII. *Interest rate*

(19) $i_L = 0.157i_s + 0.835(i_L)_{-1} + 0.335$

(20) $i_s = 1.145i_d - 0.815RR_{-1} + 0.533Du - 0.511$

where ** indicates the variable is predetermined for this model and

C_d = consumption of durables, in billions of 1954 dollars

C_{ns} = consumption of nondurables and services, in billions of 1954 dollars

D = capital consumption allowances, in billions of 1954 dollars

**Du = dummy variable: 0 for 1929–1946, 1 for 1947–1962

**F_e = exports, in billions of 1954 dollars

F_i = imports, in billions of 1954 dollars

**G = government purchases of goods and services, in billions of 1954 dollars

h = index of hours worked per week, in 1954 = 1.00

**i_d = average discount rate at all Federal Reserve banks, in percent

I_h = residential construction, in billions of 1954 dollars

I_i = stock of inventories, in billions of 1954 dollars

i_L = average yield on corporate bonds (Moody's), in percent

I_p = investment in plant and equipment, in billions of 1954 dollars

i_s = yield on prime commercial paper, four to six months, in percent

**N_g = government employees, in millions

**N_L = total labor force, in millions

**N_s = self-employed workers, in millions

N_w = wage and salary workers, in millions

p = implicit GNP deflator, in 1954 = 1.00

PB = proprietors' income, in billions of current dollars

P_{cb} = corporate profits including inventory valuation adjustment, in billions of current dollars

**p_i = implicit price deflator for imports, in 1954 = 1.00

RE = retained earnings including inventory valuation adjustment, in billions of current dollars

RI = rental and net interest income, in billions of current dollars

**RR = year-end ratio of member banks' excess to required reserves

T = personal taxes + contributions for social insurance—government and business transfer payments to individuals—interest on government debt, in billions of current dollars

T_c = corporate profits taxes, in billions of current dollars[10]

**T_i = reconciling item between net national product and national income, in billions of current dollars

W = wages and salaries and supplements, in billions of current dollars

w = annual wage rate of all employees, in thousands of dollars per year

---

[10] The variables T and T_c are endogenous. Functions are not given for these variables because of frequent changes in the tax laws. Including these functions, there are 22 equations in the model.

$**W_g$ = wage bill of government employees, in billions of current dollars

X = GNP, in billions of 1954 dollars

Y = personal disposable income, in billions of 1954 dollars

THE SUITS MODEL

A model similar to the Klein–Goldberger model was developed by the Research Seminar in Quantitative Economics at the University of Michigan under the direction of Daniel Suits.[11] This model contains about 40 equations, and, like the Klein–Goldberger model, is estimated from annual data in terms of changes in the variables. The Michigan research seminar has been making annual forecasts of the endogenous variables since 1953. The model has been reestimated each year and is occasionally respecified.

An adaptation of the Suits model was estimated with quarterly data in the late 1960's, and a version of that model was used by the President's Council of Economic Advisors in the last years of the Johnson administration.

THE BROOKINGS MODEL

A more disaggregated model of the U.S. economy has been developed by a group of economists working at the Brookings Institution.[12] This model consists of nearly 200 equations, estimated from quarterly data. The model is broken down into seven sectors: durable manufacturing, nondurable manufacturing, trade, the regulated sector, construction, farming, and residual industries (primarily services). There is some debate among economists concerning whether such a highly disaggregated model is necessary to obtain accurate predictions. The forecasting record of the Brookings model has not been significantly better than that of smaller, more aggregated models. However, the model is still in the developmental stage and the forecasting record is rather limited.

THE BUREAU OF ECONOMIC ANALYSIS MODEL

The Bureau of Economic Analysis (BEA)[13] of the Commerce Department maintains a model which is essentially an adaptation of the Klein-

[11] For a description of this model, see Daniel B. Suits, "Forecasting and Analysis with an Econometric Model," *The American Economic Review*, LII (March, 1962), 104–132.

[12] For a description of this model, see J. S. Duesenberry, G. Fromm, L. R. Klein, and E. Kuh, eds., *The Brookings Quarterly Econometric Model of the United States Economy* (Skokie, Ill.: Rand McNally & Company, 1965).

[13] Formerly the Office of Business Economics (OBE).

Goldberger model. This model contains 36 behavioral and technological equations and 13 identities. It is estimated with quarterly data and is used primarily for short-run forecasting.

THE WHARTON MODEL

The Wharton model is the most recent adaptation of the original Klein–Goldberger model.[14] This model uses quarterly data and generates short-run forecasts for each quarter, up to two years in advance on a quarterly basis. This model is more disaggregated than the original Klein–Goldberger model, yet it is smaller than the Brookings model. It contains 47 stochastic equations and 29 identities, with 76 endogenous variables. The developers of the Wharton model claim that it is the largest and most detailed model of the U.S. economy that is continuously being updated.[15] While the Brookings model is larger, it is still being developed, and has not been used as much for actual forecasting and policy planning as the Wharton model.

DISCUSSION OF THE MODELS

The econometric models of the U.S. economy developed in the 1950's were highly aggregated and based on annual data. These models have been used to make annual forecasts and have a forecasting record of about 20 years. The models developed in the 1960's were larger and more disaggregated and have been estimated with quarterly data. The largest model to date, the Brookings model, is still being specified, and most of the forecasting attempted with this model has been in the nature of simulation, where the actual values of the variables to be forecast (the endogenous variables) are already known. The Wharton model is smaller than the Brookings model, but more disaggregated than the BEA model. It has a forecasting record of about 10 years.

THE FORECASTING RECORD

All the models mentioned here are continually being respecified and reestimated, and out-of-sample forecasts are always being revised. The forecasts presented here are all from versions of the models that were specified in the late sixties.[16]

[14] For a description, see M. K. Evans and L. R. Klein, *The Wharton Econometric Forecasting Model* (Philadelphia: University of Pennsylvania, 1968).

[15] See Michael Evans and Lawrence Klein, "Experience with Econometric Analysis of the U.S. 'Konjunktur' Position," in *Is the Business Cycle Obsolete?*, ed. by Martin Brofenbrenner (New York: John Wiley & Sons, Inc., 1969), pp. 384–385.

[16] Forecasts from the models that were respecified in the early seventies can

TABLE A-2

Comparison of Short-Run Forecast Errors for the
Wharton Model and BEA Model

	Wharton	*BEA*	*Wharton*	*BEA*
	GNP (*in billions of* *current dollars*)		*GNP* (*in billions of* *1958 dollars*)	
1Q	3.5	2.5	3.7	2.9
2Q	6.2	2.6	5.7	2.6
3Q	6.9	4.1	7.7	3.7
4Q	6.5	3.7	7.3	3.4

	Wharton	*BEA*	*Wharton*	*BEA*
	Consumption (*in billions of* *current dollars*)		*Investment in Plant* *and Equipment* (*in billions of* *current dollars*)	
1Q	2.1	1.9	0.7	0.6
2Q	2.4	2.0	1.2	0.6
3Q	3.7	3.0	1.4	0.7
4Q	3.5	3.6	1.4	0.8

	Wharton	*BEA*	*Wharton*	*BEA*	*Wharton*	*BEA*
	Residential Investment (*in billions of* *current dollars*)		*GNP Deflator* (*1958 = 100*)		*Disposable Income* (*in billions of* *current dollars*)	
1Q	0.9	0.7	0.2	0.3	2.1	1.4
2Q	1.1	0.6	0.4	0.3	1.5	1.5
3Q	1.0	0.8	0.5	0.5	2.6	3.0
4Q	0.9	0.8	0.6	0.7	3.1	3.3

Source: Michael Evans and Lawrence Klein, "Experience With Econometric Analysis of the U.S. 'Konjunktur' Position," in *Is the Business Cycle Obsolete?*, ed. by Martin Bronfenbrenner (New York: John Wiley & Sons, Inc., 1969), p. 381.

A comparison of the actual forecasts and forecast errors made by the various models is shown in Tables A-2 through A-5. Table A-2 compares the short-run (quarterly) forecast record for the Wharton model and the more highly aggregated BEA model.

be found in Bert G. Hickman, ed., *Econometric Models of Cyclical Behavior,* 2 vols. (New York: Columbia University Press, 1972), Part 3, and Gary Fromm and Lawrence R. Klein, "A Comparison of Eleven Econometric Models of the United States." *The American Economic Review*, LXIII (May, 1973), 385–393.

Both the BEA and Wharton projections were made in the fourth quarter of each year, from 1952–1964, from one to four quarters in advance. The table shows the average forecast error for each quarter over the 13 year period. In most cases, the BEA results are better than those of the Wharton model.

Table A-3 compares the mean absolute percentage errors in the Wharton and Brookings models, based on simulations for 38 sample quarters, 1953(3)–1962(4). Except for business investment, the Brookings model performed slightly better than the Wharton model.

TABLE A-3

Mean Absolute Percentage Errors in the Wharton and Brookings Models (in percent)

	Wharton	Brookings
GNP (in constant dollars)	2.32	2.03
GNP (in current dollars)	2.79	2.70
GNP deflator	1.56	1.46
Aggregate business investment*	6.28	8.49
Aggregate consumption*	3.19	1.55
Disposable income (in current dollars)	2.90	1.75

* Wharton model data in current prices; Brookings model data in constant prices.
Source: Michael Evans and Lawrence Klein, *op. cit.,* p. 385.

TABLE A-4

Comparison of GNP Forecasts in the Michigan and Wharton Models (in billions of current dollars)

Year	Actual GNP	Michigan Forecast	Error	Wharton Forecast	Error
1959	483	464	−19		
1960	503	493	−10		
1961	519	521	2		
1962	556	560	4		
1963	584	578	−6	585	1
1964	623	619	−4	625	2
1965	666	652	−14	662	−4
1966	732	725	−7	728	−4
1967	781	794	13	784	3
Average absolute					
error: 1959–1967			8.8		
1963–1967			8.8		2.8

Source: Michael Evans, *Macroeconomic Activity* (New York: Harper & Row, Publishers, 1969), pp. 516–517.

TABLE A-5

Actual and Predicted U.S. GNP, Annual Rates by Quarters
1952(3)–1964(2) in the Wharton Model (in billions of current dollars)

Quarter	Actual	Predicted	Error	Error (in percent)
1952(3)	345.4	352.9	−7.5	−2.2
(4)	357.9	358.8	−0.9	−0.3
1953(1)	356.4	365.5	−0.1	−0.03
(2)	367.7	361.6	6.1	1.6
(3)	365.9	359.0	6.9	1.9
(4)	361.1	355.5	5.6	1.6
1954(1)	360.5	354.5	6.0	1.7
(2)	359.8	353.2	6.6	1.8
(3)	364.8	358.8	6.0	1.7
(4)	372.9	360.6	12.3	3.3
1955(1)	388.2	372.3	15.9	4.1
(2)	392.7	377.6	15.1	3.8
(3)	402.4	383.5	18.9	4.7
(4)	410.0	386.6	23.4	5.7
1956(1)	410.7	384.8	25.9	6.3
(2)	416.7	392.9	23.8	5.7
(3)	420.6	398.4	22.2	5.3
(4)	429.9	406.2	23.7	5.5
1957(1)	436.9	416.4	20.5	4.7
(2)	439.9	421.8	18.1	4.1
(3)	446.3	427.7	18.6	4.2
(4)	441.1	431.6	9.5	2.2
1958(1)	434.5	437.6	−3.1	−0.7
(2)	438.4	443.9	−5.5	−1.3
(3)	450.5	456.2	−5.7	−1.3
(4)	464.8	468.3	−3.5	−0.7
1959(1)	473.8	467.7	6.1	1.3
(2)	486.9	470.6	16.3	3.3
(3)	484.0	460.7	23.3	4.8
(4)	488.1	470.6	17.5	3.6
1960(1)	503.0	475.5	27.5	5.5
(2)	504.3	473.6	30.7	6.1
(3)	504.2	479.6	24.6	4.9
(4)	502.8	488.0	14.8	3.0
1961(1)	503.5	497.0	6.5	1.3
(2)	515.2	508.1	7.1	1.4
(3)	524.3	518.4	5.9	1.1
(4)	537.9	529.1	8.8	1.6
1962(1)	547.3	538.1	9.2	1.7
(2)	557.2	549.2	8.0	1.4
(3)	564.4	556.2	8.2	1.5
(4)	572.0	563.2	8.8	1.5
1963(1)	577.0	566.7	10.3	1.8
(2)	583.2	569.8	13.4	2.3
(3)	593.0	578.4	14.6	2.5
(4)	603.6	589.3	14.3	2.4
1964(1)	613.7	597.3	16.4	2.7
(2)	624.5	611.4	13.1	2.1

Source: Michael Evans and Lawrence Klein, *op. cit.*, p. 387.

Table A-4 compares annual GNP forecasts for the Michigan and Wharton models. Clearly, the Wharton forecasts are superior.

For most of the models, forecast errors for real GNP are lower than for money GNP.[17] This can be explained by errors in predicting price change. All of the well-known econometric models of the U.S. economy are essentially aggregate demand models, either Keynesian or monetarist, and hence do not contain structural equations that give good price forecasts when the inflation is generated by a wage-price spiral in slack labor and product markets. Even in the forecast period of the mid-sixties, prices tended to drift upward, a drift not fully accounted for in the models. The recent experience with stagflation in the U.S. economy has caused econometric model-builders to turn attention to the specification of their price equations. Hopefully new theoretical developments in the field of forecasting price expectations and other variables affecting wages and prices will improve the forecasting ability of our macroeconomic models in the seventies.

Although the models developed in the 1960's have a better forecasting record than the older, annual models, it is not clear that the highly disaggregated models (Wharton and Brookings) will perform better than a smaller model (BEA). Smaller models have the advantage of fewer data requirements, fewer equations to respecify and reestimate, as well as a certain simplicity which makes them easier to work with. A model such as the Brookings model with 200 equations is so complicated that no one individual can really be held responsible for it. At this writing, it has been in the development stage for 5 years and its forecasting record in simulation has not been as good as that of the BEA model.

Table A-5 shows the forecasting errors for predicting current dollar GNP in the Wharton model. These quarterly predictions for the period 1952(3)–1964(2) were obtained by simulation in which the actual values of GNP were known, but not used in the sample from which the structural parameters were estimated. Note that the model generally underestimates the true values of GNP.[18]

IMPLICATIONS FOR FISCAL POLICY

In addition to comparing the forecasting records of the econometric models of the U.S. economy, it is also interesting to look at their estimated fiscal policy multipliers. Table A-6 shows the period multipliers of the

---

[17] For a more detailed discussion of this point see Gary Fromm, "Implications to and from Economic Theory in Models of Complex Systems," *American Journal of Agricultural Economics*, LV (May, 1973), 259–271.

[18] For a more detailed discussion of these and other econometric models of the U.S. economy and an analysis of their forecasting records see Bert G. Hickman, ed., *Econometric Models of Cyclical Behavior, op. cit.*

TABLE A-6

Period Multipliers of the BEA, Brookings, and Wharton Models

	Δ GNP / Δ government nondefense expenditures		
Quarters of Change	BEA	Brookings	Wharton
1	1.1	1.8	1.2
2	1.5	2.3	1.5
3	1.7	2.7	1.7
4	1.9	2.8	1.8
5	1.9	2.8	1.9
6	1.9	2.9	2.0
7	1.9	2.9	2.1
8	1.9	2.9	2.2
12	1.9	3.0	2.4
16	2.1	3.1	2.6
20	2.5	3.0	2.5
24	2.9	3.1	2.3
28	3.1	3.3	2.3
32	3.1	3.4	2.3
36	3.2	3.7	2.8
40	3.3	3.8	3.9

	Δ GNP / Δ personal taxes		
Quarters of Change	BEA	Brookings	Wharton
1	0.4	1.0	0.4
2	0.8	1.4	0.7
3	1.1	1.6	0.9
4	1.3	1.8	1.0
5	1.5	1.9	1.2
6	1.7	2.0	1.3
7	1.8	2.2	1.4
8	1.8	2.3	1.5
12	1.8	2.6	1.7
16	1.8	2.8	1.5
20	2.2	2.8	1.2
24	2.7	2.9	0.7
28	3.2	3.2	0.4
32	3.3	3.5	0.4
36	3.3	4.0	0.7
40	3.5	4.7	1.6

Source: Gary Fromm and Lawrence R. Klein, "A Comparison of Eleven Econometric Models of the United States," *The American Economic Review*, LXIII (May, 1973), 391–392.

BEA, Brookings, and Wharton models for a simulated $1-billion increase in government nondefense expenditures. There is relatively uniform agreement among the models with respect to the timing and magnitude of the fiscal policy impact. As shown in the second part of Table A-6, there is less agreement on the impact of a $1-billion decrease in personal taxes. This is probably so because the tax multiplier involves an extra possibility of error, since the marginal propensity to consume appears in the numerator.[19]

A-4 SOME ADDITIONAL PROBLEMS OF SPECIFICATION

In the text we developed the multiplier analysis for forecasting policy targets for known values of the policy instruments, and for policy planning, that is, finding required values for the policy instruments when the targets are known. In this section we shall consider some additional multiplier problems. The foreign sector will be ignored for simplicity.

INCOME SHARES AND THE MULTIPLIER

As was demonstrated in Chapters 3 and 4, the value of the national income multiplier depends upon the marginal propensity to spend out of national income by consumers, business, and government. Recalling the aggregate demand identity and the national income equilibrium condition,

$$Y = D \equiv C + I + G$$

and expressing spending in each sector in terms of the autonomous and induced components,

$$C = a + bY$$
$$I = h + dY$$
$$G = G_0$$

the national income equilibrium condition is expressed as

$$Y = a + h + G_0 + (b + d)Y$$

and the national income multiplier is found to be

---

[19] For additional analysis of differences in the fiscal policy multipliers of these models see Gary Fromm and Lawrence R. Klein, "A Comparison of Eleven Econometric Models of the United States," *The American Economic Review,* LXIII (May, 1973), 385–393.

$$\frac{\Delta Y}{\Delta D} = \frac{1}{1 - b - d}$$

where ΔD is an autonomous change in spending from any sector.

In specifying the relationships in a macroeconomic model, consumption is generally assumed to be a function of disposable personal income, and business investment is a function business income. Thus, in an econometric model, the parameters to be estimated are typically the marginal propensity to consume out of disposable income (the regression coefficient for disposable income in the consumption function) and the marginal propensity to invest out of business income (the regression coefficient for the business profits variable in the investment equation). How can these parameters estimated from the behavioral relationships be used to formulate a national income multiplier which requires estimates of the marginal propensity to consume and invest out of national income?

National income can be broken down into the shares going to each sector:

$$Y \equiv Y_D + Y_B + Y_G$$

where

Y = national income
Y_D = disposable personal income
Y_B = business income net of taxes
Y_G = government income (tax receipts)

Suppose the distribution of income going to households, business, and government is known, and that

$$Y_D = kY$$
$$Y_B = lY$$
$$Y_G = mY$$

where

$$k + l + m = 1$$

and k, l, and m represent the percentage share of national income going to households, business, and government, respectively.

Suppose the behavioral equations, the consumption and investment functions, have been numerically specified, and that

$$C = \hat{\alpha} + \hat{\beta} Y_D$$

and

$$I = \hat{\gamma} + \hat{\delta} Y_B$$

Substituting the income shares equations into these equations, the relationships between consumption and investment and national income are found:

$$C = \hat{\alpha} + \hat{\beta}kY$$
$$I = \hat{\gamma} + \hat{\delta}lY$$

where $\hat{\beta}k$ is the marginal propensity to consume from national income and $\hat{\delta}l$ is the marginal propensity to invest from national income.

   Suppose

$$\hat{\beta} = 0.9$$

and

$$\hat{\delta} = 1.2$$

with households receiving 60 percent of national income and business receiving 20 percent. Then the marginal propensity to consume from national income is

$$b = k\hat{\beta} = 0.6(0.9) = 0.54$$

and the marginal propensity to invest from national income is

$$d = l\hat{\delta} = 0.2(1.2) = 0.24$$

Therefore,

$$\frac{\Delta Y}{\Delta D} = \frac{1}{1 - b - d} = \frac{1}{1 - 0.54 - 0.24} = 4.545$$

Suppose the share going to households rises to 70 percent and that going to business falls to 15 percent. Then, if $\hat{\beta}$ and $\hat{\delta}$ are unaffected by the change in income distribution

$$b = 0.7(0.9) = 0.63$$

and

$$d = 0.15(1.2) = 0.18$$

and the multiplier becomes

$$\frac{\Delta Y}{\Delta D} = \frac{1}{1 - b - d} = \frac{1}{1 - 0.63 - 0.18} = 5.263$$

Thus, from a knowledge of relative income shares and the numerical parameter estimates of the consumption and investment functions, an estimate of the national income multiplier can be obtained.

Dynamic Instability in a Multiplier Model

If the denominator of the multiplier becomes zero, its value becomes infinite, while if it is negative, the analysis is meaningless.[20] This implies the restriction that

$$b + d < 1$$

That is, the sum of the marginal induced effects be less than unity. Since

$$b + s = 1$$

where s is the marginal propensity to save from national income, this implies that the marginal propensity to invest must be less than the marginal propensity to save; that is,

$$s > d$$

if the multiplier analysis is to produce meaningful results.
   Suppose

$$s < d$$

so that a change in income will induce a greater change in investment than saving. If the economy were previously in equilibrium, then after the change,

$$I > S$$

That is, investment would exceed saving. Presumably interest rates would have to rise to discourage investment and stimulate saving.
   In this case the IS curve would have a positive slope, since at higher levels of income, higher interest rates would be required to maintain national income equilibrium with saving equal to investment. A positively sloped IS curve may cause the national income equilibrium to be unstable. As demonstrated in Chapter 13, whether or not an equilibrium will be unstable depends upon the shape of the functional relationships in the model.

---

[20] The analysis is meaningless in that it predicts that an autonomous increase in spending ultimately reduces the level of total spending which, as we shall see, does not occur.

It also depends upon the specific assumptions about behavior in the system, that is, the dynamic adjustment process.

Consider a system described by the *IS–LM* model of Chapter 8, with a product market lag and no lag in the money market. This implies that the interest rate adjusts instantaneously to a displacement of the general equilibrium so as to maintain continual equilibrium in the money market while the equilibrium between saving and investment is achieved only after the passage of time. Given these assumptions, the system will adjust along the *LM* curve, representing positions of money market equilibrium.

Suppose the economy is in general equilibrium. An increase in the money supply will cause the *LM* curve to shift rightward, displacing the old equilibrium.

If the *IS* curve is negatively sloped, the system will adjust to a new general equilibrium, as shown in case I in Figure A-3. Originally, the *LM* curve is LM_1, with income, Y_1, and the interest rate, i_1. An increase in the money supply causes the *LM* curve to shift to LM_2. The interest rate adjusts instantaneously to restore money market equilibrium, falling to i'_1. After a lag, income gradually increases in response to the reduction in the interest rate, and the interest rate rises with income as the transactions demand for money increases. The process of adjustment continues until equilibrium is attained in the product market at Y_2 and the rate of interest is i_2.

In case II of Figure A-3, the adjustment process is similar. Initially, the *LM* curve is LM_1 and income and the interest rate are Y_1 and i_1, respectively. An increase in the money supply causes the *LM* curve to shift to LM_2 and the interest rate declines to i'_1, to maintain money market equilibrium. The decline in the interest rate stimulates investment and causes income to increase. Notice, however, that since the *IS* curve is positively sloped, the change in income will induce more investment than saving, since the marginal propensity to invest is greater than the marginal propensity to save. Other things being equal, once an initial increase in income takes place, increases in investment will exceed increases in saving, income will increase indefinitely, and a new equilibrium will never be reached. In this example, however, increases in income cause the transactions demand for money to increase and the interest rate to rise. In case II, the interest rate rises rapidly enough in response to increases in income to dampen investment causing it to be equated with saving and restoring a new equilibrium at Y_2 and i_2.

In case III, however, increases in the interest rate are not sufficient to restore equilibrium in the product market. The interest rate does not rise rapidly enough in response to the increased demand for transactions balances to dampen investment to the level required to restore the saving–investment equality. While an equilibrium consistent with LM_2 is defined at Y_2 and i_2, it will never be attained (it is technically unstable), and income

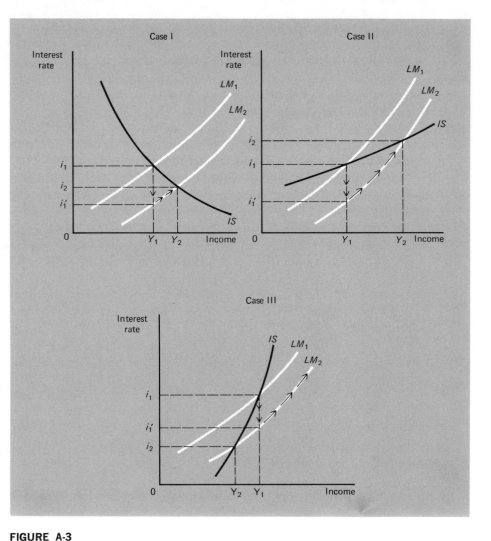

FIGURE A-3

Dynamic Adjustment in the IS–LM Model
with a Product Market Lag

will increase indefinitely unless restrained by measures external to the
model.

Given a positively sloped *IS* curve, implying that the marginal propensity to invest exceeds the marginal propensity to save, the adjustment
process described in this example will restore equilibrium only if the *IS*
curve is flatter than the *LM* curve. A new equilibrium is most likely to be

restored the smaller the difference is between the marginal propensity to invest and the marginal propensity to save and the greater is the rise in the interest rate associated with a given increase in income.

QUESTIONS FOR STUDY AND REVIEW

1. Why is specification such an important part of building an econometric model? How does the specification process differ from estimation?

2. Econometric models are stochastic rather than exact. What does this mean, and what does it imply for their usefulness for forecasting and policy planning?

3. Suppose you were asked to specify and estimate one of the equations in a macroeconomic model. Select one of the relationships discussed in this text and explain in detail how you would go about the project. Include in your discussion problems of specification and estimation as well as data sources and definitions. What difficulties would you expect to encounter and what would be the limitations of your equation as a forecasting and policy-planning tool?

4. The government is considering two alternative tax schemes for financing an expenditure project. One involves an increase in personal income taxes, while the other involves a tax on business income. How would you forecast the multiplier effect, if any, of the two projects? Which would have the greater impact, and why?

ADDITIONAL READING

CHRIST, CARL, "Aggregate Econometric Models," *The American Economic Review,* XLVI (June, 1956), 385–408.

DUESENBERRY, J. S., G. FROMM, L. KLEIN, and E. KUH, eds., *The Brookings Quarterly Econometric Model of the United States.* Skokie, Ill.: Rand McNally & Company, 1965.

EVANS, MICHAEL, and LAWRENCE KLEIN, "Experience with Econometric Analysis of the U.S. 'Konjunktur' Position," in *Is the Business Cycle Obsolete?* ed. by Martin Bronfenbrenner. New York: John Wiley & Sons, Inc., 1969, pp. 359–388.

FROMM, GARY, "Implications to and from Economic Theory in Models of Complex Systems," *American Journal of Agricultural Economics,* LV (May, 1973), 259–271.

FROMM, GARY, and LAWRENCE R. KLEIN, "A Comparison of Eleven Econometric Models of the United States," *The American Economic Review,* LXIII (May, 1973), 385–393.

HICKMAN, BERT G., ed., *Econometric Models of Cyclical Behavior.* 2 vols. New York: Columbia University Press, 1972.

HICKMAN, BERT G., ed., *Quantitative Planning of Economic Policy.* Washington, D.C.: The Brookings Institution, 1965.

KLEIN, L. R., and A. S. GOLDBERGER, *An Econometric Model of the United States, 1929–1952.* Amsterdam: North-Holland Publishing Company, 1955.

SUITS, DANIEL B., "Forecasting and Analysis with an Econometric Model," *The American Economic Review,* LII (March, 1962), 104–132.

B

Appendix:
Sources and Definition
of the Data—
The National Accounts

National income models would be useless for policy planning without data for evaluating the performance of the economy and measuring the impact of public policy. Furthermore, data are required for testing the validity of the structural hypotheses—the behavioral and technological relationships—of the model and for estimating the parameters of these relationships.

Although statistical measurement is a prerequisite for policy planning, there is no point in collecting data unless they have a useful meaning in terms of the economic model. Consequently, an understanding of the theoretical basis of the planning model must precede the discussion of the techniques of national income accounting and the conceptual problems associated with collecting meaningful data. For this reason we have departed from the traditional textbook format and have placed the treatment of national accounting at the end of this book.

We have seen how macroeconomic theory can be adapted into a model for policy planning and forecasting. Before concluding our study of the design of macroeconomic policy, it remains to consider whether or not the data of the national accounts provide a close empirical approximation to the theoretical structure of the model.

B-1 THE NATIONAL ACCOUNTS AND THE DESIGN
OF MACROECONOMIC POLICY

The data of the national accounts are used for several purposes. As we have seen, they are necessary for the construction of macroeconomic policy models, both for estimating parameters in the equations of the models as well as forecasting on the basis of these relationships.

National accounts data are also used as criteria for evaluating the performance of the economy and measuring the impact of public policy. Thus, a decline in GNP, as measured by the national accounts statistics, indicates a decline in the level of economic activity and suggests a need for remedial action. If government increases spending and GNP rises, this response may be viewed as indicative of the success of the policy.

Other implications, often of dubious validity, are sometimes drawn from national accounts data. National income statistics are often viewed as measures of welfare. This is particularly true when an international or intertemporal comparison is made. Thus, since per capita GNP in the United States in 1969 was $4242 while in Sweden it was $2859, then the assumption can be made that the "standard of living" in the United States is higher than that in Sweden. Alternatively, per capita GNP in the United States in 1963 was $2878. Does this imply that Americans are better off today than in 1963? Was the standard of living in Sweden in 1969 comparable to that of the United States in 1963? Since many people believe that an increase in real GNP or national income implies an improvement in economic welfare, understanding of the sources and definitions of the data is important for evaluating these statistics in these terms.

NATIONAL ACCOUNTING AND THE KEYNESIAN REVOLUTION

Most of our data measuring national income aggregates and other variables such as price indices and unemployment rates that are needed to estimate a macroeconomic model are of post-World War II vintage. It is not surprising that national accounting developed after the Keynesian revolution, since before that time policy planning was not based on econometric models, and consequently, data were not required. Furthermore, national income and employment were not viewed as policy targets, and hence, measures of these aggregates were not required for policy design and evaluation.

Some pre-Keynesian economists, such as Simon Kuznets and Colin Clark, developed data series for national income or product because of their interest in the historical process of economic growth and development. While these data have provided a basis for statistical investigations of the prewar period, the interest of the compilers was primarily historical and descriptive. There was no serious attempt to incorporate the data into an economic model or to use them for policy planning. Consequently, the definitions employed in this early research are often quite different from those required for the theoretical analysis. Furthermore, differences in definitions often rendered the work of different compilers incomparable.

Just as Keynesian economic theory led to the development of macro-economic planning models, so did the development of these models result in the establishment of the theory and practice of national income accounting. In many respect, practical policy planning is limited by the feasibility of measuring the variables in the model. For instance, suppose the policy planner decides to incorporate Friedman's permanent income hypothesis about consumption in his model. The essential explanatory variable, permanent income, cannot be measured. Consequently, a measurable proxy variable for permanent income must be found if the hypothesis is to be tested statistically and used for forecasting. The reliability of the model now will depend upon the reliability of the proxy for explaining permanent income as well as the reliability of the permanent income hypothesis for explaining consumption.

Not only are data required to make theory operational for policy planning, but national accounting must be done within a theoretical framework if it is to be useful for economic analysis. For example, for a Keynesian model, business expenditure (investment) must be separated from expenditures of households. Furthermore, business expenditure must be broken down into inventory accumulation and investment in plant and equipment. On the other hand, we do not have a theory of aggregate demand that disaggregates spending units on the basis of body weight. Consequently there is no point in collecting data for expenditures of people weighing more than or less than 200 pounds since there is no theoretical model to which these data can be applied.

As we shall see, national accounting is not merely a process of data collection, but involves many complex conceptual problems. This is due to the requirement that the data of the national accounts measure meaningful activities and phenomena from the viewpoint of economic theory. Before turning to these problems, however, we shall examine some of the definitions and approaches of national accounting.

B-2   DEFINITIONS AND APPROACHES

The U.S. Department of Commerce computes income and expenditure accounts for the individual sectors of the economy—households, business, government, and foreign sector. It also compiles national income and product aggregates for the economy as a whole. The sector approach is useful for Keynesian analysis. The national income and product approach is useful for evaluating the overall performance of the economy and the impact of public policy. It is from the aggregated accounts that welfare implications are typically drawn. In addition, the Federal Reserve provides data on financial flows that are useful for estimating monetarist models and for financial sector analysis in Keynesian models.

Before turning to the sector accounts, it is useful to consider the definitions of the items which comprise the aggregated accounts. The account-

TABLE B-1

National Income and Product, 1972 (in billions of dollars)

Gross national product		1155.2
less: Capital consumption	102.4	
Net national product		1052.8
plus: Subsidies less surplus of		
government enterprises	1.7	
less: Indirect business taxes	109.5	
Business transfer payments	4.6	
Statistical error	−1.5	
National income		941.8
less: Corporate profits and inventory		
adjustment valuation	91.1	
Contributions for social insurance	73.7	
plus: Net interest paid by government		
and consumers	32.7	
Government transfers to persons	98.3	
Business transfers	4.6	
Dividends	26.0	
Personal income		939.2
less: Personal tax payments	142.2	
Disposable income		797.0
less: Personal consumption expenditures	726.5	
Interest paid by consumers	19.7	
Personal transfers to foreigners	1.0	
Personal saving		49.7

Source: U.S. Department of Commerce, Office of Business Economics. *Survey of Current Business* (Washington, D.C.: U.S. Government Printing Office, 1973).

ing framework which shows the relationship between the various measures of economic activity is shown in Table B-1, with data provided for 1972.

Gross national product (GNP) measures the value of the total output of goods and services during the accounting period, including consumption goods, capital goods, and exports. Only the value of final products (i.e., those goods not used up in the production of other goods during the accounting period) is included in this measure. Thus, while bread is considered a final good, the wheat from which the bread is made is an intermediate good. Since the value of the wheat is included in the price of the bread, it will be double counting to include both the wheat and the total bread value in the measure of GNP.

It may be difficult to determine which products are final products and which are intermediate. Suppose the wheat is made into flour. If the flour is used by a commercial baker who sells bread, then it is an intermediate product. On the other hand, if it is sold to a housewife who makes the bread herself, it is a final product, since a housewife's services are not counted as part of the nation's GNP.[1]

One way out of the dilemma is to use the value-added approach for measuring total output. This approach was outlined in Chapter 2. If the value of all intermediate products is subtracted from the value of output at each stage of production, then the result, value added, is exactly equal to the value of the final product.

Table B-2 shows value added for each stage in the production of a

TABLE B-2

Value Added in the Production of Bread

Stage of Production	Receipts (in cents per unit)	Cost of Intermediate Goods (in cents per unit)	Value Added (in cents per unit)
Wheat	4	0	4
Flour	6	4	2
Bread (wholesale)	12	6	6
Bread (retail)	20	12	8
Total value added (in cents per unit)			20

loaf of bread. At each stage, the value of the goods in the previous stage is subtracted from receipts to obtain value added. Total value added in each stage is exactly equal to the retail price of bread, 20 cents.

The value-added approach is used in national accounting both because of its conceptual simplicity and because firms maintain records in terms of value added for tax purposes. As we saw in Chapter 2, value

---

[1] This omission may be due primarily to measurement problems rather than to the legitimacy of categorizing housework as economic activity.

added is composed of wages, profits, interest and rent, that is, total income earned in the production process. Since this income is subject to tax, firms record it in their individual accounts. Accounts of business establishments are the principal source of data for the national accounts.

Net national product (NNP) measures the total output of goods and services after allowance is made for equipment that is worn out or rendered obsolete during the accounting period. Since some goods are used up in the production process, their value should be deducted from total output to obtain a true picture of the total performance of the economy. Since capital consumption cannot be exactly pinpointed, there is a large factor of inexact measurement in NNP. Capital consumption (depreciation) allowances are used as a measure of the value of worn-out or obsolete equipment. However, these may overstate actual depreciation since they are calculated for tax purposes. Firms will generally take the largest depreciation allowance permissible since depreciation is deducted from taxable income.

National income measures the total payments to factors of production in the form of wages, profits, interest, and rent. Conceptually, national income is exactly equal to net national product or to GNP when depreciation is included in corporate income. Within the national accounting framework, national income differs from NNP only by a few minor items which are essentially transfer payments. It is important to exclude income transfers from income actually earned in the production process. The difference between NNP and national income is definitional, however, and not theoretical.

Personal income, income received by individuals, is obtained by subtracting corporate income from national income. Transfer payments to individuals by corporations and government are included in personal income. **Disposable income** is obtained by subtracting personal tax payments from personal income.

THE SECTOR ACCOUNTS

For macroeconomic analysis with a Keynesian model, it is important that the data are broken down by sector. The Commerce Department classifies income receipt and expenditure by major economic groups—households, business, government, and foreign sector. Thus, total GNP can be viewed as the sum of the expenditures of each of these groups,

$$GNP = C + I + G + X_n$$

and national income is the total of incomes earned by each group. National income can also be broken down by type of income, that is, wages, profits, interest, and rent.[2]

Table B-3 shows receipts and expenditures for each sector. The ex-

TABLE B-3

Receipts and Expenditures of Major Economic Groups, 1972
(in billions of dollars)

	Receipts	Expenditures	Saving or Dissaving
Persons			
Disposable income less interest and transfers paid to foreigners	776.2		49.7
Consumption		726.5	
Business			
Gross retained earnings	124.4		
Gross private domestic investment		178.3	−53.9
Government			
Receipts minus transfer payments	252.2		
Purchases of goods and services		255.0	−2.8
International			
Foreign net transfers by persons and government	3.7		
Net exports		−4.6	8.4
Statistical error	−1.5		−1.5
Total	1155.2	1155.2	0

Source: U.S. Department of Commerce, Office of Business Economics. *Survey of Current Business* (Washington, D.C.: U.S. Government Printing Office, 1973).

cess of receipts over expenditures is net saving for that group. Notice that, for the economy as a whole, net saving equals zero. Table B-4 shows total saving for each sector. For the economy as a whole, saving equals investment. The absence of net saving in the aggregate or, equivalently, the saving-investment equality does not imply that the economy is in equilibrium, but merely that expenditure and investment as measured in the national accounts are *ex post* rather than *ex ante* concepts. Thus, unintended inven-

[2] While the Commerce Department also provides data for GNP by sector of origin, this categorization is not particularly relevant for macroeconomic analysis since practically all GNP originates in the business and government sectors. The breakdown is useful, however, for an indication of the proportion of GNP provided by the public sector.

Saving and Investment, 1972 (in billions of dollars)

Personal saving		49.7
Business saving		124.4
Government saving		−2.8
Federal	−15.9	
State and local	13.1	
Total saving		171.4
Capital grant received from IMF		
(special drawing rights)		0.7
Gross private domestic investment		178.3
Net foreign investment		−7.6
Total investment		170.6
Statistical error		−1.5

Source: U.S. Department of Commerce, Office of Business Economics. *Survey of Current Business* (Washington, D.C.: U.S. Government Printing Office, 1973).

tory accumulation is included in the measures of business expenditures and gross private domestic investment; and the sectoral accounts reflect the identities,

Income earned ≡ Value of output ≡ *Ex post* (actual) expenditure

Saving ≡ *Ex post* (actual) investment

Table B-5 shows national income categorized by type of income. This breakdown is useful for models which examine changes in income distribution. Suppose that the marginal propensity to consume (*MPC*) from rental or farm income is different from the *MPC* from wages and salaries. If this

National Income by Type of Income, 1972 (in billions of dollars)

Compensation of employees		707.1
Wages and salaries	627.3	
Supplements	79.7	
Business and professional income		
(unincorporated enterprises)		54.0
Corporate profits		91.1
Farm income		20.2
Rental income of persons		24.1
Net interest		45.2
Total national income		941.8

Source: U.S. Department of Commerce, Office of Business Economics. *Survey of Current Business* (Washington, D.C.: U.S. Government Printing Office, 1973).

is the case, then the aggregate *MPC* will depend upon the distribution of personal income between the various sources. Data on distributive shares are required for parameter estimation and forecasting from this model.

Many events which affect the economy have an impact on income distribution. Furthermore, as the structure of the economy changes over time, distributional shares are affected. Not only do these changes affect overall spending decisions, but they have implications for economic welfare as well. Furthermore, a breakdown by type of income earned is indicative to policy makers of the distributional impact of their programs.

FLOW OF FUNDS

The flow of funds accounts measure aggregate financial flows throughout the economy. Compiled by the Board of Governors of the Federal Reserve System, these data are useful for monetarist models or for an analysis of the financial sector in a Keynesian model.

The economy is divided into sectors: households, firms, government, foreign, and financial. The financial sector consists of the monetary authorities, banks, and other financial institutions. For each sector the sources and uses of money and credit are measured, with transactions broken down into capital flows and changes in liquid assets. In addition to these flows, financial stock data are broken down by sector into assets and liabilities.

The flow of funds accounts include both the exchange of money and credit for goods and services and pure financial transactions. They also reflect the exchange of financial assets for second-hand goods (such as used cars) not produced in the accounting period. Consequently, they incorporate more information than the national income and product accounts.

B-3   CONCEPTUAL AND THEORETICAL PROBLEMS
OF NATIONAL ACCOUNTING

Because the measurements of the national accounts must conform to the requirements of the theoretical model, national accounting involves far more than mere data collection and compilation (a massive undertaking in itself). In many cases, theoretical considerations pose conceptual difficulties for measurement that are insurmountable unless somewhat arbitrary guidelines are followed. The Commerce Department has developed certain definitions for the accounting aggregates which, while imperfect, at least contribute to a standardized system of accounts which is comparable from year to year. It is, however, important to know exactly what is included in and excluded from the various measures of economic activity which appear in the national accounts, particularly when they are used as indicators of the performance of the economy and the success or failure of economic policy or as measures of economic welfare. We shall consider some of these conceptual problems in turn.

PARTICULAR PROBLEMS OF MEASUREMENT AND DEFINITION

Depreciation. To obtain a measure of net national product, capital consumption or depreciation must be estimated. Suppose a machine wears out in five years. Two problems arise. First, how should depreciation be allocated on an annual basis? Does the useful service of the machine decline by one-fifth each year or does it remain equally efficient each year until it is replaced? Second, should the total depreciation reflect the original cost of the machine or the cost of replacing it?

In addition, there is the problem of obsolescence. A machine may be scrapped before the end of its useful life because technological change has made it obsolete. While firms will fully depreciate a machine when it has become obsolete, it is questionable whether or not obsolescence actually represents a cost of production from a theoretical point of view.

The practice of the Commerce Department is to use business estimates of depreciation as a measure of capital consumption. Because firms will select that measure which gives them the greatest tax benefit, depreciation is likely to be overestimated in the national accounts, and therefore, NNP and national income will be understated. This may affect the comparability of these measures over time if there is a change in the tax laws concerning allowable methods of depreciation.

Inventory Valuation. Changes in inventories represent an increase in output and should be included in any measure of the national product. The measurement of inventory change poses a problem when prices change over the accounting period. A firm may experience windfall capital gains from the sale of inventory when prices rise, but these gains do not represent an increase in real output.

Firms generally record inventory in terms of value rather than volume. Furthermore, the value of inventory is generally recorded at original cost. If prices are rising over the period, units sold will have a higher value than their original cost. Consequently, a measure of inventory change in value terms will overstate the actual physical change that occurred.

If prices are changing at different rates in different industries, it will be impossible to account for real inventory change by using aggregative measures. Standard national accounting practice is to incorporate an *inventory valuation adjustment,* which is negative when prices are rising and capital gains are being realized from holding inventories and positive when prices are falling and firms are experiencing capital losses from holding inventories.

Government Transactions.   The value imputed to most goods and services produced is their market price which includes production costs— wages, rent, and interest—as well as profits. Public goods and government services are not always sold on the market, however, and therefore, these goods and services must be valued at their cost of production with no provision for profits or losses. Since demand is not taken into consideration, this method may understate or overstate the value of government transactions relative to transactions in the private sector.

Transfer Payments and Capital Gains.   Some market transactions should be excluded from GNP since they do not correspond to output of goods and services. Transfer payments such as unemployment compensation and welfare payments as well as private gifts and charitable contributions are excluded. Interest on the national debt is excluded in the U.S. accounts with the rationale that the debt largely reflects the costs of our major wars and does not reflect a return on assets.

Transfers of real property such as land and second-hand goods are also excluded. For instance, if a car is sold and repurchased, the only entry in the national accounts is the salesman's commission or service charge. If the deal is privately made, it will not show up in the national accounts at all, although theoretically a charge should be imputed for the owner's effort in finding a buyer and making the transaction.

Capital gains and losses reflect changes in value not attributable to changes in real output. These are also excluded from the GNP.

Nonmonetary Transactions.   One of the most difficult problems of national accounting is to estimate the output of goods and services not traded in markets. A good bit of arbitrariness is introduced into the national accounts at this point, because only those nonmarket transactions are included for which a method has been found to impute value.

Suppose a farmer raises cows, slaughters them, and consumes the meat at home over the winter. A neighbor raises cows, sells them to the slaughterhouse, and then purchases the meat for home consumption. If nonmonetary transactions are excluded from the national accounts, then in the first instance the raising and slaughtering of cattle contribute nothing to GNP, while in the second case GNP is increased by the full retail value of the beef. Similarly, GNP would be increased if all dwellings were rented rather than owner occupied, if banks charged a service charge for checking accounts and then paid interest on the money held in them, and if housewives hired themselves out as domestic workers and employed other women in their own homes. In all the cases cited, the real output of goods and services would be substantially unaffected.

The Commerce Department has devised methods of imputing value to farm products consumed on farms, rental from owner-occupied houses, and service charges and interest on checking accounts. There has been no attempt to impute a value to a housewife's services, however. This omission may be due to the conceptual difficulties involved or it may reflect a belief that a housewife's duties do not constitute legitimate economic activity.

Definition of Economic Activity. The national accounts are designed to measure the level of economic activity. Economic activity implies the use of scarce resources to satisfy human wants. However, there is always some controversy concerning what is appropriately designated economic activity.

War involves the use of scarce resources, yet many observers feel this activity does not satisfy human wants. The production of square wheels, unsafe automobiles, and electric toothbrushes again utilize scarce resources but are of dubious utility to society. However, all of these activities, when undertaken, are included in the national accounts.

Excluded items are family activities such as the services of women as housewives and of men as householders. Illegal activities, such as gambling, bootlegging, trafficking in narcotics, and prostitution are also excluded.

The enjoyment of leisure is also excluded from the accounting definition of economic activity. While the earnings of a professional golfer are included in national income, the efforts of a weekend duffer are not accounted for. Whether or not the resources used in the enjoyment of leisure are scarce is a matter of debate. The exclusion of leisure, household, and illegal activities and the inclusion of wasteful activities is of concern when the national accounting aggregates are treated as measures of welfare.

B-4 ACCOUNTING AGGREGATES AS MEASURES OF WELFARE

Changes in GNP, NNP, and national, personal, and disposable income over time are sometimes considered to be indicative of changes in economic welfare as well as of the performance of the economy. Thus, a growth rate of 5 percent is said to be better than a rate of 2 percent. The increase in GNP from $87 billion in 1920 to $1288 billion in 1973 is taken to mean that the quality of life has improved markedly over the period.

Comparisons are also made between countries. If per capita GNP in Uganda is $400, then it is assumed that living standards there are low and that people are better off in a country such as the United States with a per capita GNP of $6100. In general, the interpretation of the national accounts aggregates in terms of welfare is erroneous, and it will be useful to consider the limitations of the national accounting aggregates from this point of view.

Intertemporal Comparisons of the National Accounts Aggregates

Intertemporal comparisons of the national aggregates, that is, over time, can be misleading for a number of reasons. Changes in statistical coverage and definitions can bias the comparison, usually favoring the later years. The main change in coverage over time is the increasing proportion of transactions occurring in the monetary sector. This is particularly true for a developing country moving from a traditional agricultural economy where most goods are produced at home and trade takes the form of barter, to a modern economy with a large monetary sector. High rates of GNP growth in these countries may reflect, in part, growth of measured transactions rather than an increase in the level of economic activity for the country as a whole.

In advanced countries, with a relatively stable proportion of total activity in the monetary economy, refinements in statistical technique will result in more extensive computation of nonmonetary transactions. Thus, the inclusion of an imputation for rental of owner-occupied homes increases GNP for that year. Estimates for previous years are no longer comparable once the scope of statistical coverage has changed.

Structural changes in the economy may produce changes in the national acounts aggregates which do not reflect changes in real output. As more and more household tasks are performed by professional service agencies, the measured GNP will increase even though the level of economic activity remains substantially unchanged. Also, the structure of output may change. Gross national product, for instance, increased quite substantially in the United States during World War II. This was due to an increase in the production of war materials and a rationing of consumer goods. Few people considered this period to be one of increased economic welfare, although it did reflect an increase in economic activity. Structural changes, unlike changes in statistical coverage, however, do not necessarily impart a steady upward bias to the measures of economic performance over time.

The introduction of new goods presents a conceptual problem for comparing national income aggregates over time. New inventions in medicine, household conveniences, and transportation may serve to render the quality of modern life incomparable to that of the past century. New goods do not necessarily represent improved living standards, however. Life with the atomic bomb, air pollution, color television, and electric toothbrushes may in some respects be inferior to that of an earlier era. And we do not (as technically we should) subtract the production of undesirable "bads" from the national accounting measure of aggregate output. For instance, noise, pollution, and crowded highways associated with the production and use of more automobiles generate disutility and would have a negative value if they were traded in markets. Yet these "externalities" are not given market values and hence are not accounted for in a measure of GNP.

If the national aggregates are to be used as indicators of economic welfare, price chances must be separated from changes in real output. If GNP rises by 10 percent and prices increase by 5 percent over the same period, then the real increase in GNP is only 5 percent. Using a price index to calculate the change in real GNP presupposes that all prices are rising at about the same rate.[3] Over time, however, relative prices are likely to fluctuate with changes in demand and relative cost conditions, presenting an *index number problem.*

The index number problem consists of finding an index of price change when prices are changing at different rates. Suppose the price of automobiles rises by 2 percent while the price of peanuts increases by 50 percent. If automobiles represent a larger component of GNP than peanuts, the 2 percent increase in automobile prices should be weighted more heavily than the 50 percent rise in peanut prices.

Consider an economy producing just two goods, automobiles and peanuts. Suppose automobile production accounts for 75 percent of GNP, while peanut production accounts for 25 percent. Suppose the money value of GNP increases by 10 percent, while automobile prices rise by 2 percent and peanut prices rise by 50 percent. What is the real change in GNP?

A price index is a weighted average of the price changes for the two goods, where the weights are determined by the importance of that good in total output. Thus, an index of price change for this economy is

$$\frac{\Delta p}{p} = 0.02(0.75) + 0.50(0.25) = 0.14$$

That is, the average increase in prices is 14 percent. If money GNP rose by 10 percent, real GNP has declined by 4 percent, the change in money GNP less the change in prices.

Suppose, however, that the rise in peanut prices has caused the demand for peanuts to decline relative to that of automobiles, so that at the end of the period, peanut production is 10 percent of GNP and automobile production is 90 percent. Using quantity weights from the end of the period,

---

[3] A detailed discussion of price indices appears in Chapter 10.

$$\frac{\Delta p}{p} = 0.02(0.9) + 0.50(0.1) = 0.068$$

the average increase in prices is 6.8 percent, and real GNP has actually increased by 3.2 percent. Notice that, in this example, the change in prices for each good did not vary. The only change was the relative importance of the two goods in total output.

Suppose that during the process of economic growth, the prices of goods and services in the fastest-growing sectors are falling relative to prices in the slower-growing sectors. If quantity weights from the earlier years are used, the index of price change will be much greater than if current year quantity weights are employed. Thus, by using current year quantity weights, the real rate of growth will be greater than if base year quantity weights are used.[4]

An index using base year weights is a Laspeyres index; one using current year weights is a Paasche index. The longer the period under examination, the greater the discrepancy between the Paasche and Laspeyres indices is likely to be. Theoretically, either index is a legitimate measure of price (or quantity) change.

One way around the index number problem is to use an average of the Paasche and Laspeyres indices. Another is to recompute the Paasche index for each accounting period and calculate the real change in GNP each time. This is the method actually practiced by the Commerce Department and the Bureau of Labor Statistics in computing the various statistical price indices for the U.S. economy.[5] However, for historical studies in which short-period data are not always available, the problem still exists. In this case it is important to determine which type of index is being used to compute a measure of real income change.

Although national income aggregates provide no indication of the distribution of the product between individuals, any measure of welfare must take it into account. A decline in real income might actually reflect an improvement in social welfare if the product were more equitably distributed.

Finally, using any measure of economic performance as a measure of welfare implies that an increase in economic activity is synonymous with an improvement in welfare. Whether or not more automobiles, bombs, beer cans, and skyscrapers represent an improvement is questionable. Fur-

[4] Equivalently, price weights can be used to formulate an index of quantity change. Notice that in the example above, base year price weights will overstate the real rate of quantity increase relative to an index using current year price weights.
[5] For a comparison of the different statistical price indices for the U.S. see Chapter 10.

thermore, the national accounts place no value on leisure. Presumably, if the workday were to increase to 12 hours, GNP would increase, but the loss in leisure would undoubtedly represent a decline in welfare.

In sum, the aggregate measures of the national accounts are very poor measures of welfare change over time. Even as measures of the intertemporal change in economic activity, narrowly defined, they must be viewed with caution because of changes in statistical coverage, definitions, economic structure, and the index number problem.

INTERNATIONAL COMPARISONS

International comparisons of national income and GNP are subject to some of the same difficulties as intertemporal comparisons. The most obvious, of course, are differences in coverage due to international differences in the percentage of total transactions made outside the household or barter unit. Per capita GNP in Uganda may be $400, but this does not imply that the value of the goods consumed by each person is only $400. It merely suggests that measured per capita transactions (usually in money) are $400. Perhaps a more comparable measure of Ugandan GNP with that of the United States is to measure GNP per person living in urban areas. However, it is clear that welfare comparisons between life in Uganda and life in the United States are largely a matter of individual values and cannot be measured by national accounting techniques, no matter how perfect and extensive the coverage.

National accounting in different countries often uses different definitions and measures things in different ways. Most of the developed noncommunist countries have attempted to standardize accounting techniques to make the aggregates as comparable as possible. Accounting practice in the USSR, however, is so different from that in the United States that Soviet measures must be revised by experts before they can be compared with those in the United States. For instance, the Soviets count intermediate as well as final goods in their measure of GNP, thus greatly overestimating total output, relative to value added.

Because of differences in demand and cost conditions, different countries have different product mixes and price structures. Since market prices are used to value goods and services, this may pose problems for comparability. Furthermore, these differences may reflect differences in value systems which should be taken into account when welfare is being compared. A country which values leisure and dislikes the trappings of modern technology may be better off with a much lower GNP than its neighbors.

Furthermore, there is considerable international variation in the proportion of GNP devoted to collective consumption such as socialized medicine, public transportation, and state-subsidized housing and education. Not only does this fact have implications for the distribution of the GNP among individuals, but it also suggests that comparisons of disposable personal income between countries will not necessarily be indicative of relative national levels of personal well-being.

Differences in price structures pose further problems for comparability since prices must be converted from one currency to another. The problem of international conversion of currency when price structures differ is equivalent to the index number problem over time. For practical purposes, the Commerce Department uses foreign exchange rates for currency conversion; however, these rates only reflect price ratios in the foreign sector and may not be indicative of international price relationships for the rest of the economy. This is particularly true for less-developed countries in which the foreign sector is often quite independent of the domestic economy. Furthermore, if a country experiences persistent balance-of-payments deficits or surpluses, foreign exchange rates do not adequately reflect relative prices even for the foreign sector.

Finally, international differences in the distribution of income must be taken into account. Some countries, such as Kuwait, have relatively high levels of per capita GNP, but the income distribution is so inequitable that the median income is far below the average or per capita level. A country with a lower level of per capita GNP, distributed more equitably, may provide a higher standard of living for most of its citizens.

Unless all of these limitations are taken into account, data from the national accounts are not a valid basis for making international comparisons of economic welfare. Even as a comparative measure of economic activity, avoiding the necessity for making the value judgments inherent in welfare comparisons, data from the national accounts should be used with caution. The more similar the countries with respect to level of development, income distribution, tastes, and product mix, the more valid the comparison is likely to be.

QUESTIONS FOR STUDY AND REVIEW

1. What is the significance of macroeconomic theory for national accounting and of national accounting for economic theory?

2. How would the following transactions appear in the national accounts?

(a) Unemployment compensation is increased by $1000 which is financed by a payroll tax of $1000.

(b) An exporter buys $500 of shirts from a manufacturer and sells them abroad for $600.

(c) An investor purchases a bond for $95 and earns 5 percent interest.

(d) An automobile manufacturer purchases $5000 of steel from a manufacturer and produces and sells a $6000 automobile.

(e) Suppose the steel in part (d) came from inventories accumulated in the previous period.

3. Discuss some of the practical and conceptual problems associated with making intertemporal and international comparisons of welfare based on data from the national accounts.

ADDITIONAL READING

COPELAND, MORRIS A., *A Study of Money Flows in the United States.* New York: National Bureau of Economic Research, 1952.

GILBERT, MILTON, and KRAVIS, IRVING, *An International Comparison of National Products and the Purchasing Power of Currencies.* Paris: Organization for European Economic Cooperation, 1954.

KUZNETS, SIMON, "National Income: A New Version," *The Review of Economics and Statistics,* XXX (1948), 151–179.

————, *National Income and Its Composition, 1919–1938.* Vol. I. New York: National Bureau of Economic Research, 1941, Chapter 1.

MISHAN, EZRA J., *The Costs of Economic Growth.* New York: Frederick A. Praeger, Inc., 1967.

National Bureau of Economic Research, *A Critique of the United States Income and Product Accounts. Studies in Income and Wealth.* Vol. XXII. Princeton, N.J.: Princeton University Press, 1958.

U.S. Department of Commerce, Office of Business Economics, "The National Income and Product Accounts of the United States, 1929–1965, Statistical Tables," supplement to *The Survey of Current Business* (August, 1966). Washington: U.S. Government Printing Office, 1966.

————, "National Income Supplement, 1954," supplement to *The Survey of Current Business* (November, 1954). Washington, D.C.: U.S. Government Printing Office, 1954.

————, "U.S. Income and Output," supplement to *The Survey of Current Business* (November, 1958). Washington, D.C.: U.S. Government Printing Office, 1958.

Index